REVENGE

REVENGE

Meghan, Harry, and the War
Between the Windsors

TOM BOWER

ATRIA PAPERBACK

New York   London   Toronto   Sydney   New Delhi

ATRIA PAPERBACK

An Imprint of Simon & Schuster, LLC
1230 Avenue of the Americas
New York, NY 10020

First Atria Paperback edition April 2024

ATRIA PAPERBACK and colophon are trademarks of Simon & Schuster, LLC

Simon & Schuster: Celebrating 100 Years of Publishing in 2024

For information about special discounts for bulk purchases, please contact Simon & Schuster
Special Sales at 1-866-506-1949 or business@simonandschuster.com.

The Simon & Schuster Speakers Bureau can bring authors to your live event.
For more information or to book an event, contact the Simon & Schuster Speakers Bureau
at 1-866-248-3049 or visit our website at www.simonspeakers.com.

Manufactured in the United States of America

1 3 5 7 9 10 8 6 4 2

Library of Congress Cataloging-in-Publication Data has been applied for.

ISBN 978-1-6680-2208-5
ISBN 978-1-6680-2209-2 (pbk)
ISBN 978-1-6680-2210-8 (ebook)

To Tom Mangold

Also by Tom Bower

*Blind Eye to Murder: Britain, America and the Purging of Nazi Germany –
A Pledge Betrayed*

Klaus Barbie: Butcher of Lyon

The Paperclip Conspiracy: The Battle for the Spoils And Secrets of Nazi Germany

Red Web: MI6 and the KGB Master Group

Maxwell: The Outsider

Tiny Rowland: A Rebel Tycoon

The Perfect English Spy: Sir Dick White and the Secret War 1935–90

Heroes of World War II

Maxwell: The Final Verdict

*Nazi Gold: The Full Story of the Fifty-Year Swiss-Nazi Conspiracy to Steal Billions
from Europe's Jews and Holocaust Survivors*

Blood Money: The Swiss, the Nazis and the Looted Billions

Fayed: The Unauthorized Biography

Branson

The Paymaster: Geoffrey Robinson, Maxwell and New Labour

Broken Dreams: Vanity, Greed and the Souring of British Football

Gordon Brown: Prime Minister

Conrad and Lady Black: Dancing on the Edge

The Squeeze: Oil, Money & Greed in the 21st Century

No Angel: The Secret Life of Bernie Ecclestone

Sweet Revenge: The Intimate Life of Simon Cowell

Branson: Behind the Mask

Broken Vows: Tony Blair – The Tragedy of Power

Rebel Prince: The Power, Passion and Defiance of Prince Charles

Dangerous Hero: Corbyn's Ruthless Plot for Power

Boris Johnson: The Gambler

Contents

Preface

She had arrived. She was in the spotlight. The excited crowd cheered – and some screamed. Dozens of lenses zoomed in – and shutters clicked. Dignitaries bowed and some fawned. Helicopters buzzed overhead. Bodyguards hovered. Police were everywhere. Unexpectedly, Meghan-mania exploded. Finally, Meghan Markle was idolised. Her lifelong ambition was being fulfilled.

On a frosty morning on 1st December, 2017, the television star glowed. Just as her new fiancé promised, she had inherited the iconic mantle of his mother, Princess Diana. From the moment she stepped out of the gleaming black Range Rover at 11:05am, the British showed their love for the 36-year-old American actress.

Nottingham is a city 130 miles north of London, famous for its associations with the Robin Hood legend. It was an unusual choice of location to introduce Meghan Markle as the Royal Family's latest member. The East Midlands city could not rival California's sun-kissed beaches, but that was a temporary irrelevance for the citizen from Los Angeles during her slow 400-yard walk through the Lace Market towards the civic centre.

'It's warmer over there,' she laughingly agreed with Cori Burns, one of a thousand people who had waited for two hours. From her pocket, Meghan thrust a handwarmer to an Australian student who had complained of the cold.

Nearby, Harry's smile was irrepressible. Meghan's hand frequently rubbed his back and squeezed his elbow. Her constant smile and animated greetings were examples of Hollywood at its best. A brief kiss by the couple sparked hysteria. Theirs, agreed the onlookers, was a match made in heaven.

Flowers, cards, a teddy bear, chocolates, two fridge-magnets and bags of local memorabilia were thrust at the visitors. 'Meghan came over and I just put my arms around her,' swooned 81-year-old Irene Hardman, a royal super-fan. 'It's so lovely to meet you,' Hardman told the future duchess. 'I'm sure you are going to have a lovely life with him. Look after him for us.'

'You're so sweet,' replied Meghan, unaware that her hugs and poses for selfies were banned by royal etiquette. 'I cried afterwards,' admitted Hardman. 'She's wonderful. They're so genuine.'

'She's seems like such a lovely, lovely person,' Sian Roberts gushed to a NBC News camera. 'I think she's going to be a really good thing for the Royal Family.' Close by, an ABC News reporter was babbling about 'pop-star frenzy'. Unsurprisingly, many Americans were fascinated by their new association with the Crown.

Even Raushana Nurzhubalina, a student from Kazakhstan, was mesmerised. She had set her alarm-clock for 6am to get a prime spot. 'It's such a honour to see the royals,' she told BBC TV. 'I'm also a fan of *Suits*, so it's a chance to see a star of that, too.'

'We need magic at the moment,' an admirer shouted at a journalist as the confident American and Harry greeted the Acting Lady Mayoress, Bell Edis. 'I'm sure you could be the People's Princess,' said the 70-year-old civic leader. 'Harry', Edis noticed, 'chuckled and smiled with his cheeky grin. I'd said the right thing.'

'Congratulations!' shouted a group of women. Four days earlier, the couple had announced their engagement. Breaking tradition, the

Queen had agreed Meghan should be fast-tracked into 'The Firm'. 'This is the country that's going to be her home now,' said the prince's spokesman, Jason Knauf. 'That means travelling around, getting to know the towns and cities.' The visit to Nottingham was the beginning of a six-month tour of Britain.

Britain's tabloid journalists noted Meghan's trendy clothes: a Canadian navy-blue cashmere coat, an Austrian black turtleneck, a British beige chino skirt and boots, and a Scottish tote bag. 'Just how you would imagine a modern princess to look,' swooned a fashion aficionado. Hours after the list of her outfits was published, their manufacturers reported a sell-out of stocks. That news pleased Jessica Mulroney, Meghan's Canadian stylist and friend. And a creative director of a London designer said 'Meghan's personal style has an effortless ease that personifies her character'. Inevitably, commentators compared Meghan with the Duchess of Cambridge. Kate came off unfavourably.

During that day, all the boxes were ticked. Visits to an HIV centre, an institute giving health information to local Africans, a group providing advice on nutrition, and Nottingham Contemporary, a centre for 'love, life and health'. The itinerary foreshadowed the routine life Meghan could expect as a member of the Royal Family. AIDS sufferers, Meghan was reminded, were a particular target of Diana's charity work. Following in Diana's footsteps was particularly important for both Harry and Meghan.

After nightfall the couple were back in Kensington Palace, sleeping in Harry's home, which was appropriately called Nottingham Cottage. Meghan voiced no regrets or foreboding about her new life. On the contrary, she was thrilled. For years, her destiny had been to be distinct from the crowd. Repeatedly frustrated after leaving college, she was never deterred by failure. Now her tenacity had been rewarded. Her lucky break had miraculously materialised. Marrying an English prince was an unexpected prize for someone seeking the American Dream – to rise from obscurity to respectable prosperity.

An essential ingredient of her trajectory had been that her story should be told on her terms. Controlling the narrative was essential to her success. As Oscar Wilde wrote, 'The truth is rarely pure, and never simple.'

The Royal Family would soon discover that Meghan Markle's expectations and ambitions might be rather different from what they, and the enthusiastic British public, were anticipating. During those first blissful weeks only hardened cynics asked whether it might even be possible that the thousand-year monarchy could be jeopardised by this unknown American actress.

CHAPTER I

Thomas

'It was love at first sight,' Thomas Markle said after Rachel Meghan Markle, his youngest daughter, was born on 4th August, 1981 at the West Park hospital in Canoga Park, Los Angeles. The 37-year-old father proudly held the newborn baby, who he repeatedly called Flower.[1]

Doria Markle, his 24-year-old wife, was sleeping, comatose after her anaesthetic for the Caesarean birth. Once Doria awoke to discover she had a daughter she pronounced her name should be Rachel. Thomas preferred Meghan. As a compromise, she was called Rachel Meghan. Within days Rachel was forgotten. In Celtic Irish, Meghan means Brave Warrior; in Welsh it means pearl.

During Meghan's first weeks her father redecorated the family bathroom in their comfortable three-storey house in Woodward Hills with angels and fairies. 'The look on his face was priceless,' recalled Tom Junior, his son from a previous marriage. Watching Thomas hold Meghan, Tom Junior could see his father was smitten: 'My dad was more in love with her than anyone else in the world and that included Doria. She became his whole life, his little princess.'

While Thomas endlessly photographed his daughter, he agreed with Doria that baby Meghan should get everything she wanted. Even as a baby, any sign of her displeasure should be instantly placated by gifts. Worshipped, their daughter would be endlessly reassured that she was special. Her parents' unconditional love inevitably shaped Meghan's character and personality.

Thomas and Doria had met in 1977 at the ABC film studios in Los Angeles. Thirty-three years old, Thomas had just been nominated for an Emmy as the lighting director of the daytime TV soap *General Hospital*. Unsurprisingly, he spotted Doria, a slim, beautiful, Black 21-year-old trainee make-up artist with a nose-stud.

After a few weeks, Doria moved into Thomas's untidy family home. 'I'm not the neatest of men,' Thomas admitted. Among papers, memorabilia and furniture, he was bringing up two adolescent children from a previous marriage, Tom Junior and Samantha. Doria found the set-up challenging. Nevertheless, the atmosphere was good. Tom Junior recalled how the Markles celebrated Thanksgiving with Doria's grandfather, mother and half-brother. 'It was really warm and inclusive,' Tom Junior recalled. 'The kind of family I had always wanted.'[2]

Their decision to marry on 23rd December, 1979 was unusual. At the time fewer than one white American man in a thousand was married to a Black woman. 'When I married Doria,' recalled Thomas, 'people asked, "What colour will your baby be?" I said, "I don't know and I don't care."'[3] On reflection, Thomas became aware that in mixed-race marriages, their child's colour becomes an issue of self-identity for the parents. And the issue is discussed before the birth.

Thomas promised Doria kindness and stability, especially after she did not qualify as a make-up artist. All was set for Thomas to start a new life. 'I like to think,' Meghan wrote in 1990 aged eight, 'he was drawn to her sweet eyes and her Afro, plus their shared love of antiques.'[4]

From the outset, however, the prospects of a long, happy union were uncertain. Twelve years younger than Thomas, Doria lived in her own world. Immersed in the teaching of a Hindu yoga guru and mystical religions, she insisted on being married by a Buddhist priest, Brother Bhaktananda in the Self-Realisation Fellowship Temple, a replica Indian temple on Sunset Boulevard. Thomas happily went along with his wife's choice. 'I loved Doria,' Thomas said. 'I didn't think how long it would last. I gave it a go because I wanted a child. This was the first child I could afford. I didn't have enough money for the other two.'

To make life easier, Thomas rented a big house in a quiet cul-de-sac in Woodward Hills, a white middle-class residential area lined with eucalyptus trees near the Bell Canyon parkland. Photographs taken soon after Meghan's birth recorded a happy family. Sitting at a table of food cooked by Doria, Thomas held Meghan surrounded by Tom Junior and Samantha.[5]

Their happiness was short-lived. Once Thomas resumed working 18-hour shifts, cracks in his relationship with Doria appeared. Meghan's parents were clearly incompatible.

Before arriving at the ABC studios, Doria had helped her father sell bric-a-brac and then she moved around California trying to be a travel agent, an importer and finally a clothing designer before finding a permanent job. Thomas says she was employed by a boyfriend to prune marijuana plants in Humboldt County. After stripping the leaves and stems, her boyfriend supplied customers across Los Angeles. As Thomas ruefully recalled, everyone in Hollywood at that time, including himself, was smoking and taking drugs, not just at home but also in restaurants and even at the Academy Awards.

In Thomas's absence at work, Tom Junior smoked cannabis with his friends in the house. Doria also regularly smoked cannabis with women friends and sometimes Jeffrey, a friend from her high school days. Doria sympathised with Tom Junior's particular problem. As part of California's integration policy he was bussed, without choice, one hour across Los Angeles to an all-Black school. Regularly, the ginger-haired boy was beaten up by other pupils. For one year Doria urged the local education authority to accept that he experienced sufficient diversity at home. Eventually his anguish was ended, but the damage to his education was beyond repair.

There was no similar rapport between Doria and Samantha.

Doria had begun to sell jewellery. Her new company, Three Cherubs, irked Samantha. The 'three' represented Doria, Thomas and Meghan. 'Why isn't it the Five Cherubs?' Samantha asked. Increasingly jealous of Meghan and already frustrated about the difficulties of becoming an actress, Samantha, now 13, told Thomas that Doria's housekeeping was unsatisfactory.[6] Doria was, according to Samantha, ordering her stepdaughter to clean the house. Samantha's resentment grew as Doria increasingly partied in the family home with girlfriends or drove back to Humboldt County to smoke marijuana.[7]

'Doria changed after we married,' admitted Thomas Markle. 'I didn't realise she would still smoke so much weed.' Even when Samantha returned home in the afternoon with schoolfriends, she found Doria sitting in a dressing-gown on the front lawn smoking a joint. Doria, Thomas and Samantha Markle agreed, was neither gentle nor loving. Thomas also discovered that Doria found caring for Meghan alone in the house difficult. And there was more.

Samantha recalls seeing photographs of Doria with women taken by Thomas on the walls of their home. Thomas was also aware that Doria was sleeping with other men.[8] 'You're being used by Doria,' Samantha told her father. The angry teenager moved out of the house.

At first, Thomas refused to intervene, then he too became angered by Doria's lifestyle. 'We just were on different paths,' he recalled without rancour. 'I was also married to my work,' he admitted. In Thomas's version, Doria's fondness for marijuana, her sex life and her antagonism towards Samantha, who had just been diagnosed with multiple sclerosis, ended the marriage.

The amicable settlement, negotiated by one lawyer, split Thomas's limited savings. The couple also agreed that in exchange for no alimony, Thomas would always support Meghan. The absence of any rancour was inspired by Thomas's delight to have a young daughter. Until then his domestic life had been troubled.

Born in 1944 in Newport, Pennsylvania, his parents, Gordon and

Doris, could trace their American roots back to the Great Migration from England in 1632. One branch of the Markle family went back to the reign of King Edward III, who died in 1377. Other forefathers arrived in the eighteenth century from Germany and Holland to work as farmers, miners and craftsmen.

Before the Second World War, Thomas's father Gordon had owned a petrol station and then worked in a shoe factory. After military service in Hawaii during the war, he became a printer at an airforce base in Harrisburg. At the end of the daily 52-mile round-trip commute to work from Newport, he returned home miserable. After dinner with his three sons – Thomas was the third child after Mick and Fred – Gordon went to his room to read pornographic magazines.

Despite her sullen husband, Doris Markle encouraged her three sons to enjoy the best of New England's outdoor life – fishing in the river and picking food in the fields and woods. She was also determined that her sons would have a good education. Mick joined the foreign service and Fred the church as a priest.

Thomas, however, was a risk-taker. Tall, thin and known as a 'cool cat', he chased local girls. Every Sunday, as the last in the line of altar-boys at the Episcopalian church, he waited for the priest to pour the last drops of wine into his mouth. Regularly, he staggered out of the building. He was unsuited for college after leaving school.

Starting as a stagehand in a local theatre, Thomas chose lighting as his speciality. Moving to Chicago he worked as a junior technician in a TV station and in a theatre. In the midst of his hectic teenage social life, he met unemployed Roslyn Loveless at a party. Within days, Roslyn was pregnant and Thomas 'did the right thing'. They married in 1964. Both were 19 years old. Born the same year, their baby daughter, Yvonne, who would later rename herself Samantha, was the elder sister of Tom Junior, born in 1966. Samantha would years later describe her mother as 'promiscuous'.[9]

Thomas Markle worked and played hard. At the end of a long day on the set he preferred to party around the clock rather than return home. Family time was limited to taking his children to a baseball match at weekends or to the TV studio while he worked. 'They were always arguing,' Samantha recalled about her parents' fractured marriage. Thomas moved out, divorced and headed for Hollywood. After scraping a living in restaurant kitchens, he finally made a breakthrough.

Living in Santa Monica and earning a good income from lighting at ABC, Thomas heard that his two children were struggling. Roslyn was partying with a series of men and her hippy friends in Albuquerque, New Mexico. Their mother, the children complained, was not spending the money he sent for them.[10]

To escape their mother, Samantha moved to live with Thomas in Santa Monica and was followed by Tom Junior. Their 'safe haven' was unstable. Sometimes working 18 hours a day, Thomas Markle struggled to give his children a better home. Neither child complained, although Tom Junior spent some of his day smoking cannabis while Samantha, occasionally dressed as a Goth, disappeared to nightclubs before arriving in the morning at the local high school. Thomas did his best. Inspired by her regular visits with her father to the Sunset Gower Studios, Samantha wanted to become a Hollywood actor. Thomas arranged a walk-on part in a TV drama, but Samantha's ambitions remained unfulfilled.

In 1977, Thomas's turbulent background was mirrored by Doria's unstable family. Divorced, remarried and then repeatedly abandoned by their partners, Doria's mother and grandmothers had brought up their children single-handed. Both their family backgrounds were unexceptional.

Doria's great-great-great grandfather was an enslaved person of William Ragland in Jonesboro, Georgia. On emancipation from six generations of slavery, Meghan would later claim, he named himself 'Wisdom'. The evidence, however, suggests that he remained Ragland.[11] After emancipation, the Raglands worked as hired hands around the original farmstead, and only at the beginning of the twentieth century did their children head for nearby towns to find work as a hall porter, a waiter and a presser in a cleaning shop. In 1954, Alvin Ragland, who would become Doria's father, met Jeanette Johnson in Cleveland. Jeanette Johnson had been abandoned by her husband with two children. To survive, she worked as a hotel lift operator. In 1956, Alvin and Jeanette married and Doria was born. Soon afterwards the family, including Jeanette's seven-year-old son Joseph Johnson, packed their belongings and drove to Los Angeles.

Doria's half-brother Joseph would recall their night-time arrival in a small town in Texas. Cold and hungry, they were told there were no rooms for Black people: 'The highway is that way. Get going. You're not welcome here.'

Once settled in Los Angeles, Joseph and Doria went to the predominantly white Jewish Fairfax High School. Alvin set up a succession of antique shops, including Twas New, and became known for a fast life, driving flash cars and chasing women. Doria's dissatisfaction of her life with Thomas Markle coincided with Alvin, her father, abandoning Jeanette for a teacher called Ava Burrows. They later married. 'Life's hard,' Doria said, agreeing with Jeanette, her mother.

In 1983, after their separation, Doria took her two-year-old daughter to live with her mother. At the same time, Thomas moved into a large converted barn on Vista Del Mar Avenue, a stylish neighbourhood close to Hollywood Boulevard. He also rented a small flat opposite the ABC studios. Later accounts that Thomas was 'plagued by money troubles from the time Meghan was a small child and this had contributed to the break-up with Doria' were untrue.[12]

Shortly after her parents' separation, Meghan was enrolled by Thomas in the Little Red School House, a favoured crèche among Hollywood's film set. Located near the ABC studios and Doria's new home, Meghan's parents adopted a fixed routine. On the days when Thomas was working an 18-hour shift, Doria and Jeanette cared for

Meghan. On the alternate days when Thomas was in meetings to plan future filming, he collected Meghan from school. He looked after her every weekend.

Moving between her parents and their different ways of life, Meghan radiated happiness. With light olive-freckled skin and curly hair, she was not identified by anyone as belonging to any particular race or culture. Racism did not appear to be a problem, especially at school. Although there were few Black people in the Hollywood Hills, Thomas Markle insists that race was never mentioned in his conversations with Meghan. Doria mentioned one incident when someone in Woodward Hills had mistakenly assumed she was Meghan's nanny. 'I didn't see any racism in that area,' insisted Thomas Markle. 'Doria never complained that it was difficult as a Black person to live there.'[13] Writing for the first time about her background in 2015, Meghan did not suggest that her mixed-race parentage – or 'biracial' as she would write – complicated her life. She praised her father for making her feel accepted.

'I had been fawning over a boxed set of Barbie dolls,' she later wrote.[14] 'It was called the Heart Family and included a mom doll, a dad doll and two children. This perfect nuclear family was only sold in sets of white dolls or black dolls…On Christmas morning, swathed in glitter-flecked wrapping paper, there I found my Heart Family: a black mom doll, a white dad doll, and a child in each colour. My dad had taken the sets apart and customised my family.'

Thomas's recollection is different. 'I gave her the dolls at her fourth birthday party in a park with her schoolfriends. Doria and her mother were also there.' He continued, 'One mother said, "I've never seen a set like that in the store."' Until Meghan publicised the gift 30 years later to illustrate her 'problems' with race, Thomas Markle could not recall Meghan ever mentioning the issue.

In 1986, Doria found caring for her five-year-old daughter too difficult. Increasingly, Meghan either went after school to the home of Ninaki 'Nikki' Priddy, Meghan's first and best schoolfriend, or was collected by Thomas and sat in the TV studio while he worked.[15]

Encouraged by Nikki Priddy's parents, the deep relationship between the two girls gave Nikki a unique insight into her friend: 'She always wanted to be famous. She just loved to be the centre of attention.' Growing up on film sets, noticed Priddy, 'made Meghan a bit of a star. We used to imagine her receiving an Oscar. She used to practise announcing herself. I knew she was going into showbusiness. Real easy.'[16]

Samantha's absence from home confirmed Meghan's impression that she was an only child. Nikki Priddy witnessed the consequence: 'She was tough, too. If you rubbed her up the wrong way, she'd make it known with the silent treatment. There was a time when we were about seven and I'd collected a bunch of insects. She didn't want to play with them. We spent two hours sitting at opposite ends of the garden with our backs to each other in silence. I'd always be the first to apologise. I just wanted to be besties again. She was stubborn. She digs her heels in the ground.'

CHAPTER 2

School

Just before her ninth birthday in 1990, Meghan's life changed. Doria announced that she had started Distant Treasures, a clothing and jewellery business. She would need to travel to markets across the country. Somewhat puzzled, Thomas never quite understood why Doria would be away for three weeks, but he didn't complain and agreed to take full responsibility for their daughter. Meghan moved permanently into the large converted barn. The assertion that she lived 'in a cramped converted garage apartment' is inaccurate.[17]

At school, Meghan was known as empathetic, for siding with those who were bullied or mistreated. Although she would later reveal, 'I was such a ham as a child,' that year she sat with her Uncle Joseph while his mother Jeanette was dying. Joseph noticed how his niece held her grandmother's hand with genuine kindness.[18]

The parents of Meghan's schoolfriends were critical to her happiness and stability. For the first four days of the school week, Meghan usually went back to the homes of Ninaki Priddy or Susan Ardakani, another friend, until her father collected her. In both homes she witnessed a happy family life. On Fridays her treat was to watch Thomas Markle on the set at the ABC studios of *General Hospital* or *Married with Children*. Introduced into the world of television stars, she loved the glamour. More importantly, she loved the camera. Posing for fun in front of the lens, she became a different person. Conscious of the focus of that glistening glass upon herself, she dreamt like many young girls in Tinseltown of her future as a Hollywood star.

Her father encouraged his daughter's dreams. Quickly she became popular among the actors and crew, making sandwiches and getting autographs of the stars. 'No one would turn her down,' laughed Thomas Markle about his daughter's popularity. Exposed to the adult world in the studio, Meghan became aware of politics and in particular American feminism. By then, the 20-year campaign fronted by Betty Friedan, Andrea Dworkin, Jane Fonda and Gloria Steinem had matured into an irreversible movement with deep roots in Hollywood.

In the mid-nineties, TV adverts stereotyped women. The American corporation Procter & Gamble used the tagline to promote Ivory Clear dishwashing liquid: 'Women all over America are fighting greasy pots and pans.' Meghan was infuriated. Why women? Why not men? Thomas Markle knew that thousands of American women were similarly annoyed. Many had sent protests to Procter & Gamble. With her father's encouragement, Meghan joined the bandwagon. She wrote to Procter & Gamble's chairman and also to Hillary Clinton, the First Lady. Like other protestors, she urged that the slogan should be changed to 'People all over America'.

After she received no reply, Thomas wrote follow-up letters demanding that the corporation and Clinton acknowledge his daughter. Nothing happened. Using his contacts, Thomas arranged for Linda Ellerbee, a host on Nickelodeon, a children's TV channel run by Lucky Duck productions, to report Meghan's protest at her school.[19] Seeing herself interviewed on the broadcast TV film report, accompanied by a re-enactment clip of her 'writing' to Clinton, naturally boosted Meghan's self-confidence.

Some weeks later, Procter & Gamble bowed to the thousands of protests and changed the advertisement's strapline. Although

Thomas knew that Meghan's letter had not influenced the executives' decision – there was no evidence that her letter was even read – he encouraged her conviction that the change was her personal victory. Retelling her story to women at the ABC studios won her popularity. They allowed her to use an office for homework. The experience would be employed by Meghan as a milestone.

The end of 1990 was a good time for the Markles. Through hard work, Thomas was flush with money. Twenty-six years later, to extract a payment from an eager journalist, Tom Junior invented the story that his father had won $750,000 in the California State Lottery. There was no lottery 'win' but Thomas did give Tom Junior money to start a flower shop and bought Samantha a car. Meghan's school fees were easily affordable for him.

At Nikki Priddy's ninth birthday party, Meghan was videoed sitting on a red blanket, wearing a gold crown and shouting with an improvised clapperboard, 'Take two'. Directing the other girls to bow and intone to her 'Your Royal Highness', she had been influenced after watching a tape of Princess Diana's fairytale wedding. Nikki Priddy noticed her friend's desire to be watched: 'Meghan always wanted to be the centre of attention. She took the starring role.'

However, compared to the family life of her friends, Meghan found the tension between her parents challenging. Over the many weekends and holidays they spent together in their pre-teens and later, Priddy admired Meghan's management of her parents in trying to keep the peace: 'For almost as long as I knew Meghan, her parents weren't together. It could be hard for her. Sometimes she felt she had to pick sides. She was always trying to make sure each of them was happy.' Priddy watched Meghan, poised as a 'natural mediator', relay messages: 'It was literally stuff like, "Tell your mother. . ." or "Tell your father. . ." Controlling her emotions is something she learnt back then.'

Although Meghan maintained her parents' divorce caused fewer problems than expected, Ninaki recalls that 'Sometimes one parent needed a little more attention, so Meghan would devote herself to that parent.'[20] Shuttled between starkly different worlds she increasingly came to rely on herself. But 'Bean' as Thomas now called her – because she loved the book *Jack and the Beanstalk* – could always count on his protection.

Thomas's protective shield automatically went up after riots broke out in parts of Los Angeles in April 1992. Film had been released showing four white policemen beating Rodney King, an unarmed Black motorist. After the police officers were acquitted by a jury of assault, parts of the city erupted in protest against the blatant racism of the verdict. Police sirens wailed as outraged Americans torched and looted their neighbourhoods.

Although the outbreaks of violence were far from their home, Thomas decided to protect Meghan. During the afternoon that the riots started he drove with her to Palm Springs.[21] Doria had refused to join them. 'I feel quite safe,' she had told Thomas in a telephone conversation. There are serious doubts that Meghan saw any violence, not even the minor looting in a store near the ABC studio. In her absence the riots spread to Sunset and Hollywood Boulevards. After five days the curfew was lifted and they returned to Los Angeles. Meghan drove past burnt-out buildings, though no houses near her home were damaged.

More than 20 years later Meghan recalled a different experience: 'I remember the curfew and I remember rushing back home and on that drive home, seeing ash fall from the sky and smelling the smoke and seeing it billow out of buildings and seeing people run out of buildings carrying bags and looting.'[22] She also saw 'men in the back of a van just holding guns and rifles'. Equally memorable was a familiar tree outside her father's home 'completely charred. And those memories don't go away.'[23]

In those later years, Meghan mentioned that the protests brought out 'the good in her community', but she must have meant her immediate community, which was predominantly white. Her version changed again in 2017. Twenty-five years after the event Meghan would tell *Vanity Fair* that as 'the ash from street fires sifted down on suburban lawns…she exclaimed, "Oh, my God, Mommy, it's snowing."

"No, Flower," Doria answered. "It's not snow. Get in the house."'[24]

Thomas Markle was incredulous when he read his daughter's version of those events. Meghan, he insists, never saw Doria after the riots erupted. Once he had collected her from school, he drove straight to Palm Springs.

According to Meghan's earlier versions, there was one racist experience which was particularly memorable. While driving together, Doria had an argument with a white driver. After he shouted racist abuse at her, Doria was visibly pained: 'I looked to my mom. Her eyes welling with hateful tears. We drove home in deafening silence, her chocolate knuckles pale from gripping the wheel so tightly.'[25] This is the only childhood incident of this kind that Meghan has spoken about publicly. She has also mentioned her experiences listening to Doria and her grandmother's stories about their family's experiences in the distant past.

Pertinently, race was not deemed to be an issue at the Little Red School, nor at the private girls Catholic Immaculate Heart School which she entered just before her twelfth birthday. Her 'battle' with Procter & Gamble, Thomas discovered during the interview, was a major influence on winning a place at the school. According to Thomas Markle, Doria did not come to the interview, and visited the school only once before Meghan's graduation ceremony.[26]

Founded in 1906, the school's declared mission was to 'celebrate more than a century of nurturing the spiritual, intellectual, social and moral development of students as they distinguish themselves as women of great heart and right conscience'. The school prided itself on attracting 'very talented and highly motivated young women' from every race and social background. Among past students were the actress Mary Tyler Moore and television personality Tyra Banks.

Thirty per cent of the school was white; the majority of pupils were multi-national, mixed race or Black. 'Race didn't come up all that much,' recalled Christine Knudsen, a white teacher. 'It's not a big deal, simply because our school is so diverse.' Since Doria only came to the school once, most assumed Meghan was Italian.[27] The school's photographer, John Dlugolecki, who regularly visited, recalled that Meghan, in his experience, noticeably never associated with Afro-American children, and 'was not considered mixed race by her peers'. Her closest friends were white. 'My self-identification was wrapped up in being the smart one,' she recalled before she was well-known.[28] Until recently, she never suggested suffering any sense of exclusion.

Race did become an issue when, aged 12, she was asked to complete in her English class a box to identify her ethnicity. 'There I was – my curly hair, my freckled face, my pale skin, my mixed race, looking down at these boxes, not wanting to mess up, but not knowing what to do. You could only choose one, but that would be to choose one parent over the other – and one half of myself over the other. My teacher told me to check the box for Caucasian. "Because that's how you look, Meghan," she said. I put down my pen. Not as an act of defiance but rather a symptom of my confusion. I couldn't bring myself to do that – to picture the pit-in-her-belly sadness my mother would feel if she were to find out. So I didn't tick a box. I left my identity blank – a question mark, an absolute incomplete – much like how I felt. When I went home that night I told my dad what had happened. He said the words that have always stayed with me, "If that happens again, you draw your own box".'[29]

By then, Thomas had established a pleasant routine. Daily for nearly ten years, he dropped Meghan off at school and, at the end of the afternoon, would either collect her or send a limousine to bring her to the studio from the Priddys' or another schoolfriend while he finished work. Dressed in her school uniform, the curly-haired girl with a gap in her front teeth sat in the wings of the set in her Catholic school uniform while the actors occasionally participated in shooting sex scenes. 'The sacred and the profane,' she would later say. 'It was a very perverse place to grow up.'[30]

At weekends there was a routine of Saturday ballet and acting classes followed by 'our club sandwich and fruit-smoothie' at an ice-cream parlour or Hamburger Hamlet. Before going in, Thomas always bought Meghan's favourite comic called 'Archie'. The hero, a red-haired teenager with freckles, was friends with Veronica, a rich girl. For more than two years – between 10 and 12 years old – Meghan not only read each week the $1.50 new issue but also an old rare issue that cost $20. After the meal, Thomas rented old dance movies to watch at home.[31]

Some weekends were spent, as in his own childhood, fishing on the Kern River and Big Bear Lake. The fish would be cooked for dinner. On long weekends, they went on road trips, including one to Elvis's Graceland home in Memphis, Tennessee. Thomas's Toyota 4 Runner was fitted with mattresses in the back for Meghan along with a TV and VCR recorder. 'We discovered,' recalled Thomas, 'that she liked the same music I did when I was a kid. Bands like The Shirelles and all the soul groups, she liked every one. Every time we would stop at a truck stop for something to eat, I bought the cassettes.'[32]

Thomas also encouraged Meghan regularly to volunteer to serve food, especially turkey dinners, to the homeless at the Hippie or Skid Row Kitchen.[33] Maria Pollia, her school's theology teacher, remembered that Meghan was 'unusually compassionate'. Thomas Markle could also take credit for the observation by the school's head teacher, Ilise Faye, that Meghan was memorable as a confident, articulate and proactive pupil: 'She had a voice. She would stand up for the underdogs, for what she believed in, and became a leader among her friends.'

Compassion and spirituality were dominant characteristics in Meghan's early teenage years. In summer she was sent by the school to the Agape International Spiritual Centre. Early every day, guided by 'trans-denominational' Christianity, students meditated and recited an Agape mantra, 'God is on my side.' She also spent four days at Kairos, a student retreat, to discuss life and religion. As at school, she was popular and successful. At a school ceremony, aged 14, she spoke about religion and charitable works.[34] After sending a depressed fellow student a handwritten note describing him as 'strong and wonderful', blessed with a 'beautiful spirit' proving how 'special you are,' her note ended, 'I am here if you ever need me.' She was voted a Kairos leader.[35]

Her empathy was also rewarded by election as the school president. Crowned the Homecoming Queen, friends said openly 'she was always destined to be remarkable'. Years later, an admiring portrait of Meghan would be accompanied by a negative assessment. While she saw herself as 'an underdog', some classmates called her 'fake' because she seemed 'perfect'.[36] The evidence suggests the opposite. She always fought, as Sonia Ardakani noticed, 'tooth and nail for the things she wanted in life'. As Sonia's daughter Suzy concluded, 'Meghan always got what she wanted.'[37] No one doubted her sincerity. But she was utterly indulged by her father. 'I spoiled her,' repeated Thomas mournfully and continued, 'So she became controlling at school, the master of ceremonies, and controlling at home too.'

In later years, Meghan appreciated her father's dedication: 'The blood, sweat and tears this man (who came from so little in a small town of Pennsylvania) invested in my future so I could grow up to have so much,' adding, 'To my dad – my thoughtful, inspiring, hardworking Daddy – Happy Father's Day.' She showed similar gratitude towards Doria. As an ex-employee of a travel agent, Doria managed to obtain cheap tickets from an airline to fly with Meghan to Mexico. Meghan's stand-out memory of that trip appears to have been a visit to the slums.[38] She never mentioned a holiday with her parents in Hawaii, paid for by Thomas Markle: 'Although we were divorced, we got together sometimes.'

Years later, on her thirty-third birthday in 2014, Meghan's memories of her childhood shifted: 'My teens were grappling with how to fit in, and what that even meant. My high school had cliques: the Black girls and white girls, the Filipina and the Latina girls. Being biracial, I fell somewhere in between. So every day during lunch, I busied myself with meetings – French club, student body, whatever one could possibly do between noon and 1pm – I was there. Not so that I was more involved, but so that I wouldn't have to eat alone.'[39] Thomas Markle disputed Meghan's later version of her school years.

In 1993, Thomas's financial security fell apart. He had loaned much of his savings to a friend for a TV business venture. The money, he complained, was stolen. He also faced a huge tax bill. On the advice of the US Revenue Service he declared himself bankrupt. Since Thomas was still earning a high salary, Meghan's life barely changed. Although she would claim that she had to work at Humphrey Yogart in Beverly Hills for $4 an hour[40] and 'grew up on the $4.99 salad bar at Sizzler',[41] Thomas is emphatic: 'She never worked when she was at school. I would not have allowed it. And she didn't need to.' Nor did she survive on Sizzler food. She ate fresh farm food and loved fish tacos, she would later admit.[42]

Not only did Thomas Markle ensure that Meghan was well fed, but at weekends he paid for extra tuition and out-of-town trips. Her ambition was never in doubt. Influenced by her frequent presence in the studios, she was set upon becoming famous. Befriending the son of a Bolivian president at school, Meghan boasted for a few days, 'I'm going to be Queen of Bolivia.'[43]

Socially, she gave the appearance of being reserved. Her parents, she said, were strict about boyfriends. Her first kiss at 13, she later told Larry King in a TV interview, was at a church summer camp with Joshua Silverstein, who went on to become a rapper.[44] Meghan, he confirmed, had taken the initiative. When allowed to meet her first boyfriend, Luis Segura, she was 'escorted' by his brother Danny Segura. The impression that she had few dates as a teenager was reinforced by her schoolfriends Suzy Ardakani and Ninaki Priddy. With Ardakani, she went horse-riding, skating and bowling. The Ardakanis became particularly fond of Meghan after Matt Ardakani, the father, was gunned down and paralysed by a deranged Vietnam veteran. Regularly, Meghan went with Suzy to sit by his hospital bed as the garage owner slowly recovered.[45]

At the same time her friendship with Ninaki Priddy became closer. In 1996, Meghan travelled with the Priddy family to Europe. After visiting Paris, they headed to London. The two girls were photographed in front of Buckingham Palace. One year later, Princess Diana was killed in a car crash in Paris. Tearfully, the two girls watched princes William and Harry walk behind the gun carriage towards Westminster Abbey, and saw the TV camera zoom in on the white flowers on Diana's coffin with a card marked 'Mummy' written by twelve-year-old Harry. The image of Diana's young sons was etched in America's memory as was the anger about her treatment by the Royal Family, and especially by Charles.

In the aftermath, the Ardakanis and Meghan re-watched a tape of Diana's 1981 wedding. Suzy gave Meghan *Diana: Her True Story*, Andrew Morton's blockbuster book that exposed the breakdown of Diana's marriage. Even in her twenties, Meghan kept her copy of Morton's expose on her bookshelf and mentioned her ambition to stay in London for one month.[46] Twenty years later she would say, 'I didn't know much about him [Harry] or the Royal Family'.[47] Ninaki Priddy contradicted her old friend. Meghan, she reflected, was 'always fascinated by the royal family' and by Diana's humanitarian work for sufferers of HIV and landmines. On her own admission,

Meghan admitted that her 'first Cinderella moment in fashion' was wearing a 'gorgeous blouse and bejewelled shoes' for the school's Miu Miu show. 'They mean so much to me,' Meghan said, 'because I felt like a princess.'[48]

Drama was her life's priority. Encouraged by Thomas Markle, she had become intensely involved in her school's theatrical productions. To help, Thomas volunteered to erect a professional lighting set on the school stage and build a light-board. He had also paid for her orthodontics – removing the gap between her front teeth.

Obeying her father, Meghan always perfected her lines and unquestioningly obeyed the director's instructions. His more important advice, after occasionally watching rehearsals, was to explain how best to hold her head, fixate her eyes, show her best profile and, most important, look sincere. Acting, he emphasised, depended on the appearance of authenticity. Drama teacher Gigi Perreau noted her strong work ethic and her self-confident performances. School reports mentioned her starring role in a three-day sell-out of *Oedipus Rex* and the great applause for her performance in a succession of musicals – *Annie*, *Damn Yankees* and *Into the Woods*.

One downside of Meghan's success was her intense jealousy, especially if someone else got the lead part. Meghan became particularly irritated after one girl at the school was employed by a Hollywood studio as an actress and two other girls had been auditioned for the film *Trace of Red*. 'She wants to be the star on the stage,' Thomas Markle noticed, 'and the star in life.' She demanded that her father pay a professional photographer to take a 'head shot'. Dutifully, Thomas circulated the photo as an 'open call' to producers across Hollywood's studios. She received no replies. 'I want to be an actress,' she kept saying.

As a treat, Thomas took her to the Emmy awards ceremony when he was nominated as the best lighting director. After they walked down the red carpet, the 17 year old said, 'Daddy, I want to be famous just like you one day.' Thomas nodded. Like so many in the town, Meghan loved glamour and celebrity. She wanted her dream to become reality. He would do anything to help make her dream come true.

In her late teens, Meghan's attitude towards Thomas started to change. In spring 1999 the musical *The Pyjama Game* was the new school play. Meghan wanted the lead part but also wanted to go for a week to the school's summer retreat. Gigi Perreau, the drama teacher, insisted that Meghan had to choose one or the other. Meghan went to the retreat. Outraged that the teacher denied her a part in the play, she urged her father not to do the lighting. He ignored her demand. Furious, he recalled, she screamed he should obey her wishes. He refused. She moved into Doria's home for a few weeks.[49] 'She was mad at me,' admitted Thomas, 'and refused to speak to me.'

Driving around Los Angeles with Ninaki Priddy during that argument, 18-year-old Meghan was being filmed by Priddy steering her car with a licence plate 'CLASSY Girl', a gift from an ex-boyfriend. Just four minutes from Thomas's house, Meghan told her friend, 'We aren't going there because my dad and I aren't on the best terms. I'd like to stop and see if I have any mail, but let's just say I doubt it.'[50] Meghan did not invite Thomas to her appearance at the local boys' school production of *Damned Yankees*. Despite her veto, he watched the performance and sent her flowers backstage. She ignored his gesture. For the first time, her father realised that his daughter intended to write the rules. That was the only school play Doria watched, according to Thomas Markle, who after directing the lighting watched nearly all Meghan's performances.

The Priddy video ended as Meghan headed for an audition in a video for the singer Shakira. If cast, the fee would be $600 for two days. After the audition, Priddy restarted filming Meghan. 'We all danced just like wild women,' she told the camera. 'I was really nervous I was going to spill out of my top coz I was shaking so much.' She was not cast.

Meghan's graduation ceremony in June 1999 was proudly watched by Thomas Markle, Doria and Thomas's mother. Giving the speech in the 'ring ceremony', the ritual of handing over responsibility to the new senior year, Meghan won awards for her academic and acting success.[51] In the school's yearbook, her photo was accompanied by a quotation of Eleanor Roosevelt's she chose: 'Women are like tea-bags, they don't realise how strong they are until they're in hot water.'[52] She undoubtedly admired both her parents. Doria, who she later described as dreadlocked and nose-ringed, was a 'nurturing' free spirit. 'We can just have so much fun together, and yet I'll still find so much solace in her support.'[53]

'Everything you do for me', she had written in one Valentine card to Thomas, 'has turned me into who I am, and I am so grateful. All I want is to make you proud and I promise, no matter what, I'll do it.'[54] Despite her gratitude for his generosity and for paying a total of £165,000 in school fees, Meghan's departure for university inevitably created tension. Thomas Markle became melancholic as his daughter prepared to leave Los Angeles.[55]

CHAPTER 3

College

Princeton was Meghan's first choice. 'It's a rich kids' school,' Thomas thought, but he agreed to ask a friend to help Meghan's entry. Despite her good grades, she was rejected. 'She was unhappy,' Thomas noticed. 'She didn't like being turned down.' Northwestern University in Chicago, ranked among the best for drama, was her next and successful choice.

Securing a place to study theatre and international relations at Northwestern was the entry card to the elite. She had chosen a private, highly selective college renowned as a favourite of rich, well-connected white students. She knew no one there. On admission, she joined the Kappa Kappa Gamma sorority, famous for its Midwestern blondes. She pledged to be philanthropic, care about her 'sisters' and abide by the motto 'aspire to be'. Thomas automatically volunteered to pay the annual $45,000 fees.

Life was good for Meghan. She loved cooking, watching films and studying drama. She made a host of new friends, including Lindsay Jill Roth, the daughter of Long Island lawyers, who became a lifelong confidante, and Larnelle Quentin Foster, an African-American man also studying drama. Spending a lot of time together at events, classes and productions with Foster, she frequently visited his east coast home. Thrilled that her son had met an ideal woman, Foster's mother, a pastor, was unaware that her son was gay. Meghan's first college boyfriend, Steve Lepore, a baseball player, moved to a North Carolina college soon after they met, thereby ending the relationship.

Later boyfriends were rated by a self-help dating bible called *The Rules*, subtitled 'Time-tested Secrets for Capturing the Heart of Mr Right', written for women seeking marriage in the shortest time available. Meghan acquired a copy soon after its publication in 1995 and brought the book to the campus. By then, she could recite passages by heart. 'In any relationship,' recalled Priddy, 'there was always an element of marriage in the back of her mind.' Each man was judged on how their domestic life, as part of a team, would 'look [like] in ten years.'[56] Thomas Markle noticed the same calculation. During his visits to Chicago he heard Meghan predict, 'That's my next boyfriend.' Once identified, she successfully seduced the man. 'She fixed it,' observed Thomas with awe. 'She had this ability to control men.' She functioned so much better with a man around, he realised. She also saved money by moving into the boyfriend's home. But Thomas was puzzled as to why she suddenly called herself Rachel. She refused to explain the switch, but by coincidence the sitcom *Friends* was the current rage, starring Jennifer Aniston as 'Rachel'.

As she had been at school, the hard-working young woman was empathetic, always willing to help the less fortunate. She shone in her charity work, including 'The Glass Slipper Project' that provided dresses for local teenage girls for their Prom; and a 30-hour dance marathon to raise money for cancer sufferers. She also excelled in drama classes, not because of obviously exceptional talent but through hard work and professionalism.

Pertinently, she resisted the invitation from Professor Linda Gates, the head of the voice programme, to study acting in a theatre. 'You can learn to be a great actress,' Gates recalled telling Meghan, 'but I'm not sure she wanted to. Theatre is where you learn to transform yourself and reach an audience – six or seven nights a week. A star actress like

Meryl Streep, trained in the theatre, can completely transform herself and go deep into a character. But Meghan was playing herself – a pretty girl who is personable and intelligent. Her strength was empathy.'[57] Throughout her life, Meghan never mentioned a theatre performance she had seen or enjoyed. Like many aspiring cinema stars, she thought theatre was dead. But, pertinently, friends could also not recall her gushing about an outstanding screen show.

To pursue her film career Meghan asked Thomas to secure a talking part for her in the TV soap *General Hospital*. Her five-line appearance was transmitted in November 2002. After two more auditions she was not offered further work. But the principal purpose had been achieved. Her brief appearance secured the all-important Screen Actors Guild union card. Thereafter, she could work as an actress. Thomas Markle paid the $6,000 fee. Her résumé, he believed, did not mention that she was mixed race.

Meghan would later claim that she encountered 'closed-mindedness' about her parentage and her parents' divorce at college. 'A dorm mate I met in my first week,' she recalled, 'asked if my parents were still together. "You said your mom is Black and your dad is white, right?" she said. I smiled meekly, waiting for what could possibly come out of her pursed lips next. "And they're divorced?" I nodded. "Oh, well that makes sense." I understood the implication and I drew back – I was scared to open this Pandora's box of discrimination, so I sat stifled, swallowing my voice.'[58] However Professor Harvey Young who focused on African-American theatre at the college did not believe that there was racism among the 15,000 students on the campus. He limited himself to a neutral observation, saying, 'Meghan was thoughtful and understood what it means to face prejudice and discrimination.'[59]

During her second year, still uncertain whether she would make it as an actress, Meghan asked her uncle Michael Markle, by then a communications expert for the US government, to arrange a five-week internship as a junior press officer at the American embassy in Buenos

Aires. 'I hated the idea of being this cliché, a girl from Los Angeles who decides to be an actress,' she explained later. 'I wanted more than that and I had always loved politics, so applied for an internship.'[60] Thomas paid for the 'study programme'. Her half-sister Samantha would later claim that Meghan was not actually employed in the embassy, but was actually at a school attached to the embassy that arranged work experience.

Towards the end of her stay, Meghan took the Foreign Service Officers Test, the preliminary to judge whether a candidate is sufficiently proficient to take the more demanding exam to enter the State Department. After never showing any interest in maths – a basic requirement to become a diplomat – she failed the three-hour exam. The following year, she returned to Buenos Aires to meet a boyfriend. Thomas Markle paid for that trip too. When Meghan called from Argentina, saying, 'I need $500 to get out of the hotel,' he sent her the money.

On her return from Argentina, she decided that she would follow the cliché – acting. Later, she would mention an introduction to an agent called Drew who was apparently impressed by her performance in a student film. 'You're going to make money,' Drew promised, 'and I'll take 10. I think you should stick around.' No one has since been able to identify 'Drew'.[61]

Graduation from Northwestern in 2003 was joyful, though tinged with anxiety as Meghan prepared to return home. Los Angeles was a Mecca for thousands of young aspiring actors. The overwhelming majority would be disappointed and end up penniless. At least she had the odds stacked in her favour. 'My dad taught me to find my light,' she would write.[62] Doria's contribution to her daughter's career was advice about skincare. Drink two litres of water daily, she suggested, use a Clarisonic brush, apply sunblock and get facials.[63]

Financed by Thomas Markle, Meghan rented a home, bought a used car and asked her father to pay for the petrol. He also converted her bathroom into a darkroom because she wanted to learn about photography. For additional income, she worked in turn as a gift-wrapper, a calligrapher for wedding invitations and as a hostess at Mirabelle, a restaurant in West Hollywood. Mirabelle's waiters were usually unemployed actors seeking parts.

Clutching a portfolio of photos, including the typical aspiring actress shot with a revealing neckline and an open midriff, Meghan began the tough routine of seeking auditions. Unlike her competitors, she could cite her appearance in *General Hospital*. She read lines with gusto to po-faced casting directors whose routine 'Thank you' at the end gave no hint of the outcome. She had learnt to control her feelings after rejection.

To outsiders her progress might have appeared meagre, but within the industry even a few inches of celluloid was notched as a success. Her brief appearance as a 'hot girl' in a film called *A Lot Like Love*, starring Ashton Kutcher, and one line in *Century City* were fleeting. But she was doing better than most of her rivals.[64]

Her search for a long-term relationship was equally frustrating. There were six months with Shaun, an actor and screenwriter raised in the Hamptons whom she had met at Northwestern. That ended after he refused to commit, and was followed by five months with actor Brett Ryland. That ended because he apparently lacked the right personality. Then followed other actors, a Latin tycoon and an inconsequential night out with Simon Rex, a male porn-star.[65] Every evening she set off saying to herself, 'You never know, tonight I might meet the man who will change my life.'

In 2004, she met Trevor Engelson in a West Hollywood bar. Tall with reddish hair, the ambitious 27-year-old graduate of cinematography at the University of Southern California was starting out as a film producer, targeting the comedy channels with his clients' scripts. In his free time, he listened to hip-hop, read voraciously, travelled endlessly and, he told a podcast, played around the clock, explaining: 'I'm Jewish and I believe you only have one shot at this life. I'm a gigantic believer that all this shit could come suddenly to an end any minute now. You should have some fun.' Starting in the post-room of an actors' agency before promotion to a production house, he had been fired for secretly undertaking a freelance production. Soon after, Engelson sold his own film script, *The Road to Freaknik*, and started a production company, Underground Films 5190.[66] Engelson looked at his competitors and thought, 'Fuck him, it'll be me.' He did not want to be the average Joe, but 'get the lottery ticket and be special'.

Insensitive and self-confident, Engelson's well-honed chat-up lines in the noisy bar impressed Meghan. Boasting that he worked and played hard – even reading screenplays every morning through his steam shower's glass door – he offered his life's philosophy: 'Hope is the greatest currency we have in this business.' Then came another favoured maxim: 'Don't give it five minutes if you're not gonna give it five years.' Ten years later, Meghan frequently intoned both these lines in speeches to young audiences as her philosophy of life.

Engelson was clever and capable of behaving well-mannered, and his family's stable background attracted Meghan. He had been brought up in the Jewish community in Great Neck, a prosperous New York commuter town. His father was an orthodontist and his mother a speech therapist. Educated at Great Neck's North High School, Trevor was known as 'Flowerhead'. His friends called themselves the Mudd Juice Posse. 'Trevor was one of the most desirable people you'd want to be in a friendship with,' recalled Larry Pretto, also raised in Great Neck. 'Honest, loyal, respectful, with a lot of humility.' Engelson's attitude to girls, said Pretto, was decent. 'He didn't just want them as notches on his bedpost. He was old-school. If they wanted to shop, or go out somewhere, he'd take them into the city. He just wanted to make them feel good about themselves. He charmed everybody.'[67]

Other contemporaries were less complimentary. They thought him brash, conceited and definitely not the genius he believed himself to be. But Engelson's promise of stability matched Meghan's needs. Or, more importantly, her illusion. Like so many lured to Hollywood she was driven by a fantasy of her future. Not just the pursuit of happiness but also the belief that Trevor could help her, emotionally and professionally. She wanted easy living and freedom from financial stress. In turn, everything about her was new to him.

Ninaki Priddy was among the first to meet Meghan's latest boyfriend: 'Trevor was big for her. He was very focused with great connections. It was an opportunity for her to establish relationships with agents. She loved it – being at his side and going to those dinners. She loved him. He was very doting.' Meghan was so besotted by the romance that she could barely keep her hands off Trevor. In public she hugged and kissed him, and adopting a babyish voice cooed, 'Trevity-Trev-Trev'. Priddy witnessed her sense of triumph. In return, Trevor gave Meghan bear hugs.

Unable to believe his own good fortune, Trevor told his friends that he had met 'the hottest chick in California'.[68] After a few months, Meghan moved into his home on Hilldale, West Hollywood. Thrilled by her catch she proclaimed, 'I've got my toothbrush in his cabinet.' Trevor discovered his beautiful woman was also a domestic goddess. 'She was definitely a curator of a beautiful life,' said Ninaki. 'She had a very specific style. She loved her hotel-style bedding – beautiful, contrasting black piping detail on crisp, white duvets. She loved everything white. Meg was a perfectionist. She liked to throw dinner parties with beautiful menus that complemented flavour profiles with amazing wines.'[69]

Priddy was describing an idealised snapshot of one evening rather than Meghan's routine life. Although Meghan, it seemed, had found a genuine partner sympathetic to her insecurity, her reality as a wannabe actress was grim. As she touted herself around the studios, auditions were followed by an inevitable 'Thank You' and rejection without reason. Survival in Hollywood, she knew, depended on avoiding the necessity to tell or face up to the truth, and denying rejection when it occurred. There was no alternative. Like a slot-machine addict, she needed to keep playing and refuse to give up until she had a hit.

'My twenties,' she wrote, 'were brutal – a constant battle with myself, judging my weight, my style, my desire to be as cool/as hip/as smart/as "whatever" as everyone else. I must have been about 24 when a casting director looked at me during an audition and said, "You need to know that you're enough. Less make-up, more Meghan."'[70]

Driving around Los Angeles in a battered Ford Explorer whose front door didn't open – she got in and out through the trunk hatch – she eventually landed brief appearances in TV films including *Love Inc*, *Deceit* and *The War at Home*. Trevor chose not to cast her in his latest comedy, *Zoom*. His 'comedy' crashed.

Hollywood, a town of competition rather than compassion, was unforgiving towards Trevor and Meghan. In 2006, both ranked among the thousands of eager, desperate and flailing unknowns blitzed by snideness and malice. Their noses were pressed against the glass, enviously beseeching the industry's moguls. Any success would depend on a mixture of hard graft, genuine talent and unexpected luck.

At last, Meghan got a break. Her fortunes changed. Howie Mandel, a comedian and host of the TV show *Deal or No Deal*, watched her reel of one-liners and her audition. Her body and looks matched his requirements. She would be one of 26 identically dressed hostesses on five-inch stiletto-heels, squeezed into tight mini-dresses to pronounce their figures, each carrying a briefcase.[71] Her half-sister Samantha believed, 'They must have stuffed her bra.'

Starting at 5:30am, Meghan was contracted until after nightfall. Seven episodes were filmed in one day. Each show paid $800. Between each episode she would change clothes. 'It's so embarrassing,' she told her father. 'It's exposure,' he consoled her. 'If you're spotted, you'll get another part. It'll take time to get there.' Thomas knew that to win stardom, Hollywood expected Meghan to do anything. Humiliation was one of the prices of winning fame.

In front of a raucous audience and loud music, the show's seductive hostesses stood near contestants carrying a briefcase containing between one cent and one million dollars. After choosing one briefcase, the contestants were offered the Deal: either 'sell' the briefcase for a fixed sum or continue in the hope of choosing the briefcase with one million dollars. Amid contrived tension, contestants were urged to take the risk.

As ever in Hollywood, sexy young women attracted rich and powerful men. Among the visitors welcomed to the studio was Donald Trump. On the set between takes, the New York businessman handed out his card and invitations to visit his golf courses. Some girls accepted and would later say that Meghan not only rejected Trump but all the other invitations. Leyla Milani, one of the other girls, would assert that Meghan never went out after the shows, but read scripts for auditions.[72] 'Meghan was never interested in casual dating. She was always looking for commitment,' wrote her approved biographer years later.[73]

Those recollections were contradicted by Brett Ratner, a successful Hollywood producer of the time. Ratner prided himself that Hilhaven Lodge, his Hollywood palace – famous as Ingrid Bergman's first home in America – was in those years 'the centre of the universe'. Proudly telling everyone, 'I'm fat and Jewish', Ratner had dated tennis champion Serena Williams for two years. Several times every week Ratner hosted all-night parties for the stars – Johnny Depp, Leonardo DiCaprio, Penélope Cruz and many more swished into his hilltop compound. 'Tons of beautiful girls came,' recalled a close friend of Ratner. Among them every weekend were the game-show girls. 'A dime a dozen' was the common quip about party girls. Meghan was one of those frequent guests. Among a clutch of stunning-looking women, she was memorable to a few unusually observant guests as conservatively dressed, and known to pose as an innocent. Yet she was usually among the last to leave as dawn broke.

By the end of the *Deal or No Deal* show, Meghan had lost her coyness. Dressed in hot pants and little else, she starred in the lifestyle magazine *Men's Health* making burgers on a grill.[74] The champion of women's empowerment later described those experiences as being 'objectified'.

Juggling her career, life with Trevor was good. Both enjoyed travelling abroad and eating the best food. They flew to Greece, Mexico and Thailand to visit recommended restaurants. Although she barely earned enough to cover her own costs, Trevor's latest film scripts had earned him an income. The downside was that they still lived beyond the fringes of Hollywood's elite. Hollywood's power-brokers were unaware they even existed. After rejection and snapshot appearances left on the cutting-room floor, Meghan was still looking for the big break.

An audition by Donna Rosenstein, a rising TV producer and casting director, was a reward for Meghan's perseverance. In a proposed series, *The Apostles*, she would play a former sex worker rescued by a Christian policeman who falls in love and marries her. In the series' pilot, Meghan played the part of an experienced young woman who argued with her husband – and provided sex advice to her neighbours. Fox Studios rejected the pilot. Then, she featured in a pilot for *Good Behavior*, a light-hearted series about a Las Vegas criminal family trying to become honest. That too was rejected. In her next part in *90210*, a successful remake of the Beverly Hills series, she memorably performed oral sex in a parked car in a public area. After two episodes, she disappeared without explanation. Next, she was given a cameo appearance snorting cocaine in *The Boys and Girls Guide to Getting Down*. In 2009, she appeared in *Get Him to the Greek*. Roger Ebert of the *Chicago Sun-Times* called it a 'fundamentally sound movie' but missed Meghan, who had no lines and was not given a credit.

Even worse, her brief appearance in *Fringe*, a sci-fi film, was edited out. 'That was heart-breaking for her,' recalled Nick Collins, her agent and a partner of the Gersh Agency from the beginning. 'There are people who shut down when that happens, and other people who say "I can do it, I'm going to show them". Meghan is in the second group.' In Hollywood's ratings, any appearance in a series, even if the project was rejected, was marked a 'success'. Casting agents noticed her string of appearances.

Her reward for tenacity came in 2010. Brett Ratner contracted Meghan for a 35-second appearance in his film *Horrible Bosses*. Cast as a FedEx delivery girl, Meghan mixed for the first time with Hollywood's royalty including Jennifer Aniston, Kevin Spacey and Donald Sutherland. On the set of the profitable film, she introduced herself: 'Mr Sutherland, I hear I'm going to fall in love with you before lunch-break.' He laughed. 'I resisted the very major urge to squeal,' Meghan wrote.[75] Rating the film with two stars, the *Guardian* called it an 'occasionally amusing but mostly crude, charmless and misjudged comedy'. On the back of those experiences, Trevor cast her in small roles in his films, *The Candidate* and *Remember Me*. Both flopped.

Eight years into her bid for stardom, Meghan recorded the horrors of her professional life in Working Actress, an 'anonymous' blog: 'I'm not going to lie. I've spent many days curled up in bed with a loaf of bread and some wine. A one-woman pity party. It's awful and ridiculous.'[76] On another evening, she continued, 'I've had to freeze my acting union membership, borrow money, work jobs that I hated, endure being treated like shit on a set, kiss actors with smelly breath and cry for hours on end because I just didn't think I could take it anymore.'[77]

The reasons for her rejection were common. Hollywood was full of good-looking ambitious actresses but very few had star quality. Critical to cinematic success was identity. Natural stars like Meryl Streep, Nicole Kidman and Rachel Weisz project a gravity on to the big screen to lock in the audience's eyes. Meghan lacked charisma. On screen, she generated no magic. Although she was undoubtedly attractive, directors found her unexciting and ordinary. The audience's emotions and curiosity, they believed, would not be excited by her appearance. Like the vast majority of wannabes, Meghan portrayed her own wants and needs, and not the requirements of the role. She was her own person. She could not convincingly become another person. She never played a part which she could adapt to herself. Lacking natural mystery, she remained a B actress struggling with one-liners that might end up on the cutting-room floor.

'No thanks' after an audition fuelled Meghan's belief that the casting director had not understood her. She needed to try harder, and the next day would certainly be different. In Hollywood, rejection was not a stigma or humiliation. After five years, her reel was substantial. Jobbing actors, she was reassured, earned a good income from constant employment.

Repeatedly, she looked for explanations as the rejections piled up. 'I wasn't Black enough for the Black roles,' she wrote, 'and I wasn't white enough for the white roles, leaving me somewhere in the middle as the ethnic chameleon who couldn't book a job.'[78] In an article for *Elle* in 2015, Meghan described how she was asked 'every week of her life, often every day' what she was and where she came from, as people struggled to place her ethnicity. Rather than accept she was not an outstanding actress, she stressed: 'It was the first time I put a name to feeling too light in the Black community, too mixed in the white community.'

Five years later, she rephrased her story. In *Allure* magazine, she dated her first realisation of 'colourism' during an African-American studies class at Northwestern.[79]

Thomas disputes this. 'Race was never an issue throughout Meghan's childhood,' insists Thomas Markle, 'or her years in Hollywood. I was surprised when she brought it up. With the exception of the box at school and a driver shouting at Doria, Meghan never mentioned race.' Meghan, he insisted, 'was never the underdog.'[80]

Similarly, Thomas Markle insists that Meghan never blamed racism for rejection at auditions. 'Didn't come up,' he said.

In mid-2010, Nick Collins sent his client for an audition in an office block in Santa Monica, Los Angeles. The American producers were looking for an attractive young woman to play Rachel Zane, an aspiring lawyer unable to pass the exams. In the low-budget soap series set in a New York law firm, Zane would have an affair with Mike Ross, a brilliant young man with a photographic memory.

Called *Suits*, Aaron Korsh, the 43-year-old writer of the potential series, based the narrative on his five years on Wall Street. Korsh had quit his bank to work for eight years as an assistant writer in a film production company. On the verge of giving up, he took a gamble to write *Suits* built on his experiences on Wall Street. Loyalty within a 'family' of employees was Korsh's forceful theme. Bankers were portrayed being asked to do things in the office that offended their morality but loyalty – 'a two-way street' – compelled them to oblige.

After reading the script, the producers suggested Korsh switch the drama to a lawyers' office. Once adapted, the producers started auditions for the pilot. Korsh had 'no image' for the part of Rachel Zane except that she was intelligent, likeable, worldly-wise, sexy and, to match the loyalty theme, totally trustworthy. Her role required that she would go to any lengths to help those she was working with.

Rachel Zane's 'loyalty' dilemma was profound. Mike Ross, a self-serving beguiling fraudster, lacked any loyalty. Yet he invoked loyalty to demand a favour from honest Rachel Zane. Korsh explored how Zane reacted to the danger of violating her ethical boundaries. The parallel conundrum was whether Mike's outstanding qualifications made him a better human being.

As a last-minute thought about the part before the audition, Meghan ditched a colourful jumper and jeans and bought a $35 little black dress. 'I don't think I did a good job,' she lamented to Nick Collins afterwards. 'I really wanted that part.'[81]

Back in his Santa Monica office, Korsh was excited. 'We all looked at each other,' he recalled, 'like "Wow this is the one." I think it's because Meghan had the ability to be smart and sharp without losing her sweetness.' Although the producers agreed they would seek diversity among the cast, Korsh recalls, 'I didn't know that Meghan was mixed race when she was piloted. She was just the best.' Korsh's admission challenges Meghan's complaint that her career had been stymied by her colour.

Cast on 24th August, 2010, Meghan shot the pilot in New York and, as usual, waited to hear whether a network would buy the series. At the beginning of 2011, Meghan was told that USA Network, a cable corporation, had commissioned one season of 12 episodes. Years of hustling had paid off. She would earn a regular income of $50,000 per episode. That would be $600,000 after nine months' work. Reflecting on her earlier pessimism, she explained: 'It was a really good lesson in perspective. I think we are always going to be our own worst critics.'[82]

There was one surprise. To save money, filming would start in April in Toronto and not as anticipated in New York. Every member of the cast was upset, except Meghan. To the producers' bemusement, Meghan was keen to set up her permanent home in Toronto rather than commute like all the other actors from Los Angeles. Unexpectedly, she also revealed that she would stay in Toronto beyond November, after filming ended. Leaving Los Angeles and Trevor, Meghan told the producers, was not a downside. She did not explain why she wanted to leave Los Angeles. One friend speculated that she had agreed that Trevor's 'super cheesy. Like a guy who wears those Adidas slippers (with a suit) to a fancy event.'[83] Another friend suggested that while Meghan could commit herself to Trevor, she did not like being possessed.

Meghan needed to be in total control. If necessary, *Suits* was her get-out card from the relationship.

CHAPTER 4

Suits

Trevor Engelson sensed the tension. Six years after he and Meghan had met, they flew to Belize for a holiday. Soon after they arrived, he proposed. Marriage, he believed, would secure their relationship. Despite the five-hour flight between Los Angeles and Toronto, he hoped that regular commuting and telephone calls would minimise the barriers. Meghan seemed to be thrilled by the idea.

Shortly after saying, 'Yes', Meghan telephoned her best friend. 'She called me immediately,' recalled Ninaki Priddy. 'She was ecstatic and sent me some beautiful pictures. This was the man she wanted to have children with.'[84] Soon after returning to Los Angeles, Meghan rushed to see Ninaki. 'Meghan came to show me the ring when she got home and was so excited. She asked me to be maid of honour. We were hugging each other and crying. There was no doubt about her love for Trevor. Meg used to tell me she couldn't imagine a life without him. She said if anything were to happen to him she wouldn't be able to go on.' More than ever, Meghan relied on Priddy: 'I think when you're an only child in that situation your friends do become your family.' As for Trevor, Priddy was sure he 'would have walked the earth to make the marriage work'.

Every aspect of Meghan's life was changing. For a start, her mother's life had finally stabilised, although the cause was upsetting.

In March 2011, Doria's 82-year-old father Alvin died after falling and hitting his head on the pavement. She inherited some money and his house in Windsor Hills, a Black middle-class area. At the same time, she began studying for a degree in social work at the University of Southern California.[85]

Thomas Markle's life also changed. At the age of 67 he retired and, relying solely on his pension, moved to Mexico. In Rosarito, a coastal town merely 20 miles from the American border, he could live cheaply in the sun. At first he rented a beach hut and then moved into a bungalow on a cliff above the sea. The rent was just $850 a month. The downside of retirement was losing his Hollywood status, but after spending 50 years surrounded by people, he wanted peace. With the Pacific lapping on the wide, empty beach below, he lived among the debris of a lifetime in Hollywood. 'I've never been a neat person,' he admitted.

With few friends, the solitary, proud man filled his time watching old films, walking around the town and taking photographs. Regularly, he telephoned his two elder children, especially his daughter Samantha. His relationship with Meghan was different. 'I don't want to come to Mexico,' she said during one of their weekly calls. He in turn refused Meghan's invitations to travel to Toronto. He feared an argument. After seeing the first episodes of *Suits*, he was critical of the director's lighting – and the whole production.

Meghan disliked his criticism, Thomas recalled. 'She began talking down to me. Suddenly, there was a command in her voice. She'd outgrown me. She gave the impression that she didn't need me anymore. I began to think that I didn't understand Meghan anymore.'[86] The previously compassionate creature was becoming a woman of strong opinions and bigger ambitions. Flush with money, her sense of duty and obligation began to slip. She finally had status. She was being taken seriously. Aaron Korsh actually wanted to know her as a person.

Before leaving for Toronto, Korsh and Meghan had met for lunch at the King's Road Café in Hollywood. To his delight, Meghan revealed herself to be a foodie. In the development of the series, Korsh decided that his team of writers would incorporate her interest into the scripts. The influence went two ways. Keen to absorb new ideas, Meghan was especially interested in Korsh's depiction of loyalty and authority.

There was a caveat. Although finally established after years on the periphery, Meghan was the youngest of the cast. Ranked sixth actor in the series she would not be mentioned in the publicity for the launch. Not least because, by common consent, she was not the best actor in the show.[87]

Uncertain if *Suits* would be recommissioned after the first series, Meghan needed a safety-net, just in case. Like all actors she was plagued by insecurity. Seeking work, she sent her reel to Phaedra Harris, the casting director of *Dysfunctional Friends* in Hollywood, a highbrow comedy. 'She was aggressive in a good way,' recalled Harris. 'She was very tenacious, driven.' Meghan was momentarily considered for a minor part, but the film's schedule clashed with *Suits*'s.[88] Although she wanted to live separately, Meghan had no alternative but to rely on Trevor.

Life in Toronto was not glamorous. And the long hours made it hard work. Early each day, Meghan was collected by car from her small rented house in a tree-lined road in the Annex neighbourhood. The driver dropped her outside a downtown concrete hanger. Filming *Suits* was a familiar experience. Nurtured since childhood to embrace fellow actors, crew and directors, her professionalism shone. 'She was kind and sweet,' recalled a producer, 'knew her lines and was easy to talk to.'

During those first months, the *Suits* cast became her 'surrogate family'. Two actors, Rick Hoffman and Gina Torres, became particular friends. Sometimes they went to bars and clubs after a day's filming. But usually Meghan returned home to cook for herself, do yoga, and Skype with Trevor, encouraging him to fly to Toronto.[89] Often, she admitted, she spent time on the internet 'trolling for girlfriends'.

Frequently, she called Ninaki Priddy. 'It was an exciting time,' recalled her old friend.

Before the first *Suits* episode was broadcast on 23rd June, 2011, Trevor posted a message on Facebook urging people to watch his 'bad-ass fiancée'. The enthusiastic reviews spread hope that the small audience would grow. Meghan's excitement was doubled by her wedding, which was planned for 10th September, 2011, in Jamaica.

Three weeks before the big party, *The Schmoes Know*, a live podcast by Trevor with two friends, highlighted the difference between him and Meghan. Swigging from a hip-flask, Trevor described how he feared a splash on his suit while using a urinal. One of his friends suggested that Meghan be invited to appear on their podcast. 'She's a big deal, fuck off,' snapped Trevor.[90] Casual, earthy, untidy and unpunctual, Trevor knew he was marrying a self-disciplined perfectionist.

Shortly before flying to celebrate in Jamaica, Trevor and Meghan married on 16th August in a civil ceremony in Los Angeles. Neither Thomas nor Doria were invited, and the date was deliberately classified as 'confidential' by the couple to prevent outsiders – without a court order – discovering the details.

A total of 102 guests including Meghan's parents were invited to a four-day beach party at the Jamaica Inn, famous as a haunt of Ian Fleming, Marilyn Monroe and Arthur Miller. Meghan booked all 55 rooms and villas. Guests paid for their own accommodation. Thomas Markle contributed $20,000 to the costs, partly by selling shares worth $6,000. 'They didn't expect the money,' recalled Thomas, 'but I offered it. It's my daughter.' In return, Meghan and Trevor gave him a 'certificate' for a journey anywhere in the world, which he did not use.

Wheelchair-bound with multiple sclerosis, Samantha volunteered to stay away. She was represented by her daughter. None of Doria's family appeared. Thomas believes that none could have afforded the fare and the accommodation. In addition to the couple's friends from Hollywood and New York, there was a large contingent from the cast of *Suits*. The chemistry of working together as a 'family' had created a special magic. Meghan's empathy and professionalism had won universal affection. Always the easiest to agree to schedule changes, the producers appreciated that she never got worked up. By then, many noticed the close relationship between Meghan and Patrick J. Adams playing Ross. 'We grew up together over the course of the show,' Adams would say about their special bond.[91]

The night before the wedding ceremony, Trevor described in his speech during the dinner a book he had prepared about his and Meghan's lives. The book's conclusion, said Trevor, was his pledge to give Meghan 'the family home she never has had'. Thomas's and Doria's jaws fell. 'We looked aghast at each other,' said Thomas. 'She had had two good families and all the love and attention any child could want.' Both wondered what Meghan had told Trevor about her childhood. Why had she concealed her past? Or why had she distorted her origins? What other 'secrets', Thomas wondered, had his daughter told Trevor? For the first time, Thomas feared that his cooling relationship with Meghan would be fractured by her inaccurate statements. In Jamaica, however, Thomas Markle would not let Meghan's fantasies interfere with his pride, although another characteristic of hers emerged.

'She controlled the whole wedding like a sergeant,' he noticed. 'There were times for everyone to be ready in costumes, for games and for meals. I couldn't understand what she was trying to achieve. She even forbade everyone from taking photos.' Despite her instructions, his beloved daughter was getting married and he disobeyed: 'I went ahead and snapped.'

Ninaki Priddy was the maid of honour: 'I started crying the moment I saw her in her dress. Meg literally shone with happiness. We'd been like sisters since we were two years old, so I knew she'd always wanted to get married. To see her finally doing that was...well, it was a big deal. It was such a moving wedding. It was so beautiful to watch, beautiful to be a part of. They loved each other so much. She married her eternal love.'[92]

Dressed in a white suit bought by Meghan, Thomas walked his daughter with Doria down to the beach for the ceremony. Trevor's father was waiting under the chuppah, the canopy for a traditional Jewish ceremony. His mother sat in front. Both Trevor's parents were unhappy that their son was not marrying someone Jewish, and in particular that he was marrying Meghan. From their first introduction, both had disliked Meghan's aloof self-interest. Over the years, she had shown neither loyalty nor intimacy to the Engelsons. Neither believed she would be willing to make the sacrifices for the creation of a proper family home. Trevor had ignored their opposition to the marriage. Since their son was determined to marry Meghan, there was no alternative but to make the best of the situation.

Trevor's father officiated at the ceremony. In her own written vow, Meghan promised to love and cherish Trevor. At the end, Trevor stamped on a bag of glass. Shattering the glass symbolises for Jewish people the fragility of relationships and reminded Meghan that maintaining relationships required special care. A roar of approval and cheers burst out and the party began. With reggae music in the background, the guests began drinking rum and lager and smoking the cannabis handed out to everyone in small bags by the couple. Unnoticed by the guests, Meghan demanded the official video of the party. To Thomas Markle's surprise, she destroyed it soon after the wedding. She wanted no visual record of the marriage. By default, only her father's photos survived.

On their return to Los Angeles, the couple lived in a small house off Sunset Boulevard. While Meghan waited to hear whether *Suits* had been recommissioned, Thomas Markle's mother became seriously ill in Los Feliz, his latest Los Angeles home. With increasing dementia and after a kitchen fire, Doris Markle moved to a residential home. Tom Junior met Meghan during a visit. 'I saw the private side of Meghan, a genuinely caring, loving person. She had an amazing relationship with Doris, even though she didn't know her that well.'[93] Doris died on 25th November, 2011. Thomas Markle's two brothers met Meghan and Trevor for the first time at the funeral.

By then, Meghan had celebrated the good news that American Network had commissioned a second series. To celebrate, she bought a £4,800 Cartier watch. On the back was engraved 'To M.M. From M.M.'

The second season would attract a bigger audience – about a million viewers, mostly young.[94] One cliffhanger was whether Rachel and Mike would forge an intimate relationship. The sub-plot focused on Mike's personal life. He had a crush on Rachel Zane but he was having a relationship with Jenny, who in turn was the ex-girlfriend of Mike's drug-dealing former best friend Trevor. At the end of the series, Mike and Rachel consummated their relationship.

Meghan began to identify with the character: 'I happen to really love Rachel, I love how ambitious she is, always trying to take the bull by its horns, and savvy. She's sort of become someone that I could see as a friend, which makes it a lot sweeter to play.' In particular, Meghan liked the fact Rachel had 'encyclopaedic knowledge of the law', and that she was to many viewers 'love interest' or 'eye candy'.[95]

A new theme inserted by the producers was Rachel's father's disappointment that his daughter was failing her exams. Although race was not contentious in the series, they cast Wendell Pierce, the Black actor, as the father. Pleased that the producers had acknowledged that she was mixed-race, she had uttered one reference in the first series. 'Do you think this is a year-round tan?' Meghan had asked her boyfriend. Wendell Pierce's introduction provoked a racist response from a handful of viewers. 'Ew, she's Black?' was one Twitter comment. 'I used to think she was hot.' Race still remained unmentioned by Meghan, apart from a solitary protest in an unexceptional daytime Canadian TV show.[96]

Introducing herself as Meghan Engelson, she returned to Toronto to film the second season of *Suits*. Regularly, Trevor arrived from Los Angeles to work from her house. The struggling producer 'would have walked the earth to make their marriage work', according to Priddy. Trevor did not notice that his wife, free from the constraints of her past in Los Angeles, avoided the daily compromises of marriage. Liberated by her financial security, Meghan began to identify with her character, Rachel Zane. Wearing Tom Ford pencil skirts, speaking about contracts and clients, she was becoming like Zane, an empowered, sassy, professional woman. Inevitably, her relationship with Trevor began to change.

Toronto is not a large community. Unlike in Los Angeles, Meghan was a noticed fish in a small pond. For the first time she had status. She began to make new friends. One was Jessica Mulroney, an aspiring fashion stylist, whom she met in a fitness studio.[97] Jessica's husband, Ben Mulroney, was not only famous as a TV host but as the son of the former Canadian prime minister Brian Mulroney, a pillar of Canada's establishment. Naturally, Jessica was also a friend of Sophie Grégoire-Trudeau, the wife of Justin Trudeau, whose father Pierre had been Canada's prime minister for four years. As a leading parliamentary member of Canada's Liberal party, Justin was tipped to become prime minister. Added to that, there was Markus Anderson, a Canadian businessman who had just returned from London to open a Toronto branch of Soho House, a members' club for the city's socially ambitious fashionistas.

The combination of life on the film set, occasional recognition on the street in Toronto and her new social life with Canada's dynastic families changed Meghan. She was mixing with an elite. Compared to her financially strapped struggle in Los Angeles and a loud-mouth husband unable to deliver fame, her new life in Toronto was what she had always dreamed of. Money was the decisive influence. With a growing taste for luxury, the finest clothes and jewellery and the promise of a glittering presence on the red carpet, celebrity was within reach. Absent from Trevor, she promoted her importance through Instagram. Launching a new account on 24th May, 2012, she introduced herself with images of *Forbes* magazine, plus Rachel Maddow's *Drift* – a book describing the balance of power between America's politicians and the military – and pages from her *Suits* script.[98]

On her return trips to Los Angeles to live with Trevor, Meghan realised that her future in Hollywood was bleak. In the world of paparazzi, parties and producers she was still unknown and excluded. Trevor faced the same fate. He was a good man – unrecognised and unknown – going nowhere. In Hollywood, they would neither be famous nor rich. Impatient, she began to chase an achievable dream.

'There is Meghan Before Fame and Meghan After Fame,' summed up Priddy glancing through a photograph album. Unapologetically, Meghan started cancelling lunches with her old Los Angeles friend at the last moment, explaining how she feared that she would be recognised. Priddy felt a new coolness: 'The tone of her voice, her mannerisms, the way she laughed didn't seem real to me anymore. Her time became increasingly important. When she was in town, she'd want you to drop everything to see her. If I was busy, it would be, "Why don't you want to see me? I'm here. Let's hang out!"' On other occasions, she refused Priddy's suggestions to meet for lunch. Priddy felt awkward. 'It was like a light switched off. We began to talk less. I felt if I questioned her behaviour I'd be left on the outside.' Fearful for their friendship, Priddy preferred not to know the truth.[99] Meghan had changed. She had become sharp, clear and even cruel. More than ever, her emotions were concealed.

Trevor noticed his wife's transformation. During holidays together in New Zealand and Vietnam his ostensible complaint was serious food poisoning, after agreeing with Meghan's suggestion that they try the local food. There was a more serious problem. The holiday was a curtain-raiser to a critical discussion. At 31, under pressure from

Trevor, Meghan was thinking of children. He wanted them, she did not. With her career breakthrough, motherhood was impractical.

Instead, she searched for a dog, as she wrote, 'to keep me company in Toronto.'[100] In December 2012, she headed for Spot Rescue, a pet adoption agency in Los Angeles offering rescued dogs. She chose Bogart, a six-week-old yellow 'Labrador mix'. But there was a problem. The same dog had been chosen by someone else. To beat her competitor, Meghan recruited Priddy and other friends to bombard the agency in an email chain in her support. The dog, wrote Meghan, was guaranteed happiness in the '*Suits* Family'. 'I felt that she was playing the *Suits* card,' recalled Priddy, 'to try to get what she wanted. I felt she had developed a sense of entitlement because she was on the show. It left a sour taste in my mouth.'

Several days later, Meghan recorded her success on Instagram. Posting a photo of herself holding Bogart, she thanked the American daytime TV talk-show host Ellen DeGeneres for sending her to the agency: 'You told me to adopt this sweet pup yesterday, and I'm so happy I did. Thanks a million!'[101] Dropping names on Instagram, Meghan realised, boosted her importance. By February 2013, in successive Instagram posts Bogart was anointed by Meghan as a social media star 'showered with love'.[102]

This was noticed by the royal biographer Sally Bedell Smith. Her son David had bought Bogart's brother puppy at the same time. Meghan emailed David to organise a reunion of the puppies on Malibu beach. 'Reunited for the first time,' Meghan wrote on Instagram with an attached video after the dogs romped together for one hour. 'They were beyond happy. #puppylove #bogart #rescue pup. Oh my God, how sweet!' One month after the dogs' beach party, Meghan was in Toronto, apparently more in love with Bogart than Trevor. Her dog was a perfect conversation starter when she walked through the nearby Trinity Bellwoods Park.[103]

'Watch *Suits* tonight…so proud of my amazing wife,' Trevor posted on 24th January, 2013 – and then went to the Oscars in Los Angeles without Meghan. Omid Scobie, Meghan's self-styled spokesman, would interpret that as a snub.

Scobie is an unusual journalist. Critics have highlighted that his face changed after working in Japan for *US Weekly*, and Richard Eden, in the *Daily Mail*, suggested that his age has also varied. Some would say that as the royal editor for *Harper's Bazaar*, the Anglo-Iranian is a propagandist. Employed by *Heat* magazine, he became friends with Dan Wakeford who would become the editor of *People* magazine in 2019. He is treated by some media as the spokesman for Meghan and Harry.

According to Scobie, Meghan had always mentioned her dream to go to the Oscars – especially as a star. In reality she refused to join her husband. Trevor, she knew, was spending every night in bars, supposedly to get work. Living apart had made them incompatible. 'Living the dream' of *Suits* success, she decided that Trevor's demand that they have children did not match her ambitions. She told friends in Toronto that she did not want children with him. His charm had worn thin. His expectations from their relationship were unacceptable. No one could live with her, except on her terms.

Some who knew Trevor were not surprised by her decision. They cast him as a 'brash acquired taste'. Often he acted with self-importance. She had learnt a lot from him, and his financial support had been invaluable, but there was nothing more to absorb, nothing more to gain. He had been an opportunity – a starter marriage. He was no longer her family – or, was the latest family she no longer had.

The cast of *Suits* was her new family. Importantly, in the third series of *Suits* her fee was increased to $75,000 per episode and the run was increased to 16 episodes. Her total annual income would be £1.2 million. For the first time, there was the prospect of residuals. Money gave her the right to change her mind and do what she wanted and when. With her own money she felt there was no duty or obligation to anyone but herself. In hindsight, her marriage seemed to be transactional.

A FedEx envelope delivered to Trevor's home was a bombshell. Inside was Meghan's diamond engagement ring and her wedding ring. There was no note. The end of the marriage in spring 2013 came 'totally out of the blue' observed a friend. Trevor was left 'feeling that he was a piece of something stuck to the bottom of her shoe.'[104]

Searching for explanations, some suspected that Meghan was having an affair with an actor on *Suits*. Perhaps Trevor was having one too in Los Angeles? Nothing emerged to contradict one truth: totally unsentimental about their eight-year relationship Meghan had decided to move on.[105] 'We didn't see each other and we had drifted apart,' Meghan explained to a friend. She knew what she wanted and understood who she was. Abby Wathen, an actress, recalled meeting Meghan about that time. 'I was destroyed by my own divorce,' said the actress, but 'she was empowered.'[106] By taking back total control of her life she would do with men what men had previously done to women. Engelson was the past – and irrelevant.

Meghan called Priddy to announce that her 15-month marriage was over. 'I don't believe she gave him enough of an opportunity,' said Priddy, still shocked by events five years later. 'I think there was an element of "out of sight, out of mind" for Meghan. The way she handled it, Trevor definitely had the rug pulled out from under him. He was hurt.'[107] Splitting from Trevor, Priddy realised, showed that 'Meghan was calculating – very calculating – in the way she handled people and relationships. She is very strategic in the way she cultivated circles of friends. Once she decides you're not part of her life, she can be very cold. It's this shut-down mechanism she has. There's nothing to negotiate. She made her decision and that's it.'[108]

After reflection Priddy called Meghan, but the shutters had fallen: 'She wouldn't confide in me. It was obvious to me she wasn't the friend I'd grown up with anymore. She had a new circle of friends.' Priddy was shaken. 'The end of our friendship was like a death. I mourned it for quite a while.'

Looking for solace, Trevor called Thomas Markle. Meghan, he discovered, had not told her father the news. Both men were surprised. 'I explained to Trevor that Meghan's real love was being an actor, probably more so than anything else. You marry the business – I keep telling people that. I married the business. Meghan married the business. That ruins a lot of your relationships. I think what she did was dedicate herself to her show.'

Thomas did not tell Trevor a more hurtful truth: 'Meghan has outgrown you, just as she outgrew me.'[109] Thomas called Doria. It hurt that she already knew. 'Trevor was mean to her,' said Doria without further explanation. 'He did bad things.' Thomas was puzzled. Meghan, he thought, had possibly invented something. Or he had misjudged Trevor.

The Engelson family was less sanguine. Devastated by Meghan's betrayal of their son and themselves, Leslie Engelson was particularly hurt. Meghan's cold-heartedness left both of them deeply unhappy. Their hurt was compounded after Meghan posted photos of herself on 8th April at an ice-hockey match at the Air Canada Centre. She was watching Michael Del Zotto, a Canadian ice-hockey star nine years younger than herself. Her affections for Del Zotto, she wrote, were 'The Best'. On 22nd April, she posted more photos of herself watching Del Zotto play at Madison Square Garden in New York. Both would deny a relationship. Leslie Engelson was not convinced. In their close-knit world, she said, daughters-in-law are not unfaithful. The Engelsons blamed Trevor's mistake to marry a girl from a broken family without a common background and no sense of loyalty towards her new family.

Although Trevor resisted invitations to explain, he did tell a friend that domestic life with Meghan bore no relationship to the demure young woman who fluttered her eyelids on TV screens. Marrying a 'mercurial, dramatic, shouty and difficult' actress who demanded a role in his films had been a challenge.[110]

In retaliation, Meghan's friends portrayed Trevor as envious and resentful of her success in *Suits*. Until then, Trevor had enjoyed Meghan's dependence on him. Thereafter, speculated Omid Scobie, repeating what her friends had said, Trevor had refused to 'support her acting career'. She was not invited to the Oscars because he 'didn't want to share the spotlight.'[111]

Moving swiftly to end the marriage, Meghan filed for divorce on 7th August, 2013, citing 'irreconcilable differences'.[112] Two weeks later the papers were served on Trevor. Neither hired a lawyer to negotiate their agreement to divorce. They parted without any financial arrangement. The case was finalised on 7th March, 2014. Meghan kept Bogart.

In the months after the divorce a different Trevor emerged. For some months he dated Charlotte McKinney, a blonde *Men's Health* model. Eventually, he married Tracey Kurland, the daughter of a billionaire. He would frequently be seen darting around Los Angeles in a particularly flashy Porsche. 'Sinking with the cream,' insiders carped about a man whose fame was his association with Meghan.

Meghan showed no sign of remorse about Trevor's inevitably hurt feelings. At 32 she was free. Free of all the baggage of her parents, marriage and hustling in Hollywood. Two years later she would describe her next step: 'You create the identity you want for yourself, just as my ancestors did when they were given their freedom.'[113] She added, 'I dream pretty big, but truly I had no idea my life could be so awesome. I am the luckiest girl in the world, without question.'[114]

On reflection, some decided that Meghan was reinventing herself. 'I love my character,' Meghan told Larry King in a TV interview broadcast on a digital channel to promote the third season of *Suits*. 'Rachel Zane is ambitious and sassy.' Unintentionally, Aaron Korsh, the series' creator, was remoulding the actress's own character. 'I see

Rachel,' said Meghan, 'as such a good friend. I root for her; I'm almost like a fan. Rachel is like the ultimate best friend – who has a closet that I always borrow things from in my personal life.'[115] As she said later, 'ambition' was what she and Rachel Zane had in common.[116]

'I'm part of the horse-and-pony show this year,' she wrote in her anonymous blog about American Network's launch of *Suits* to prospective advertisers in New York. 'They'll roll out the red carpet in a major way because they want me on show – "the talent", they call us.' Clearly excited by her introduction to first-class flights, chauffeurs and luxury hotels, she continued, 'This is part of the job and it's fucking awesome. If you are pursuing television, then realise that you have already sold out and take your big, fancy pay-check because you can now. Flashing those pearly whites (ahem, veneers) and working the carpet with your sexy little body (ahem, Spanx) is part of the job description you jumped on board for when you signed on that dotted line.'

In her fantasy, the unknown actress cast herself as a celebrity coping with the chore of recognition and being pestered for photos.[117] In reality, little had changed since she left school. She ached for fame – and a new relationship.

As part of the promotion for the cable network in July 2013, Meghan and Patrick J. Adams, alias Mike Ross in *Suits*, were interviewed by Larry King in a small, dark room in a cheap New York hotel. Meghan looked unusually unattractive with greasy hair, rumpled clothes and peaky eyes. Throughout the soft interview she gazed adoringly at Adams. While Adams described his character as a cross between Mark Zuckerberg and Steve Jobs, Meghan edged closer to her fellow actor. Asked a direct question, Adams emphatically denied to King that he and Meghan had a sexual relationship. King clearly disbelieved Adams. Meghan smiled.

Later that year, she arrived in Europe with a mission.

CHAPTER 5

Manhunt

Meghan flew across the Atlantic in November 2013 to secure contracts for work – and on a manhunt. To promote herself, she had hired Sunshine Sachs, a PR agency in Los Angeles famous for crisis management and known to represent Ben Affleck, Bon Jovi, Aerosmith, Leonardo DiCaprio, Justin Timberlake, Jennifer Lopez, Snoop Dogg and Natalie Portman. The firm denied reports that they represented disgraced movie mogul Harvey Weinstein in 2015.

Ken Sunshine, a 69-year-old former political consultant turned publicist, was a well-connected Democrat who had worked for a series of presidential and mayoral candidates, including George McGovern, Mario Cuomo, the young Bill de Blasio, and proudly for the Clintons. The agency promoted itself as a crisis management group, and its detractors would smirk that Sunshine was sunny by name but murky by deeds. 'We don't play it safe, we're not genteel,' Ken Sunshine had said. 'We name names and battle the media when we have to.' The agency was accused of doctoring their clients' Wiki entries to remove negative material.

Among Sunshine's trusted partners was Keleigh Thomas Morgan, a pleasant-looking middle-aged woman. Sunshine Sachs were paid about $7,500 per month to transform an unknown actress into a global celebrity. Among their earliest attempts to make a star of Meghan was an appearance in January 2013 at an *Elle* magazine 'celebration' in West Hollywood of Women in Television. Media coverage of the event only made brief mention Meghan Markle.[118]

Meghan's first stop was Trinity College, Dublin. The student organisers of the college's Philosophical Society had sent out hundreds of invitations to celebrities to address their annual conference. Previous speakers included Angela Merkel, Joe Biden and Nancy Pelosi. Among the very few replies that year was Meghan's. She accepted the invitation. Some students were sceptical that an audience would be attracted to hear from the unknown 'Rachel Zane'.

Fearing a disappointment, they decided in advance to award her the plastic Bram Stoker medal rather than the prestigious Honorary Patronage. The pessimists proved to be wrong. Packed wall to wall, Meghan wowed the students wearing a jumper, distressed skinny ripped jeans, black stilettos and holding a Louis Vuitton bag. Quite clearly, *Suits* had a cult audience. The students admired Meghan's undisguised self-identification with Rachel Zane: 'She's layered and humanised. Even though she seems so confident, she really has all those insecurities and vulnerabilities, and I relate to that as a woman, and I think fans will too.' At the end, she headed to Dicey's, a popular haunt for students, to promote E2 drinks.[119]

Next stop was London. Neil Ransome, a jobbing publicity agent at the Insanity Group, had been hired to negotiate publicity for Meghan in the tabloids. Before her arrival, Ransome had approached dozens of gossip and showbiz journalists. He was universally ignored. No one had heard of Meghan Markle or *Suits*. After incessantly 'pestering' Katie Hind, a junior reporter at the *Sunday People*, a comparatively small-circulation newspaper, Ransome secured her reluctant agreement to meet Meghan.[120]

On a cold evening, the two women drank Prosecco on the rooftop of the Sanctum Soho hotel. In her engaging manner Meghan admitted that she was not keen on American men and had discounted finding a husband in Canada. By contrast, she liked how Englishmen called women 'darling' and were 'suckers for a compliment'.[121] She hoped for the opportunity to meet the right Englishman, she said. Not least, she proclaimed, because she 'excelled' at networking. She had developed that skill 'down to a fine art'. Hind was bemused.

Unexpectedly, Meghan next asked Katie Hind about Ashley Cole, the Chelsea and England footballer. Proudly, Meghan showed a photo of Cole on her iPhone. Cole, explained Meghan, had followed her on Twitter and they had exchanged messages. Hind's advice was emphatic. Cole was infamously unfaithful to his wife, was unreliable and known for his erratic lifestyle. Meghan's face, Hind noticed, became 'downcast' and 'disappointed'.[122] Strangely, Cole would deny that he ever exchanged messages with Meghan. He recalled that the cast of *Suits* sent him a message that they liked him and he returned an acknowledgement. Thereafter, Cole claimed, nothing happened. Meghan's presentation of Cole as a possible boyfriend, he suggested, was a fantasy. Cole's famous football friends recall a different version. Meghan, Cole had boasted to those teammates, was chasing him.

With that, Meghan and Hind, both 32 years old, discussed their common problem. They were single and searching for a permanent relationship. Neither had a solution. The night ended with Meghan heading back to her nearby hotel and Hind noting that the American craved publicity. However, despite Meghan's enthusiasm Hind decided she was not worth mentioning in her newspaper. She was not a story.

The following night was Meghan's big chance. She had been flown to London to co-host a TV gala with fashion model Oliver Cheshire, whom she didn't know. Standing on the red carpet in Leicester Square, Meghan grinned. At that moment, grasping Cheshire's hand, there was nothing she wanted more than her photo to feature in next day's tabloid newspapers. She prayed for publicity. The editors rejected her plea. Their readers had no interest in Miss Nobody.

Inside the cinema, Meghan met Lizzie Cundy, a glamour-seeking

TV personality. Over a drink Meghan confessed that Hollywood was brutal and she had failed to make a breakthrough. Her ambition was to feature on an English reality show like *Made in Chelsea* – and she wanted an English boyfriend. 'Do you know any famous guys?' she asked. 'I'm single and I really love English men. Do you know any man who's free?' Once again, she mentioned Ashley Cole. 'He's following me on Twitter.' Cundy's own marriage to a footballer had hit the rocks. She was not keen on Cole. Meghan seemed disappointed. At the end of the evening, Meghan returned to her hotel alone. Her tips to the paparazzi and Ransome's efforts had produced just one passing mention in a *Daily Mail* gossip column. There was no photograph.[123]

The only good news was that Nick Ede, a fixer paid by Sunshine Sachs to book her appearance at the TV gala, had also arranged for her to meet Jonathan Shalit, a successful and likeable TV agent. 'I want to be a TV celebrity chef like Gordon Ramsay,' Meghan told Shalit in his office. Or, she volunteered, she would be happy to appear in any other non-scripted TV show. Shalit was excited. She was charming, good-looking and admired by the small audience for *Suits*. He was unaware that while Meghan liked eating good food, her cooking skills were limited. Other than blender-made vegetable soup her specialities were plain pasta, roast chicken, barbecued hamburgers and steak. The rest of her food was bought ready-made. Rather than cook, she imagined fronting a TV programme to tour the world tasting food. A short video of her tasting pickles in Brooklyn for Ora TV exposed her limitations.[124] There was neither magic nor magnetism. The programme idea evaporated.

Undeterred, Shalit arranged an audition for *Strictly Come Dancing*. Reluctantly she declined. Tied to a *Suits* contract for nine months in the year, the timing clashed with filming in Britain. Disappointed, Shalit bid her farewell. She returned to Toronto without either new work or a new man.

CHAPTER 6

Influencer

On Meghan's thirty-third birthday in August 2014, under the headline 'Birthday Suit', she posted a seductive topless side-shot of herself. Her self-justification for 'self-objectifying' was pertinent: 'I don't see beauty and empowerment as separate things. Self-empowerment and women's rights, I put them in the beauty section.'[125] The photo was the highpoint of a year's work to reinvent herself as an Influencer.

Uncertain how long her income from *Suits* would last and unusually careful with money, Meghan had registered a slew of websites – Posh Beauty, Spoon Me Fork Me, Lalitots and Foodiepup – to leverage her celebrity. The idea was not original. Meghan had observed Hollywood's royalty – including Angelina Jolie and Emma Watson, famous for her role in the Harry Potter film series – become profitable Influencers. Meghan's skill was to absorb and copy those she admired and to also learn from their mistakes. With her new proximity to Toronto's aspiring Influencers at Soho House, she followed Sophie Trudeau's attempt to establish herself as a 'gender equality activist' and an ambassador for the 'I Am A Girl' initiative; and she watched Jessica Mulroney floundering in her search for an online identity. The trick, she realised, was to create a Brand.

Laced through a narrative of her opinions and lifestyle, she promoted fashionable causes and celebrities with endorsements and praise.

Interspersed in the gush, she promoted fashion and cosmetics for a fee. As a self-proclaimed 'inspiration junkie', she charged the manufacturers to be associated with a high-priced, ultra-fashionable star. For the first year, none of her websites took off.[126]

Her next idea was The Tig, named after the Italian wine Tignanello and designed by Jake Rosenberg, the Canadian-born designer of *Coveteur* magazine. Meghan described herself as 'the editor-in-chief of my lifestyle brand' – a website to flaunt wealth, luxury clothes, a glamorous jet-setter's lifestyle and wellness. 'The Tig,' she wrote, 'is a hub for the discerning palate – those with a hunger for food, travel, fashion and beauty…and to be a breeding ground for ideas and excitement – for an inspired lifestyle.' Registered in 2014 as a product of Frim Fram Inc, a Californian company, The Tig was launched in May 2014.

Meghan's routine was to leave early in the morning for the studio and, after a day's filming for *Suits*, head for the gym. On her return home she spent the evening scouring the internet for ideas. The assiduous researcher combed the highbrow *Economist* and lowbrow *Darling* magazines for snippets. She trawled other websites for ideas, sought free products from luxury brands like Hermès in exchange for promoting their handbags, and emailed endless celebrities for comment and endorsement. To build her credibility she needed to be associated with stars – if possible with a photograph to prove their friendship. The celebrity hunter's strength was to seize every opportunity and never take 'No' for an answer.[127]

Sweet-talking her entry into a charity football match on an artificial indoor beach at New York's Pier 40 on the Hudson River, she met among other players Serena Williams, the 23-time Grand Slam tournament tennis singles champion. In Meghan's version on her website, 'We hit it off immediately, taking pictures, laughing and chatting not about tennis or acting but about good old-fashioned girly stuff. So began our friendship.' Noticeably, no photo of Meghan with Williams appeared on The Tig. Brett Ratner, the Hollywood film producer and long-term boyfriend of Williams, never heard her mention Meghan. Although Meghan had never been seen holding a tennis racket, she wrote how she and Serena were united by 'our endless ambition'.

Similarly, she secured an introduction to Ivanka Trump, the daughter of the New York property tycoon. 'When we have drinks,' she told her followers, 'I will make sure I order whatever she does – because this woman seems to have the formula for success (and happiness) down pat.' Ivanka's 'beautiful designs' of shoes, furniture and clothes were afterwards embraced on The Tig. Not mentioned was Meghan's rejection of Donald Trump's invitation to party with him while working on *Deal or No Deal*. Also not mentioned was *Variety* magazine's report announcing the fifth season of *Suits*. Meghan had been again listed sixth and last in the cast-list.[128] The audience, however, was increasing towards three million.

To build her profile as an opinionated life-loving star, Meghan hit on a tested formula. She conjured up intimate, personal 'revelations' that, laced with colourful fantasies, did not have a totally faithful relation to the whole truth. Presenting herself as a racy Hollywood goddess, she mentioned her love of good food, 'copious amounts of rosé', spicy tequila cocktails and neat Scotch. Describing herself in one post as a 'saintly hippy', she disparaged fancy restaurants and pledged herself as good company, 'embracing every little second of it'.

She stipulated her ideal man. Dressed in a linen shirt, she visualised him barefoot on a beach, eating a slice of pizza and inviting her for a drink on the way home. Presents of lingerie from him were 'always nice'. Be the bold adventurer, she advised: 'I think it's important to roll with the punches and enjoy every minute of it. If he makes you laugh, that helps.'[129] The result was a website reflecting a woman of conviction with commercial sensitivity, a chancer with perhaps a limited sense of humour.

On that thirty-third birthday, she reminisced about her struggles as a teenager and as an actress. She summed up her recipe for happiness as a single woman: 'You need to know that you're enough. A mantra that has now ingrained itself so deeply within me that not a day goes by without hearing it chime in my head. That five pounds lost won't make you happier, that more make-up won't make you prettier, that the now iconic saying from Jerry Maguire – "You complete me" – frankly, isn't true. You are complete with or without a partner. You are enough just as you are. So for my birthday, here's what I would like as a gift: I want you to be kind to yourself. I want you to challenge yourself. I want you to stop gossiping, to try a food that scares you, to buy a coffee for someone just because, to tell someone you love them… and then to tell yourself right back. I want you to find your happiness. I did. And it's never felt so good. I am enough.'

The homily on The Tig did not always entirely reflect her own life or occasionally even her personal values. As a purely commercial venture she understood her market and how to compartmentalise between her real life and the fantasy life she offered her increasing number of followers, which was now heading towards the 100,000-mark. Conjuring fantasies was her unique selling-point. The most noteworthy in Meghan's list composed for 'A Guide to Living Well' was the entry under the heading 'Non-Negotiable' – 'Kindness'.

That summer, she met Cory Vitiello, a Toronto restaurateur famous for his burgers and his clientele. The handsome 35 year old welcomed Hollywood celebrities who were filming in Toronto to the Harbord Room. Vitiello was known for dating several well-known Canadian women including Belinda Stronach, a glamorous, multi-millionaire businesswoman and politician. On 10th July, 2014, after eating at his restaurant with the *Suits* cast, Meghan wrote a gushing review in The Tig. Cory was dubbed 'my very favourite chef'.

Shortly afterwards, Vitiello ended a relationship and started to date Meghan.[130] Together they rented a three-bedroomed home in the city's Annex district. Through Cory, the life and soul of many parties and sought after by many women, Meghan was introduced to 'everyone' in Toronto. Swiftly, she became a fixture of the city's social life. Pertinently, Cory Vitiello never featured on The Tig. In the transactional nature of Meghan's relationships with men and women, keeping Cory anonymous was compatible with her own search for fame.

CHAPTER 7

The Irishman

Few British men were more famous in the summer of 2014 than the Northern Ireland golfer Rory McIlroy. On 10th August, shortly after winning the Open Championship in Britain, the 25 year old won the PGA Championship by one stroke in Kentucky.[131]

At 2am the following morning in New York, McIlroy walked into the Fitzpatrick hotel on 57th Street and Lexington Avenue. Everyone who saw him over the following days recalls the golf champion as 'hot, hot, hot'. He partied non-stop across Manhattan for 24 hours with his entourage. Without a break, he next flew in a private jet across the Atlantic to Manchester to collect a prize at Old Trafford. After more celebrations with United's footballers he jetted back to Manhattan to appear on TV and join Tiger Woods to promote golf's big brands. By 19th August he was looking for relaxing fun. McIlroy had just split from his blonde fiancée, Danish tennis ace Caroline Wozniacki, and was reported to be chasing brunettes.

All the rage in America at that moment was the ice-bucket challenge. Famous personalities nominated each other to be drenched with iced water to raise money for research into motor neurone disease. Celebrities promoted themselves by posting a video of their ordeal. Unexpectedly, McIlroy nominated Meghan to drench herself with ice.[132] Not un-coincidentally, Meghan was staying with a friend close to the Fitzpatrick hotel where McIlroy had a suite. She accepted the challenge, on condition that Rory came to her friend's apartment and personally poured the bucket over her on the balcony.

After the video was posted, the two went to Fitzpatrick's hotel for a drink. They were spotted in the small bar by the hotel's owner, John Fitzpatrick. The 54-year-old American Irishman was renowned as chairman of the American Ireland Fund, as a major promoter of a united Ireland, as a philanthropist donating millions to charities, and as a friend of, and donor to, the Clintons. He had hosted their New York fundraisers since 1991. 'He's at the front of the grid,' wryly observed a businessman. Famous for exuding charm as the benefactor of hospitality, the confirmed bachelor was frequently photographed escorting beautiful women – and famous for giving them generous gifts, especially Louboutin stilettos. Media attention flattered his ego.

'I was in the bar of my hotel,' Fitzpatrick recalled, 'and I saw Rory McIlroy. I walked over and he was with Meghan Markle.[133] I was a huge fan of *Suits*. Sarah Rafferty, the lead in the series, became a good friend.' Fitzpatrick invited the couple for dinner at Cipriani. By midnight, as the golfer and Meghan were photographed sitting close together, Fitzpatrick was hosting a party of 20.[134]

The following morning, McIlroy arrived at the Ringwood golf course 30 miles away to play in a new competition. Worse for wear after a hectic night, he fell back to 101st place. Nevertheless, he refused to sleep as usual near the golf course to be ready the following day. Instead he drove back to New York to see Meghan. His performance suffered. 'I wasn't quite on my game,' he confessed. 'I was enjoying myself.'

Back in Toronto at the end of the week, with Cory Vitiello, Meghan gushed about the golfer in The Tig:

'Ah yes. Rory McIlroy. THE Rory McIlroy. Whispered (and shouted) to be the foremost golfer in the world, loved by Tiger, respected by Palmer, and dumper of frigid water on to my lone head for the ALS Ice Bucket Challenge. That Rory McIlroy. He is a force who has the propensity to actually work hard and play hard – relishing intense practices to substantiate his title, embracing nights of sipping Opus One (his bold and impressive choice of wine) and indulging in group dinners at Cipriani – for the balance, of course. And yet, beyond his work/play ethic, the most endearing quality of this man is his character – as real and honest as they come, appreciating a simple smile, never shunning a fan photo, enjoying a plate of pasta with veal ragu, and expressing a love for his parents that is rarely seen in men his age. Or at any age, to be honest. He is not just the real deal... he is real. And perhaps that is what makes him even more cherished. A critical darling and fan favorite – it's for good reason – he is born and raised in Holywood, Ireland – a long cry from my hometown of Hollywood, California – and yet, he, alone, could be the impetus for his Holywood's own Walk of Fame. I imagine they would be glad to welcome that gilded boulevard in his honor. Today's Tig Talk is with the courteous, classy, and ever-so talented, Rory McIlroy – who, by the way, had the kindness and wherewithal to not put the two full bags of ice I bought into the bucket – he wanted me to raise awareness for ALS and yet also survive the challenge. For that I am most grateful.'

Keen to use their close relationship to promote herself, she encouraged the media to publish photographs of McIlroy and her. As she would later admit, she 'occasionally set up a paparazzi photo or let info slip out to the press'.[135]

Asked by Cory Vitiello whether she was having a relationship with McIlroy, Meghan insisted their time together was innocent. He believed her. At the time, she anticipated meeting McIlroy and Fitzpatrick again in Dublin eight weeks later.

Meghan had lobbied hard to be invited to the One Young World conference in Dublin. She knew that celebrity in Hollywood was enhanced by philanthropy and activism. To secure her first platform she asked Misan Harriman, an Anglo-Nigerian photographer, for a favour. Harriman's friend, the tennis champion Boris Becker, was about to address over a thousand young people at a One Young World conference in Dublin. Could Becker, asked Harriman, get a slot for Meghan?

Becker introduced Meghan to his agent, Gina Nelthorpe-Cowne, a glamorous South African based in London. Her speciality was to negotiate appearances by famous people in conferences, advertisements and campaigns. Having booked another client, Bob Geldof, to speak in Dublin, she was well placed to ask the conference organiser Kate Robertson to give Meghan a slot. The actress wanted to speak about gender equality and 'positive change'.

Robertson was cool on the idea. Nobody, including her, knew Meghan Markle. That changed after she spoke to her daughter. The young fan of *Suits* was instantly enthusiastic. Meghan was booked. Unlike the stars, Meghan would not receive a fee, only expenses. Excited about her trip, she posted a message to an Irish friend of McIlroy: 'Lock something down. I head out there October 14-17. Have a wonderful night X MM.'[136]

'When I first arrived at Meghan's hotel room in Dublin,' Nelthorpe-Cowne recalled, 'she was in a towelling bathrobe with her hair tied back. We just clicked. We hugged as if we had known each other for ages. She was delightful – warm and personable.'[137] Nelthorpe-Cowne sympathised with Meghan's obvious purpose in Dublin – to promote her profile, increase her income and become influential.

Nelthorpe-Cowne noticed that her new client walked gracefully on four-inch heels and embraced well-wishers, as well as being beautiful and charismatic. Meghan had perfected the art of a double-handed greeting. She made everyone feel they were the only person in the room. Even the star guests, including Mary Robinson, Ireland's former president, and Kofi Annan, the former United Nations' Secretary General, were drawn to the flash of her engaging smile and the flicker of an eyelid. Nelthorpe-Cowne was also charmed. As for Meghan, seeing the famous politicians in the front row as she began her speech, her self-importance soared.[138]

Identifying herself as a mixed-race woman she spoke about her childhood, the 'box' at school to identify her race, and her feeling of exclusion. But she gave no hint of personally suffering racism, nor did she mention discrimination, and she did not question the status of a mixed-race woman in a white society. Rather, she accepted European values. She made no attempt to describe a personal mission or offer an agenda to change the world. The totality of her speech was to urge her audience to admire her own personal experience and adopt her mantra of togetherness.

No one could argue against those sentiments. The enthusiastic applause, especially by the politicians in the front row, confirmed that her performance had gone down well. In her own mind, as she later described, she had been elevated into the ranks of the powerful. That explained her unusual reaction as she headed towards the hotel lift. A young man politely beckoned her to enter in front of him. 'I don't need that,' she snapped, delivering a tirade to the startled man until the end of the ride.

In the background was Cory. He had flown from Toronto with Meghan, some would suggest in a Netjet paid for by Rory McIlroy. He was introduced as a famous chef. Everyone agreed that he was somewhat quiet. Clearly, he was not a Gordon Ramsay type.

That same night, Friday 17th, Meghan left the hotel for dinner with Rory McIlroy at the upmarket restaurant Fade Street Social. She was spotted looking 'smitten', gazing intently at McIlroy.[139] 'They sat beside each other looking very cosy and chatted all night,' reported Alexandra Ryan in a newspaper gossip column. That was Meghan's third night in Dublin. On a previous night John Fitzpatrick would describe his dinner with her, and later implied that she and McIlroy had secretly met.[140] Meghan's Irish friends assumed that she and McIlroy had also met unseen, earlier during her visit.

Not surprisingly the newspaper report annoyed Cory Vitiello. Again he challenged Meghan. Had there been an affair? he asked angrily. Emphatically, Meghan denied that she had betrayed Cory. She and McIlroy were just friends, she said. Once more he believed her. Her agent called Ryan for a correction. 'They're madly in love,' Alexandra Ryan wrote the following day about Meghan and Cory. 'The two of them were sewn at the hip the entire time they spent in Ireland.'[141] Meghan was relieved. The golfer was not her future, and Cory was still her Toronto facilitator.

Before the two flew on to Paris for the weekend, Gina Nelthorpe-Cowne promised her new client an exciting future as a 'showcased asset'. She would arrange fee-paying engagements for Meghan as a public speaker and she would negotiate a deal for Meghan as the face of a major fashion or skin-care brand. 'I want to be the Face of L'Oreal,' Meghan had declared seriously. 'I have legs as long as a mile.'[142] Their relationship was sealed with a kiss. In her emails to Gina thanking her for her support, Meghan signed her messages, 'Sending love, XOXOXO hugs and kisses, MM'.

* * *

Back in Toronto's Soho House, Meghan's 'Girl Squad' was growing in number and importance. Sophie Trudeau's husband had been elected the Liberal party's leader and was forecast to become the country's prime minister. Martina Sorbara, a singer and a new friend, was the daughter of a Canadian politician. And Jessica Mulroney was still searching for recognition as a social media personality. Her search for fame, including an association with a grocery chain, had faltered but her relationship with Meghan had grown stronger.

Many could not understand Meghan's attachment to Mulroney. She was widely regarded as a bit of a WAG – as similar to a glamour-seeking footballer's wife. Meghan's friendship with Mulroney, observed Shinan Govani, Toronto's leading newspaper diarist, was either the result of 'poor judgement or because there was no one else'. There was another unseen characteristic. Meghan suffered terrible envy – of the other woman's wealth, looks and social success. What at school and in Hollywood was classed as healthy ambition had metamorphosed into jealousy. Increasingly, envy coloured so much of her life.

Meghan regarded the Soho House group as allies to more than just a jobbing actress. The politicians' applause for her speech in Dublin confirmed her new importance: 'I want to use whatever status I have as an actress to make a tangible impact.' The internet was critical to her plans. Apart from promoting products on The Tig in return for gifts or payment,[143] she liked to spread joy to her followers.

'In case no one has told you today,' she wrote to her readers one evening, 'you deserve endless pizza and love, and you have a nice butt.' Everyone, in her opinion, should be free to choose their own reality and values. Sexual attraction increasingly featured on her website. At the same time she was becoming intolerant of ideas that did not match her own. She had little patience for other people's values. In her world she simply got angry with people who refused to agree with her.

Uppermost in her mind was her image. Convinced that she was on the cusp of international celebrity, she had become preoccupied with Rachel Zane's character. Constantly, she absorbed Aaron Korsh's vision for Zane, the feisty opportunist with extraordinary manipulative skills. To her delight, Korsh inserted her own personal interests into the script. Zane became a foodie. He also agreed to limit the number of love scenes with her dressed in just a bra.

Korsh also introduced Meghan to the most expensive clothes. Calling Meghan 'Little Fox', Jolie Andreatta, the series' costume designer, dressed the actress in Dior, Prada, Burberry and similar labels.[144] For many viewers, the focus of the series became the outfits. Meghan credited Andreatta with influencing her understanding of fashion, especially the power of the white shirts, Tom Ford pencil skirts and the importance of 'The Fit'. To her disappointment, Andreatta said in an interview that Meghan was not her favourite actress to dress.[145]

Anything critical alarmed Meghan. Trawling the internet, she read that a handful of viewers had protested that Zane was about to start an affair. She was alarmed that she, Meghan Markle, was personally blamed. Her own reputation, she feared, was threatened by her portrayal in *Suits* as an 'unfaithful woman'. Worried about the potential backlash, she beseeched Korsh to end that storyline and the affair.[146] Korsh agreed, aware that he was not only writing a good story but also shaping Meghan's real-life character and personality. Strangely, Meghan would later claim, 'I don't read any press, I haven't even read press for *Suits*.'[147]

Absorbing Korsh's interpretation of loyalty and power-play, Meghan was pleased to be cast in what she saw as her true colours, the compassionate mould he was creating. At the end of each day's shoot, seeing the huge amounts of food thrown away, she organised its distribution to Toronto's homeless.

In that new image Meghan placed her status above reality. She wanted wider recognition. During autumn 2014 she featured in *When Sparks Fly* for Hallmark Channel TV about a journalist discovering surprises on an assignment in her hometown. The film flopped. Next, to obtain more exposure as an activist and philanthropist, she signed up to a Pentagon-sponsored trip with a group of American entertainers flying on Air Force Two between US military bases in Spain, Italy, Turkey and Britain.[148]

Led by the chairman of the Joint Chiefs of Staff, General Martin Dempsey, the service families at every stop were puzzled. Meghan's biographical description, mentioning that she was 'actively involved in the socio-political arena', that she had 'worked' at the American embassy in Buenos Aires, and that she 'now works closely with the United Nations Women', made no impression on the audiences.[149] Few knew her name or understood her peppery speech about *Suits*, and she looked pained when asked to sing, especially 'White Christmas'.[150]

Her anchor throughout this time was Cory Vitiello. Thanks partly to him she enjoyed life in Toronto. Joanne Vitiello, his mother, was convinced that Meghan was a saint. Unlike the Engelsons five years previously, Joanne welcomed Meghan as her son's potential future wife. At the outset Meghan seemed tempted. In December 2014 she flew with Cory to Florida for the Miami Art Week. Invited by Markus Anderson to stay at the Soho Beach House, she was as usual hunting for contacts.

Anderson arranged for her to sit during lunch next to Misha Nonoo, an aspiring fashion designer, the daughter of a Bahraini father and English mother. 'I am very spiritual,' Nonoo had once said. 'I meditate twice a day and I love gong baths and sound healing.'[151] Nonoo, Meghan later wrote on The Tig, was 'the kind of woman you instantly adore'. Like Meghan, Nonoo was eager to climb the greasy pole. And to Meghan's admiration, Nonoo had stepped up in the world. At a three-day wedding party in Venice she had married Alexander Gilkes, an old Etonian friend of Princes William and Harry. Meghan became persuaded that Nonoo's apparently rich British husband was an ideal type for herself.

Shortly after Christmas, Meghan flew to Los Angeles with Vitiello. Staying at the house of another actress from *Suits*, she invited Thomas and Doria for lunch. During a pleasant day she gave both parents a gift of $5,000. Thomas met Cory for the first time. 'Just a nice guy. Not special,' Thomas concluded. Cory quickly forgot the event. Seven weeks later, Cory was absent from Meghan's Valentine post on The Tig.[152]

'This Valentine's Day,' she wrote, 'I will be with friends, running amock [sic] through the streets of New York, likely imbibing some cocktail that's oddly pink, and jumping over icy mounds in my new shoes through the salted snowy streets of the West Village. But those shoes, by the way, were my gift to myself. Because I've worked hard, because I'm not going to wait for someone to buy me the things I covet (nor do I want to), and because I want to treat myself as well as I treat those dearest to me. Because I am my own funny Valentine.'

Pertinently, she conjured a fantasy to describe herself as single and in a 'funk'. The solution, she explained after chatting with her '*Suits* sister wives', was self-love. She should give herself the same love and acceptance, she concluded, as she showed to everyone else. 'I decided to be my own Valentine.'

Meghan had decided that her long-term future was not with Cory. She had set her sights higher. New York, she decided, was the key to her ambition. She wanted to emulate her idols, Angelina Jolie and Emma Watson.

CHAPTER 8

Hillary

'I've often escorted Meghan around New York,' John Fitzpatrick recalled 'and she often stayed at my hotel in Manhattan.'[153] Fitzpatrick understood Meghan's ambition – she wanted to meet and spend time with celebrities. Automatically, he invited her to the best restaurants, especially Le Bilboquet, pronounced by Fitzpatrick as 'Bill Buckley'. Priding itself as one of New York's snobbiest restaurants on the Upper East Side, people had to beg for a table to sit near famous actors or even Bill Clinton.

Among New York hotelier Fitzpatrick's many attractions for Meghan was his close relationship with the Clintons. In 2015 he proudly hosted Hillary's fundraising campaign in the city as she sought the presidency in the following year's election. As New York's former senator and the Secretary of State, no one was better connected than Hillary Clinton.

By then, Meghan had focused on Emma Watson and her ambassador-ship for the UN Women's programme. Meghan set her sights on securing the same appointment. Fitzpatrick could help. A request from Hillary Clinton's office to Phumzile Mlambo Ngcuka, head of UN Women at the headquarters in New York, secured the vital introduction Meghan sought.

Elizabeth Nyamayaro, a Zimbabwean employee of the United

Nations campaign to promote women's rights and eradicate gender inequality by 2030, telephoned Meghan and asked her whether she would like to become a 'women's advocate for political participation' in Africa. That was exactly the opportunity Meghan wanted.

Nyamayaro dressed in outstanding clothes, and with her distinctive voice dominated a room. She never expected to stand quietly in a corner. Nor would Meghan. From the outset there were the ingredients for a disagreement between these two. Nyamayaro suggested that Meghan should do one week's internship in New York and then front a promotional video advocating female leadership. To accommodate her timetable it would be shot in Toronto. Matt Hassell, the creative director of the advertising agency KBS, was asked by Nyamayaro to fly down to New York from Toronto to meet the 'famous celebrity' who would be the video's star.

Amid secrecy about the celebrity's identity, Hassell wondered who it might be. Meryl Streep or another Hollywood star? When Nyamayaro revealed it was Meghan Markle, Hassell was dumbfounded. 'Who?' he and his producer Brenda Surminski asked themselves. Neither had ever heard of Meghan or *Suits*. 'Wonderful,' they politely chimed, as Meghan joined the conversation by Zoom.

Introduced to the actress, both advertising executives were struck by Meghan's insistence that she, the star, would be in control. Her illusion of grandeur continued during the video shoot at George Brown College in Toronto. Everyone, it seemed, was there to serve her. Only Nyamayaro refused to oblige. Throughout the day they disagreed about the script. The video was shot, but the result was practically unusable.

Nevertheless, in February 2015 Meghan flew with Nyamayaro 9,000 miles from New York to Rwanda, a landlocked country in central Africa, to speak to women about the importance of gender equality.

Rwanda had been the site of an appalling tragedy. In the early 1990s, a genocidal civil war between two tribes – the Tutsis and the Hutus

– had ended after the brutal death of about 800,000 Tutsi civilians. Paul Kagame, a Tutsi army officer, had emerged in 2000 from the bloodbath to become the country's president, receiving 90 per cent of the popular vote. By 2015, Kagame was widely accused of being complicit in mass murder. Many of his political opponents had been found dead, not only in Rwanda but across Africa, and Hutu refugees in neighbouring Congo were being slaughtered by the Rwandan army.

Nevertheless, led by Britain's former prime minister Tony Blair, many in the world community paraded Kagame as a model African democrat. The UN, like Blair, ignored a 2014 report by the US State Department about murderous oppression in Rwanda. Similarly, they discounted the US Congress hearings in 2015 about Kagame's propensity to murder his opponents.[154]

As a regular reader of the *Economist*, Meghan would have been aware of Kagame's reputation, but if she wanted to ingratiate herself with Nyamayaro she had no choice but to support him. In Nyamayaro's opinion, Kagame was responsible for making Rwanda an 'exemplary model of female leadership to every country'. In her admiration for the dictator, Nyamayaro described Rwanda's women politicians as 'phenomenal'.[155] She did not acknowledge that the female MPs were merely rubber-stamping Kagame's edicts.

Accordingly, in her first speech in Rwanda, Meghan praised the president: 'We need more men like that.' During a week of meeting female Rwandan politicians she was excited that 64 per cent of Rwandan senators were women.[156] She did not mention that one reason for that was the murder of Rwandan men during the tribal genocide. Just as intimidated as the men, the female politicians did not question their leader's luxurious lifestyle. Travelling across the world in his large private jet, Kagame stayed in $2,000-per-night hotels while his countrymen's average daily wage was $2.

Styling herself as an Angel of Mercy, Meghan did not question the president's largesse. Overnighting in air-conditioned luxury, she visited the wretched Gihembe refugee camp to ask the distraught women how they coped with life. Their replies were barely listed. Back before nightfall in Kigali, the capital, she recorded on her Instagram account about the trip, 'This type of work feeds my soul.'[157] She did not appear to be troubled by the contrast that a short distance away impoverished people barely survived. 'My life shifts from refugee camps to red carpets,' she wrote on The Tig. 'I choose them both because these worlds can, in fact, coexist.'[158]

On her next trip to London, Meghan spoke to Gina Nelthorpe-Cowne about Elizabeth Nyamayaro as 'a real friend'. Through the UN executive, she explained, she was certain to secure greater public exposure. 'I take very seriously being a role model for young women,' she explained.[159] Within a short time, she expected Nyamayaro to promote her from UN advocate to UN ambassador, the same senior rank as Emma Watson.

In September 2014, as a UN Ambassador for Women, Watson had launched the UN's HeForShe campaign at the UN headquarters in New York. Her impassioned speech about gender equality captured global headlines. Watson was praised by Phumzile Mlambo-Ngcuka: 'We are thrilled and honoured to work with Emma, whom we believe embodies the values of UN Women.' Dreaming of the same stardom, Meghan wrote in her Working Actress blog, 'I work long hours, I travel for press, my mind memorises. My mind spins. My days blur. My nights are restless. My hair is primped, my face is painted, my name is recognised, my star meter is rising, my life is changing.'[160]

Gina Nelthorpe-Cowne noticed the change. Her agency had arranged for Meghan to stay for free at the five-star Dorchester in Park Lane. Although she was unknown, Meghan insisted that she be registered using an alias. Soon after the booking was confirmed, Meghan announced that she could not stay in that hotel. The owner, the Sultan of Brunei Hassanal Bolkiah – whose Dorchester Collection included the Beverly Hills Hotel in Los Angeles and the Le Meurice in Paris – had recently suggested that adulterers and homosexuals should be punished according to sharia law; and that women who had abortions should be publicly flogged. Another hotel willing to provide free accommodation in return for Meghan agreeing to promote it was found. 'She was protective of her image,' said Nelthorpe-Cowne, 'and didn't want to do anything that would compromise that.'

The news in London, however, was disappointing. Despite Nelthorpe-Cowne's incessant pitch to clients for speaking events – highlighting Meghan as a strong, entrepreneurial, fluent woman of substance – she was rejected. The reason was always the same: she was unknown, and so was *Suits*. Without a profile, Meghan was told, she could not attract British media attention and therefore would not be hired for engagements. Meghan did not hide her frustration.

After consulting her agent and publicists Meghan spotted an opportunity. Until then she had mentioned race publicly twice – once in December 2012 at the Third Annual Witness Uganda Concert in Los Angeles, and again in an anti-racism video for the US charity, Erase the Hate. Her published record produced no other examples of her publicly mentioning racism. In fact, throughout her appearances during the first series of *Suits*, her mixed race was barely mentioned, not least because most viewers thought she was white. That, she decided, should change, especially after her Black father was introduced into the second *Suits* series. Having reconsidered her past, she decided she would sincerely present herself as a survivor of racism.

The challenge was to find a platform to launch her rebranding. She chose *Elle* magazine in America. One eyewitness described how Meghan 'breezed' into *Elle*'s office and met Justine Harman, one of the magazine's editors. At one moment in their conversation Meghan sought to ingratiate herself, and offered to write the place-cards for Harman's wedding. After successfully pitching her idea for an article, Meghan embroidered it with a twist. Meghan suggested to *Elle* that she should travel to the island of Malta to search for her mixed-race roots.

Somewhere in the distant past, she recalled, grandmother Markle mentioned that her father's great-great-great Irish grandmother Mary Bird lived in Malta with an English soldier called Thomas Bird. They married and a child was born in Malta in 1862. To give the story greater attraction, Mary Bird was said to have been employed as a cook in 1856 at Windsor Castle.

Harman had no reason to question Meghan or her suggestion that she travel to Malta with Gina Nelthorpe-Cowne. *Elle* magazine arranged with the Maltese tourist authority that, in exchange for a free trip, Meghan's published article would not only describe Meghan's origins on the island but also promote the local food, wine and beaches, and be the backdrop for a fashion shoot.[161]

'This trip', wrote Meghan soon after, 'was mostly about trying to understand where I came from, my identity. There is something so lovely about fitting in a piece of the puzzle.' Meghan also posted, 'Before I came, people were telling me, "When you go to Malta, everyone will look like you," and I started to say, "Oh my gosh, I do sort of blend in," and it's the loveliest feeling.'[162]

To Nelthorpe-Cowne's surprise, the moment they landed on the island Meghan decided against finding her white ancestry. That was not surprising. Meghan had no 'ancestry' in Malta. The nineteenth-century soldier Thomas Bird married Mary McCue in Donnybrook, Dublin in January 1860 (clearly excluding any employment in Windsor Castle). Bird was posted with his wife to India and briefly to Malta. Soon after a son was born they moved to Canada, where Thomas died.[163] Mary remarried and became Mary White.[164] Thomas Markle would dispute that his mother ever conjured the story about the Markles' connection to Malta.[165]

Did Meghan, Nelthorpe-Cowne later wonder, ever intend to look for ancestors? She doubted it: 'Everything she does is carefully curated and forensically planned.' The sensitive soul searching for her roots was replaced by what Nelthorpe-Cowne identified as 'the businesswoman first and foremost'. Money, Nelthorpe-Cowne concluded, was Meghan's priority.

During the trip, visiting restaurants and vineyards, Kurt Arrigo, a well-known local photographer hired by the Maltese tourist authority, photographed Meghan in numerous locations with endless changes of clothes. During those days Meghan spoke to Gina about branding herself as a foodie, as a beauty and fashion expert, and as an advocate of wellness. During her time in Malta, she did not speak about race, politics, nor her father, and never mentioned Serena Williams and all the other celebrities she claimed to be her friends on her website.

On their return to London, Meghan told Nelthorpe-Cowne, 'You're really special for me. We have a special friendship.' By then Nelthorpe-Cowne admitted to herself, 'I had fallen under Meghan's spell, as everyone did. Not only did she exude warmth and sincerity but she made you feel that you were the only person in the world that mattered. She's a girl's girl and we had shared many stories.'

Unfortunately for the Maltese tourist authority, Meghan's published article in *Elle* made no mention of Malta. The island's restaurants, wines and beaches were forgotten. Arrigo's photographs were not used.[166]

In a well-written article for the magazine headlined, 'Meghan Markle: I'm More Than An "Other"', Meghan introduced what she called 'the dichotomy' of being mixed race in response to *Elle*'s invitation 'to share my story.' Although it was her own initiative to tell her story, she wrote, 'I'll be honest, I was scared.' While she had previously hinted in social media about her background, 'Today I am choosing to be braver, to go a bit deeper, and to share a much bigger picture of that with you.' She retold the familiar three stories: the Barbie dolls, the school questionnaire's ethnicity box and the student at Northwestern commenting about her background. She complained about 'this world of not fitting in, and of harbouring my emotions so tightly under my ethnically nondescript (and not so thick) skin.' Asserting that she was an outsider occupying 'a murky area…a haze around how people connected with me,' she concluded: 'While my mixed heritage may have created a grey area surrounding my self-identification, keeping on both sides of the fence, I have come to embrace that...to voice my pride in being a strong, confident mixed-race woman.'

Curiously, while she mentioned in a Tig post in 2015 travelling to Malta at *Elle*'s request,[167] the reference to *Elle* was removed in 2017.[168]

The *Elle* article was used by Nelthorpe-Cowne as leverage to invite 30 potential buyers of Meghan the Brand to Home House, a private members' club in central London. Meghan appeared in a discussion with Emmanuel Jal – a Sudanese child soldier and musician – speaking about feminism and women's empowerment. She did not mention race. The result was disappointing. The audience dismissed her as uninteresting. L'Oreal and all the other cosmetic firms had rejected the invitation to feature Meghan as the face of their brand. The only glimmer of hope was an offer of a possible contract from a lesser-known Swiss watchmaker.

In the post-mortem, Meghan was not keen to hear the bad news. Nelthorpe-Cowne promised to keep trying.

Depending on the question, Meghan had either hit a roadblock or reached a crossroads in her career. John Fitzpatrick came to the rescue. He invited Meghan to the St Patrick's Day reception on 17th March, 2015, at the White House. The previous night, Fitzpatrick had hosted the annual American Ireland Fund's dinner for 200 Irish and American celebrities. Fitzpatrick's description of his relationship with Meghan appeared to be accurate: 'She was dating a celebrity chef which was on and off [and] she was kind of seeing someone.' He continued, 'Officially I was not dating her – we were best friends.'[169]

To a fanfare, Meghan entered the White House with Fitzpatrick, a truly exciting moment for every American. 'This is my friend Meghan. Do you know her?' Fitzpatrick asked Ryan Tubridy, a popular Irish radio and TV host.[170] She also met Stephanie Roche, then a

Houston Dash football player, with whom she would later open the city's Irish consulate.

Her most memorable introduction was to Barack Obama. The president had walked over to meet Fitzpatrick and spoke to Meghan. 'She was over the moon,' said Fitzpatrick.[171] From the White House the couple drove to the Willard Hotel, Fitzpatrick's headquarters. A handful of important Irish power-brokers had been invited to his reception before going on to the Irish ambassador's residence for a night of partying. To Fitzpatrick's surprise, over 30 friends arrived. He asked Meghan to help serve drinks. 'She got behind the bar,' he recalled with fondness. Thanks to Fitzpatrick, Meghan returned to Toronto invigorated about her future.

In March 2015, Meghan had good reason to believe she was on an upwards trajectory. Not only was she meeting the Democratic party's aristocracy but, with Hillary Clinton's support, Elizabeth Nyamayaro had agreed that she could address a UN Women conference in New York. That week, UN Women was hosting two conferences. The principal conference for VIPs, addressed the previous year by Emma Watson, was held at the UN's headquarters. A second meeting for children and minor personalities was held on 10th March at an off-Broadway theatre.[172]

Nyamayaro told Meghan that she could speak at the second conference as a UN Women's Advocate for Women's Leadership and Political Participation. One keynote speaker would be Priyanka Chopra, the Indian actress and a former Miss World. Others addressing the 2,000 audience would be the UN Secretary General Ban Ki-moon and Hillary Clinton. Although Meghan's name did not feature in the press release or the programme's publicity, Meghan invited her mother for 'the most important event of my life.'[173] She planned to emulate Emma Watson's stardom as a feminist. She would claim to have been inspired to become an actress by Julia Roberts.[174]

In her brief address, Meghan fluently recited the story of her childhood protest to Procter & Gamble, the reply she received from Hillary Clinton and how single-handedly she had changed Procter & Gamble's campaign. 'It was at that moment that I realised the magnitude of my actions. At the age of 11, I had created my small level of impact by standing up for equality.' No one doubted her plausible self-congratulation.

. After the acclaim for her achievement, she denounced the low representation of women in parliaments. Referring to her visit to Rwanda she said, 'I've always wanted to be a woman who works. And this type of work is what feeds my soul and fuels my purpose.' More contentious was her praise for President Kagame. She said about a man accused of atrocities, 'We need more men like that.'[175] She repeated Emma Watson's feminist sentiments. 'I am so proud', she concluded, 'to be a woman and a feminist, and this evening I am extremely proud to stand before you on this significant day which serves as a reminder to all of us how far we've come, but also amid celebration a reminder of the road ahead.'[176]

The audience enthusiastically applauded. Ban Ki-moon stood and shook her hand. In the aftermath Meghan described the event as a watershed in her life. Over the following years, many got the impression she had spoken in the United Nations' General Assembly's auditorium alongside Emma Watson.[177] Few realised that Watson did not speak to the UN that year and that Meghan had addressed a sideshow audience.

Soon afterwards, Meghan urged Elizabeth Nyamayaro to introduce her to Emma Watson. Nyamayaro refused. Never deterred, Meghan asked Nyamayaro to promote her to UN Ambassador. Phumzile Mlambo Ngcuka, the South African director of UN Women, was doubtful. Meghan's cause could not have been helped by giving the impression to some people that while she did speakabout politics, philosophy and ideology, her apparent all-consuming passion for the empowerment of women was in reality focused on self-promotion and the empowerment of Meghan Markle. Whatever the reason, Nyamayaro refused Meghan's request to be promoted to ambassador. Meghan resigned from HeForShe and cut her ties with UN Women. Yet remarkably, despite the unpublicised split, she continued to cite publicly her UN Women experience as proof of her philanthropy. Outsiders never glimpsed the truth about the rupture or the reasons.

In Meghan's mind, both UN officials had underestimated her importance. By then, The Tig's posts were attracting nearly one million followers on Instagram, and she had over 250,000 followers on Twitter. Having passed the milestone of 1,000 posts on The Tig, she was finally a self-made businesswoman.

As an Influencer dependent on freebies, clothes on loan and payments for product promotions, she earned fees by endorsing several well-known brands: Bobbi Brown make-up, Lanvin fashion, Sentaler coats and Reitmans, Toronto's leading mid-market fashion retailer. Accompanied by attractive photographs of herself, she successively featured a pink blusher called Orgasm, herself in bed with her two dogs Bogart and Guy, described as 'nuggets' and her 'tag team', and described foreign travel with friends and visits to restaurants. Citing Amanda Chantal Bacon and Gwyneth Paltrow, she vigorously recommended Moon Dust, a blend of herbs, plant extracts and minerals, to vigorously 'enhance your beauty, brain, body, sexual energy, sleep and spirit'. She applauded ashwagandha as 'a root which aids the thyroid'. She forgot to add that the root was endorsed by the *Kama Sutra* to improve sexual satisfaction. Occasionally she mentioned that while walking in the nearby park, her dogs attracted admirers.

To personalise The Tig, the promotions were enhanced by Meghan's recollections: 'I was born and raised in Los Angeles, a California girl who lives by the ethos that most things can be cured with either yoga, the beach or a few avocados. I'm being cheeky, clearly.' She referred to her 'hippie-dippie-California-girl sensibility of all things clean and green'. She described herself as 'opinionated, driven and with a deep desire to effect change.' Regretfully, she said, 'I'm not very tall, so when I wear a short skirt I've got to be really conscious…Being yourself is the prettiest thing a person can be.'[178]

Making a virtue of single life in Toronto, she presented herself on YouTube as a great cook enjoying Spanish, Italian and other local restaurants. To keep fit, she ran six miles a day, did hot yoga and Platinum Pilates, and liked acupuncture and cupping. She started the day with a cup of hot water with a slice of lemon, some steel-cut oats mixed with almonds, bananas, agave syrup and soy milk and then 'grabbed' a smoothie.[179]

Being a humanitarian and a 'global citizen' dedicated to women's 'self-empowerment', and opposed to Brexit and Donald Trump, she advised: 'Travel often, getting lost will help you find yourself.' As for herself, she trilled about her glittering career to fulfil her 'genuine' desire to use her fame to make the world a better place. The proof of influence, she claimed, was her friendship with so many celebrities.

As a 'world-class networker', Meghan enjoyed flashing names on The Tig. There were frequent mentions of meeting Serena Williams; she was 'proud' of her friend Millie Mackintosh, the 'Quality Street heiress' and *Made in Chelsea* star whom she had met at Soho Farmhouse; and after a recent dinner of pasta and veal ragu she classed her close friend Rory McIlroy as 'not just the real deal – he is real. Courteous, class and ever so talented.' In the run-up to the 2016 presidential elections, she also praised her friend Ivanka Trump as 'staggeringly beautiful…but so incredibly savvy and intelligent that she's not just carved a niche for herself under her father's famed Trump notoriety, she's undoubtedly created her own empire. It's so easy to knock girls who come from privilege…but I always remember Ivanka being different.'[180]

To overcome her misfortune of not knowing sufficient celebrities, she name-checked those she had never met including Elizabeth Hurley: 'Thanks Liz for making me aspire to act like a lady and feel like a woman'; and similarly Heidi Klum – 'the most beautiful woman I have ever seen…Like the kind of chick you would want to grab a drink with.' She was careful not to mention the personalities she met through John Fitzpatrick. The Clintons and the American Irish set would not welcome gushing references on her blog. Her relationship with Fitzpatrick remained secret. Cory Vitiello remained invisible.

There was a downside. Toronto was not the most natural place to meet international celebrities regularly. Thanks to Cory's restaurants she had become an expert on food, and through *Suits'* expensive wardrobe she had become a fashionista. Through Cory she had weaved her way into the city's rhythms, but Jessica Mulroney was a source of even better introductions. The ambitious networker had given Meghan the opportunity to meet Canada's Establishment – the Thomsons, Westons and Rogers.

None, however, could provide the breakthrough she wanted beyond Canada. Hollywood fame remained elusive.

CHAPTER 9

Watershed

Among Hollywood's players, Lori Sale is a feisty, fast-speaking well-known agent, famous for securing marketing and branding contracts for her clients. In early 2015, Rick Genow, a Hollywood entertainment lawyer, contacted Sale. The lawyer explained that he represented Meghan Markle, the actress and host of The Tig. Could Sale, he asked, secure a brand contract for his client, who was based in Toronto?

Sale had never heard of Meghan or *Suits*, but concluded that even an ensemble actor on a cable show who was a minor celebrity could be placed. After meeting the actress, Sale pitched her new client to Jeannie Vondjidis-Miller, the head of marketing of Reitmans, Canada's largest women's clothing retailer. The 90-year-old business offered inexpensive clothes through its 700 stores to an ageing and declining clientele. Sale's call came just as Vondjidis-Miller was pondering who should front their campaign to re-energise the brand.

The idea of Meghan Markle, the young fashion-savvy celebrity, as a 'brand ambassador' had already been raised by Marc Lanouette, an executive at Tank, the store's advertising agency. In the midst of *Suits'* successful fifth season Meghan had already persuaded the store to promote their clothes on The Tig. Accordingly, Sale was pushing at an open door to negotiate a two-year contract to start in June 2015. For nine days' work – filming the commercial, photoshoots, the launch and TV promotion – Meghan would be paid $162,100 plus 7 per cent royalties on the sale of all the products associated with her campaign.

This was a watershed moment for Meghan. No serious Hollywood star, she knew, would associate herself with Reitmans, a brand whose clothes cost under C$100 (£60). And for only $15,000 a day! After income tax and agent's commission she would be left with half that amount. She longed to be the face of Ralph Lauren, not Reitmans. That choice eluded her. At least no one outside Canada would see the campaign.

Filming started on 6th August. Meghan checked into Montreal's Ritz hotel. A list of demands preceded her. She requested in her room and on location green juices, vegetables and 'high-end' bottled water. Evian and Fiji were rejected in favour of a designer brand. The two-day shoot went well, but ended on a sour note. The car to take her back to the airport was not booked. Meghan exploded, but she made her flight. The campaign – TV commercials, billboards and social media – was estimated to have increased Reitmans' sales by over 15 per cent. The company told Sale they would use Meghan the following year.

Meghan had good reason to feel semi-successful. The Tig, UN Women and Reitmans had given her a sense of achievement. But it wasn't enough. As she had said about Rachel Zane's constant struggle to survive and succeed at the beginning of season five, amid the conflicts of emotions and divided loyalties when Mike Ross is convicted of fraud, 'Rachel's just not willing to cave, she never gives up. She might be in love, but this won't put her off her endgame.'[181]

Hard graft had secured an advance in Meghan's career.[182] The downside was that every small success was accompanied by disappointment on the bigger stage. Hollywood repeatedly rejected her.

The previous year, casting director Anna Kennedy had invited Meghan to audition in Los Angeles. Reg Traviss, a British director, was looking for a female lead for *Anti-Social*, a gritty crime thriller based in London. Wilting in the Los Angeles heat, Traviss was instantly impressed by the cool, charming Meghan. Booked for the film, she arrived in London amid acrimony that her demand for first-class transatlantic fares and luxury accommodation had been rejected. Traviss complained that she was unhelpful in every way during the shoot. Gregg Sulkin, her younger co-star, also discovered that despite their close relationship Meghan was high-maintenance. The omens for when the film was completed in 2015 were bad.

During that same trip to London she went with Gina Nelthorpe-Cowne to a small meeting addressed by Emma Watson, her hero and role model. At the end, she asked to meet Watson. The actress rejected the request. The snub was mortifying. In hindsight, Gina was not surprised. Watson's rebuff was not mentioned when Meghan described her UN role in The Tig. 'I was in London,' she wrote to her followers, 'to support Emma Watson in her HeForShe Initiative for UN Women.'[183] Meghan's skill was to conceal setbacks, even describing Elizabeth Nyamayaro as 'my mentor'. The Hollywood lesson was ingrained: never admit rejection, keep positive and just keep on trying.

The reality of her life in 2015 was a struggle to get on and stay on the fast-moving carousel. Her imperative was to earn more money. She needed a breakthrough. With Lori Sale's help she did secure a succession of sponsored appearances: lunch with Cable Telecommunications in Chicago; mention of her name in Marchesa Voyage for Shop Style; and appearances at events for Air Canada, Equinox and at a self-esteem project on International Girls' Day hosted by Dove in Toronto.[184] For $40,000, Meghan was expected by Dove to arrive, 'do a social pose' and speak 'promotionally' to Dove's delegates.

One unpaid highlight of the merry-go-round was Markus Anderson's invitation to celebrate the opening of Soho House in Istanbul. Endlessly posing for photographs with other guests, she was disappointed that unlike the celebrities at the party she was not named in the pictures published by the media.[185]

Meghan's anonymity beyond Toronto was irritating to her. Even the Swiss watch manufacturer was still considering whether to hire Meghan. In a bid to persuade the chief executive, she and Gina Nelthorpe-Cowne waited in a London hotel lounge to perform another pitch. 'She was done up to the nines, looking stunning,' observed Nelthorpe-Cowne. Meghan asked a waiter for a speciality tea. Served in a German-style mug, Meghan looked at the tankard familiar in a beer festival and exclaimed, 'I can't have this. This is just not on brand. Take it back.' The waiter returned with a china cup and saucer. The meeting ended without a contract.

Weeks later, she returned to London to watch a rough cut of *Anti-Social*. 'It's awful,' a friend told her at the end of the private viewing. 'It's really bad and an embarrassment for you.' Meghan agreed that the film, her thirteenth brief appearance, was best buried. She refused to give up. 'I've never wanted to be a lady who lunches,' she had said sincerely. Earning money was her priority.

Thomas Markle had noticed the change in his daughter. Ever since he had contributed to Meghan's wedding he'd been short of money. Meghan had offset his problems by part-financing the purchase of a new car (the rest was paid by a loan), and helped him move home. His latest written request provoked a phone call from Toronto. 'I've checked with Andrew,' said Meghan referring to her business manager, 'and I've given you $20,000 over the last two years.'

'I'm shocked you're keeping such a close track of the money,' spluttered Thomas, reeling that she knew 'to the last dime' how much she had given him. Compared to the £500,000 he had spent on her education, he said 'the $20,000 is a spit in the bucket.' Meghan remained silent, but her anger was obvious. Her suggestion that Thomas fly to Toronto was rejected by him. On his fixed income, he could not afford the fare.

The cooling relationship and his unwillingness to visit Canada sealed Meghan's arrangements for Christmas 2015. The holiday would be spent with Cory Vitiello's family. Joanne Vitiello hosted her large family with the hope that her son and Meghan would soon marry. Meghan ticked all her boxes. 'Very smart, very bright, very caring, very sincere,' she said.[186] Joanne Vitiello had not noticed the strains in the relationship.

Cory was weary of Meghan's prima-donna behaviour. Entering restaurants she demanded a special table, the entitlement of every famous actress; and her name-dropping whenever she returned from New York was becoming insufferable.[187] 'You're not Nicole Kidman,' he snapped at her.

There was also her apparent unwillingness to allow any publicity about their relationship. Asked by a magazine to name five people she would invite for a dinner party, she mentioned American chefs Anthony Bourdain and Mario Batali, Gwyneth Paltrow, Jamie Oliver and a girlfriend. Not Cory. Irritatingly, she was even appearing as a celebrity guest on the Food Network's TV show *Chopped Junior* as an expert praising the 'real sort of farm-fresh to table food' that reminded her of what she had eaten growing up in California.[188] Cory had been used to secure that appearance but felt unthanked for his help. Meghan's homily that 'kindness' was 'non-negotiable' appeared to have been forgotten.[189]

For his part, although unhappy, Cory was incapable of ending the relationship. In private, Meghan could not conceal her own impatience.

CHAPTER 10

Rwanda

Meghan Markle's second visit to Rwanda in January 2016 was markedly different from her first trip.

To Meghan's good fortune, Matt Hassell, KBS's creative director in Toronto responsible for the UN Women campaign, had fallen under her spell. Some would even say he was besotted by her. When an Evangelical Christian charity, World Vision Canada (WVC), told Hassell about its search for a celebrity to promote its work in Rwanda, he insisted that Meghan was ideal. Lara Dewar, WVC's chief marketing officer and a *Suits* fan – the series had now been running for five years – was also enthusiastic. Meghan, she agreed, could be titled an 'ambassador'.

Brenda Surminski, KBS's producer, called Meghan. Within 30 minutes the actress had agreed to travel to Rwanda to promote World Vision's project to build water wells in destitute villages. This would be some revenge after the negativity of the UN executives. Surminski would produce the film of her visit. Difficulties arose soon after Meghan had signed the contract and Surminski began to plan the trip.

The actress insisted on flying to Rwanda first-class and to be accompanied by Gabor Jurina, a Canadian fashion photographer.[190] Michael Goyette, an American hair and make-up stylist, was also listed as travelling with Gabor. 'Only Michael,' explained Meghan, 'knows how to work with my Black hair.' Naturally curly, she had used a treatment called Keratin to create her hair's silky straight look. Meghan's demands sent the costs well above the budget. Surminski, the film's producer, World Vision decided, could no longer travel to Rwanda.

In two air-conditioned mini-vans, Meghan and her team of three World Vision marketing executives, a Canadian cameraman plus an advertising account executive, and several suitcases containing a selection of fashion outfits, were driven for 90 minutes from Kigali's best five-star hotel to Gashora. For generations the village women and children had walked every day several miles to fill their jerry-cans in a dirty river. The result was constant illness. The commissioning of a well, financed by World Vision to deliver fresh water, was a major event – marked by Meghan's arrival in January 2016.

To the villagers' surprise, after Meghan was filmed with the children playing under the clean water bursting from the tap, she disappeared with Gabor Jurina. For hours Jurina photographed the perfectly coiffured actress hugging, squeezing and smiling with the village children. Each pose was followed by a change of clothing. 'Meghan is a true humanitarian,' Lara Dewar would say. Speaking of Meghan's 'authenticity', Dewar praised her involvement with the children, letting them sit on her lap for the photographer.[191]

Once she returned to the village, Meghan was filmed admiring children painting images of their lives on paper supplied by the charity. The Watercolor Project, conceived by Matt Hassell's staff, illustrated the value of the charity's work to supply clean water. Strangely, Dewar would wrongly claim that Meghan was the 'creator' of the Project.[192] Throughout the four-day trip Meghan was impeccably considerate to the accompanying team. She ensured there would be no repeat of her UN experience.[193]

Back in Toronto, Meghan hosted a party to raise funds for another well. Thanks to her, the Mulroneys and other Toronto stars came to Lumas, a downtown gallery, to see the children's paintings. Their money, Meghan explained to the guests, would allow more village children to go to school rather than spend their day carrying water.[194] 'This water is not just a life source for this community,' Meghan said in the video's commentary, 'but can really be a source for creative imagination and dreaming and hoping for something even greater than they can even imagine. You'll feel really good at the end of the day knowing that you've been part of that.'[195]

Her efforts that evening raised C$15,000 (about £9,000), enough to build another well.[196] The box was ticked. At the end, Surminski was puzzled. Celebrities using a desolate African village as the backdrop for fashion shoots was 'mind-blowing'. Meghan, she concluded, had 'opportunistically orchestrated the trip to pose as a philanthropist.' Moreover, her ambitions were so obvious. She was 'on a path with visions of something good happening at the end, but her destination was unknown'. Gabor Jurina posted the fashion photographs on his website. Eight months later, they would be more valuable.

The Rwandan trip coincided with the end of the fifth season of *Suits*. The series climax was to be Rachel Zane on the verge of marrying Mike Ross. At the last moment the script was changed. Ross went to prison for fraud and told Zane he could not marry her. Filming the sixth series had started, and series seven was about to be commissioned. Meghan's fee for series seven was increased to $175,000 per episode. The star, Gabriel Macht, who played Harvey Specter, was paid $500,000 per episode. Despite the reassurance of her improved fee, Meghan sensed that Rachel Zane's 'life' was nearing the end. Few TV series even lasted seven seasons and the end would be sudden. Although that proved unduly pessimistic – the network commissioned another two seasons – Meghan was nervous about her professional fate. Once her contract ended, her acting career would need to be relaunched.

Hollywood's traditions ruled that an actor's transition from TV to films was very difficult. Once the audience had identified an actor with one character, the actor needed an absence to restore their 'anonymity' and then recapture public interest. In Hollywood, George Clooney was hailed as virtually unique, a pathfinder for making a conspicuous success of that transition. Others including Jennifer Aniston would follow, but they had become global stars. Identified by the small audience as Rachel Zane, Meghan would struggle financially during a fallow period while the same audience 'forgot' Zane. She could not expect much TV work and her poor experience over the previous five years confirmed that Hollywood did not beckon. She needed to reassess her life.

A break came during a trip to New York. To promote *Suits* she reappeared on the Larry King show.[197] In a pre-prepared performance she laid out her familiar presentation. First, her successful campaign against Procter & Gamble's advertisement, praise for President Kagame and her campaign to empower women: 'I want to be a feminist and also feminine…No matter how you look, you should be taken seriously… Just be true to yourself.'

The other soundbites repeated The Tig's messages of reassurance to women: 'You're more fabulous if you do something of value in this world…You must be kind to yourself…Talk to ourselves like we are our own best friend…You need to champion yourself.' Portraying herself as modest, low-cost and undemanding, she revealed that she liked to take risks but was vulnerable and alone: 'I don't have a mentor. I need a lot of help. I don't have a sound-box.' Finally, she advised viewers, 'If it's worth five minutes, then give it five years.' Few would have realised that she was repeating Trevor Engelson's pick-up line. What she said was always so predictable.

Once again, John Fitzpatrick afforded Meghan a welcome break from Toronto's routine. The three-star Fitzpatrick hotel in central Manhattan was not the type of venue where Meghan liked to be seen. In the midst of winter she would prefer to have been holding her glass uptown in the Carlyle or The Mark. Brand Meghan was about top-end luxury in clothes, food and travel. She made the exception because Fitzpatrick had become her passport to the heart of America's political establishment. The garrulous Irish-American philanthropist offered her a chance to break the mould of her life in Toronto.

On 17th February, 2016, Fitzpatrick was hosting another fundraiser for Hillary Clinton. Thirty rich Irish-Americans were enjoying themselves in his private apartment with Bill Clinton. No one was insulted that Hillary could not break off from her campaign. Many were also delighted that Fitzpatrick had invited Liam Neeson, the star of *Michael Collins*, a Hollywood drama about the Irish revolutionary leader. For Fitzpatrick, who supported a united Ireland, Neeson/Collins was a hero. Eagerly, Meghan agreed to be photographed standing between Neeson and Fitzpatrick. To her misfortune, the badly lit photo failed to portray her beauty. Moreover, it spoke volumes for Meghan's insignificance that the Hollywood star would later insist that he had never met Meghan.[198] Despite the photograph, his memory about Meghan was blank. Meghan remained forgettable, but she did not forget the event. Hanging out among the famous in Clinton's world was an incentive to move on.

Soon after the New York visit, Meghan flew to the Cayman Islands. Gina Nelthorpe-Cowne had arranged for her to address a financial company's annual conference. Fixing the gig had been a hard sell. Meghan's main selling-point was her low cost. As an unknown her fee was $15,000 plus expenses, and a business-class air ticket. Her request for first-class was rejected. Although Meghan could only make the same speech about women's rights that she had delivered to the UN in 2014 and every occasion since then, Nelthorpe-Cowne promised a good performance.

Once the contract was agreed, Meghan urged Nelthorpe-Cowne to arrange for Jessica Mulroney to be included in the trip at the client's expense. 'She's my best friend,' said Meghan, 'and I need her as my beautician and stylist.' More important, Meghan needed Mulroney to provide a confidante's reassurance. Meghan's wish was granted. Throughout the trip, Meghan repeatedly asked Mulroney, 'What shall I do after acting?'

Meghan faced not only a professional challenge but a personal crisis. At 35 she wanted children. Although Cory Vitiello was a good man and would be a good parent, he was deemed to be unsuitable as the father of Meghan's child. A chef with limited ambitions in a country which she perceived as unglamorous, Cory's horizons were too limited. 'There are only so many times you can discuss a recipe,' a friend reported, echoing Meghan's sentiment. 'And then there is nothing else.' Although it was Cory's social importance in Toronto that had propelled Meghan's status, the chef's value had dwindled. He could not further Meghan's ambitions. She wanted real celebrity, many millions of dollars and personal glory.

Her high-octane visits to New York sealed the fate of their relationship. After every trip, he cursed her ego as 'out-of-control star-fucking'. She recoiled. For Meghan, life with Cory, as with Trevor, had become unfulfilling. She would only live with Cory on her terms. After one divorce she would avoid another mistake. Repeatedly, she asked a friend whether she should end the relationship because, she revealed, she no longer loved Cory.[199]

Attempts over the previous year to find a new boyfriend had floundered. On several occasions she had swapped messages with Matt Cardle, a winner of the television show *The X Factor*, suggesting that they meet.[200] Her attempts ended after Cardle met the woman he eventually married. Approaches to other single celebrities while she lived with Cory remained unknown to the chef. Despite his suspicions, Cory tweeted that month, 'I am so proud of my lady.' Professionally, she remained on the same spot on the treadmill. World Vision had reappointed her as a global ambassador, and she could also look forward to a second season filming her own Reitmans clothes collection.

With her face across city billboards and on social media she would be famous among Canadians. But, as ever, that was not enough.

'I want to be a success at home,' she repeated during the Cayman trip. She feared that returning to Los Angeles would end in grief. Nelthorpe-Cowne offered a solution. 'Come to London,' she suggested. Meghan's best hope, Nelthorpe-Cowne explained, was to break through in Britain and, on the strength of that success, bounce back to Los Angeles. 'I'll introduce you to Matthew Freud,' said Nelthorpe-Cowne, although she secretly feared that the well-established Freuds PR agency would not be interested in an unknown actress. 'Freuds could create your brand in Britain,' continued Nelthorpe-Cowne.

The word 'brand' triggered Meghan's interest. 'OK,' she agreed. 'But I don't want to stay long. I want to go back to Los Angeles. I want to be a success in Los Angeles, my home.' There was another incentive. Moving to London would solve the Cory problem. The final break from him was delayed.

Some members of the *Suits* team noticed that Meghan's tone during the filming of the sixth series was sharper, slightly aggressive. Reflecting her frustrated ambition, her prospects after the series were grinding to a halt. Other than The Tig, there was only *The Game*, an Australian coffee-table book edited by Samantha Brett.[201] Forty 'trail-blazing women' including Meghan had described their lives.

In her section, Meghan recalled as a schoolgirl helping at the soup kitchen on Los Angeles' Skid Row. Maria Pollia, her theology teacher, had 'told me that life is about putting others' needs above your own fears…Remember that someone needs us, and that your act of giving/helping/doing can truly become an act of grace once you get out of your head.'[202] Her teacher's homily, she said, 'has stuck with me my old whole life'. She also wrote that to earn money as a teenager she had served customers at Humphrey Yogart in Beverly Hills for $4 an hour. Thomas Markle was puzzled when he read that. 'She never worked while she was at school,' he insisted.

The scenario of her impoverished youth grew as she became part of the Clintons' and the Democrats' set. In early April she flew to New York for another of John Fitzpatrick's eve-of-primary celebrations at his hotel. Two hundred supporters cheered both Clintons in the bar decorated with Irish flags.[203] Meghan voiced her support for Hillary Clinton in Toronto's late TV *The Nightly Show*. On the same show she condemned Donald Trump as 'divisive' and 'misogynist', a vote-loser among women for 'the kind of world that he's painting'. Trump, she said, 'has made it easy to see that you really don't want that'. Americans were urged to vote for Hillary Clinton. Her opinion provoked no registered comments on social media.

Meghan had reached a turning-point. After spending a few days with Cory in New York she was certain their relationship was over. Getting him out of their jointly rented house would be difficult, she suspected, and Toronto's gossips would enjoy a damaging field-day. In addition her frustrating failure to find an exciting career follow-up to *Suits*, and her weariness of life in Canada, all coalesced during two days in Montreal in spring 2016.

CHAPTER 11

Reitmans – Take Two

On 13th March, Meghan flew into Montreal for the second Reitmans shoot. As she entered the location – an old restaurant called Auberge Saint-Gabriel – for the day's filming, the tension was uncomfortable.

The contract for eight days' work paid Meghan $202,628 plus 7 per cent royalties. The total C$4 million budget, shaped around Meghan's fashion credibility, was billed as 'aspirational without being alienating'.[204] Jeannie Vondjidis-Miller, the head of marketing, described Meghan as the 'National Spokesperson' for Reitmans. 'We wanted someone with a point of view,' she said. Very soon, many of the creative team associated with the campaign were exhausted by Meghan's point of view.

Discussions about the commercial's concept – or storyline – had started in February. The 35-second commercial for the summer campaign was called 'The Label'. Meghan, the creative directors employed by the Tank agency and John Grammatico, the film director, disagreed about the 'concept' that ended with Meghan delivering the tag-line 'Reitmans…Really'. Over several weeks Meghan had denounced Tank's storyboard: a handsome man asks Meghan to dance at a party, in order to be able to read the label on her dress. Could such a beautiful woman really be wearing a Reitmans dress?

'Seriously, this doesn't make sense!' Meghan exclaimed about the storyboard. 'I'm a brash American and if my name is going to be on something, I'm going to have my say.'[205] Tank's account manager, Emmanuelle Thaon, and creative director Sophie Gaudet were reluctant to make changes. In their opinion, Meghan offered no worthwhile alternative ideas, other than suggesting that a Caribbean location with a Hollywood budget would be better. In Meghan's judgement, the advertising agency's executives had promised Reitmans more than they could deliver for the budget.

On 4th March the arguments reached their climax. After ferocious exchanges a few script changes were made, only to be rejected by Meghan again. 'She bulldozed her way through and never said a nice word,' complained one of the team. No one stood up to her. As the argument reached a climax, Meghan cut the telephone line. That evening, John Grammatico, a director known as a professional without an ego, emailed Tank's creative director. He urged her to agree to a solution to avoid expensive time-wasting confrontations during the actual filming. Meghan, Grammatico suggested, was not completely wrong. The agency was focusing the commercial on Reitmans' label and the dress. Like all stars, Meghan wanted the focus to be on herself. 'She needs to be flattered,' he wrote, 'and she's right. Celebrities want to be the hero.'

The solution was to 'put Meghan in charge, because she's beautiful and famous and she's in control'. Rather than the man looking at the label, suggested Grammatico, he should look at Meghan. Reluctantly, the creative director agreed. The script was rewritten by Grammatico. His script had punch. At the end of their dance, unknown but jealous women watching the dancers try to get a peek at the label on Meghan's stunning dress and are confronted by Meghan. As she turns around on the dance floor, she tells the women with a smile, 'Reitmans… Really'. Grammatico's solution was accepted. But the seeds of discord had been sown.

One year after the first campaign, Meghan was less enamoured that her 'brand' was attached to Reitmans. Not only was she associated with a downmarket label, but their new clothes were decidedly unappealing. In addition, her sense of entitlement had grown. To prove her importance she demanded additional special treatment. Unhappy that her executive suite for C$1,531 per night at the Place d'Armes hotel in Montreal was only a master bedroom, living-room and powder-room, Meghan demanded that the agency reserve a bigger suite at the more expensive Gault hotel. 'She insists,' said her agent. The production team resisted. 'She wants photographs of the hotel rooms and the rooms assigned to her on the set,' shouted her agent.

Next, Meghan demanded that she be registered in the hotel under an alias, Jane Smith. 'Her identity must be kept secret,' said her agent, Lori Sale. 'Meghan doesn't want to be hassled by the hotel staff, other guests or photographers.' The production team were flummoxed. No one in French-speaking Montreal knew Meghan. In the event, the hotel refused the request. Registered under her own name, no paparazzi gathered outside the hotel.

Inside the hotel room, Meghan's complaints hit another high. Ignoring the flower displays, bottles of her favourite wine and even a special calligraphy pen carefully laid out on the tables, she criticised the hotel's Tempurpedic bathrobe and slippers. She wanted Dior. The tea was the wrong blend and the vegan green juice was warm.

Meghan's arrival on the set at 7:10am was anticipated. 'The Princess is coming,' sniggered one assistant. Hard-faced, Meghan entered the restaurant avoiding eye contact with the crew. Her agent had demanded that only the designated few on the set were authorised to speak to her. That order had been passed among the 58 members of the Canadian production team. With a forced smile, she disappeared upstairs to her dressing-room. The whisper across the production team was equally poisonous: 'She's fake-sweet.'

Two hours had been allocated for completing her hair and make-up and, at her last-minute request, to paint her nails. Animatedly during that session, Meghan talked about life with Felix, her trusted hairdresser. The manicurist, a woman in her late thirties, joined the conversation. According to those involved, Meghan was rude and unpleasant. The manicurist was stunned. There was silence as her nails were finished. The manicurist was dismissed. She left the location in tears. 'This unusual situation caused me stress,' she later confessed. 'It still haunts me.'

Throughout the day Meghan appeared for her shots escorted by her entourage – Felix the hairdresser and Marco the make-up artist – and then returned to her room. Both were ordered never to leave her side. 'She was always fed up,' one crew member noted, 'sighing, huffing and rolling her eyes at things. It was heavy-going working with her.' Another noticed that she would be 'super sweet' with Felix and Marco and then within seconds turn to the crew and be 'super-disagreeable'. The own-brand Reitmans' clothes she was expected to wear, said Meghan, were unsatisfactory. Definitely inferior to Chanel.

Meghan's complaints sparked members of the team to make mock faces behind her back. 'She's here for her ego, not the art,' said another unimpressed team member. Occasionally, she openly refused to follow John Grammatico's directions or asked him to change his angle. Grammatico patiently explained his intentions. No one dared to contradict Meghan. Keeping their jobs depended on satisfying her demands. The only consolation was Meghan's actual performance. In front of the lens she transformed herself into a warm, glamorous icon. The camera loved her and she loved the camera.

The downside was the arguments. At the end of 12 hours' filming, the crew wrapped to avoid triple-time payments. Seventeen shots had been prepared on the storyboard. Because of the disagreements, Grammatico had been unable to record two critical shots.

The following day, the mood deteriorated. The new location was in a loft on Saint Pierre Street. Over 12 hours Meghan would shoot a video of fashion tips for the website. Since the technical requirements were lower than for a commercial, the lighting and sound equipment were noticeably inferior. At 7:10am Meghan arrived, giving some the impression that she was unconvinced by the campaign. To satisfy another of her demands, the wardrobe staff had bought a pair of expensive Aquazzura beige suede shoes chosen by Meghan.

From her dressing-room, Meghan was heard complaining about the production, the clothes, the style and the script. In particular she implied that Jeannie Vondjidis-Miller, the Reitmans marketing executive, lacked fashion sense. In retaliation, members of the team began to speak in French. 'Meghan was offended,' recalled one person. 'She took it personally.'

During the filming, Meghan was asked: 'What Canadian woman inspires you?' She laughed and asked for examples. 'None of them inspires me,' she replied. 'You can't make me say something I don't want to or don't believe in.'

Again, no one dared challenge the star, except John Grammatico. 'I don't like the shot,' Meghan complained. Initially, her demands for changes to the angles were rejected. Towards the end of the day, Grammatico relented. 'Whatever...' he sighed, and obeyed. At the end, they were eye-balling one another.

'It's a wrap,' shouted the assistant at exactly 7pm. Meghan's agent had already called to warn that her client would not film one extra minute. She was in a hurry. There was none of the customary 'Thank you' or 'See you again'. Meghan departed. To the surprise of the wardrobe staff she forgot to leave behind the Aquazzura shoes. Mistakenly, she walked out of the apartment wearing them. 'That's the last time we'll work together,' Grammatico muttered, accurately.

'It's nice to suffer with you,' grumbled one account executive to a cameraman. 'She is definitely the meanest person I've ever met. Just saying,' Jean Malek, the third director, posted on Facebook. Another female member of the team would be more specific. A long-time fan of *Suits* and Meghan, that person had looked forward to working with the actress: 'Instead, I thought she was a bit of a bully filled with a narcissist entitlement complex that had everyone walk on eggshells, as well as the agency and production teams work around the clock under tremendous stress with no demonstration of appreciation at all. More often than not, sarcastic, condescending, demeaning criticism.'

The fall-out threatened the third day of filming – Meghan would be modelling Reitmans jeans. To rescue the campaign, Reitmans' retail president, Walter Lamothe, met Lori Sale in a Los Angeles hotel. During the filming, Lamothe said, Meghan had gone into make-up and had ranted about the crew, creative staff and Reitmans' executives. 'She's off the rails,' one of them said. The problem, explained Lamothe, was whether Meghan was willing to complete the contract and promote the range on TV.

The agent called Meghan. 'That kind of behaviour will never happen again,' Meghan was told. In plain language the agent ordered her client to send handwritten apologies and fulfil her contract. No apologies were forthcoming but, on Meghan's insistence, another production company was employed for the third day's filming.

Unsurprisingly, the fear Meghan generated made some of her team reluctant to describe their experiences. Jeannie Vondjidis-Miller, seen on the second day's shoot reduced to tears and who left Reitmans after the filming, went to another extreme. Recently she described her relationship with Meghan as 'Excellent. I thoroughly enjoyed the collaboration and her input was well received. She was kind, thoughtful and conducted herself as a professional.'[206]

Viewers would never realise the turmoil associated with the production. Loving the camera, Meghan became a different person during the brief minutes of filming. The results of the well-shot commercial portrayed Meghan at her best. A separate film of Meghan's work to design four dresses for the Meghan Markle Range was professional.[207] Her approved portrayal sat oddly with her later comments about having watched *Married with Children* being shot with her father 20 years earlier: 'I saw how the women were objectified, and I knew I didn't want to be looked at like that.'[208] One Facebook comment suggested that the Reitmans campaign had landed her in the same trap: 'She looks like she's heading into a porn set. We can't even properly see the dress.' During a special TV programme, Jessica Mulroney agreed. She called one outfit 'a porno-pose dress with pussy-bow'.[209]

In the post-production of the advertisements Meghan sent countless comments and demands about changes to the colour of her lipstick and her waistline. One request regarding a photograph of her sitting down with open sandals generated particular mirth: 'Please fix my feet for me – I get slaughtered online for [sic] people picking apart my feet, sadly. There's a scar on my left foot + my right foot isn't the prettiest (long toe etc) – if you can soften that so that it doesn't distract from the shot that would be amazing. Silly I know. But trust me...'

To launch the new campaign in Toronto, Reitmans hosted a lunch on 5th April for fashion journalists. Jessica Mulroney's prospective presence propelled Meghan into a hysterical spin. The table décor, the flowers and the menu, she screamed to her agent Lori Sale in Los Angeles, were all terrible. 'What will Jessica Mulroney say?' she wailed. Sale pointed out that her small audience in Los Angeles had never heard of Mulroney.

On TV, Mulroney would praise Reitmans' faux-leather leggings and cashmere-blend poncho. On the same live programme Meghan promoted clothes manufactured by Forever 21. The company was criticised for paying its workers in Los Angeles as little as $4 an hour, and an average of $7 per hour, scoring 2 out of 5 on 'Ethical Labour Practices', and 2/5 on 'Efforts to Reduce Waste'.[210]

Once the dust settled, Reitmans were satisfied. The commercials were credited with increasing their sales by over 20 per cent.[211] Forgetting her anger, Meghan spoke about the TV advert and the billboards with her face across Canada as life-changing. 'It's a huge moment,' she said.[212]

CHAPTER 12

Limbo

Befriending celebrities united Meghan and Markus Anderson, Soho House's manager in Toronto, in a common cause. Both were looking for famous people to enhance their professional fortunes.

That quest was particularly important for Meghan in spring 2016. In preparation for another trip to London in June, she needed more contacts in the capital. Knowing the importance Meghan attached to celebrities, Anderson introduced her to Princess Eugenie, the daughter of Prince Andrew and Sarah Ferguson. Like her parents, Eugenie appreciated freebies and hob-nobbing with the rich and famous.[213] After the meeting, Meghan considered calling the princess during her next visit to London. Eugenie was the type who could help her.

Before the filming of *Suits* broke for the summer holidays, Meghan and Cory once again discussed how to end their relationship. He would need to move out of their joint home. Some thought she was hedging her bets. Others believed her subsequent explanation for the breakdown that Cory 'didn't want to settle down.'[214] In truth, Cory was relieved that she had taken the initiative before she left for Europe.

As agreed, Nelthorpe-Cowne had arranged with difficulty free accommodation in the five-star Carlton Tower hotel in Knightsbridge. In return for posing for the hotel magazine's front cover and other promotional publicity on The Tig, and her Instagram and Twitter accounts, she could stay for one week.

'My colleague and I walked to her room at the Carlton,' recalled Nelthorpe-Cowne, 'and en route was this parrot sitting in a cage. Meghan looked at this parrot and looked at my colleague and said, "I can't stay here because of the parrot."'

The 'colleague's' description of the scene was more colourful: 'Meghan went completely ballistic. It was really unpleasant.'

Meghan immediately checked out. Nelthorpe-Cowne arranged accommodation at the Soho Hotel. 'I realised that she was absolutely right, of course,' said Nelthorpe-Cowne. 'Wild animals belong in the wild and not in cages.'

Once settled in her room, Meghan came down for lunch with Nelthorpe-Cowne's co-director and a widely respected literary agent, Adrian Singston, and his assistant. Weeks earlier, Meghan had asked Singston to draft a synopsis for a proposed book to be written by her based on The Tig. Titled *Think Beautiful*, Meghan's purpose was to leverage her brand by promoting the products, restaurants and places featured on her website to comprehensively help women to better themselves. After her outburst at the hotel, Singston was uncertain how Meghan would behave. Over the previous months, many at the agency had become wary of their client. They thought Meghan's mood was unpredictable. Regularly she called the agency to demand they make reservations at restaurants or events in anticipation of her arrival in London. Inevitably, she would cancel or change her requirements. During those telephone calls, Singston was distraught by what he witnessed. He saw a young woman reduced to tears by what she called 'Meghan's passive aggressive tone.'

On this occasion, Meghan calmly sat down for lunch. Her metabolism required the right amount of food at a precise time. But as she ate, she quietly directed her venom at Singston. His synopsis, said Meghan, contained a proposed chapter called, 'How to be a better woman'. The chapter focused on a woman's choices to improve her sexual attraction.

Meghan, said Sington, seethed at him. She complained that he had inserted sex into her proposal. He was surprised. Meghan regularly posted messages on The Tig recommending potions and poses to secure a man's interest. But Meghan was following a now familiar pattern. On this occasion, her anger was directed at the experienced agent. She seemed to delight in humiliating people. Her raison d'etre, concluded Sington, appeared to be manipulating men. Was it, he wondered, a result of her 'terrible envy'? At the end of the meal, she left for her room. 'She's one of the most unpleasant people we've ever dealt with,' Sington later told Nelthorpe-Cowne. By then, Meghan had also told the agency, 'Forget the book and forget him. I never want to be in the same room as him again.'

Later that same afternoon, Meghan once again met the Swiss watch manufacturer. Finally, a promotional contract was agreed. The contract, if completed, could have been worth $500,000.

In the evening, Meghan spoke again to Nelthorpe-Cowne about finding an Englishman to marry. Yet again she mentioned the footballer Ashley Cole. Nelthorpe-Cowne was surprised. Not only had she heard about Cole's unpleasant past, but in a recent interview with *GQ* magazine Meghan had explained how a man could impress her with kindness, confidence and finding the right line between funny and vulgar. She disliked men who spent too long in the bathroom but loved how 'British guys dress for the cold'.[215] Ashley Cole fulfilled few of her requirements but raised the suspicion, despite his denials, of a relationship.

Meghan then headed to the Mediterranean to spend a few weeks in Ibiza and Amalfi with Markus Anderson, Jessica Mulroney and Misha Nonoo. The four were kindred spirits, each of them yearning to be part of the jet-set. The thrill of boarding a private plane and flying anywhere in the world on command was one of their dreams.

In reality Meghan's day-to-day life, was utterly conventional. There was no danger, no risk, no threat to her survival. She was not part of a notable set. Her life was a performance to a limited audience on a tiny stage. Part of the crowd, she passed through air terminals, taxis and hotels in almost complete anonymity. Her problems were familiar to all unknown, unmarried actors in their mid-thirties – fear of loneliness and personal and financial insecurity.

Professionally, she could not complain about unfulfilled potential. She had never struck out to be different, or to rebel, or judge herself against spectacular theatrical performances. The impression was of a person satisfied with herself. She rarely confessed to a lack of self-confidence. Her self-criticism was limited to cosmetic superficialities. The Tig never hinted at an intellectual curiosity or a hinterland. She was never heard to suffer any restlessness to beat a new challenge. The biggest influence on her life so far appears to have been the character Aaron Korsh created, Rachel Zane, an ambitious, fluent, sexy, shallow fashionista with a passion for food.

Marriage, and finding a well-financed partner, was uppermost in the holiday-makers' conversations on the Mediterranean beaches and over meals. By then, Misha Nonoo's marriage was on the rocks. She had discovered the shortcomings of being among Britain's upper classes. Although Alexander Gilkes claimed friendships with Princes William and Harry, Princess Eugenie and Madonna, his financial acumen was unimpressive. His business was unprofitable. Nonoo feared that any divorce settlement would stipulate her paying him money.

Meghan was also witnessing the perils of finance. Her father was about to file for bankruptcy for the second time. In September 2016 he owed a credit-card company £24,600 ($30,000) and owed £49,000 in tax. The credit-card debt had soared with 28 per cent interest charges. Unsurprisingly, Meghan was preoccupied by her own financial security – and finding a husband.

Finding Meghan a suitable Englishman became a pressing issue.

Her prospects were discussed after she landed at Hydra, an island south of Athens. Her best friend Lindsay Roth was hosting a weekend's hen-party before marrying a British actuary. Prince Harry came up in the conversation. Nonoo had met him through Gilkes. Harry was certainly eligible, but was known as feckless towards women.

From Greece, Meghan headed to London to promote *Suits* and herself. Once more she met Lizzie Cundy. Again they discussed Meghan's chance of appearing in a similar show to *Made in Chelsea*. She also reaffirmed her everlasting interest in Englishmen. Yet again, Cundy could offer no one suitable.

Meghan had been hired to wear Ralph Lauren during the Wimbledon fortnight. The tournament started on 27th June. Fortuitously for Meghan, Ralph Lauren's newly appointed publicist was Violet von Westenholz, a well-connected 31-year-old socialite. Her father, Piers, an interior decorator and antique dealer, was an old friend of Prince Charles's wife Camilla. During Charles's weekend visits to the Westenholz' Hertfordshire country home and during joint family holidays, their children Violet and Harry had played together. During a conversation with Westenholz at Wimbledon, Meghan mentioned that connection. In her empathetic manner, she persuaded Violet, a sensitive soul, to arrange a blind date with Harry. Before agreeing, Westenholz sent Harry photos of Meghan.

Meghan had also arranged to meet Piers Morgan later that day, the colourful former newspaper editor. Over the previous weeks they had exchanged several Twitter messages. Morgan was impressed by Meghan's performance in *Suits* and she was as ever keen to persuade British journalists to take her seriously – and build up a profile.

They met at the Scarsdale Tavern in Kensington, Morgan's favourite pub. By his account they enjoyed their conversation. Meghan asked Morgan to invite her on to *Good Morning Britain*, his TV breakfast show. His enthusiastic reply, she knew, was not a commitment. As she got into a taxi after 90 minutes, he bid farewell thinking she was heading to a Mayfair club. He had no idea who she hoped to meet during her visit.

Only in hindsight did he realise that she would be ultimately heading for an audition demanding her most compelling performance.

Soon after, in remarkably colourful language, Harry approved von Westenholz's suggestion of meeting Meghan.

Once the meeting was agreed, Meghan asked Markus Anderson to reserve a private room at London's Soho House. On the eve of their meeting, Meghan sent her father a note ending, 'I love you with all my heart now and forever, Love Bean.' Since she had always sent him a Valentine card, he was not surprised by the affection.[216]

At lunchtime on Friday 1st July, Meghan and Gina Nelthorpe-Cowne met at The Delaunay, a fashionable restaurant in Aldwych near Covent Garden. To her regret, Nelthorpe-Cowne could not report any success in launching Meghan's career in London.

Surprisingly, Meghan seemed uninterested. Before they started eating she whispered, 'I'm going on a date tonight.'

'Who with?' asked Nelthorpe-Cowne. She couldn't hear the reply: 'Meghan whispered so quietly I had to ask her to repeat it.' When she did, Nelthorpe-Cowne was incredulous. 'I couldn't believe what I was hearing, but I think she could barely believe it either. We were both extremely excited. I jokingly asked if she knew what she was letting herself in for and she said: "Well, it's going to be an experience and at least it will be a fun night."'

Gazing at her client, Nelthorpe-Cowne thought, 'I looked at how stunning she was and I just thought: "There's no way he's going to be able to resist her."'

As Meghan carried on whispering with excitement, Nelthorpe-Cowne interrupted, 'Do you know what you're doing? Do you know anything about him?'

Meghan replied, 'I've googled Harry. I've gone deeply into his life.'

Nelthorpe-Cowne was left in no doubt that Meghan had carefully researched every aspect of Harry and his past life. She understood precisely the man she was meeting: needy, volatile, unhappy and seeking a soulmate.[217]

'I understood where she was coming from,' Nelthorpe-Cowne recalled. 'Her dream of bagging a prince was even written in one of her old blogs.' At Kate's wedding to Prince William in 2011, Meghan had written: 'Little girls dream of being princesses. And grown women seem to retain this childhood fantasy. Just look at the pomp and circumstance surrounding the Royal Wedding and endless conversations about Princess Kate.'

Nelthorpe-Cowne left the restaurant with one thought: 'Meghan is dreaming big.'[218]

CHAPTER 13

A Troubled Prince

In 2016, Prince Harry was a damaged, insecure and under-employed 31 year old. Over the previous 15 years he had become notorious in the media as a wild party animal. Yet despite a series of incidents – dressing up as a Nazi for a party, calling a fellow Sandhurst cadet 'a Paki', and drunkenly attacking a photographer outside a nightclub – Harry was always forgiven after apologies by a Buckingham Palace spokesman.

Unlike his father, Harry was widely adored as a good lad who many men and women wanted to protect. But beyond the public's gaze Harry had become over recent months lonely and forlorn. Watching William's happiness with Kate and their two children he had become vulnerable. Meghan Markle's research of Harry highlighted the reasons for his unhappiness, but even she could not have grasped the depths of his despair before they met.

The loss of a parent is a tragedy for any child. The loss is often mitigated by love from the surviving parent, by grandparents and sometimes by a step-parent. But in 1997, when Diana died shortly before his thirteenth birthday, Harry was unusually helpless.

Throughout his childhood Diana had tolerated her son's problems. Without constraints, young Harry was known to his mother's staff as a contrarian who did the opposite of what he was told. As he grew up he became increasingly undisciplined. His father and his wider family watched helplessly as the boy refused to behave and rejected education. After he unsuccessfully tried to pass his entrance exam to Eton, his relations recognised that Harry's ignorance was spilling over into arrogance. That reality was concealed during Diana's funeral.

The image of the grieving boy walking behind Diana's coffin through London evoked heartfelt sympathy across the world. Harry would claim that the funeral had a profound effect. 'I think the hardest thing was the walk,' said William in 2017. 'It was a very long, lonely walk. It was that balance between duty and family – and that was what we had to do.'[219] Harry's anchor over the following months were his grandparents, his father Charles and his loving nanny, Tiggy Legge-Bourke. 'He was there for us,' Harry said in his early twenties of Charles. 'He tried to do his best and to make sure we were protected and looked after. But, you know, he was going through the same grieving process.'[220]

Harry's most important relationship was with William. Two years older, William was more intelligent but as the older brother more affected by his parents' tempestuous relationship.

'I hate you, Papa. I hate you so much,' he shouted at Charles while witnessing yet another argument with Diana. 'Why do you make Mummy cry all the time?'[221]

Unforgiving towards Charles, William explained to Harry the reality of their father's adultery. Both blamed Camilla for their mother's unhappiness and the destruction of their parents' marriage. They resented that in the aftermath of their parents' divorce Charles had devoted his time to shoring up his faltering status and consolidating his relationship with Camilla. After Diana's death, Charles's attempts to build a close relationship with his sons were undermined by his adultery. William was outrightly antagonistic towards Charles; while Harry, after entering Eton on his second attempt, was slightly more tolerant. Both for some time avoided meeting Camilla when she was staying in Clarence House, Charles's London home. Their dislike was reignited after Camilla was blamed for Tiggy Legge-Bourke's departure.

Bound together through divorce, tragedy and anger, the brothers' survival depended upon their mutual dependence. Caring for Harry from the day he was born, William was as unhappy as his brother. Rude at school, 'Basher' Wills could not resist asserting his privilege, sometimes violently, reminding outsiders of his destiny as the future king.[222]

Seeking peace and acceptance, Charles tolerated that audacity. Spending his time with Camilla or away on official duties, Charles turned a blind eye to his wayward teenage sons. He had converted a basement in Highgrove for their weekend parties. In his absence, the club, renowned for generous supplies of alcohol and tolerance of drugs, was hosted by hot-headed William with Harry in close support. Whenever trouble erupted, Harry invariably took the blame to protect the heir and conceal his explosive temper.

In 2000, after William left school for a gap year, 'Hash Harry', aged 15, renamed Highgrove's basement as Club H. The host became notorious for excessive drinking and smoking. Two years later, after William had started at St Andrews university, the *News of the World* illegally tapped a mobile telephone, discovered the Highgrove parties and proclaimed: 'World Exclusive – Harry's Drugs Shame'. The newspaper's headline in January 2002 was somewhat contrived. William was probably more culpable than Harry but, as Charles's advisor Mark Bolland insisted, 'William has to look perfect and Harry has to take the strain.' In protecting the heir, Harry did not protest. William liked to be in control and Harry uncritically accepted his brother's power.

However, the newspaper's dishonesty rankled. Harry was aware that the *News of the World*, convinced that Charles was not his father, was seeking a strand of his hair to check whether the DNA matched that of James Hewitt, Diana's boyfriend for five years. The newspaper failed, and Buckingham Palace dismissed the suggestion by explaining that their affair had started more than one year after Harry's birth. But his own legitimacy troubled Harry. Some in the Palace were convinced that Diana did have an unnamed lover after William's birth and that man, rather than Charles, was Harry's father. She was known to have had an affair with Barry Mannakee, her protection officer in 1985, the year after Harry's birth. It was still not known whether she also had a lover in late 1983.

The rumours disquieted Harry, not least because quite apart from Charles there were other embarrassing burdens. Until the serialisation in June 1992 of Andrew Morton's book, *Diana: Her True Story*, few believed that Charles had abandoned Diana or that she was unhappy. Because Diana was rich and beautiful, there weren't many that truly thought her problems could be so serious.

Buckingham Palace distrusted the book's veracity until the *Sun* published a sound tape of Diana, alias 'Squidgy', speaking to James Gilbey, a married boyfriend, and the *Sunday Mirror* published a tape of Charles speaking to Camilla in the most lurid, sexual terms. Among Charles's asides was his joke that he could end up as a Tampax with his 'luck to be chucked down a lavatory…and never going down'.

The sensational portrayal of Diana, lonely and distraught, damaged Charles. Thereafter the Royal Family's scandals were rarely off the front pages. In quick succession, Prince Andrew and Sarah Ferguson separated, Princess Anne divorced Mark Phillips, and on 9th December, 1992, Diana and Charles legally separated. While the ruins of Windsor Castle were still being repaired after a fire, Jonathan Dimbleby's authorised biography of Charles and his TV documentary in 1994 not only confirmed the heir's long-term relationship with Camilla. It also led to the exposure of Diana's five-year affair with Captain James Hewitt, which had ended in 1991.

In the Battle of the Waleses, Diana scored the last penalty in a *Panorama* interview in November 1995. 'There were three of us in this marriage,' she told the BBC, 'so it was a bit crowded.' Neither Charles nor Diana considered the damage to their children these interviews caused, justifying Harry's complaint years later: 'All sorts of grief and lies and misconceptions are coming to you from every angle.'[223]

The brothers grew up convinced that the media had killed their mother. Saintly Diana, in their opinion, was destroyed by journalists who pursued her relentlessly. For years the paparazzi had chased and provoked their mother for profit. A single photograph could be worth thousands of pounds. She had fallen victim to their dishonesty.

Neither prince wanted to accept that Diana played the media for her own advantage. Regularly, she tipped off photographers about her whereabouts and posed for pictures. She eagerly collaborated with journalists to wreak revenge on Charles, especially with Andrew Morton, the *Daily Mail*'s Richard Kay, and Martin Bashir, on the basis of his deception. Her motives were complex and sown during her own unhappy childhood and later, as she tried to pick up the pieces of her wrecked life. Neither son understood what those close to Diana witnessed: their mother's remorseless self-destruction.

They were too young to understand her intimate relationships with a series of racy men. Most spectacularly, her profound unhappiness had driven her to take a bizarre decision in the summer of 1997, and rely on Mohamed Al-Fayed, the serially dishonest Egyptian businessman who owned Harrods. Some would blame Diana's longing for publicity. Others explained that her reaction to the perpetual onslaught of allegations that she was inadequate, incompetent, mentally ill and unfaithful to her husband was to respond to the criticism head-on, rather than allow her critics and the media to triumph.

No one underestimated Diana's own excitement about the global interest she aroused. She was an icon exuding breathtaking glamour and beauty. Her magic and mystery intensified every time she met the sick and sad. Seeing herself as a casualty who searched for fellow victims to both share and alleviate their suffering, she eluded any universally agreed description. Controversial in life, she left a troubling legacy.

During his twenties William visited his mother's family and friends to try to fill in the gaps about Diana. Harry resisted that disturbing tour. He preferred to believe the Hollywood fiction that his mother had been murdered by the paparazzi's relentless pursuit of her into the Paris tunnel. 'I think it was a classic case of don't let yourself think about your mum,' he would later explain, 'and the grief and the hurt that comes with it, because it's never going to bring her back and it's only going to make you more sad. My way of dealing with it was just basically shutting it out, locking it out.'[224]

Years after Diana's death, Harry recalled complaining to his father about the turmoil he was suffering at school as a member of the Royal Family and the legacy of a broken family. Profoundly unhappy, Harry wilfully destroyed other boys' property at Eton, once cutting up the pencil-case of a fellow student. 'Well, it was like that for me,' Charles allegedly said to him, 'so it's going to be like that for you.' Harry observed, 'That doesn't make sense. Just because you suffered doesn't mean that your kids have to suffer.'[225]

Throughout his life Harry forgot that Diana was also a victim of a broken family. Her own mother, alias The Bolter, abandoned Diana aged nine for another man. Diana spent her wrecked childhood shuttling between her selfish parents. And while Harry was at school Diana had endless affairs, often with married men.

Amid that emotional maelstrom Harry gained merely two A levels. After five years at Eton, Britain's best-known school, Harry scored a grade B in art and a grade D in geography. Most Etonians would expect to achieve at least three As. Harry's results reflected his record stuck at the bottom of his class. Unsuited for university, he needed a career. 'I spent many years kicking my heels and I didn't want to grow up,' he admitted.[226] Angry and emotional, his male friends tolerated his wish to be the naughtiest in the room. At a loss, Harry was frequently seen in nightclubs, especially Boujis in Kensington, with 'society blondes', leaving in the early hours, sometimes covered in vomit after a drunken wrestle with friends. One pub banned him for allegedly calling a barman a 'fucking frog'. Pessimistic and cynical, he cursed the media for reporting those incidents.

Most girls made little noticeable impression on him until 2004 when he met Chelsy Davy, an attractive, intelligent, independently minded university graduate from a Zimbabwean farming family. Both were party animals enjoying drugs, drinking and sex. Davy discovered his need for a girlfriend who could also be like a mother. 'The trouble is,' Harry later told General Richard Dannatt over a drink in Kensington Palace, 'I'm not like any other young man. It's difficult to be normal.'[227]

William avoided those problems. In 2004 he was not seeking a substitute for Diana. He was in a deep relationship with a fellow student at the University of St Andrews, Kate Middleton, and anchored into her calm, middle-class, 'ordinary' family. Confident as an undergraduate, he also understood the expectations of being an heir. During his school years at Eton he had regularly walked across the bridge for Sunday lunch with the Queen and Prince Philip in Windsor Castle. During those afternoons, the monarch had given gentle advice to her grandson, guiding him to resist controversy. He should not be meddlesome like his father, nor attract criticism for his taste in ostentatious luxury.[228]

By contrast, no one seemed willing to solve Harry's raw misery. Permanently frustrated, he appeared alternatively charming, spoiled, badly educated, simple-minded and demanding. Cooped up in Kensington Palace he could not escape the royal straitjacket – the formality of the staff and their rigid requirements. Even friends had difficulty defining his interests in life.

Harry's salvation was the army. In 2005 he applied to enter the military academy at Sandhurst. His examiners were perplexed by his childish answers in the entry exam. Had he not been the Prince he would have been rejected. 'Being in the army', he later said, 'was the best escape I've ever had. I felt as though I was really achieving something. I have a deep understanding of all sorts of people from different backgrounds and felt I was part of a team.'[229]

His transformation started with his secret posting to Afghanistan's Helmand province in 2007 as a forward air controller. 'I wasn't a prince, I was just Harry,' he said, reminiscing about his joy at being Officer Wales. From behind Camp Bastion's high walls he saw nothing of the country except during missions to kill the enemy, shot from the swooping helicopter. Orders were obeyed, but he could not have known whether the dead were hapless innocents or Taliban fighters. He could not understand the complications of that country, nor consider the hopelessness of the Allied plan to build a viable, liberal nation. Harry never questioned his military mission.

Ten weeks after arriving, his posting was leaked by a German magazine. The security threat was unmanageable. He had to be hastily evacuated. 'I felt very resentful,' he said, adding another reason to loathe the media after newspapers published photographs of him in 2012 playing nude pool with strip girls in Las Vegas.[230] 'Too much soldier, not enough prince,' quipped Harry in regret.

Further training as an army helicopter pilot led to a second 20-week tour in Helmand. Reluctantly, he left the army in 2015. Contrary to the version propagated by the Sussexes' self-styled 'spokesman' and the royal editor for *Harper's Bazaar*, Omid Scobie, that he had taken a 'tough decision' to leave, Harry had no choice.[231] His lack of academic qualifications barred him from further promotion.

Harry's return to civilian life and the resumption of royal duties were undermined by Chelsy Davy's decision to end their relationship. After their wild years together she wanted to settle down, but not as a member of the Royal Family. The uncompromising rules, restrictions, exposure and expectations were unacceptable to her. She wanted a normal life.

Harry at first rekindled his relationship with an aspiring actress, Cressida Bonas, daughter of Lady Mary-Gaye Curzon, who was one of the most beautiful women of her generation. Like Harry, Bonas was interested in mental illness.[232] She too in 2014 left Harry, a man who always feared photographers and demanded protection.[233] Both women, like others Harry met, discovered that he lacked class, was unromantic, unserious, short-tempered and imperious. Throughout their relationship, he had behaved without generosity. In a dig at him on his engagement to Meghan, Bonas would post a message alongside a sketch of a boy and girl on swings: 'No matter how educated, talented, rich or cool you believe you are, how you treat people ultimately tells it all.' She added the comment, 'Truth.'

Returning to civilian life after the army was harder than Harry expected. Finding a worthwhile job alongside his royal duties aggravated what he called the 'total chaos' caused by his personal problems.

He had first recognised his problems three years earlier in 2012. 'I just didn't know what was wrong with me,' he later said. 'I had probably been very close to a complete breakdown on numerous occasions.' He added, 'Anyone can suffer from mental health problems, [even] a member of the Royal Family.'[234] Before he left the army in 2014 William had been his saviour: 'My brother was a huge blessing. He kept saying, "This is not right, this is not normal – you need to talk about stuff."'[235] On William's advice, he visited a therapist. 'Once I started doing therapy,' he later said, 'it was like the bubble burst.' The therapist stoked his anger.[236]

Like Diana, Harry found respite from his torment by helping fellow sufferers. In 2013 he was inspired to create an international athletic and sports competition for injured soldiers, especially those who had served in Iraq and Afghanistan. Called the Invictus Games for the 'Unconquered', he won the admiration of former servicemen. He listened sincerely to those less fortunate than himself. 'I have a job I absolutely love,' said a man who felt needed. His natural talent to empathise during royal visits, just as his mother had done, broke down barriers with the wider public. Hugging children, laughing and joshing with athletes, Harry had found an outlet for his emotions.

His race against Usain Bolt during a visit to Jamaica reinforced the monarchy's popularity, whose zenith was marked by the Queen's Diamond Jubilee in 2012. Guitarist Brian May played on Buckingham

Palace's roof and the Queen appeared in a film with 'James Bond', the actor Daniel Craig, skydiving into the 2012 London Olympics. Two billion viewers had watched William and Kate marry on 29th April the previous year. The Queen became the world's best-known and admired celebrity. Harry, the charming prince, became the second most popular royal after the Queen.

Among royalists there was additional relief that Harry and William were so close. Even better, the public saw Harry laughing with William and Kate on-stage to champion the Royal Foundation, a charity established by the trio for their special causes, especially mental health. Harry described his main role in life was to support William as king.[237]

Beyond the Invictus Games and his ceremonial duties Harry's purpose remained elusive. Some speculated that he resented his brother. Perhaps he begrudged being the fall-guy for William during their teenage years. Others believed he was jealous that William was happily married with two children. Some wondered after the birth of Prince George whether he had been destabilised, now that his responsibility as the 'spare' had disappeared. His importance within the Royal Family would certainly diminish. The pressure of public life, he revealed, was intolerable. 'Every single time I was in any room with loads of people, which is quite often,' he said, 'I was just pouring with sweat…my heart beating – boom, boom, boom, boom – literally, just like a washing machine.'[238]

In May 2016, Roya Nikkhah, the *Sunday Times* royal correspondent, met Harry at Kensington Palace. During their wide-ranging conversation about Harry's happiness in the army, his commitment and concern about society and his sorrow about his mother's death, Harry presented the official line about his overarching duty to the monarchy – 'I absolutely adore my grandmother and I would take on everything she wants us to'. He also revealed his melancholia. 'The idea of family and marriage,' he said, would be 'absolutely fantastic'. Finding a wife, he admitted, was stymied by the few 'opportunities to get out there and meet people.'[239]

Four years later, on 12th January 2020, Nikkhah would be struck by the transformation of the charming, funny prince she had met over the years. Harry had 'become [a] sullen, haunted rebel.' One year after that, Harry candidly admitted 'I was thinking, I don't want this job. I don't want to be here.'[240]

In hindsight, many came to believe that back in 2016 Harry was already looking to escape.

On Friday 1st July, Harry was in France with his father, brother and David Cameron, the prime minister. They were visiting the Somme to commemorate the hundredth anniversary of the start of the battle.

At the end of a solemn day, the group returned to London. Harry sped off from Northolt airport towards Soho, unaware of how the next hours would change his life.

CHAPTER 14

The Catch

Harry had never heard of Meghan Markle, but he trusted the judgement of his childhood friend Violet von Westenholz. Nothing would be lost meeting the unknown actress for a drink. A close friend would later say that one question Harry asked very carefully of von Westenholz was about Meghan's appearance. Exactly what did she mean about Meghan's background? Her biography on Google was enticing.

Meghan's google search was more forensic. As the master of online research for The Tig, she instinctively searched Google for information.[241] The fun-loving prince, she discovered, had adopted Diana's compassion as a prop to support his own emotional needs. He had not only set up the Invictus Games but was also involved with Sentable, a charity he created in Diana's memory to help HIV sufferers in Lesotho. Saving Africa's animals was clearly also important for him. Her two visits to Rwanda would prove useful. Her philanthropic activism was an advantage.

Meeting Harry on 1st July, 2016 came at a critical moment for Meghan. Nearly 35, she mentioned to Gina that her biological clock was ticking. She wanted children. If they clicked she could fulfil her ambition for global celebrity. She knew exactly how, during their conversation, she could reassure him. 'She was the one,' Harry later revealed. 'The very first time we met.'

Early the following morning Meghan called Gina Nelthorpe-Cowne. 'He's lovely, adorable and such a gentleman,' she gushed.

'Will you meet again?' asked Nelthorpe-Cowne.

'I hope so. We left on good terms.'

By the end of the conversation, Nelthorpe-Cowne shared Meghan's excitement: 'We were both in heaven, like teenagers, about the news.'

'We're meeting again,' Meghan told Gina Nelthorpe-Cowne over lunch. 'He's really lovely,' she sighed.

On 3rd July, Meghan posted on Instagram a picture of two Love Heart sweets with the message 'Kiss Me' and 'Love Hearts in London'. Her friends understood the circumstances and the climax of the four-day relationship. On the morning of 4th July, dressed in Ralph Lauren, she returned to Wimbledon. She thanked Violet von Westenholtz for the introduction. After watching Serena Williams win her match against Svetlana Kuznetsova, she drove directly to Heathrow to fly back to Toronto for filming of *Suits*. 'Gutted to be leaving London,' she posted shortly before leaving.

Two weeks later Harry secretly flew to Toronto. He stayed for about one week in the house of a friend of Meghan's, probably Jessica Mulroney. With Cory still sharing her home, the situation for Meghan was tricky but manageable.

Since she had carefully researched Harry's life, Meghan knew exactly how to make him feel loved and appreciated. So long as she looked at him with intense affection and trust, she would not trigger his insecurity or paranoia. To reassure him that he was admired for himself she would tell him what he wanted to hear, especially about the importance of his ambitions and principles. Free of fear and suspicion, Harry succumbed to a person who offered much more than affection. 'I think that very early on,' Meghan said later, 'when we realised we were going to commit to each other, we knew we had to invest the time and energy and whatever it took to make that happen.'[242]

Naturally, she could not keep the relationship secret. Although

Harry had warned her about the need for silence to give them time to establish their relationship away from the media spotlight, her closest Toronto friends were told, and so was Thomas Markle. 'Daddy,' she said early in the month, 'I've met this new guy and I really like him.' The very next day she revealed, 'Daddy, he's an Englishman.' On the fourth phone call in July, she revealed, 'Daddy, he's a prince.'

At the end of the week, after he returned to London, Meghan was convinced that her spell was cast and the relationship with Harry would be sealed. She told Cory that their affair was over. Unaware of the circumstances, he was relieved. The final months had been unpleasant. Packing his belongings, he moved in mid-July into an apartment with Richard Lambert, a British-born friend renowned in Toronto as an owner of bars and nightclubs. Meghan stayed in the house, removing the evidence of Cory's presence. She awaited Harry's first visit to her home.

Coincidentally, during those weeks she happened to be asked questions about Britain on a TV quiz show. Not surprisingly, the Californian could not answer what 'apples and pears' means in Cockney rhyming slang (stairs), nor could she identify the three national animals of Britain's kingdoms (the lion, unicorn and dragon). 'Am I supposed to know that?' she asked. No one understood the relevance of her question.[243]

Four weeks after she first met Harry, Meghan set off on a whirlwind tour. First, to New York in early August for Lindsay Roth's wedding, which coincided with her thirty-fifth birthday. From there, she flew to Italy with Jessica Mulroney for a brief holiday in Positano. Then she headed to Rwanda as World Vision's ambassador. Finally, she arrived back in London for the first time since meeting Harry in June.

Over lunch, Meghan showed Gina Nelthorpe-Cowne photographs of Rwanda's famous silverback gorillas, before getting down to business. 'Things are going really well,' she revealed and added, 'He's asked me to come to Botswana.' Nelthorpe-Cowne was incredulous. 'I understood straightaway,' she recalled, 'that Meghan would mesmerise that broken-hearted young boy we saw following his mother's coffin. I was almost as excited as she was about her conquest. Anyone taken to Botswana in those circumstances would fall in love.'[244] On reflection, Nelthorpe-Cowne remembers foreseeing problems.

'Have you any idea what you're doing?' she asked. Harry, she explained, was clearly thinking about marriage. 'Do you realise you won't be able to make any more movies? Royal duties will be your life.'

'Gina, save it,' Meghan snapped. Nelthorpe-Cowne was taken aback by the steel in Meghan's voice. Holding up her hand, Meghan continued: 'Stop. Be quiet. I don't want to hear any negativity. This is a happy time for us.' Stopped in her tracks, Nelthorpe-Cowne looked at the hard fury in Meghan's eyes. At that stage, she failed to grasp the full significance of the moment. Meghan's plan was working. Harry was within her web.

Years later, Meghan sought to portray herself as cautious about going to Botswana. 'Is it crazy to go away like this?' she allegedly asked her friends. 'It wasn't something she had done before,' wrote Omid Scobie.[245] That portrayal of coy uncertainty was barely convincing. She knew that any association with Harry – even if it ended abruptly – would establish her as a super-celebrity.

Botswana, said Harry, was his second home. He had been introduced to the country in 1997 by Geoffrey Kent, the successful travel entrepreneur and manager of Charles's polo team. In the aftermath of Diana's death, the bereaved boy fell in love with the smell of the African bush and Botswana's rich animal life. From Botswana he had flown with Charles to Pretoria to meet Nelson Mandela. His escort, Mark Dyer, a former Welsh Guards officer and equerry to Charles, became Harry's mentor. Thereafter, Harry spent most Augusts in southern Africa. Frequently he visited Botswana and Malawi to work on programmes to care for elephants and rhinos. On 6th August, 2016, the *Sun* reported his presence in Natal. He had been to the raucously drunken wedding of George McCorquodale, a cousin.

Two weeks later, Meghan flew to Botswana for a second bush holiday with Harry. Living secretly in a tented camp overlooking a river and lush hills, their five days were filled with watching the wild animals, swimming and eating. Following in the footsteps of Chelsy Davy and Cressida Bonas, she was the fourth girlfriend Harry had taken to Botswana. Like them, Meghan was the type to whom Harry could confess his secrets. He could fall in love with her because she could save him from what he feared about himself. 'It was absolutely amazing to get to know her as quickly as I did,' Harry later said. Those days were 'crucial to me to make sure we really got to know each other'. By the time they returned to London they had agreed that in future, while keeping their relationship a secret, they should not be apart for more than two weeks.

On their return to London, Meghan immediately called Gina Nelthorpe-Cowne – from Harry's home in Kensington Palace – to arrange to meet for lunch that day. Soon after she sat down, Meghan pulled out her phone. 'She showed me the most wonderful photographs of the two of them. They were so clearly already in love.' Nelthorpe-Cowne said, concluding, 'The deal was sealed. Harry and Meghan knew they would be together.' Any doubts were swept aside by Meghan: 'I'm in love. Euphoric. He's the right father for my children.'

In a burst of girl-talk the conversation revealed her concern to spend enough time with him. She needed, Meghan explained, to prevent Harry escaping. She was not going to let him get away.

'Well, you know what you're letting yourself in for,' Gina Nelthorpe-Cowne said in a deliberately supportive voice. 'This is serious. This is the end of your normal life, the end of your privacy – everything.'

Meghan smiled.

'I knew then', recalled Nelthorpe-Cowne, 'that they were certain to get married.'

'OK, I'm happy for you, Meghan,' she said. 'Do me a favour. Use your platform to save the environment.'

'Yes, I will,' replied Meghan.

Their intimacy suddenly evaporated. Meghan, Nelthorpe-Cowne feared, was no longer a genuine friend. Focused on what she wanted, she wasn't going to listen to anything that cast a shadow.

Naturally, Meghan did not reveal all her feelings to Nelthorpe-Cowne. As she would say one year later about marrying into the Royal Family, 'I do not see it as giving anything up. I see it as a change. It is a new chapter.' As became evident in later months, Harry's commitment and talk of duty and self-denial was unattractive to the actress. The idea that there would be serious restrictions on her life as a member of the Royal Family had not occurred to her.[246] 'We're going to change the world,' Meghan said solemnly to Nelthorpe-Cowne. 'With Harry by my side, we can change the world.'

Sworn to silence, Nelthorpe-Cowne told no one, including her husband, about Meghan's revelations to her. The media was totally unaware of the relationship.

At the end of September 2016, Meghan was booked by Nelthorpe-Cowne to address 1,300 delegates at the One Young World Summit in Ottawa. Billed as among 'the brightest young leaders from around the world', Meghan was listed as a 'UN Woman Advocate for Women's Leadership and Political Participation' and 'a global ambassador for World Vision.'[247] As usual, Meghan urged her agent to generate publicity around her speech. 'I also want to be photographed with Justin Trudeau and Kofi Annan,' she told Nelthorpe-Cowne. 'It's really important. Very important.'

To satisfy her demands, Nelthorpe-Cowne also arranged for Meghan to feature in a special edition of *Vanity Fair* as an 'exceptional young leader'. Meghan was seated with the chosen 'leaders' in a minibus outside the conference centre waiting to be driven to the photoshoot. Seeing Meghan through the open door, a young female reporter asked her a benign question. 'Talk to my agent,' snapped Meghan. 'Gina. Just sort this out.' Nelthorpe-Cowne was 'taken aback and a little shocked'. Until that moment, in her eyes, Meghan had always been warm and accommodating to everyone. Meghan had changed. 'She was only a feminist when it suited her,' concluded Nelthorpe-Cowne.

Back at the hotel, Meghan had a new demand. Once her relationship with Harry was known and she spent more time in London, she explained, she would need a special media relations team. 'I want you to handle it, Gina,' said Meghan. Since she had no money, she continued, and the kudos would be immeasurable, she expected her agent to work without payment. Gina politely refused. She was not a PR agency and lacked the staff and expertise. However, she could promise Meghan that once the Harry connection was known, her commercial appeal, especially in America, would increase. Meghan was insulted by Nelthorpe-Cowne's rejection of her proposal.

That evening, Meghan was photographed with Justin Trudeau, Canada's prime minister. Unexpectedly, Kofi Annan had left Ottawa the same day, missing the dinner. The chance for the photograph was lost. Nelthorpe-Cowne watched her client fume. The following morning, Meghan announced that she would not make her speech. She was returning immediately to Toronto. *Suits*' directors required urgent filming.

'But you've agreed to make a speech,' implored Nelthorpe-Cowne.

'I'll leave it up to you. You're my agent. Sort it.'

In the midst of her rebuke, a young woman interrupted her.

'Don't these people have manners?' asked Meghan. 'She didn't even greet me.'

Embarrassed, Gina Nelthorpe-Cowne rushed back to her room and for the first time in her long career burst into tears. Since Meghan and Harry had become an item, she realised, her client had become a different woman: 'There was a big change after that.'

The change was partly influenced by Harry's obsession with the importance of protection, bodyguards and privileged status. Regularly, Harry flew first class on commercial flights to Toronto. Wearing a baseball hat, he slipped off the plane unnoticed to a car waiting on the tarmac. While he lived in Meghan's house, bodyguards sat around the clock in a SUV parked nearby. The same bodyguards escorted him to the local shops and around the city.[248]

In alternate weeks, Meghan flew to London. On arrival at Heathrow she received special treatment organised by Harry. First to disembark, she was driven to a VIP facility for processing her passport and then sped in a chauffeured car to London. There she stayed in Nottingham Cottage, Harry's two-bedroom home within Kensington Palace, a secluded and guarded compound near Kensington High Street.

Those privileges influenced her reaction to an encounter in the first-class airport lounge on a return trip. An airline official asked her to move to another seat to make way for a group of male Colombian dignitaries. Without protest, she picked up her bag.

In the future, she pledged, no one would ask her to move.

CHAPTER 15

Exposed

In Meghan Markle's life, little happened by chance. Beyond the empathetic smiles was a woman who distrusted spontaneity and liked to control every aspect of her life. In late September 2016 nothing was more important than her relationship with Harry.

She decided that her past story needed adjustment. On 9th October, 2016, a PR agency in Los Angeles changed her Wikipedia entry. The reference to the *Deal or No Deal* game show was removed, along with the description of her carrying case number 24. The technician also deleted the reference to being a fashion model. A section headed 'humanitarian work' was inserted. That described her visits to Rwanda and Afghanistan, and her New York speech for United Nations Women and The Tig.[249]

Two weeks later, Meghan sent Gina Nelthorpe-Cowne an email announcing the end of her acting and commercial career. Their contract was terminated. Nelthorpe-Cowne was disappointed: 'I realised it meant losing her as a friend as well as a client.' Meghan's timing had been carefully planned.

Harry was back in Toronto. On Saturday 22nd October, Meghan took him to a Hallowe'en party at Soho House. Dressed in costumes, they went with his cousin Eugenie and her boyfriend. As Meghan later admitted, the four 'snuck out...to have just one fun night on the town before it was out in the world that we were a couple.'[250] The previous night, Meghan had posted a photo of herself on Instagram with a pumpkin and a photo of her 'secret Hallowe'en date'. Most at the party were in no doubt that Meghan was 'outing' Harry. For her own good reasons she wanted the relationship to be publicised. In media hype, some would call it the 'Greatest Story since the Abdication'.

Camilla Tominey of the *Sunday Express* revealed the affair on 30th October. Alerted from London, Harry left Meghan's Toronto home unseen early that morning and headed for the airport before journalists arrived. 'It has the ring of truth,' confirmed the Palace about the global sensation creating a frenzy outside Meghan's house. She emerged, smiling to a crowd of photographers, and drove to the *Suits* studio.

Soon afterwards she posted more photos of herself on The Tig.[251] Among them were shots of two visits to London, herself at the Soho Farmhouse in Oxfordshire, and pictures showing that she and Harry were wearing identical bracelets. Separate posts featured a jigsaw and a cup of tea. Another showed two cuddling bananas with the caption, 'Sleep tight X'. Journalists received numerous tips about the clothes and accessories Meghan was wearing. One hundred thousand new followers signed up to her account. 'Princess Meghan Markle,' asked one, 'which banana is Harry?' Meghan was clearly not concerned about her privacy at that particular moment.[252]

In Los Angeles that morning, Ninaki Priddy, Meghan's oldest friend and maid of honour at her Jamaican wedding, and a victim of Meghan's ghosting, smiled. Meghan's long fascination with the Royal Family had landed her the ultimate prize. She re-read Meghan's post on The Tig: 'Little girls dream of being princesses – and grown women seem to retain this fantasy – just look at the pomp and circumstances surrounding the royal wedding and endless conversations about Princess Kate.'[253]

The British media was ecstatic. 'He's been happier than he's been for many years,' reported *The Times*.[254] The tabloids went into overdrive. In unison, America's media whooped that the Royal Family was lucky. Meghan, proclaimed an American newspaper, was the 'feminist princess of our dreams'. Buckingham Palace's website agreed: Meghan was 'proud to be a woman and a feminist'. Inevitably, the media instantly launched a hunt to discover the truth about the little-known actress. The first reports were positive. Schoolteachers and former pupils in Los Angeles universally sang her praises. In Toronto, Reitmans could not believe their luck. The news coincided with the launch of Meghan's collection. Meghan saying 'Reitmans…Really' boosted sales.

Just one day later, the media's tone changed. Journalists called at her father's shabby Hollywood apartment. Standing at the open door, a pregnant woman explained that he was travelling in Mexico. 'There's no way of contacting him,' she said. 'I never know when he's going to come back.'[255]

Delighted that her father lived in a remote area north of Rosarito where his discovery was unlikely, Meghan telephoned Thomas Markle. 'Lay low,' she ordered. By then Doria was under siege by journalists. Meghan ordered Doria not to say a word. Allegedly, some journalists offered Doria money for an interview, tried to enter her home illegally and harassed her as she walked on the pavement. Doria said nothing.[256] Guards were later posted outside her home.

By then, newspapers reported that Thomas Markle had filed twice for bankruptcy and that several years earlier Doria had also filed for bankruptcy with credit-card debts of $52,750. Meghan's half-brother, Tom Junior, had also been declared bankrupt. Then it got worse for Meghan. Without considering the consequences, she did not call Samantha Markle or Tom Junior, or any of the Raglands. The price for cutting out her extended family was immediate.

Samantha Markle gave a series of ferocious media interviews –

although she would later claim to have been misquoted. On Radar Online, an American website, Samantha criticised Meghan for her 'lack of emotional and financial support' towards her father since she became a famous actor. 'Watch out, Harry,' Samantha told the *Daily Mail*. 'The Royal Family,' she said, 'would be appalled by what [Meghan's] done to her own family. The truth would kill her relationship with Prince Harry. He wouldn't want to date her anymore because it puts her in a bad public light.'[257] In the *Mirror*, Samantha dubbed Meghan a 'pushy social climber'. Later she added that Meghan was 'a social climber with a soft spot for gingers'. In the *Sun*, Samantha proclaimed that 'her behaviour is certainly not befitting of a Royal Family member'. Meghan, she said, 'is narcissistic and selfish'. Meghan and Samantha had not seen each other since Samantha's graduation in 2008. A photo showed them smiling together eight years earlier.

At first, Tom Junior contradicted Samantha. 'Meghan didn't turn her back on everybody in the family,' he said. 'She's worked very hard to get where she's at.' But then his attitude altered and he joined the attack. Meghan telephoned her father. She asked that he order his two children to stop speaking. 'I can't stop them,' said Thomas Markle. 'They're my children too.'

Inevitably, 'the family at war' prompted a further outburst on social media. The digital headlines were lurid. Among the least offensive was the description of Meghan as a 'gold digger'. Another critic carped that her latest Reitmans promotion portraits had been photoshopped to give her a smaller waist, bigger breasts, and had removed a mole on her lip.[258] Among the more embarrassing clips on Pornhub was a scene from *Suits* of her wearing a bra and kissing another actor, a suspicious video of her topless on a yacht, and a fabricated topless photo.

While the social media trolls raged, traditional journalists hit a block. The media had expected Harry to marry a *Tatler* girl with a titled father. The disbelief that a 35-year-old Californian actress could become a dutiful consort sparked lurid reporting. Page after page described the sex scenes in *Suits*, speculated about her divorce and questioned her past. Both Trevor Engelson and Cory Vitiello remained stonily silent. Approaches to Meghan's other former boyfriends produced little new.

Faced with that lack of co-operation the media raked over Meghan's gushing praise in 2013 for ice-hockey star Michael del Zotto. Had she been unfaithful to Trevor Engelson? they asked.[259] 'When Meghan met Harry,' said one anonymous man, 'I messaged Trevor and said, "He got your leftovers".' Hollywood also stayed silent. Few had heard of Meghan, and those who had rejected her after auditions refused to speak. All agreed that this was not the right time to make a new enemy. The exception were some of the cast of *Suits*. Loudly they sang her praises.

In that fevered atmosphere, the Mail Online ran an article headlined 'Harry's girl is (almost) straight outta Compton: Gang-scarred home of her mother revealed – so will he be dropping by for tea?' The article wove together various racial stereotypes, lamenting Doria's 'gang-scarred' Los Angeles neighbourhood, Crenshaw, and its 'tatty one-storey homes', and listing crime statistics for the area.

After one week, even the *Sun* felt sympathy for Meghan. Under the headline, 'Let's give Harry's girl a chance', the paper urged that 'the poor girl doesn't stand a chance. She is getting slaughtered from all angles before the relationship gets off the ground.'[260]

Harry believed that he had good reason to fear the media. Earlier that year he had complained that every girl he met had been bombarded by journalists. As he fretted about how to protect Meghan before 'the massive invasion that is inevitably going to happen to her privacy', the *Daily Mail* also showed some sympathy. 'Harry's tragedy,' wrote Jan Moir, was that 'no sane girl would marry him.' After Samantha's attacks, Moir had pity 'for the poor girl' thrown into the tabloid's pit. Meghan, she suspected, would surely follow Chelsy Davy and Cressida Bonas and 'flee for the hills' to enjoy happy obscurity and avoid 'a life sentence…

in a royal court…corroded by an endless appetite for royal news' and 'skirmishes with bloodless courtiers'.

Prophetically, Moir warned that if the couple did eventually marry, their relationship would, with a 'hop and a skip', lead to 'despair and being stripped of all royal titles and dignity'. The good news, Moir noted, was that at the Hallowe'en party, Harry 'showed his maturity by leaving his Nazi uniform at home'.[261]

Unknown to the media and public, Meghan was staying in Nottingham Cottage. Every day she read the newspapers and watched the TV reports. By the end of the week she became extremely upset. Disingenuously, Harry later told the BBC, 'We were hit so hard at the beginning with a lot of mistruths that I made the choice not to read anything positive or negative.'[262]

Meghan was more candid. After scrutinising the websites she felt 'sick' about the narrative castigating her as a social climber 'from the ghetto' whose goal was to marry-up. That was 'not making sense'. She had 'never put any focus on that,' it was said.[263] Insisting that she needed protection from tabloids intent on destroying her reputation, Meghan ordered her North American publicist to describe her as a bewildered victim of fake news.[264] No journalist, Harry knew, would believe that. Fearing that he could lose the girl of his dreams, and his future wife, he was distraught.

Months earlier, at the outset of their relationship, Harry had assumed Meghan's acting career had prepared her for the inevitable media interest. Unlike Chelsy Davy, Meghan said she could cope. For more than ten years she had sought publicity from the tabloids. To be mentioned inside any newspaper, even at the bottom of the page, was her dream. Finally, she was in play, and on the front pages.

To Meghan's misfortune she failed to understand that Hollywood publicity is about favours, mutual agreements, payments and dishonest journalism. Buckingham Palace lacked those levers over Britain's newspapers. Fleet Street's delight was to publish raw reality without

Hollywood's cosmetic cover-ups. Moreover, the Palace had no influence beyond Britain, especially against the frequently vicious and inaccurate social media. Meghan preferred to suggest she did not understand those limitations. Instead, she identified the newspapers' 'racial undertones'. The media's curiosity and questioning the suitability of her background to be a royal was damned as racist.

At the outset, only one tabloid had described Meghan as 'not in the society blonde-style of girls' that Harry normally dated. Days later, Rachel Johnson in the *Mail on Sunday* was more succinct: 'Miss Markle's mother is a dreadlocked African-American lady from the wrong side of the tracks who lives in Los Angeles, and even the sourest spinster has to admit that the 35-year-old actress is extremely easy on the eye.' She added, 'Genetically, she is blessed. If there is issue from her alleged union with Prince Harry, the Windsors will thicken their watery, thin blue blood and Spencer pale skin and ginger hair with some rich and exotic DNA.'[265] Two out of thousands of comments had racist overtones. Racist undertones were read in many of the other comments.

Meghan's complaints to Harry about the media were no different than those of his previous girlfriends, except that her complaints were about widespread racism. 'Meghan,' Omid Scobie, who frequently described himself as an Anglo-Iranian, would later write, 'didn't want to be defined by [race].' He immediately contradicted himself by quoting Meghan's article in *Elle*: 'To say who I am, to share where I'm from, to voice my pride in being a strong, confident mixed-race woman.'[266] Until the recent rise of Black Lives Matter, Meghan had been relatively silent about race, but her stance had altered after associating with international charities. Implicit in championing her mixed race, her critics would say that Meghan was joining those criticising white people.

Called the 'First Black Princess', she attracted emphatic support from Black American women. On the internet, they rejoiced: 'Secure the palace, Sis!' Others were more cautious. Mixed-race girls, they believed, enjoyed advantages denied to Black women by white men. 'Meghan Markle is the type of Black,' wrote Elaine Musiwa in American *Vogue*, 'that the majority of right-leaning white America wishes we all could be, if there were to be Blackness at all.'[267] Musiwa particularly identified mixed-race girls' 'familiarity with whiteness. It showed in the way they held themselves.' Having triggered these conflicting emotions, the turmoil alternatively delighted, irritated and confused Meghan.

The Harry/Meghan relationship shifted into unknown territory. Previous liaisons always focused on the girl's background, but never her race. Equally unusual, no previous girlfriend had such a colourful past as Meghan. But most pertinent was Meghan's political activism. Some journalists instantly spotted that introducing an uncompromising American into the Royal Family guaranteed problems. Added to that was Meghan's conviction that she, and only she, should control her image and the media's narrative about herself. Within two weeks, the Harry/Meghan relationship was transformed into an unprecedented battle between the couple and the media.

Those close to Harry believed that he had long harboured a fantasy to be told what to do by a woman. In his search for maternal sympathy, Meghan promised to be an understanding mother figure as well as an adoring lover. For the first time in Harry's life he was prepared to obey a woman. To secure Meghan's loyalty, he would change himself to match her expectations.

For her part Meghan knew by then that she was pushing a man eager for revenge against the media and his family. His personal relationships had been damaged by the *News of the World*'s phone hacking, not least when their journalists suddenly appeared during his supposedly secret meetings with Chelsy Davy.[268] Even more pertinently he blamed Diana's death on the media. Feeling 'deeply disappointed' that he had been unable to protect his mother he eagerly declared war against his enemy – the newspapers – to protect Meghan.

Nothing could be done without the assistance of his key aide, Jason Knauf, a New Zealand-born 34 year old recruited by the Palace from the Royal Bank of Scotland. Following Palace protocol, Knauf had mastered the standard procedure to stonewall media inquiries about Meghan. There would be no interviews, no briefing about her private life and no comment about any controversy. Only after considerable discussion did the Palace agree to a concession. 'This is going to be her home now,' Knauf revealed. Contrary to Meghan's later complaint that Knauf and his staff were 'amateurs, learning on the job and flip-flopping', he was following the traditional dictum that royals 'don't complain, don't explain'.[269] Beyond that, Knauf's task was to advise and protect Harry from pitfalls and himself. The publicist fell at the first hurdle.

Anxious to please, Knauf lacked both the authority and the experience to reason with Harry that the British media has never uncritically venerated the royals. Knauf's natural course would have been to remind Harry that Charles had suffered considerably more humiliation than Meghan – from Diana, the Tampax tape, *Spitting Image* on television and a series of books, especially that by Paul Burrell, Diana's valet. Camilla had also been mercilessly ridiculed. In reply to Harry's anger that he would not tolerate suffering like his mother, Knauf failed to reply that his mother's strength and appeal was her ability to mock herself. To persuade Harry to dampen his anger and swerve away from confrontation with the media required the sophistication of age and wisdom. Unable to summon the support of Charles or the Queen, Knauf succumbed to Harry's fury.

In order to pacify Meghan's anger, Knauf agreed to issue a statement on Harry's behalf damning the media for their description of Meghan. Harry dictated the sentiments for Knauf to fashion into a statement. Committing Knauf to a conundrum, Meghan demanded that the statement should reflect the parallel between her potential fate and Diana's. Knauf suggested that over-dramatising Meghan's distress would backfire, but Harry was adamant. If Meghan's wish to be equated with Diana was not satisfied, insisted Harry, he would probably lose her. Knauf acquiesced.

To reinforce his attack, Harry asked William for support. His brother hesitated. Attacking the media was perilous. Harry, he also feared, was committing himself too quickly to Meghan. She was, after all, still just another girlfriend. To William's regret, Harry was obeying Meghan's orders. That was unwise.[270] Harry was adamant. Despite his unease, William capitulated. 'The Duke of Cambridge,' read the draft statement, 'absolutely understands the situation concerning privacy and supports the need for Prince Harry to support those closest to him.'[271]

In the final statement issued by Harry on 8th November, five months after meeting Meghan, the media was denounced for orchestrating a 'wave of abuse and harassment', for their 'outright sexism and racism' towards Meghan and the 'bombardment of nearly every friend, co-worker and loved one in her life'. Harry complained about 'the smear on the front page of a national newspaper; the racial undertones of comment pieces; and the outright sexism and racism of social media trolls and web article comments'. The statement continued: 'To those who would reply that this was "the price she has to pay" and "this is all part of the game", he strongly disagrees. This is not a game – it is her life and his…It should stop before any further damage is done.'

The media – and much of the British public – were bemused. Neither Harry nor Meghan were young innocents. Since 2011, Meghan had exposed herself to the media. Journalists mockingly pointed out that those who lived by Instagram risked 'dying' by Instagram. Similarly, Harry had flaunted his international partying. Despite public warmth towards him he was undoubtedly privileged – pocketing millions of pounds of public money every year and enjoying spectacular homes and comforts. He could not expect the benefits of royalty and simultaneously the privacy of normal people. Harry also experienced an unusual blowback. Newspapers commented for the first time that the couple had played the race card. Reporting of Meghan and her past was being interpreted by them as racism.[272]

Two days later on 10th November, Richard Kay, the *Daily Mail*'s senior royal writer, was strolling outside his newspaper's office in Kensington High Street. To his surprise he spotted Meghan. Until then, no one realised that she was in London. Following her back from Kensington's most expensive food shop carrying a bulging bag adorned with the slogan 'Alleviate Poverty' to Kensington Palace, Kay concluded that if Harry and Meghan were living together their relationship was more serious than anyone had previously realised.

Tellingly, Meghan confirmed Kay's suspicions. Despite her new anger about social media she posted a photo of herself on Instagram wearing a necklace with 'M' and 'H' and her dog wearing a Union Jack jumper.[273] 'My cup runneth over,' Meghan told a Vancouver newspaper, 'and I'm the luckiest girl in the world'. She described herself as an 'aspirational girl-next-door', a 'brash American' and mentioned that her mother had always cautioned her to dress less sexily because she should 'never give the milk away for free.' Palace officials were as confused as journalists were incredulous. Meghan was simultaneously castigating and feeding the media.

Fearing the worst, from bitter experience, the Palace stepped in to control Meghan's life. Aaron Korsh was told to submit all future *Suits* scripts to Nick Collins, Meghan's agent. Scripts were thereafter forwarded to Kensington Palace for approval. Orders for changes of words were sent back from London to Los Angeles. The most important demand concerned Meghan's last scene at her 'wedding' to Mike. No photographs, the Palace ordered, were to be shot of Meghan wearing a wedding dress. Between filming, she was always to wear a jacket over the dress.

The atmosphere in the studio changed. Some actors and staff discovered that Meghan's attitude occasionally stiffened. Sometimes she arrived late and her empathy occasionally morphed into near-arrogance.

Meghan had markedly shifted from the early days when she held a prayer meeting with the *Suits* cast before filming started.[274] Tongue-in-cheek, the *Suits* scriptwriters took a licence with Zane's final words before she says, 'I do.' Thinking of Harry, Meghan delivered the lines to her on-stage husband Mike, 'You are the strongest man I have ever met and you make me stronger…you're the husband I've always wanted and I can't wait to start our adventure together.'

Harry appeared to have changed, too. Previously in private, he appeared 'tense and irritable'. Yet in a series of interviews with Angela Levin, the journalist witnessed a Harry more relaxed about his role in life. During visits to schools for deprived children, hospitals for wounded servicemen and emergency centres, he was unusually accessible. Joking and compassionate, he was winning universal applause.[275]

During those weeks, Harry met Charles and Camilla at Clarence House. In Harry's version, the conversation alternated between serious and joking and touched three topics.[276] First, Harry was told that Meghan should continue with her acting career. Second, Scotland Yard could not automatically be expected to pay for his girlfriend's 24-hour protection. And third, according to Harry, someone speculated about what his future child would 'look like'. In one version, Camilla remarked, 'Wouldn't it be funny if your child had ginger Afro hair?' Harry laughed. Subsequently, Meghan's reaction to that conversation turned Harry's amusement into fury.[277]

Four years later, Harry described the aftermath of those conversations as 'really hard' and 'awkward'.[278] But none of his previous girlfriends had given up work or been protected by the police. Harry also knew that Charles's limited income from the Duchy of Cornwall meant the annual allowance to himself would never exceed £1.5 million, a substantial amount by most standards. Finally, in his view, any family speculation about a child's appearance was (unfortunately) seen by his elders as light-hearted. A conversation with Meghan would change that assumption. More important, and unspoken, Harry knew that his role as a senior royal would diminish within a decade. His salvation would be Meghan. Under no circumstances could he lose her.

On Meghan's next arrival in London, Harry was standing on the tarmac at Heathrow with a police escort. At his insistence that racists posed a danger, two SO14 officers were assigned to protect the visitor. After his conversation with Charles, Harry's demand for a dedicated female bodyguard for Meghan had been approved and was being processed. Meghan sped out of the airport towards Kensington. This was indeed the super-celebrity lifestyle for which she had always yearned.

Gina Nelthorpe-Cowne was among the first to notice a change. In a routine friendly message she asked Meghan permission to use a photograph from the Ottawa youth summit. Instead of her usual personal approval, Meghan's lawyers rejected the request. Across London, Millie Mackintosh, the TV star, found herself cut off from her friend.

Lizzie Cundy also discovered the new reality. 'Oh my God,' she had texted to Meghan. 'I heard about Harry.' Meghan had replied, 'Yes. We'll try and hook up.' Thereafter, there was no reply to Cundy's texts. 'I was literally ghosted by her,' confessed Cundy. 'She ditched everyone.'

To his surprise, Piers Morgan was also ignored. 'Meghan Markle,' he later said, 'is a self-obsessed professional actress who has landed the role of her life and is determined to milk it for all she's worth. She's spent most of the past 20 years cosying up to people until they serve no more use to her, then airbrushing them out of her life without so much as: "Goodbye, loser!" I know because I was one of them.'[279]

At the time, none of those people realised they were not isolated cases but part of a pattern. Meghan, some would say, was 'picky', dismissing those who didn't share her 'vision'. Even Thomas Markle was reprimanded. 'How do you like the new series?' she asked about *Suits* during a telephone conversation. 'I would like it if I could see you,' Thomas replied. 'It's so badly lit.' Meghan exploded. 'She got mad at me and ended the call,' Thomas remembered.

Soon after Harry and Meghan's relationship was exposed, Harry invited Meghan to join his weekend shoot at Sandringham. With the Queen's permission he had invited 16 friends to arrive for dinner on Friday night, shoot on Saturday and leave after lunch on Sunday. Most of the guests were old friends from Eton with their wives or girlfriends. All of them were employed by international banks and auction houses or were estate owners and racehorse trainers. All were bonded by common assumptions, principles and loyalties.

Like other shooting weekends, Harry was looking forward to endless banter, jokes – and a lot of drinking. He had not anticipated Meghan's reaction. Their jokes involving sexism, feminism and transgender people ricocheted around the living-rooms and dining-rooms. Without hesitation, Meghan challenged every guest whose conversation contravened her values. According to Harry's friends, again and again she reprimanded them about the slightest inappropriate nuance. Nobody was exempt. Harry's world would not be her world. Beyond Harry's hearing, the friends questioned Meghan's 'wokery'. Meghan was a dampener on the party, they concluded. She lacked any sense of humour. Driving home after Sunday lunch, the texts pinged between the cars: 'OMG what about HER?' said one; 'Harry must be fucking nuts'; and, 'She's a total nightmare' were others.

Besotted, Harry was unaware of his friends' reaction. In late 2016, Harry also assumed that Meghan and Kate would be firm friends. He appeared not to have realised that Meghan had nothing in common with Kate Middleton apart from both coming from aspiring, hardworking families.

Kate was born in 1982 into a contented middle-class family. Her father Michael was a former BA flight dispatcher who met her mother Carole, then employed as a secretary for British European Airways, at Heathrow. Brought up in a council flat, Carole's mother, the child of former miners in County Durham, had bought a small house and encouraged Carole's ambitions. By the age of 32, Carole had married, given birth to three children and set up a home-based business in the family's Berkshire home. Party Pieces offered everything for children's parties. Regularly, the Middleton children took packages to the local post-office.

Admired as a tough businesswoman, Carole was credited as particularly shrewd after Kate met William at two teenage parties. After she discovered that William had registered to study history of art at St Andrews university, Carole discussed and agreed that her daughter would switch from Edinburgh to St Andrews, register for the same course and take a gap-year so that both would be contemporaries. Thereafter, Kate had a happy but occasionally fraught eight-year relationship as William's girlfriend.

During those years, marked by breaks, pauses and indecision in his relationship with Kate, William spent weekends and Mediterranean holidays with the Middletons, a solid, unpretentious and discreet family. Friends of the Middletons would insist that the parents were innocents, at the mercy of the grand Norfolk families angry that their eligible daughters had been overlooked by William. But despite the Queen's invitations to Kate to visit Sandringham and by Charles to Clarence House, William refused to be pressured into marriage. While the media mocked 'Waity Katie' and mimicked her mother with 'Doors to Manual' because she had worked for an airline, William remained mindful of his own parents' misery.

In November 2010, aged 28, William finally proposed. The wedding, six months later, was a spectacular success with a substantial global TV audience. The raucous celebrations in Buckingham Palace ended on a foreboding note. At 2am, Harry, the worse for wear, went to the microphone to announce the party was over on the orders of his father. The newly-weds departed in a Fiat Uno.

Meghan was staying in Nottingham Cottage at a particularly

sensitive time for the Cambridges. To minimise his strained relationship with Charles and to build a normal family protected from Palace pressure, William had in 2011 moved with his family to Anmer Hall, adjacent to the Sandringham estate in Norfolk. Five years later, the Cambridges returned to London. William's two children were about to start school and the Duke of Edinburgh's imminent retirement required the Cambridges to undertake more royal duties. Their home, 1A Kensington Palace, spread over 22 rooms with two kitchens, was directly opposite Harry's two-bedroom cottage.

In those early weeks Meghan enjoyed the pomp and illusion of aristocratic power. She assumed the Windsors could not ignore her professional success. Compared to the Californian actress who had successfully overcome the traumas of her parents' divorce and survived the struggle to establish her career, Kate appeared to have smoothly glided towards the apex of British society. A few hiccups could not compare to the humiliation of the insecure actress, suddenly aware that the flop film *Anti-Social* was about to be re-released in London. A re-cut trailer featured her emerging from a shower to kiss a boyfriend.[280]

The messiness of Meghan's past – divorced parents, the Hollywood zoo, her own failed marriage, impetuous years in Toronto, and countless relationships – contrasted with the appearance of Kate's unsullied cool confidence. As a future Queen she seemed somewhat aloof and suspicious. In reality, Kate was shy and unpretentious. Some would say that her reticence reflected a woman without the same interests as Meghan. A clash between the two women was likely.

During the first weeks, any tension passed unnoticed. At Harry's request, to cement Meghan into the family, Palace officials swiftly encouraged the impression that Kate's close relationship with Harry would automatically extend the Trio to become the Fab Four.[281]

To ease the transformation, Harry was portrayed by Miguel Head, his publicist, as a changed man enjoying a close relationship with Charles, who also 'gets on very well with Prince William'. Harry, a man with 'genuine charm' and a 'hypnotically seductive power' towards girls, was portrayed as relaxed about not being a future king.[282] No longer the 'naughty' boy, he was promoted as the charity superstar 'taking his royal duties seriously'.

To Harry's good fortune, everyone assumed he was respectful and loyal. At ceremonies, he rarely seemed blasé or weary. Rather, there was a natural charm and sincere curiosity about everyone he met. Working with William he had led a Concert for Diana at Wembley that included star performers such as Elton John and Tom Jones. He had established the Invictus Games and Sentebale, the charity in Lesotho that helped sick children and HIV sufferers. Latterly, with William and Kate he had created a mental health charity, Heads Together. If there were any differences between Harry and William, they would, with Kate's help, be overcome by co-operation.[283] Caught up in the enthusiasm for Meghan, Hugo Vickers, an experienced royal biographer, told the *Daily Telegraph*, 'Jolly well let him marry her.'[284]

Insiders were less sure. Harry, they noticed, was influenced by Meghan's Californian lifestyle. Although she was no longer a passionate reader – William Faulkner's *The Sound and the Fury*, she said, was the most 'influential' book she had read – she had given him *Eight Steps to Happiness* and *The Motivation Manifesto*, two American books about inspiration and life's choices.[285] He appeared to have absorbed their message. Gradually, his language had become less English, less military.

Some of his outings were unusual. Harry had arranged to visit the Natural History Museum after it was closed. Meghan, he explained, wanted to commune with the dinosaurs in private.[286] Any doubts about her influence were dispelled soon after. Harry openly disparaged Donald Trump as 'a serious threat to human rights'.[287] One lingering puzzle was how Harry would reconcile his newfound Californian liberalism with his love of shooting pheasants and partridges. The answer was that Harry would do anything to impress his girlfriend.

On 24th November, 2016, while Harry was representing the Queen in St Lucia, Meghan was in Los Angeles for Thanksgiving. To celebrate the holiday she invited her father and mother for dinner. Instead of meeting at Doria's home, Harry had arranged with Arthur Landon, an old schoolfriend and the son of a former British army officer enriched by his relationship with the Sultan of Oman, for Meghan to use the Landons' Hollywood home. Set in a huge plot of land, the stunning mansion was empty. Thomas arrived with two pecan pies while Meghan and Doria cooked the turkey. Neither Thomas nor Doria had ever entered a house as luxurious. While both parents were impressed by their daughter's new status, there was nothing particularly unusual about the reunion. Ever since their divorce Thomas and Doria had met regularly. Occasionally, on his return trips to Los Angeles, Thomas and Doria 'got back together' overnight in Doria's house, where she cooked a meal and washed his clothes.

Over dinner their six-hour conversation was only about old times. Meghan disclosed nothing about her new life or plans, and neither parent asked about her future. The dinner was briefly interrupted by a telephone call from Harry. In a cursory manner, the prince wished Thomas a happy Thanksgiving. He said nothing about meeting him. At the end of the meal Thomas refused Meghan's invitation to stay the night and drove back to Mexico. In hindsight he believed that his daughter had 'not yet reached the point of entitlement'. Nor did she suggest that she imagined living in Britain or marrying Harry.

At the end of his two-week official tour of the Caribbean, Harry broke the published schedule and, rather than flying back to London from Barbados, headed for Toronto. Harry's breach of protocol was ignored, although Meghan's exhortation on The Tig to her followers to reduce fuel emissions to protect 'good ol Mama Earth' looked odd for a couple who had crossed the Atlantic four times in five weeks and were booked to spend the new year in the Norwegian Arctic Circle.[288]

During Meghan's pre-Christmas visit to London she was not shy of publicity. Newspapers favourably reported that she and Harry spent 15 minutes buying a Christmas tree in Battersea. They were also noticed in a theatre watching the award-winning *The Curious Incident of the Dog in the Night-Time*. One newspaper published photographs of Meghan as a child. They were bought from Tracy Dooley, her former sister-in-law by marriage to Tom Junior. Meghan, said Dooley, was 'lovely' and 'always in good spirits'. Tom Junior agreed: 'She'll always be our princess…She's a very giving person.'[289]

The only outspoken doubter was the *Daily Mail*'s Jan Moir: 'Do you really expect Meghan,' she asked Harry rhetorically, 'to give up her career and move to the UK?' Harry, she speculated, might follow the Duke of Windsor into exile.[290]

Anonymous voices recalled that Diana and Sarah 'Fergie' Ferguson were praised at the beginning of their royal journey as a breath of fresh air. Fergie turned out to be an appallingly bad risk.

Thomas Markle, a keen photographer, shot hundreds of frames of his beloved 'Flower' or 'Bean', as he called his daughter Meghan. Having emotionally and financially supported Meghan until she first married, Thomas felt aggrieved that he was ghosted after her marriage to Harry. © Thomas Markle

Despite the happy photos of Harry and William with Princess Diana and
Prince Charles, their childhood was scarred by their parents' arguments
and their acrimonious divorce.

Harry failed to understand Diana's close relationship with the media. He blamed the media for his mother's death. Prince Harry served as a forward air controller in the Afghanistan conflict (*above*), until his posting was leaked by a German tabloid.

© Ben Rosser/BFA.com

Meghan's relationship with Trevor Engelson (*above left*), her first husband, was close until she moved permanently to Toronto to film *Suits* in 2011. Their marriage lasted less than two years. Her Toronto boyfriend, Cory Vitiello (*above right*), a well-known chef, was relieved when his relationship with Meghan ended. Throughout, Vitiello was suspicious about Meghan's close relationship with golfer Rory McIlroy (*below*).

Meghan's speech at a UN Women conference in 2015 marked the beginning of her quest to be known as a global activist. She split with the UN less than two years later.

Meghan and Gina Nelthorpe-Cowne, her then agent, on a trip to Malta. Gina would later speak of being blanked by her former client.

During her time in Toronto, Meghan became close to Jessica Mulroney *(top left)* and Misha Nonoo *(far right)*. Both are prominent members of the Toronto social scene.

Violet Von Westenholz is widely credited with setting up Meghan and Harry, having met Meghan at Wimbledon in 2016.

Through John Fitzpatrick, an American-Irish hotel owner in New York, Meghan met the Clintons in 2015. Fitzpatrick, a generous, close friend of Meghan's, encouraged Hillary Clinton to become a key ally in Meghan's quest for fame. Later, Hillary supported Meghan's condemnation of the Royal Family.

CHAPTER 16

Hiccups

Meghan spent Christmas 2016 in a Santa Monica hotel. Thomas and Doria joined her there. Thomas was still glowing from Meghan's message on Father's Day in June. Superimposed on a photo of herself as a baby with him, she wrote:

'Happy Father's Day, Daddy. I'm still your buckaroo and to this day your hugs are still the best in the whole wide world. Thanks for my work ethic…for the importance of handwritten thank you notes and for giving me the signature Markle nose. I love you so, Bean.'[291]

At the end of dinner Meghan said to her father, 'Stay here for the night.' He declined. He drove back to Mexico, unaware that it was the last time he would see his daughter.

In late January, Meghan had the shock she dreaded. While filming the seventh series of *Suits* in Toronto she heard that the *Daily Mail* had published photos of her wedding to Trevor (first published in an American magazine), alongside an unflattering portrait of the Markle family. Contrary to the loving image presented by Tracy Dooley one month earlier, the Markles were portrayed as infamous for boozing, bust-ups and bankruptcy. Twice-married Tom Junior, a former bankrupt and heavy drinker, was not speaking to his father or sister. Samantha, Meghan's wheelchair-bound half-sister, was described as a twice-divorced mother of three who had also been bankrupt and lost custody of her children. Doria's past was reported to be shrouded in mystery. While she currently worked as an 'older adults' therapist' at a Los Angeles charity, the records showed that she had faced eviction while unemployed. No one could explain why Meghan had lived throughout her school years with Thomas. Where was Doria, journalists asked, during those ten years?[292]

Other newspapers were more positive. In the *Daily Telegraph*, Allison Pearson asked, 'Is it just me or are Prince Harry and Meghan Markle utterly adorable and a source of endless fascination?...I can't wait for Duchess Meghan...' The *Daily Mail* crushingly compared 'frumpy', 'straight-laced' Kate who never really worked after university, with the 'glam' actress.[293]

Once again, Meghan's attitude towards the media dictated her relationship with Harry. She craved publicity, but only on her terms. Any reports or photographs which were not wholeheartedly uncritical and personally approved by her and her Californian publicists were deemed hostile. Total control was essential. She appeared unwilling to accept that her demands were futile in London.

On one day Meghan was prepared to be guided by Jason Knauf and the Palace's media experts, but on another day she rejected their advice. A telephone call from Knauf advised her that wearing her 'M' and 'H' necklace only encouraged photographers and the media. That was precisely infringing the privacy she sought. 'Close to tears, and completely distraught,' she called a friend and pleaded, 'I can't win. They make out like I'm to blame for these pictures, that it looks like I'm encouraging them. I don't know what to say.' According to an admirer, 'She felt damned if she did and damned if she didn't.'[294] To some in the Palace, Meghan's emotional torment appeared unreasonable. But for Harry, Meghan's distress caused him to become increasingly paranoid. Any adverse reports prompted wild criticism of his staff.

A seminal moment occurred during their trip to Jamaica in March 2017 to celebrate the marriage of Tom 'Skippy' Inskip, Harry's Etonian friend who had been present in Las Vegas during Harry's nude romp. Harry flew premium economy from London; Meghan arrived from Toronto in a friend's private jet.

About 40 guests, including Harry's oldest friends, gathered for the three-day party at the Round Hill Hotel in Montego Bay. All the parents in attendance fondly remembered giving Harry cottage pie and comfort during his teenage years. The close-knit group keenly anticipated meeting Meghan. They were quickly disappointed. Not only did she quibble about the food, but behaved 'princessy', refusing to engage with Harry's friends. 'She wasn't interested in us,' said one mother.

Since this was the first important event Meghan and Harry had appeared at together, there was certain to be media interest. Secluded in the resort's most isolated villa, Harry spotted a photographer in the bushes. Although he was wearing a swimming costume, he became incandescent.[295] Harry's friends were puzzled by his particularly violent outburst considering the frequency of similar previous incidents in his life. Their suspicion of Meghan increased; the sentiment was mutual. Meghan disliked Inskip and his crowd. Their jokes and their attitude towards the world were unacceptable to her. The photographs were never published.

Over the following weeks Harry's friends agreed that he was rushing too fast towards marriage. Uneasy about the influence on Harry of the woman who had suddenly walked into their lives, their instincts warned them to beware of the intruder. Several shared their fears with William. Inskip was among the first to tell Harry to be cautious. Best to be sure, he said. William spoke next. 'Don't feel like you need to rush this,' he said to his brother. 'Take as much time as you need to get to know this girl.' After all, he had known Kate for eight years before he proposed.[296]

Furious about the closing ranks, Harry told Meghan. Both agreed that they were victims of racism. William, fumed Harry, was a snob.

An odd charge, since Kate was as middle class as Meghan. But Harry's anger was deep-rooted. He had long resented William's superiority and the fact that he was about to become sixth in succession. 'I'm not the important one,' he had once said. Overwhelmed by his sense of inferiority, his relationships with Inskip and William were breaking down.

Beyond the Palace few understood Harry's intentions. Over the previous six months, since their affair had been exposed, Harry and Meghan had prevented the public properly understanding their relationship. The occasional newspaper story and social media post was never accompanied by a meaningful photograph showing them as a couple.

Four months after moving into Kensington Palace, Meghan was more confident. She calculated that any scepticism about her suitability would be mollified. She chose to ignore the officials' fear that a Californian actress with a past would not accept the severe restrictions placed on members of the Royal Family.

Meghan's visit to India in January 2017 for World Vision illustrated the problem. Spearheading a worthwhile campaign targeted at 100 million young girls compelled to stay away from school while they menstruated, she railed with heartfelt conviction in a speech against India's conservative men who denied girls sanitary pads. Conditioned by discrimination, she said, the girls missed school and suffered unnecessary poverty.[297]

Before leaving for India, Harry failed to caution Meghan. While her campaign was acceptable for an actress, it was totally inappropriate for a potential member of the Royal Family to stir controversy among men in a Commonwealth country who did not believe they were oppressive. Palace officials were not silent. On Meghan's return to London it was explained to her by one official that she would need to accept restrictions. Meghan smiled and rejected any advice. She had decided that she did not want to become a muted royal. Her two visits to Rwanda and one to India would continue to be cited as evidence of her being 'heavily involved in philanthropic and advocacy work.'[298]

Nearly one year after the couple had first met, Meghan decided she should be appropriately introduced to the public. The prince agreed. A photo would be contrived at a polo match. On 6th May, Meghan stood with Mark Dyer, now the owner of The Sands End pub in Fulham, and his American wife Amanda Kline, watching Harry play in Ascot. After the game ended, photographers were given the right angle to record the couple kissing.[299] Five weeks later, American magazines published photographs of Meghan looking decidedly sultry to promote *Suits*.[300]

Considering her new life and the need to refresh the series, Aaron Korsh, the writer of *Suits*, planned to write Meghan out of the series at the end of the 2017 season. The news for Meghan from her agent Nick Collins was not encouraging. No film producer was offering her any major roles and no serious Hollywood director spoke about featuring Meghan in his movie or new TV series. Just as she feared, her acting career was stymied. Her income after 2017 would plummet.

At the same time, a Palace official cautioned her that The Tig was not suitable for someone living in Kensington Palace. Over the previous three years she had posted over 2,000 messages and included 100 articles about herself from magazines and newspapers to nearly one million followers. At the beginning of April, she addressed those loyalists: 'After close to three beautiful years on this adventure with you, it's time to say goodbye to The Tig. What began as a passion project… evolved into an amazing community of inspiration, support, fun and frivolity. You've made my days brighter and filled this experience with so much joy…Keep finding those Tig moments of discovery, keep laughing and taking risks, and keep being "the change you wish to see in the world."' She added: 'Above all, don't ever forget your worth. As I've told you time and time again: you, my sweet friend, you are enough.'[301]

Although her financial security was fragile, the termination of her

Hollywood roots was not final. While she resigned as a director of her company, Frim Fram Inc, Andrew Meyer, her business manager at Freemark Financial, and Rick Genow, her lawyer, remained as directors. Just in case.

Meanwhile, Meghan's future was being considered by Palace officials in the midst of another developing royal crisis. William had been criticised for skiing in Switzerland rather than attending a Commonwealth Day service in Westminster Abbey, and Prince Andrew's behaviour was even more troubling. Banned in 2011 from representing Britain as a trade ambassador after a succession of complaints about his crude behaviour, 'Air Miles Andy' was exposed by the media to be notorious for his travel expenses and taking loans from unsuitable businessmen.

Worse, the exposure of his relationship with the convicted American paedophile Jeffrey Epstein was certain to embarrass the Queen. Although the photograph of the two men walking in New York's Central Park had been published by the *News of the World* in February 2011, Epstein's 2007 conviction for paedophilia had resurfaced for scrutiny in Florida in 2017. 'Randy Andy's' serial misconduct was scrutinised by Christopher Geidt, the Queen's tall, authoritative private secretary wearing Whitehall's most polished black shoes. Where that would lead was uncertain.

Geidt's greater concern, shared by Prince Philip, was the risk that Charles posed to the monarchy. Charles's image as an adulterer and an old-fashioned meddler, the Palace believed, needed to be transformed. To become popular, Charles should refrain from controversy and emerge as a discreet moderniser with a common touch. That, Charles knew, required William and Harry's help.

Summoning his two sons, Charles's agenda at their meeting was familiar. Ever since Prince Philip had told the family's Way Ahead meeting in 1996 that, to survive, the monarchy needed to slim down, Charles had tried to reduce the numbers appearing on Buckingham Palace's balcony. Among the first to be cut after 2002 was Prince

Andrew and his daughters. By 2012, Charles had limited the numbers to merely six – the Queen, Charles and Camilla, William and Kate, and Harry. Over the following years, there were always doubts whether the slimmed-down version would survive. Would pressure from the minor royals compel Charles to allow them to reappear on the balcony? That argument re-emerged in August 2017.

With Philip's retirement, and in anticipation of the Queen undertaking fewer public duties, the monarchy's future rested upon William and Kate. The couple were to be promoted as a focal point for the nation. Eventually, their children would also be asked to represent the monarchy. In that scenario Harry would be heavily engaged for the next ten years and then, as his royal duties declined, he would be free to pursue his own life. Harry agreed to the plan without mentioning his frustrations. Organising his charities and starring at a few public meetings was not satisfactory in the long term. Living in a small house in Kensington Palace was becoming joyless. Life with Meghan promised an escape. Geidt suspected that Harry, with Meghan's influence, was looking for an alternative future.

Looming was the broadcast of a 'soul-searching' TV documentary made by William and Harry about Diana. That was certain to cause problems, highlighting Geidt's inability to co-ordinate, let alone control, the four princes – Charles, Harry, William and Andrew. He feared that their antics made protecting their privacy harder and could damage the monarchy. Excessive exposure risked reducing the public's respect for the Royal Family. Too late, Geidt discovered that Harry had been encouraged by Meghan to 'share his truth' about his mental state.

Harry first disclosed his mental anguish at a Heads Together event in Kensington Palace on 25th July, 2016. 'Anyone', he told the audience, 'can suffer from mental health problems, [even] a member of the Royal Family'. To encourage others to speak about their mental health, the young royal appeared at ease with himself and his role: a confident, charming, increasingly gracious man relaxed in the knowledge that the public was on his side. His talent was to make people feel he was one of them. Praised by many for his courage and honesty, few realised in 2016 that the apparently 'fun' prince had sought psychiatric help. He had taken up boxing to control his aggression.

Harry struck a chord. The public's sympathy increased. Meghan added a twist. Encouraged by Meghan that his old British stiff upper-lip should be replaced by honest confession, Harry offered himself to Bryony Gordon, a British journalist at the *Daily Telegraph*, as a haunted victim addressing the catastrophic impact of Diana's death on his life. Ignoring Geidt's concerns he laid bare his 'total chaos' since 2012 to a woman who confessed to having also suffered from personal problems – alcoholism, depression and drug addiction.[302]

'I just didn't know what was wrong with me,' he told Gordon. 'I had probably been very close to a complete breakdown on numerous occasions.' He thanked William for urging him to seek psychiatric help. Life had become better 'once I off-loaded my stuff to somebody else'. The analysis he revealed was unsurprising: 'Losing my mum at the age of 12 and therefore shutting down all of my emotions for the last 20 years has had a quite serious effect on not only my personal life but my work as well…My way of dealing with it was sticking my head in the sand, refusing ever to think about my mum, because why would that help? It's only going to make you sad.' Working for Invictus and meeting injured soldiers had helped 'park' his own issues to listen to others. They loved him for listening to their problems. He added later, 'Keeping quiet was only ever going to make it worse.' Speaking about his personal problems had become a priority.[303]

Harry's promise of future confessions alarmed Geidt. The potential damage, the senior official decided, required a plan of action. He acted on the widespread assumption that he would remain in office until the Queen died.

To reassert the Queen's unquestioned authority, Geidt summoned all 500 of the royals' staff from across Britain to a meeting in Buckingham Palace on 4th May. The pretext was the anticipated last official engagement of 96-year-old Prince Philip – his 22,219th – in August. Geidt told his audience that Philip's retirement was 'an opportunity to pause, reflect and refocus on the family'. The discordant relations among the royals and their self-indulgence, he implied, had to end. Everyone should work to serve the Queen. All the palaces would be subject to Buckingham Palace's overriding veto. Co-ordinating the courts of Buckingham Palace, Kensington Palace and Clarence House had been an unfulfilled ambition of his for years.

The reaction from two princes to Geidt's initiative was hostile. His well-meaning attempt backfired. Out of self-interest, Charles and Andrew were united in outrage. Neither saw Geidt as an ally. Both asked the Queen to dismiss her private secretary.[304] Their mother was too weak to resist. Geidt's demise coincided with his suspicions about Meghan's influence on Harry.

Even Geidt had not anticipated Harry's self-destructive confession to Angela Levin for *Newsweek* magazine the following month.[305] 'Is there any one of the Royal Family,' Harry asked the journalist, 'who wants to be king or queen? I don't think so, but we will carry out our duties at the right time.' Speaking for William and himself he placed the brothers together on one pedestal: 'We are involved in modernising the British monarchy. We are not doing this for ourselves but for the greater good of the people.'

That was a surprise for those who criticised the work-shy brothers for fulfilling just a fraction of the engagements of other royals, including their grandparents. Even more flippant was Harry's warning that an 'ordinary' Royal Family would take away The Firm's mystery. 'It's a tricky balancing act,' he pontificated. 'We don't want to dilute the magic. The British public and the whole world need institutions like it.'

There was a novelty in Harry, as a constitutional expert, suggesting that he and William would decide the monarchy's fate: 'We want to make sure the monarchy lasts and are passionate about what it stands for,' he said. 'But it can't go on as it has done under the Queen. There will be changes and pressure to get them right.' He suggested that the Queen endorsed their right to decide the future. 'The Queen…tells us to take our time,' he said. 'The monarchy is a force for good and we want to carry on the positive atmosphere that the Queen has achieved for over 60 years, but we won't be trying to fill her boots.'

Harry then became introspective. 'I sometimes still feel I am living in a goldfish bowl, but I now manage it better…I am now fired up and energised and love charity stuff, meeting people and making them laugh.' After saying that he should not have been asked to walk behind his mother's coffin – 'No child should be asked to do that' – he confessed about his later life. 'I was like, "Oh my God, get me out of here now."'[306]

Harry then turned to his most significant revelation. Highlighting that his role as the 'spare' had disappeared he admitted, 'I feel there is just a smallish window when people are interested in me before [William's children Prince George and Princess Charlotte] take over, and I've got to make the most of it.' Anticipating insignificance he repeated his hope that he would make something of his life or he would consider turning his back on privilege, because he 'wanted out' of the Royal Family to live an 'ordinary life'.[307]

This was a new Harry. Liberated by Meghan he was wilfully careless of the consequences of his 'truth'. Even his praise for *The Crown*, Netflix's hugely popular fictionalised drama about his grandmother and the House of Windsor, broke the party-line about the series' systematic fabrication. 'It's great but I wish they'd stopped at the end of the first series,' Harry said. 'They absolutely must not move on to the younger generation.'[308] This was the same Harry who demanded privacy and who said, 'I believe a leopard can change its spots.'

The *Newsweek* interview was praised as honest and heartfelt, and few openly questioned Harry's wisdom. His confession was a curtain-raiser to the brothers' TV documentary, *Diana, Our Mother*. Introduced by William, the heir explained that 20 years after her death many did not know the real person. Viewers witnessed the brothers' emotion, grief and anger, especially towards Charles. Despite ferocious arguments between father and son, William refused to mention Charles in the film.[309] The brothers blamed Charles and Camilla for their beloved mother's misery and death.

Christopher Geidt's worst fears had materialised. The divisions between the three palaces were irreconcilable. Charles's and Camilla's popularity ratings fell sharply, and Charles's hope that William and Harry would agree to support Camilla as a future queen was again uncertain.

Amid the unrest, Geidt departed on 31st July, 2017. The loyal official was followed by the resignation of Samantha Cohen, an Australian-born assistant private secretary who had served in the Palace for nearly 20 years. 'Turmoil at the Palace as Queen's Right Hand Man to Quit' was the headline, anticipating mayhem.

Geidt's successor, Edward Young, his portly deputy, was not as highly rated. At the outset Young made a fundamental error. Instead of insisting that in the interests of the monarchy's well-being, Geidt's plans for co-ordination between the palaces was a non-negotiable condition for him accepting the post, he allowed the princes to take control. Thereafter, Young lacked the authority to influence the media strategy in the other palaces.[310]

Amid those seismic changes, no outsider in London had yet grasped the importance of Meghan's influence. For most she remained invisible. But in New York, Jane Sarkin, *Vanity Fair*'s features editor, properly understood the Californian's ambitions.

CHAPTER 17

Vanity Fair

Jane Sarkin pitched to Graydon Carter, the magazine's famous editor-in-chief, that Meghan should be offered not only an interview in the illustrious magazine but also a guarantee to feature on the front cover. Carter, famed as a man ahead of the curve, had never heard of Meghan or of *Suits*. Nevertheless, he was persuaded that Harry's latest girlfriend was destined to change the Royal Family. When the call came, Meghan was ecstatic.

The messenger was Keleigh Thomas Morgan, a partner at Sunshine Sachs, the Los Angeles public relations agency. After the agency's years of struggle to get Meghan noticed, *Vanity Fair*'s approach proved that her relationship with Harry was priceless.

For Meghan, Keleigh Thomas Morgan's news was electrifying. Thousands of Hollywood wannabes, she knew, had begged Graydon Carter for *Vanity Fair*'s recognition. Getting the cover photo was the ultimate prize, an endorsement of enduring celebrity. She would be globally famous forever. The amazing bonus was the magazine's offer that Peter Lindbergh, the famous German fashion photographer, would spend a day with Meghan in a London studio.

Living with Harry had already transformed her life. The feature could even prompt Harry to announce their engagement – delayed, according to Harry, until the Queen's formal approval on her return from Balmoral in the autumn.

Harry had proposed to Meghan in Nottingham Cottage one evening while she cooked roast chicken, going down on one knee to utter the traditional offer. She could hardly wait to say 'Yes'. Harry gave her a ring that he had commissioned, with two of Diana's diamonds set in yellow Botswana gold.[311] He was particularly proud of his design. Meghan did not conceal her excitement, even though she was secretly determined to have the ring redesigned as soon as possible.[312]

Harry next called Thomas Markle asking for his approval. 'Yes, so long as you don't raise your hand against her,' replied Thomas. Within less than five minutes the conversation was over. Thomas was sworn to secrecy. Harry did not suggest that they would meet before the wedding.

The engagement was unknown to Keleigh Thomas Morgan as she gave a carefully measured response to *Vanity Fair*. Of course, Meghan would be delighted but she 'doesn't want a piece about her. It should represent her as a major actor and especially as an activist and philanthropist.' The interview would introduce Meghan to the world. And, Thomas Morgan added, the peg for the interview should emphasise the 100th episode of *Suits*. Harry, she revealed, had only agreed to the article because, as Meghan declared, the producers wanted to celebrate *Suits*' centenary.

By then, Meghan's relationship with some *Suits* actors was troubled. An argument had erupted over Sarah Rafferty. Meghan had asked Lori Sale, her merchandising agent, to consider representing Rafferty, a redhead older than her, for commercial endorsement contracts. The two met and Sale was enthusiastic. Hearing the news, Meghan called and accused Sale of a conflict of interest.

Sale was perplexed. Not only had Meghan asked her to represent Rafferty but the two actresses were not competitors. Meghan's behaviour hardly chimed with her recent plea on a TV programme about self-esteem to be 'Kind to yourself – and not to be so judgemental and so unkind – I wouldn't treat my best friend that way.'[313] Sale was the latest to discover the nature of Meghan's sincerity. She was two characters, one concealed and one fictional, with a baffling tendency to switch from idolising to belittling a friend.

Once again, Meghan was accused of being manipulative – a criticism which several *Suits* actors shared but did not disclose to outsiders. Meghan's behaviour remained a secret among the *Suits* family, and was unknown to the *Vanity Fair* team.

Sam Kashner, a long-standing contributing editor at the magazine, was assigned to the interview. Known for high-profile cover stories about Jennifer Lawrence, Nicole Kidman, Rosamund Pike and Lee Radziwill, the sister of Jacqueline Onassis, Kashner had previously lived in Toronto. 'I don't know who this woman is and I've never heard of *Suits*,' Kashner told his editor before flying to Toronto in late June.

Contrary to Omid Scobie's assertion that Meghan wanted 'to tell the world "I'm in love"' and did the 'interview with Harry's blessing,'[314] Kashner arrived in the pouring rain at Meghan's home knowing that his interviewee was under strict orders from both Harry and Keleigh Thomas Morgan. Aware that Diana and Sarah Ferguson had destroyed themselves in interviews, Harry had ordered Meghan to maintain tight-lipped silence about sensitive subjects – Donald Trump, race, their relationship and especially himself. He was not to be mentioned.

At 12:30, Kashner watched Meghan prepare lunch in a tiny kitchen. The local market, she explained, sold wonderful quiche, goat's cheese, vegetables and special breads. 'I baked a cake,' she added. As she darted in and out, pummelling him with questions about his school, marriage and work, Kashner began to sense a reversal of roles. Always conscious of Janet Malcolm's quip that journalism is seduction followed by betrayal, he sensed that Meghan was the seductress.

Looking around, Kashner noticed that the kitchen walls were covered with photos of herself and the books piled on the coffee table were picture guides and history books of London. 'Only the A-Z of London's streets was missing,' he thought, uncertain whether she had actually read any books about Britain. Even before they sat down to eat, Kashner felt uneasy. Both knew that a lot was riding on the interview, and both understood that the critical issue of Harry had been vetoed.

Meghan spoke, he realised, knowing that she had the winning ticket but avoiding giving an impression of triumphalism. However, as she spoke about 'my speech to the United Nations' and her success as an 11 year old against Procter & Gamble, Kashner thought to himself, 'It's hard to know if she's genuine. She's an actress.' He had no reason to doubt her version that 'Every day after school for ten years I was on the set of *Married…with Children*, which was a really funny and perverse place for a little girl in a Catholic school uniform to grow up.' Kashner could not know that Thomas Markle insisted that the studio visit was her Friday treat.[315] Nor could he know that when he understood her to have spent her 'senior year' working at the US embassy in Argentina, it was just five weeks.

'You're not the typical journalist,' Meghan said coyly over lunch. 'I like you, especially your stuttering.' In the brief silence which followed, Meghan failed to grasp that Kashner felt he was being played. It was a cat-and-mouse game, he reasoned, and she was calculating how to take advantage of the cards played. 'She knows the marks she wants to hit,' he thought. 'She won't hit her goal by being genuine,' he concluded.

After lunch, she kicked off her shoes. Tucking her legs on to the seat, Meghan visibly relaxed and, to Kashner, appeared sexy. This was the moment to probe and pry.

'Tell me about Harry,' said Kashner, not expecting an answer.

'We're a couple. We're in love,' Meghan unexpectedly replied into the recording device.

Clearly prepared, she baulked when asked, 'What does love mean?' Instead, she asked Kashner about his marriage.

Eventually she uttered, 'I'm sure there will be a time when we will have to come forward and present ourselves and have stories to tell, but I hope what people will understand is that this is our time. This is for us. It's part of what makes it so special, that it's just ours. But we're happy. Personally, I love a great love story.'

Bullseye. Kashner was quietly elated. Tellingly, she added: 'I'm still the same person I am. I've never defined myself by my relationship.' She wanted him to know that she was an independent woman who would not be defined by her relationship with Harry.

Unexpectedly, Markus Anderson arrived. Their conversation was interrupted. 'I wanted you to meet some of my friends,' explained Meghan about the Soho House manager and social fixer standing in the doorway, holding a bottle of wine. Baffled, Kashner became more puzzled as the two engaged in an incomprehensible conversation. 'I felt played, orchestrated,' he recalled.

After a time, Meghan returned to their conversation and her agenda: her work for women. To her misfortune, Kashner was unconvinced. 'Actors doing "good work" is slippery,' he thought, sensing something jarred about The Tig, a commercial operation, operating alongside charity. 'The proof,' he thought, 'will be if she goes to Rwanda and India after she's married.'

'Markus will take you to the airport,' offered Meghan. 'No, I'll take a cab,' replied Kashner, anxious to escape. Over the next few days he called those who Meghan had recommended as her friends. Serena Williams denied she was Meghan's friend but just an acquaintance. She gave him an enigmatic quote: 'You've got to be who you are, Meghan. You can't hide.'

Kashner's unease grew. Soon after he had returned to New York, Meghan sent him a bottle of spices from the market. 'Meghan's snow job,' he decided.

The photoshoot on a London rooftop, Peter Linbergh reported, was a 'delight', despite Meghan's refusal to look sexy. Not only did she refuse to take off any clothes but she insisted that she should look 'covered up'. Her freckles, she insisted, should not be retouched. A standard white shirt and black and white tulle ball-gown, she believed, would win Palace approval. Instead, the milestone in her life endangered a myth.

Sunshine Sachs had demanded that the magazine satisfy Meghan's requirement that she be presented as a philanthropist and activist, without considering one problem: *Vanity Fair's* scrupulous researchers could find no evidence of Meghan's global philanthropy and activism. Those in the public eye, *Vanity Fair's* editors had discovered, sometimes found difficulty living up to their self-created publicity. 'Hollywood philanthropy is PR philanthropy,' Graydon Carter often observed. Actors' philanthropy, in his opinion, was superficial rather than a deep commitment. What others called Liberal Hollywood's Zeitgeist, to go with the flow. Eventually, the fable threatened to consume the person. Keleigh Thomas Morgan gave the impression she expected that reality to be glossed over.

Reading Kashner's completed interview, *Vanity Fair's* editor 'knew the article was a huge coup for the magazine'. The familiar and well-rehearsed profile gush about the dilemma of ticking the race box at school, the mixed-race dolls and the Los Angeles riots was good colour, but her revelation was sensational: 'We're a couple. We're in love' was guaranteed front-page headlines. Meghan's interview took the Royal Family into uncharted waters. Intentionally, she had revealed her master plan.

As the magazine was printed, Meghan was celebrating her thirty-sixth birthday with Harry in Botswana. Accompanied by a team of bodyguards, she had travelled like royalty and was cared for like the princess she soon expected to be.

Meghan had brought with her to Botswana a copy of *Pride*, a small-circulation magazine aimed at mixed-race and Black Britons. The magazine featured an interview with her. She described her fight against racial prejudice and the importance of female empowerment delivered by appointing women to senior positions. As a 'woman of colour,' she told the magazine, she felt an 'obligation' to speak about being half-Black.[316] *Vanity Fair*, she imagined, would blast her same message across the globe.

Pre-publication copies of the magazine were released to Sunshine Sachs and Buckingham Palace in early September. The stunning front-cover photograph of Meghan was covered by the headline 'She's Just Wild About Harry'. Meghan's unprecedented brazenness took Buckingham Palace by surprise – and electrified the British media. Like a thunderclap, the interview triggered sensational reactions: Meghan had used her relationship with Harry to promote herself. The Hollywoodisation of the royal family had sealed Meghan's fate as Harry's fiancée.

Within hours, Meghan called Ken Sunshine and Keleigh Thomas Morgan. Hysterically, she described Buckingham Palace's fury at 'Wild About Harry'. Sunshine Sachs, said Meghan, should have ensured that her comments about Harry were removed. Why wasn't the focus on her philanthropy and activism?

Ken Sunshine feared that Meghan would fire his agency. Puzzled why Buckingham Palace was angry, he called the magazine's editor to deliver what he imagined to be the ultimate threat. 'You're going to have to deal with the Queen on this,' he said. The furious monarch, he imagined, like Trump, would pick up the phone and berate the editor. The editor was bemused. Meghan, Ken Sunshine was told, 'didn't get the cover in her own name or as a feminist, but because of who she was likely to marry'.

Destabilised by the furore, Meghan texted Kashner: 'Gutted and deflated'. Soon afterwards, she called him: 'I'm very disappointed in you because I thought this could have been an actual friendship. I don't now think that can happen.' Kashner, she implied, had 'queered the deal' with Harry.

Kashner was puzzled. How could she hate a blatant puff-piece? Then her feelings were explained. Of course, she hated the title 'Wild About Harry' because she was promoting her philanthropy. She was equally furious that her childhood battle with Procter & Gamble was omitted. Kashner resisted revealing that *Vanity Fair*'s fact-checkers had adamantly decided that her story was possibly false. After consulting Procter & Gamble and advertising historians, the fact-checkers concluded there was no proof that the incident had ever happened. There was also no evidence, as Meghan claimed, that she received a reply from Hillary Clinton.[317] Unknown to Kashner, Thomas Markle knew that both Hillary Clinton and Procter & Gamble had ignored Meghan's letters. Her 'campaign' was fictitious, invented by an adoring father.

'She complained because she wasn't presented in the way she wanted,' recalled Kashner. 'She demanded that the media do what she expects. I felt manipulated and betrayed.' *Vanity Fair* did however agree to one 'correction'. Meghan insisted that she had met Harry in July, not May. The magazine published the change but unknowingly collaborated with a smokescreen about their relationship inspired by Meghan. Meghan insisted on the change. There was speculation that until mid-July, she was still living with Cory Vitiello.

As the anger subsided, Meghan reconsidered her fate. The producers and cast of *Suits* were 'awestruck' that an actor from their cult series with a mere 1.5 million audience had made *Vanity Fair*'s cover. Their only disappointment was that the royal relationship did not improve the ratings. Not by a single per centage.

On the positive side, Harry remained utterly loyal. As Sarah Vine, a *Daily Mail* columnist, concluded, Meghan had 'ticked this box' and customised her relationship as 'a new chapter'.

Left unanswered was Vine's rhetorical question. Did Meghan imagine that joining the Windsors was just another 'spicy chapter' in her life but on 'a grander stage'?

Reversing the narrative was impossible. Through Kashner, Meghan had made clear to Buckingham Palace that she would be unwilling to obey their rules. Protocol was irrelevant to her. Unlike the other young women who married the Windsors she would not remain silent.

In London, Harry's family and their senior advisors were subdued. This was not an issue, as some would later assert, about the Palace's handling or mismanagement of Meghan. Nothing could be done. The besotted prince ignored the warnings that Meghan spelled trouble for the Palace.

CHAPTER 18

Spotlight

In early September 2017, Kate revealed that she was expecting her third child. Prone to sickness in pregnancy, she curtailed her public appearances. Since the *Vanity Fair* article had increased the Cambridges' suspicion of Meghan, the actress discovered that her neighbour in Kensington Palace had even less time for her.[318]

By then, Harry had introduced Meghan to Diana's two sisters, Jane and Sarah, and her best friend Julia Samuel. Harry assumed that Diana's family and friends would see a similarity between Diana and his fiancée. Both, he said, shared the same problems. He was disappointed. No one agreed that his vulnerable mother had anything in common with his girlfriend. More discomforting for him, they thought Meghan would not fit in with the Royal Family.

Their unease was voiced by Charles Spencer, Diana's brother. At William's request, Spencer weighed in. Three times married, Spencer cautioned his nephew to reconsider his haste towards marriage.[319] His advice provoked a bitter reaction.

'This was going to be really hard,' Harry would later reflect on establishing Meghan's place in the family.[320] One of his recurring concerns was insufficient money if they married. Although Harry annually received about £1.5 million from Charles, Meghan had been advised to continue acting to supplement their income.[321] By that point, Meghan knew from her agent Nick Collins that her acting prospects were limited.[322] Omid Scobie, her official biographer, would accurately summarise her exit from Hollywood. 'She wanted a more meaningful career,' he wrote. 'She could be doing so much more with her platform.' Her frustration remained. She was tantalisingly close to sealing her future, but nothing was official.

Harry betrayed no tension when he arrived in Toronto for the third Invictus Games, bringing together wounded athletes from 17 nations for eight days. The *Vanity Fair* article, and the coincidence that the city was also Meghan's home, transformed the event into a media circus.[323] Before the games started, Harry's publicists made sure that his personal interest in depression and suicide was noted by the media. Dutifully, they reported that his meetings in the city had highlighted mental illness and the importance of the Royal Foundation's Heads Together campaign to help sufferers. The next photo-call was also approved by Harry.

Meghan's arrival in the stadium's public area on 25th September with Markus Anderson was carefully planned. Melodramatically, Harry insisted that a Scotland Yard detective stood nearby. Meghan was there not only to cement her relationship with Harry but also to showcase her vision as Harry's future wife.

To help designer Misha Nonoo, she wore a classic white 'husband shirt' from her friend's new collection. Praised by some for wearing distressed 'Mother Denim' jeans to soften the look, others criticised the deliberate tears in the fabric to suggest: 'I don't give a damn.' Women found Meghan's cool, minimalist style – her polished casual look – 'relatable' for their own wardrobe. The 'Meghan effect', she noted with satisfaction, sparked a dramatic increase in orders for the clothes and sunglasses she wore. Her relationship with Harry promised considerable commercial benefits.[324]

Unknown to the media at the time was Meghan's admiration of Carolyn Bessette, the wife of John Kennedy Jnr. Although the fashion publicist and former president's son had died in a plane crash in 1999, she remained a style icon. Meghan had already decided that her wedding dress should be modelled on Bessette's. Others would draw a parallel about the previously unknown Bessette ensnaring America's most desirable bachelor prince.

After establishing her presence, Meghan prodded Jason Knauf to choreograph the critical photograph. With the media in place, Harry and Meghan arrived hand in hand to watch a tennis match. With an adoring look, Meghan posed alongside Harry, touching and stroking him while the cameras ceaselessly clicked. Her life's work had prepared her for that moment.[325] Five days later, she landed her reward.

Just one year earlier, Meghan had entreated Gina Nelthorpe-Cowne to fix a photo opportunity with Justin Trudeau. Now, not only Trudeau but also Melania Trump, the president's wife, and Barack Obama with Joe and Jill Biden were in Harry's box in the stadium.

'How's it going with Meghan?' Obama asked Harry, shortly before she was escorted into the box.[326] Leaking that exchange to the media, and arranging for photographers to see Doria laughing with Harry in the box, confirmed Meghan's status. The message to Buckingham Palace from Toronto was uncompromising. Their marriage plans were irrevocable.

'Come up to Toronto and help me,' Meghan told her father. He hesitated. He could not afford a ticket and the expenses. He could hear Meghan's anger when her request was rejected. However, after later seeing that his daughter had posed for a photo with Doria, he asked whether, if he did fly north, they could also pose together 'to take the heat off me'.

At first Meghan agreed and volunteered to pay the fare. 'He's only coming to get his photo,' Doria told Meghan. Within hours, Meghan told her father that he should not come. Thomas was puzzled. He was unaware that Doria had flown weeks earlier to London to meet Harry. Meghan had not invited him.[327]

Unsuspicious of his daughter and her mother, Thomas sought reconciliation among his children. With good intentions, he gave Meghan's telephone number to Samantha. The reaction from his younger daughter was nuclear. Meghan screamed in fury down the line to Mexico and changed her telephone number. Her calls to Thomas markedly declined. Staring at the Pacific from his bungalow, Thomas Markle struggled to recognise his daughter's behaviour.

Shortly afterwards, Meghan filmed her last scenes for *Suits*. She was giving up professional acting forever. Among those who bid farewell to her was Wendell Pierce, Rachel Zane's 'father' for four years. 'You always have a friend in me,' he said to Meghan. He never heard from her again, he said later. He too was ghosted.[328]

CHAPTER 19

Engagement

To please Harry, the Queen agreed to ditch centuries of tradition. Meghan would be fast-tracked into the Royal Family before the wedding.

Two weeks after the Invictus Games ended on 12th October, Harry introduced Meghan to the Queen in Buckingham Palace.[329] Over tea and sandwiches, the monarch formally approved her grandson's engagement. The 91 year old had no choice. Apparently, she had already met Meghan in Windsor Park. In a fleeting, unexpected encounter, Meghan would claim to have performed an unrehearsed botched curtsey.[330] During the formal meeting in the Palace, Harry would describe how the Queen's corgis, who had for the previous 33 years barked at him, lay at Meghan's feet and wagged their tails. Meghan described the scene as 'very sweet'.[331]

One month later, Meghan finished packing her belongings in Toronto and flew to London to start her new life, or 'chapter' as she preferred to call it. Successful entry into the Royal Family required effort and imagination. Most newcomers had been defeated. Not only had Diana and Sarah Ferguson been ousted but Princess Anne's first husband Mark Phillips and his family had been ignored. Even the Middletons had been rudely snubbed by several women in the court until William demanded better behaviour.

Meghan was the beneficiary of those misjudgements. In anticipation of the engagement's formal announcement, Palace officials agreed that to ease her transition into the family she needed guidance about the restrictions accepted by all members of the Royal Family. Harry would claim that he had forewarned Meghan: 'You know what you're letting yourself in for. It's a big deal and it's not easy for anybody.'[332]

If so, no one directly asked Meghan whether she understood that the British monarchy had only survived – with the support of 70 per cent of Britons – by seeking to remain soberly uncontroversial. No one spelled out to her that monarchists were unaware that most of the changes made to ensure the Crown's modernisation and survival had been imperceptible. But then, no one recalls that Meghan asked any detailed questions before the engagement was officially announced on 27th November, 2017.

At 10am, wearing a white coat, later changing into a £56,000 Ralph & Russo dress, a label favoured by Naomi Campbell and Jennifer Lopez, Meghan entered Kensington Palace's Sunken Garden. With Harry beaming, the photographers were given time to produce their best shot. They noted Meghan's eyes fixed on her fiancé and recorded her rubbing Harry's back as they walked back to the Palace. Her conspicuous tactile reassurance would become a feature of their public appearances. To some it was maternal. To others, proprietorial.

The fashionistas were excited. Unlike Kate who wore a high-street Reiss dress for her engagement announcement, Meghan was not wearing an 'ethical' garment. Her clothes and accessories, worn with a 'confident sense of style', were praised as 'authentic'. 'Meghan is very in-the-know,' gushed one commentator. 'She just gets beauty. Her approach is very effortless. She just wants to look like a better version of herself.'[333] No one dared to comment on the genius of Meghan's street-smart, showbiz performance. With her reassurance, Harry expected to be seen by the public and media precisely as he wanted.

In a 20-minute BBC TV interview which followed, Harry revealed to Mishal Husain that from the first moment they met he knew that Meghan was 'The One'. Poised and self-confident, Meghan said that at the early meetings she knew nothing about Harry. Without a blink, she declared that she had done no research about Harry before the blind date. Everything she had discovered had occurred, she said, during an 18-month 'really authentic and organic learning curve…investing time and energy to make it happen.' In that period, she had 'learned about him by focusing on who we are as a couple'.

Then, without a flicker of doubt, she volunteered that 'Catherine has been absolutely wonderful.' 'Amazing,' agreed Harry, 'as has William as well. Fantastic support.' Harry's whole family had given 'absolutely solid support'. Diana, he was sure, was present for 'this crazy journey'. She and Meghan would be 'as thick as thieves…I think she would be over the moon, jumping up and down – you know, so excited for me.' Finally, Harry revealed that he had called Thomas Markle to ask for Meghan's hand.

Next, to move on from the image created by *Vanity Fair*, Meghan presented herself as a victim of the brutal media world: 'I've never been part of tabloid culture and lived a relatively quiet life,' she explained. 'There's a misconception that because I worked in the entertainment industry, this would be something that I would be familiar with.'

Presenting herself as a contrast to Kate, she said: 'I do not see [marrying Harry] as giving anything up. I see it as a change. It is a new chapter.' She would use her 'new platform' with Harry. 'Both of us have passions for wanting to make change for good. There's a lot to do.' At their first meeting, they agreed about 'the different things that we wanted to do in the world and how passionate we were about seeing change'.

Harry agreed: 'We're a fantastic team…and over time we hope to have as much impact as possible.'

Meghan added: 'Once you have access or a voice that people are going to listen to, with that comes a lot of responsibility which I take seriously.'[334] The subtext was unambiguous: as a member of the Royal

Family she would campaign for her causes and ignore the royal gospel of uncontroversial impartiality.

With few exceptions the newspapers were ecstatic. Journalist Robert Lacey welcomed a mixed-raced descendant from enslaved ancestors into the royal family as a 'brilliant step forward'. Meghan, he was certain, would enhance the Royal Family's appeal, especially among minorities and the young.[335] In the *Daily Telegraph* she was hailed as 'the best thing to happen to The Firm for decades and is arguably more charismatic than the rest of them put together.'[336] The *Sunday Times* agreed: 'She can make the case for a 21st century monarchy.'[337] Others were thankful that Harry had not chosen a 'boring Sloane or a weedy aristo…It's all too fabulous and so is she.'[338]

Richard Kay, a *Daily Mail* journalist close to Diana, was similarly enthusiastic: 'Intoxicated by a young woman who has not only had to make her way in the world but had to overcome its prejudices too,' Harry had chosen a woman who Diana would have wanted to be. Indeed, Kay speculated, Meghan could be 'the next Diana in terms of global appeal'. With a new Diana, the monarchy's future looked 'fascinating'. Sarah Vine noted that Meghan, three years older than Harry, was like a mother, caring and encouraging him. 'She provides an older, stable presence for the little lost boy…she will be giving up everything to marry the Prince.'[339] Trevor Phillips, an outstanding Black commentator, spoke for many: 'It's a very big deal that she has talked of her pride in her ethnicity. For people of colour that will be seen as a very positive, modern approach and immensely welcome.'[340]

Inevitably, there were a few cynics. 'She doesn't ride and hates shooting?' asked one. 'Will she fit into the aristos who surround Harry?'[341] Another knowingly asked whether Harry's closest friends, 'Skippy' Inskip and Guy Pelly, liked Meghan. Ninaki Priddy, her childhood friend, fired the most hostile comment: 'Princess Pushy gets exactly what she wants and Harry has fallen for her play. She has always been fascinated by the Royal Family. She wants to be Princess

Diana 2. She will play her role ably, but my advice to him is to tread cautiously.'[342] Disillusioned by her treatment by Meghan, Priddy sold her story and a large photo album for nearly £150,000.

Even Trevor Engelson joined in. Tongue in cheek, he pitched a film about a divorced man arguing about his children's custody with his ex-wife after she married a prince.

After scrutinising her TV interview, Stephen Glover, a cautious observer, identified Meghan's 'skills of self-promotion' and that with her 'acute commercial brain [she] is far from being a shrinking violet'. If Meghan has embarked on 'a mission to promote Brand Markle,' suggested Glover, she was destined to conflict with the 'cautious Brand Windsor'. He concluded: 'The last thing the Royal Family needs is a vocal activist from across the pond noisily embracing global causes.'[343]

Worldwide reports ignored those suspicions. The American media gushed about 'the most eligible bachelor in the world'. The *New York Post* headline 'She's gorgeous, she's talented, she's philanthropic' was echoed by the *Washington Post*'s 'She's American and she's awesome'. Meghan's biography was flattering: 'Like her royal beau, Markle is a passionate humanitarian. She does frequent advocacy work for the United Nations and World Vision Canada, travelling internationally to promote gender equality and access to clean water.' The four trips over two years had proved invaluable.

Buckingham Palace had also scrutinised Meghan's interests. Astutely, the Queen persuaded Samantha Cohen to withdraw her resignation, which had been submitted after Geidt was dismissed. The mother of three agreed, as private secretary, to help Meghan through the wedding and beyond. Under Cohen, a team of 14 young, intelligent and experienced officials, including Jason Knauf, was assembled to introduce Meghan sensitively to the quirks and expectations of royal life and service to the nation. There would be, said the Palace, six months of listening and learning: 'She is going to proceed with humility.' Among the additional staff was Lieutenant Colonel Nana

Kofi Twumasi-Ankrah of the Household and Lady Susan Hussey, a lady-in-waiting to the Queen since 1960. Hussey and other close companions of the Queen visited Meghan in Nottingham Cottage to offer help and advice.

Considering the importance of making a mixed-race woman welcome, Cohen's team tactfully sought to understand Meghan's concerns, her priorities and how her ambitions could be realised. For hours they discussed resolutions to problems and how she should feel as part of the Royal Family. In response, Meghan was insistent that she would not allow Buckingham Palace to shape her. She would remain independent. She did not want The Firm to dictate her thoughts and activities. There was a certainty in her attitude. Few underestimated the elephant in the room – Meghan's resolutely independent attitude – but no one anticipated the battle to come. The courtiers expected her to join their society with unquestioned loyalty to the Crown.

In her subsequent interview with Oprah Winfrey and other interviews, Meghan denounced the Palace staff for failing to discuss her needs and objectives from the outset. But before the Oprah interview, Omid Scobie accurately reflected Meghan's opinion, and that contradicted the version Meghan offered to the world later on TV: 'The Queen was wonderful, warm and generous towards the new Duchess,' he wrote. 'She made sure Meghan knew what was going on.'[344] Scobie added, 'Charles made sure Meghan was supported as she navigated the ups and downs of life in the public eye.'

Meghan did not feel the same towards Kate. Within a short time she complained that Kate had not adequately welcomed her. The difference of background and experience made them unlikely soulmates.[345] There could be little intimacy. In her personal relationships Meghan had rarely tolerated or compromised with a woman of starkly different interests. Kate was recognised as an adversary who had to be reckoned with.

The differences were not apparent during Meghan's first public engagement – the beginning of a six-month tour of Britain. On a frosty morning on 1st December a large crowd waited for the couple in Nottingham. The moment they were seen, Meghan-mania exploded. 'We need magic at the moment,' one of her many admirers shouted as the confident and relaxed American greeted the crowds alongside Harry. She even gave a hand-warmer to a woman who complained of the cold. Harry and Meghan were ready to be loved by the British public.

The favourable media coverage excited Meghan. Drawing comparisons with Kate, one writer reported that unlike Meghan the Duchess of Cambridge was too formal and not as glamorously dressed. Reflecting with her staff in Kensington Palace on her popularity, Meghan credited her success with being uniquely special, an attitude reinforced by Harry. Diana's stardust, Harry suggested, was falling on to Meghan. None of Meghan's staff volunteered that only by being a member of the Royal Family was Meghan special. Less than one month after the engagement was announced, one member of her staff asked herself, 'She'll be famous, but will she be a royal?'

Meghan's fear was her family. In her telephone calls to Thomas Markle in Rosarito, Meghan continued to urge him to 'lay low'. He was ordered not only to say nothing but not even appear in public. His address was still unknown.

On 6th December, 2017, Meghan's order to Thomas Markle became worthless.[346] The manhunt was over. Tom Junior had sold his father's address to a journalist. A *Daily Mirror* reporter was outside Thomas Markle's house when he emerged that day. Asked whether he would escort Meghan down the aisle, Thomas replied, 'Yes, I'd love to.' Then he added, 'I'm very pleased. I'm delighted. I'm sorry. You know I can't talk.'

He had done his best. The first photographs showed a dishevelled, overweight man. The following day, Thomas was stopped in the narrow road outside his house. 'A present for you,' said a British journalist, thrusting a bottle of champagne and a packet of British tea at the surprised man. Within hours, an army of journalists and photographers were packed into the narrow, dusty road outside his bungalow.

'All hell's broken loose,' he told his daughter from his cramped living-room. 'I'm besieged.' Meghan was thrust into a frenzy made worse by his story about the champagne.

'That could be considered a bribe,' snapped Harry, listening to the call. Thomas was bewildered. A 'bribe'? What did Harry mean?

'I'm being harassed every time I leave home,' he pleaded. 'This is crazy. I'm surrounded. I need help.'

'Don't speak to anyone,' ordered Harry, clearly unable to imagine the chaos in Markle's isolated community. 'Don't talk to the media. They will eat you alive.'

'Can you help me get rid of these people?' asked Thomas.

'Don't speak to anyone,' repeated Harry unsympathetically.

Doria, Thomas knew, was getting help. Why was Meghan denying him the same assistance, he wondered? Although Meghan would later claim that Jason Knauf 'had spoken to my father on many occasions', Thomas Markle heard nothing from London.[347] Thomas understood that Meghan was keen to exercise her control. She could not risk Thomas at large. Similarly, she could not risk the rest of the Markle and Ragland family speaking beyond her remit.

'This is really weird,' Thomas told Samantha Markle. Meghan's voice, Thomas decided, was strange. 'When Harry is in the room, she is sweet but when he steps out of the room she is a different person — mean and controlling.'[348]

To his surprise, he had not received a Christmas card. More peculiar was Meghan's suggestion that Thomas Markle cut himself off from Samantha and Tom Junior.

'You don't need them,' she said.

'I'm not disowning my kids,' Thomas Markle replied. 'That's crazy.'

'Then I have nothing more to say,' said Meghan. 'We have nothing more to talk about.'[349]

After glimpses of the couple at the Invictus Games in Toronto, Meghan's formal introduction to the British public in Nottingham on 1 December 2017 was a stunning success.

© Christopher Furlong/Getty

Four weeks later, her appearance for Christmas with the Royal Family at Sandringham signalled the Queen's unprecedented enthusiasm to welcome Meghan into the Windsor family.

Left: Lord Geidt, the Queen's Private Secretary of ten years, was forced out by drives to remain independent from Buckingham Palace.

Right: Edward Young, Geidt's successor, lacked the crucial authority to influence the media strategy in other palaces.

Below: Keleigh Thomas Morgan, Meghan's Los Angeles publicist before and after her marriage to Harry, promoted Meghan's interests – and ignored the Royal Family's concerns.

Above: Jason Knauf worked closely with Meghan and Harry as their spokesperson, and would become entangled in their lengthy court battles.

The stunning wedding at Windsor Castle on 19 May 2018 was hailed as proof of the monarchy's embrace of multi-culturalism.

In the run-up to the wedding, Meghan nurtured her relationship with Doria, her mother, but left Thomas Markle unprotected from the media. Outraged that a photo carrying four cans of beer falsely labelled him as an alcoholic, Thomas suffered under the pressure. Sick, he could not fly to London for the ceremony.

Initially, anxieties over Meghan's insistence that she would use her new 'platform' to campaign ignoring the monarchy's strict impartiality seemed unfounded. She appeared happily with the Queen, at Wimbledon with Kate Middleton and at Ascot with Camilla and Charles.

Unveiling the Fab Four before the wedding in 2017 was planned to establish the modern monarchy, and the quartet appeared united in public into 2018, seen here at a Heads Together conference and the Commonwealth Service that year.

Above: The Sussexes' official visit to Australia and the South Pacific in the same year seemed on the surface to be successful. In reality, the couple simmered amid acrimony.

© Richard Pohle/Getty

Left: Tensions broke through at Wimbledon in 2019, where the Duchesses appeared strained and barely spoke to one another.

© Karwai Tang/Getty

Right: The Sussexes' South African Tour was pitted with controversy. As well as the now-famous interview with ITV's Tom Bradby describing her poor mental health, she told a group of women that she had paid for her own college fees, which angered her father.

Left: The couple's first child, Archie, was born in May 2019 and accompanied them on their tour.

© Pool/Samir Hussein/Getty

Harry realised that he had been sidelined from the Royal Family while watching the Queen's Christmas Day address in 2019. His family photo was not on the Queen's desk. On the couple's return to London in March 2020 for their farewell, they staged a brilliant photograph in the City but the Royal Family's frozen faces during the Commonwealth service in Westminster Abbey seemed to confirm their anger with the Sussexes.

Post Megxit and the bombshell Oprah interview, the Sussexes must rely on maintaining a level of global celebrity in order to fund their lavish lifestyle. They have signed multi-million dollar deals with Netflix and Spotify, and their philanthropic endeavours – here, pictured with the Mayor and the Governor of New York State whilst there on a trip – are all well-documented.

Although the Sussexes were invited to celebrate the Queen's Jubilee in June 2022, they were seated far from the senior royals in St Paul's and agreed not to pose in public.

Thomas Markle now suspected that Doria was forcing the division. At the same time he believed Meghan had told Doria not to speak to Thomas. 'Doria was feeding anger and spite to Meghan,' complained Thomas. Doria, he reluctantly believed, saw an 'opportunity' that Meghan would pay off Doria's debts for college and also buy her a new car. For the first time, his calls to Doria were ignored. 'She's obeying Meghan's command,' he concluded.

In Kensington Palace, the couple were in the midst of self-created turmoil. The TV documentary marking the twentieth anniversary of Diana's death had been memorable for Harry's outspoken damnation of the media for causing his mother's death. He forgot Diana's countless provocative poses for photographers, especially those in a turquoise swimsuit in the South of France just before she died; and that she was killed by a drunken driver encouraged to be reckless by Dodi Fayed. She was not wearing a seatbelt.

That documentary had been preceded by Prince Harry in Africa, a TV documentary about his charity Sentable. Harry revealed that he wanted to spend the rest of his life working in Africa. 'Now I'm so energised, fired up,' he said. 'And now for me, I can see exactly where I want to take [my life].' Africa was his future.

'I am struck by how happy he seems, how comfortable in his own skin,' reported Bryony Gordon in the *Daily Telegraph*. Portraying Harry as a 'rock-solid role model', Gordon believed that Harry's 'lightness of touch' confirmed that his demons were expunged. The message he sends out to young people, she continued, is 'be kind to yourself, do good things and everything else will follow.'[350] Gordon made those pronouncements to promote Harry's Mad World podcast, which described his descent into 'total chaos'.

Unmentioned was Harry's gratitude to Meghan for introducing him to Eye Movement Desensitisation and Reprocessing, a treatment to unlock distressing memories.[351] Harry's confessions were matched by Meghan's latest revelation: 'I give things a lot of thought and I try to be as sensitive and thoughtful as possible to how it'll make someone feel.'[352] Their Palace staff were encountering a different experience.

Meghan had told BBC TV in her engagement interview that she was marrying Harry and joining the Royal Family on her terms. In their staff's private discussions with Meghan she spoke about launching a campaign to empower women, and voiced her frustration about the Royal Family's ingrained tradition to avoid controversy.

Meghan's opinions raised sensitive questions for Samantha Cohen. Could a 36 year old who deemed herself to be professionally successful adopt the British propensity for understatement? Could she ditch Hollywood's hyperbole in favour of the Palace's low-key, repetitive 'No comment'? How could an ambitious, career-minded, outspoken, Californian actress understand the Royal Family's immutable hierarchy and rigid protocols? One staff member silently questioned whether the Californian really wanted to exchange the sunshine and ocean breeze for rainy Britain, and whether Harry would be tempted to exchange the grouse moors for Beverly Hills.

All of those questions remained unanswered. Meghan offered no willingness to compromise. She interpreted their acquiescent smiles as agreement rather than polite exasperation. She was not impressed by their aristocratic manner and mannerisms. Even their wealth was gauche. She did not want to dress, speak and even think like them. Silently, Cohen's staff judged Meghan's refusal to understand the non-negotiable requirements of royalty as irresponsible self-indulgence. In the run-up to Christmas 2017 both sides blamed a clash of cultures.[353]

Meghan was used to starting the day early. She was a doer, she wanted action. Emails to her staff arrived before breakfast, some as early as 5am. The sin was not the emails but her irritation about the staff's response. Meghan never explained whether she expected the staff to reply instantly to her 5am messages, or whether she was merely getting on with her day. 'They preferred a more genteel pace,' her friends would say about her staff, and disliked the 'American work ethic'.

That criticism deliberately disguised a profound change in Meghan's behaviour. Stories surfaced that Meghan's orders to Melissa Touabti, her PA, to buy special red blankets for a Sandringham shooting party had ended in screams.[354] Touabti, complained Meghan, had failed to buy the right blankets.[355] At the same time it was said that Amy Pickerill, a chief aide, also felt that Meghan exerted an attitude of entitlement which reduced her to tears. Meghan, she concluded, was unwilling to listen to advice.

Somewhere in her journey between Toronto and Kensington Palace, Meghan's famed empathy had disappeared. Some would say she had absorbed the performances of Toronto's elite or that of a Hollywood mogul. Others would blame Harry's own short-tempered arrogance towards his staff as her model. Whatever the explanation, a Kensington Palace official had to ask Harry and Meghan to speak to their staff with more understanding. 'It's not my job to coddle people,' Meghan reportedly replied.[356] Naturally, no one was aware of the previous complaints during the Reitmans shoot or Adrian Sington's experience.

Beyond the Palace walls the fairytale was flourishing. Buckingham Palace briefed the media that the couple's wedding plans were for a 'ceremony designed to incorporate both families, their wide circle of friends and welcome the public into their lives'. The process was underway for Meghan to become a British citizen and for her baptism into the Church of England by the Archbishop of Canterbury.

Mindful that Meghan appealed both to youth and the diverse communities, the Queen wanted to accelerate Meghan's membership of the Royal Family before the marriage. In a break from tradition, to please Harry and under pressure from Charles, Meghan was invited to the Christmas lunch for Buckingham Palace's staff, to the Royal Household party at Windsor Castle, and to spend Christmas with 30 family members at Sandringham. Harry and Meghan would stay with Kate and William at Anmer Hall on the Sandringham estate. At every event Meghan behaved and dressed impeccably.

On Christmas Day, a larger crowd than usual watched the 'Fab Four' smilingly walk together to the church. Universally, everyone assumed that the two families would establish a happy new dynasty for the next 40 years. Holding hands, Harry and Meghan waited for the Queen to arrive. After the service Meghan curtsied nervously to the Queen. Three years later Harry would claim that despite appearances there was 'a lack of support and lack of understanding' for Meghan.[357]

On Boxing Day, Harry missed Sandringham's traditional pheasant shoot to present as the guest editor the BBC Radio 4's *Today* programme. The scoop was his interview with Barack Obama, recorded in Toronto during the Invictus Games. He described his Christmas as 'fantastic'. It was, he said, Meghan's introduction to his wider family. 'It's the family I suppose she's never had,' said Harry live on air. His comment may have seemed innocuous to his domestic audience, but his remark sparked bewildered fury among the Markles. During his wedding speech in Jamaica, Trevor Engelson had said exactly the same.

Thomas Markle could not imagine how Meghan described her childhood to Harry. Was it as an abandoned orphan, desperate for rescue? Thomas was hurt. He had made huge efforts to provide Meghan with a loving home. Even after his divorce from Doria she had been invited to their Christmas Day celebrations. Samantha Markle was adamant that Meghan had two very happy homes before she went to college. In a Twitter post to Harry, she warned: 'If she will treat our family this way, she'll treat your family this way.'

Their anger with Meghan was cut short by the arrest of Tom Junior after a drunken brawl with his fiancée in Oregon. Although Tom had put a gun to Darlene's head he was released, and instead she was jailed.[358] The circus once again highlighted Meghan's conundrum. She wanted her 'problem family' cut out of the narrative.

Like other Markles, Tom Junior expected an invitation to the wedding. After all, he had regularly played with Meghan as a child and often saw her until she went to Canada. Similarly, Thomas's brothers, Fred, an Eastern Orthodox priest who baptised the Markle babies with water from the Jordan, and Mick, the retired State Department official who helped Meghan enrol into the student course in Buenos Aires, anticipated flying to London. And of course Samantha too expected a seat in the chapel. But no invitations had arrived. Meghan had not even suggested that she and Harry would fly to Los Angeles or Mexico to meet Thomas Markle.

When she flew with Harry to celebrate the new year in his cousin David Linley's home in the south of France, Meghan suspected trouble was brewing. Thomas, still obeying orders to remain silent, began to suspect that Meghan was ashamed of her past. Immersed in royalty, her family was being filtered out – or ghosted.

In London, Lady Susan Hussey had shortly before enjoyed lunch with a group of theatre executives and directors. While discussing the possibility that Meghan might become associated with the National Theatre after the wedding, Hussey became unexpectedly serious about the couple's future. 'That will all end in tears,' warned Hussey. 'Mark my words.'

CHAPTER 20

Aggravation

Meghan's last appearance in *Suits* was the perfect springboard for the continuation of her tour across Britain, which had been arranged by Kensington Palace.

Mobbed in the city centres of Cardiff and Birmingham, Meghan arrived in Belfast. After seeing an exhibition about the peace initiative at Lisburn, her spokesman said that she had 'praised the warmth of the Belfast people'. Those accompanying Meghan were struck by her clear lack of interest in the island's history, which was strange considering her strong relationship with John Fitzpatrick.[359]

By the time she reached Edinburgh she was distinctly unroyal. Instead of keeping her distance she autographed a book, agreed to selfies and, with Harry's encouragement, allowed the public to hug her. Some complained that she was playing to the cameras, giving distinctly unroyal 'high-fives', wearing inappropriate clothes, and walking in front of Harry.

In 'glutinous actress mode [she] was acting herself in some future episode of TV's *The Crown*,' commented Jan Moir in the *Daily Mail*. 'Where is all this going? Too many layers of custard compassion is all going to make us feel a little bit sick.'[360]

Moir's criticism coincided with Ninaki Priddy's sale of more memories to the same newspaper. In Meghan's opinion she was being 'maliciously' depicted by her discarded friend 'as a conniving social climber who had her sights on snagging a prince ever since she was in high school.'[361] Priddy's assessment was about to be shared by another of Meghan's friends.

The highlight of Meghan's trip to Edinburgh was a visit to Social Bites, a centre to help the homeless managed by Josh Littlejohn. By coincidence Littlejohn was also a client of Gina Nelthorpe-Cowne. At Littlejohn's suggestion she was included in the 20 people awaiting Harry and Meghan in the centre. Before they arrived, the 20 were divided into two groups – one to meet each of the couple.

'I used to work with Meghan,' Gina told a Palace official. 'I'd like to meet her again.'

'No problem,' he replied, directing her to Meghan's group. Fifteen minutes later, as the crowd outside roared their welcome to the arriving couple, the Palace official pulled Gina aside. 'Sorry, you're in the wrong group. We made a mistake. Please move to Harry's group.'

The couple entered and split up. 'I used to work with Meghan,' Nelthorpe-Cowne told Harry directly. 'Did she make me go to your group?' Harry didn't reply. Moments later, Meghan looked away from Nelthorpe-Cowne. In disbelief, she walked towards Meghan. With obvious embarrassment, a Palace official 'body-blocked' her.

'I realised I was of no value to her anymore,' lamented Nelthorpe-Cowne. 'I realised she only surrounds herself with people who can elevate her. Meghan has a way of closing the door on the past.'[362] Meghan had ignored a cardinal royal rule: avoid offending anyone.

In Kensington Palace, Meghan's staff reluctantly admitted a problem. Meghan, they realised, did not understand one reality: she was the centre of attention, listened to with respect and even admiration, simply because she was marrying Harry. Insensitive to their message delivered in the politest terms – 'I just wonder whether you might consider...' – she spoke with certainty implying, they assumed, that she had little to learn.

Harry did not understand that his fianceé was confusing being famous with being a royal. Hollywood's celebrities boosted their sponsorship opportunities, film ratings and Instagram followers by small acts: bashing President Trump at the Oscars, kneeling during the national anthem or setting up charities that benefited themselves more than the cause.

By contrast, royals survived and prospered by casting a light on others' achievements rather than their own, celebrating national occasions, championing their country abroad, and providing comfort to others during tragedies. The royal world is expected to be one of altruism, history, tradition and low-key patronage for no personal gain. Hence the despair which arose after reports of the vulgar antics of Princes Charles and Andrew.

Despite long conversations with her staff, Meghan did not want to grasp that the Palace's operations were low-budget and ultra-cautious. Royals were present to open events, smile and encourage, not to promote themselves. Princess Diana never created her own big-budget charities or even employed a full-time press secretary. The Queen was admired because she kept her opinions to herself. Meghan, however, had pledged to 'hit the ground running'. She had added in her much-used trope: 'I want to make a tangible impact…this kind of work feeds my soul.'

Kate had become irritated by her neighbour. Unlike her own cautious approach 'to learn the ropes' before engaging in royal duties, Meghan was running – but what was her destination? And who was she running with? Did she realise that the Royal Family ran together under the monarch, not as competitive individuals?

Anxious to help Meghan's bid for the spotlight, Palace officials looked for appropriate opportunities to promote her as a philanthropist. They spotted the Al-Manaar mosque near Grenfell Tower in west London, which had been destroyed by a fire in June 2017 that caused 72 deaths. An international group of women survivors had established the Hubb Community Kitchen to cook their own local specialities twice a week for their fellow displaced. Capitalising on Meghan's interest in food, and to enhance her reputation as an activist, the Palace organised a visit. Later it released photos of Meghan wearing an apron, washing rice, tasting the food and stacking dishes. 'Immediately I felt connected to this community kitchen,' she later wrote. 'It is a place for women to laugh, grieve, cry and cook together.'[363]

The more important step was the preparations to appoint Meghan as a vice-president of the Commonwealth Trust, a voluntary international organisation of 54 countries inspired by the Queen's dedication to multi-racialism. Sixty per cent of the Commonwealth's population was under thirty years old. Standing with political leaders at a Commonwealth Youth Forum reception to promote women's empowerment, Meghan had watched as Harry was proclaimed the Trust's president. 'In my new role,' he said, 'I will work to support the Queen, my father the Prince of Wales and my brother William.' With Meghan appointed as an ambassador to the Commonwealth, he continued, their priority would be to support the Commonwealth's 2.5 billion people.[364] As an ambassador to the Commonwealth, Meghan was reassured. It certainly outranked being an ambassador for UN Women.

The downside came in the form of racist remarks on social media. Kensington Palace's Instagram account was read by seven million followers, and received a racist barb by the girlfriend of a UKIP leader. The post by the supporter of the anti-EU United Kingdom Independence Party deeply upset Meghan and Harry. That single post would be repeatedly cited by the couple to suggest that Palace 'officials were overwhelmed by threats made from multiple sources'.[365] The officials replied that they were overwhelmed by demands from Harry and Meghan to remove any criticism, rather than a few threats on social media.

Throughout those weeks, Meghan was hectically directing the wedding plans. Inevitably there was tension. The wisest realised that much depended on the relationship between Meghan and Kate. Their stark differences could not be easily bridged – or concealed.

To avoid the daily comparison between their accommodation in Kensington Palace, Meghan decided she needed an alternative home. She wanted to escape from Kensington Palace. A substitute for California's beaches was found near Soho Farmhouse, a private club in Chipping Norton in Oxfordshire. In early 2018, Harry rented a converted Cotswold barn on the Great Tew estate. In that setting Meghan could entertain her American friends and invite Harry's crowd. The only group missing were Meghan's British friends. There were very few of them.

In order to counter any suggestions that Meghan had not been welcomed fully into the Royal Family, her reintroduction to the public was staged on 28th February, 2018, three months before the wedding. Pulling every lever, Samantha Cohen and Jason Knauf encouraged the media to elevate the unveiling of the 'Fab Four' as joint patrons of the Royal Foundation.

The Foundation enjoyed special status. As the focal point for William, Kate and Harry's philanthropic work, the Foundation emphasised help for mental health sufferers. The three royals were patrons of the Foundation with limited influence on its direct activities. That power was exercised by the Foundation's executives, an unimpressive group criticised for ineptly moving the royals around like chess pieces. While William, Kate and Harry had become accustomed to their motley behaviour, Meghan's arrival as a natural recruit for the Foundation's philanthropic work disturbed the rhythm of the executives' habits. Her feminism also upset their ingrained conservatism.

'Right now,' enthused Meghan to the audience, 'with so many campaigns like MeToo and Time's Up, there's no better time to continue to shine a light on women feeling empowered and people supporting them.' She continued to the cameras, 'You'll often hear people say, "Well you're helping people find their voice" and I fundamentally disagree with that, because women don't need to find a voice. They have a voice, they need to feel empowered to use it, and people need to be encouraged to listen.'

Ignoring Kate's frozen expression Meghan spoke about inclusivity and diversity; she spoke with conviction about her virtuous thoughts to end universal injustice and of her protests about the number of scenes in *Suits* that required her to emerge from a shower wearing a towel. She posed as the trailblazer – fighting for what she believed – as 'the feminist princess of our dreams' who boldly pronounced Harry to be a feminist.[366]

The audience's reaction was mixed. Many of the young were impressed. But to many others women in Britain did not appear to be silenced. Indeed, the monarch, the prime minister, the president of the Supreme Court and many senior civil servants, industrialists and media editors were women. Moreover, Meghan was only sitting on the platform, as she later liked to say, as 'a mother, feminist and advocate', because of Harry. Marriage would make her rich and titled, but not famous because of any personal achievement. She was piloting an unscripted storyline way beyond Rachel Zane's scope.

While Meghan spoke, Harry spotted William's rictus grin. Virtue-signalling from a platform ignored the royals' role impartially to foster national unity. She had not been invited to join the Royal Foundation to reinvent the Royal Family's customs. Meghan, William silently feared, did not understand that the public expected mystique not familiarity. Was she trying to upstage Kate? Did she realise that there was a pecking order in the constitutional monarchy? As hard as she might try, Meghan could not win because Kate would be the queen and Meghan would remain a duchess. Had Harry ever explained to Meghan that royal protocol meant that they would always walk behind William and Kate? Had Harry dared to explain his diminishing role in the Royal Family? Or had he avoided that truth out of fear of losing Meghan?

'Wedding first,' Harry whispered loudly.

'We can multi-task,' Meghan replied to the unexpected interruption. Instead of speaking about mental health she had been swept up by her vision of a modern monarchy. She imagined herself as centre-stage rather than recognising the reality of standing on the periphery. Her self-deception was understandable.

As the discomfort among the four became obvious, William tried to restore harmony. The Crown, he volunteered, should be 'relevant to their generation' but the Four should 'not reinvent the wheel'.

Asked by a member of the audience about disagreements, the four laughed. Disputes, they acknowledged, existed. 'They come so thick and fast,' said Harry. 'Working as a family does have its challenges.'

'We don't know,' William admitted when asked whether their disagreements had been resolved. In the jovial atmosphere of goodwill towards Meghan, few of the audience realised that Kate's smiling expression concealed irritation. Her publicists had already briefed the media that compared to Meghan's £1,415 dark navy outfit, Kate's dress cost £99. Behind the stoicism of the future queen was disappointment. Particularly about Meghan's treatment of their shared staff, their disagreements about the management of the Foundation, and more recently Harry's grumpiness towards William.

Over the preceding months, Charles had sought to improve his relations with William. The heir was fearful of a crisis when the Queen died. One possible consequence of the national trauma after the beloved monarch's death would be the nature of his coronation. The organisers had not yet finalised the size, pomp and duration of the ceremony. The religious tone was undecided. Among Charles's other concerns was securing William's agreement that Camilla be crowned as queen. To capture his eldest son's support for easing the difficult transition, Charles assigned more public duties to William and Kate. They would represent the modern faces of Britain's best values. Everything depended on skilfully managing the transition from the Queen's reign.

Aggravation

Orchestrating the changing of the guard at the Palace is usually executed with military precision. The departure of Christopher Geidt was an exception. Just before Geidt's farewell party in Buckingham Palace in early March 2018, Charles had been present nearby at St James's Palace to witness Meghan's baptism by the Archbishop of Canterbury. But Charles and his brother Andrew refused the invitation to pay respect to Geidt. They boycotted the party.[367]

The tension could not be concealed. Mark Leishman, Charles's private secretary, had also resigned. And just before the party the Queen hosted a ceremony to award Geidt his third knighthood in six years. Edward Young, Geidt's successor, would be challenged to manage the growing and inevitable crisis within the family. Few had confidence he could rise to the task.

None of this was visible to the public as the Queen led her family into the Commonwealth Day service at Westminster Abbey 12 days later on 12th March. Only a handful of insiders noticed Meghan's irritation that she walked, as hierarchy stipulated, behind Kate rather than as her equal.

CHAPTER 21

Tears

Thomas Markle was feeling isolated. 'I haven't received an invitation to the wedding,' he told Meghan from his bungalow.

'It must have got lost in the post,' she replied.

Knowing that a British consulate official had visited Doria with an official scroll and she had also received a formal invitation to the wedding, Thomas concluded, 'She's bullshitting me. This is Doria's work.'

'Just lay low,' Meghan urged Thomas during the telephone call.

Some in the Palace were puzzled by Meghan's refusal to fly discreetly to Los Angeles with Harry and meet her father. After all, Doria was in regular contact with Kensington Palace about the arrangements. Meghan had even flown to Los Angeles to show her mother the sketches for her wedding dress and to arrange for Oscar de la Renta to make Doria's outfit – a pale green coat and dress with a matching fascinator.[368]

During the visit Meghan had not suggested that Thomas Markle drive up to Los Angeles. She had only arranged for a Beverly Hills tailor to take Thomas's measurements for a suit which would be made in London. Thomas presented himself at the tailors under a pseudonym. He was told to fly to London on 16th May, arriving merely two days before the wedding to try on the finished suit. Doria was also to arrive in London shortly before the wedding, without the time to overcome any jet-lag. Meghan wanted to minimise any chance of embarrassment. Was she afraid that Thomas might reveal truths about her family that she would prefer left unsaid? Or worse, would Harry take fright once he met Thomas and even break off the marriage?

Thomas's discomfort was aggravated by his family's unhappiness. None of Thomas's other children or brothers had been invited to the wedding. 'Uncalled for,' the former diplomat Michael Markle dubbed Meghan's 'indifference'. He added, 'I'm upset and surprised. Meghan has climbed socially and left us behind – that's how I feel.'[369] Tom Junior was equally damning: 'She's torn our entire family apart.' Samantha speculated that Meghan was ashamed of white working-class men. Equally disappointed were Doria's relations, especially her half-brother Joseph Johnson. He had cared for Meghan until she left for college. After Joseph died in 2021, his widow complained that Meghan failed to send her any condolences.

Palace gossip related that the publicity departments of some famous designer labels – Chanel, Dior, Armani, Givenchy and others – had been surprised by calls from a member of Meghan's staff with a request: Meghan would be delighted if the House were to bequeath a handbag, shoes or an accessory to Kensington Palace in the near future. These items would be treated as goodwill gifts, the publicists were told. The women were puzzled by what they called 'the Duchess's discount'. In the past, their offers of gifts to Kate had been rejected on the principle that the Royal Family did not accept freebies. Meghan's staff, it appeared, were not worried by that rule.

The troublesome Palace rumours coincided with Kate giving birth to her third child, Louis. Five hours later, perfectly made up and posing on the steps of St Mary's hospital for the cameras, Kate introduced the latest royal baby to the world, then smiled and drove off with William. Harry was reconciled to the fact he was now, as sixth in line, no longer the 'spare'. He relied on his partnership with Meghan to reposition himself.

A casualty of the royal birth was that night's TV documentary featuring Camilla. With the focus on Kate there was less interest in the documentary, which had preoccupied Charles. Fearful of Camilla's unpopularity and the opinion polls reporting that a majority of Britons would prefer William to follow the Queen, Charles had asked his sons to praise Camilla in the documentary. Both refused.[370]

Witnessing those disagreements, Meghan was determined to dictate the terms of her own public image. She would control how the public should perceive her, and also the tone of the marriage ceremony. Hollywood, she knew, would love the images of an American princess with the backdrop of a medieval castle and the interior of the fifteenth-century church.

On Meghan's visit to inspect St George's Chapel, her guide mentioned the tombs of kings within the walls. The history and constitutional relevance of those granite stones did not register with Meghan. Even the grave of George III, who lost America as a British colony in 1776, passed unnoticed. After one year in England, Meghan showed little understanding of Harry's family or his country. She was unconcerned that Charles and Camilla, as divorcees, had not been allowed to marry in the chapel. To embed Meghan into the royal family, this breach of constitutional practice had been approved by the Queen. Taking this for granted, Meghan appeared convinced that their milestone marriage would, in Harry's words, keep the monarchy popular.

Meghan's behaviour was fuelling Palace speculation about Kate's anger over her treatment of their shared staff. Meghan's requests, they complained, were delivered as commands rather than inquiries about whether something would be possible. The team of handpicked professional women preparing for the wedding were the target of her complaints. Among the several disputes was the choice of music for the wedding (undecided until the last days), the menu at the reception (constantly changed), the guest-list (not only old friends but many of Harry's cousins, uncles and aunts were excluded), whether the guest-list should, as usual, be published (Meghan's veto was final), the seating arrangements in St George's Chapel, Meghan's wedding dress (frequently re-cut), whether air-freshener could be used in the chapel (Meghan's request was rejected), the mounting cost (Charles agreed to increase the budget) and – not least – which tiara Meghan could wear.

No member of Buckingham Palace's staff is closer to the Queen than Angela Kelly, the 61-year-old personal advisor of the Queen's wardrobe. Devoted to the monarch, Kelly's many duties include caring for the royal collection of tiaras. Invited to the Palace's secure room, Meghan alighted on a tiara sparkling with emeralds. Her choice was approved by Harry. Kelly suggested that its Russian origin made it unsuitable. Harry became angry. 'He had been downright rude,' *The Times* was told.[371] Kelly reported the unhappy exchange to the Queen. Harry was summoned by his grandmother to a private meeting. 'He was put firmly in his place,' *The Times* reported.

Shortly before the wedding the approved tiara featured in a second tiara dispute. Meghan's hairdresser flew from New York to rehearse his work around the tiara, Queen Mary's Diamond Bandeau. Meghan asked that the tiara be delivered to the stylist's room. Kelly refused. Tiaras, she said, were not released for hairdressing rehearsals. Harry again became irate, accusing Kelly of being unhelpful.[372] 'What Meghan wants, Meghan gets,' he shouted.

Harry was now called 'The Hostage' by some of his staff.[373] Less frivolous was the realisation that Meghan did not seem disturbed by arousing anyone's displeasure. Tradition, hierarchy and family relations did not deter her from annoying anyone – and that included the Queen.

The tension troubled Kate when she arrived with Charlotte, her three-year-old daughter, at a fitting for the bridesmaids' dresses. By then, Kate was irritated by complaints of Meghan bullying her staff. One had complained that she was offhand. Another that her temperament was haughty, displaying little sympathy for those outside her circle.

W. H. Auden, the poet, had summarised this kind of dilemma: 'Private faces in public places are wiser and nicer than public faces in private places.'

Since she had just given birth to Louis, Kate was too fatigued to cope with a disagreement about whether the bridesmaids should wear tights. Following protocol, Kate believed they should. The Californian was uninterested in royal tradition. Her insistence was supported by Jessica Mulroney, present as an advisor and the mother of another bridesmaid, Ivy. Some would say that Meghan compared Ivy favourably against Charlotte. Others were surprised by Meghan's close attachment to Mulroney.

That disagreement was followed by an argument about the length of Charlotte's hem. Kate thought it was too short, and anyway did not fit. Melissa Touabti, Meghan's assistant, and the dress-fitters employed by Givenchy's Clare Waight Keller witnessed Meghan emphatically reject Kate's observation. Compromise was not a trait Meghan embraced. The stand-offs, Kate decided, confirmed the complaints by Touabti and other members of staff about Meghan. Kate burst into tears. Kirstie Allsopp, a friend of Camilla, would later confirm that Kate was reduced to tears by Meghan bullying her staff.[374]

After leaving that unhappy scene Kate decided to make amends. She crossed the Kensington Palace corridor and presented Meghan with a bunch of flowers. Kate also told Meghan not to speak rudely to her staff. 'That's unacceptable.'[375] What followed can never be irrefutably established. In Kate's version, Meghan slammed the door in her face and threw the flowers in a dustbin. Meghan would tell Oprah Winfrey that the tears were shed by her, not Kate, and the flowers were an apology.[376] 'I think that's where everything changed,' Meghan rightly said.

After the first report of Kate's tears was published by Camilla Tominey in the *Daily Telegraph*, Meghan would claim that it was the 'beginning of real character assassination'. The Palace spokesman refused her request to set the record straight.[377]

CHAPTER 22

Humiliation

In Rosarito, Thomas Markle was feeling abandoned. 'I was being chased and harassed on a daily basis by the media. I didn't know who to turn to. The people at the Palace gave me no help at all. I felt utterly isolated.'[378] Not only did Meghan fail to telephone, but Jason Knauf, his Palace contact, never returned his calls. Thomas Markle was fretting. 'I was hung out to dry,' he later said.[379]

Thrust into the spotlight, Thomas had become upset by the portrayal of him online and in newspapers across the world as a scruffy, obese, alcoholic hermit. Trolls on social media accused him of undermining and failing to defend Meghan. He was embarrassed by the contrast of his lifestyle with Meghan's glamour. British newspapers asked why no recent photo of Meghan and her father had appeared; they speculated that Harry had not met him under orders from Meghan; and they questioned why he kept changing his mobile number.[380]

As the ridicule increased, Meghan delivered a wounding blow. In a rare telephone call Thomas had told Harry that he wanted to give a short speech at the wedding reception. Shortly after this, Meghan called to say that it was not possible. 'That hurt,' Thomas admitted. 'It was the worst blow.'[381] The award-winning lighting director was a proud man. He wanted public acknowledgement, even admiration, as the father of this remarkable young woman.

Samantha Markle listened to his repeated complaints. By then she had been approached by Jeff Rayner, a British photographer based in Los Angeles. Rayner offered to photograph Thomas preparing for the wedding. Samantha told her father that the photos would show he was not a recluse. 'The media was unfairly making him look bad,' she later said, 'so I suggested he do positive photos for his benefit and that of the Royal Family.'[382] Although in an early phone conversation Harry had warned Thomas Markle not to deal with any media because 'they will eat you alive', Thomas agreed to Samantha's suggestion.

Thomas met Rayner at a restaurant in Rosarito. 'You look dishevelled and fat,' said Rayner, laying out snatched media photos of Thomas. One of Thomas carrying four cans of beer implied that Meghan's father was a heavy drinker. 'We're going to make you look great,' said Rayner. Anxious not to appear as if the photos were staged, Thomas urged that Rayner should take long-distance 'candid shots'. They signed an agreement. He would be paid $1,500 plus 30 per cent of the royalties.

On 27th March, Rayner photographed staged shots of Markle in Rosarito glancing through a book of 'images of Britain' at a Starbucks, reading news stories about Meghan and Harry in an internet café, and being measured by a tailor for a wedding suit. The 'tailor' was David Flores, a 17-year-old student and shop assistant at a party shop. Flores was paid $15 (£11) to hold the tape-measure Markle produced. 'These don't look like candid shots,' Thomas told Rayner. 'Don't worry,' said Rayner. 'No one will know.' Gullible and desperate, Thomas trusted Rayner. The photographer would wait until the right moment to sell his prize.

In London, rumours about Meghan's discourtesy towards her staff seeped out of the Palace. 'I think the pressure to escape from The Firm is crushing,' predicted Germaine Greer, a republican feminist. 'She bolted before. She was out of the door. I think she'll bolt. I hope in a way she'll bolt, but maybe she'll take Harry with her.'

Camilla Long, the acerbic columnist, agreed: 'I think it's unlikely Meghan hasn't already mapped out the big sit-down interview with Oprah after the divorce is over and she's fled to America. She has already written her lines about the "healing process" and will monetise a public "personal development."' Long was to prove uncannily accurate. Oprah Winfrey had called at Kensington Palace to discuss an interview before the wedding. Flattered that she now ranked among the superstars, Meghan had been told by her officials to reject the offer. She would wait, she told Oprah, 'until the time was right'.[383]

Those first shots triggered other sceptical comments. Was this, asked Patrick Jephson, Diana's former private secretary, a genuine love story by a woman prepared to sacrifice for duty, or was she seeking a stage in her lust for fame?[384] Could she, he speculated, distinguish between her celebrity as an actress and her new global fame derived purely by association with Harry?

Even the most discreet Palace officials were voicing similar exasperation. Meghan picked up the vibes. A close friend would reflect her anger. The critics, she said, were racially motivated: 'Find me a woman of colour in a senior position who has not been accused of being too angry, too scary, too whatever in the workplace.'[385]

On the eve of the wedding, Patrick Jephson privately feared that Meghan would use the race card to rebut any unfavourable news stories. 'It will be really tragic,' Jephson said, 'if Meghan and her husband got into the habit of firing ethnic warning shots at the very same media that will reliably trumpet all their good work for years to come.'

Jephson was also concerned by Harry's conviction that Meghan had much in common with Diana. That illusion, Jephson believed, was dangerous. As Diana and Fergie discovered, warned Jephson, Meghan should not overestimate her worth. As a newcomer to the 'dynasty business' her sole purpose was to preserve the monarchy as the focus of national unity. The Windsors would be ruthless against any threat posed by an aggressor.[386] Jephson knew Diana better than Harry. He had seen her 'spread happiness' but he had also witnessed her weaknesses. Working outside the system, Diana ignored advice, kept her officials in the dark and, as a loose cannon beyond anyone's control, was eventually cast out. Meghan, Jephson feared, was replicating Diana's worst characteristics. Not, as Harry believed, her best characteristics.

In late April, as the countdown to the wedding on 19th May began, Jeff Rayner offered Thomas Markle's photographs to newspapers. After the first ones appeared abroad, Knauf alerted Meghan. She called her father. Asked whether he had co-operated with a photographer, Thomas replied 'No'. At Meghan's request, the Palace officially denied that Thomas Markle had co-operated with Rayner. Thomas Markle, said Knauf, was suffering from media intrusion – being 'followed and harassed' by photographers. He warned the media to respect Markle's privacy and to stop further harassment. Everyone believed Knauf's denial.

On 3rd May, two weeks before the wedding, Thomas Markle drove to a first-aid station in Rosarito with chest pains. Years earlier, he had received nitro-glycerine treatment for irregular heartbeats. Paramedics told him that he was in the midst of a heart attack and should go immediately to the local hospital. After a few hours of poor care, and despite suspected congestive heart failure, he discharged himself. Over the following days he told Meghan about his health problems. He also told her how much he was looking forward to wearing his new suit and shoes, and that, during a trip to Los Angeles, he had left flowers at Doria's house for Mother's Day. By now, Rayner was selling the photographs across the world and expecting to earn over £100,000. One photo was published by the *Sun* as an 'exclusive'.

On 11th May, Harry and Meghan called Thomas Markle. During the conversation, they asked if he did co-operate with Rayner.[387]

'No,' said Thomas.

'If you're lying to me,' said Harry, 'my children's life will be in danger.'

'What are you talking about?' shouted Thomas, angered by Harry's tirade. 'You haven't got any children.'

On 11th May, Thomas also texted Meghan: 'I know your hard work to make me look good. [sic] Thank you. I'm getting excited. It's all so close now. I can't wait to walk you down the aisle.'[388]

The Markles' lives permanently changed on Sunday 13th May. The *Mail on Sunday* exposed Thomas Markle's complicity with Jeff Rayner. A grainy CCTV image recorded outside the Rosarito internet café showed Thomas following Rayner holding a long-lensed camera. Other informants, including David Flores the 'tailor', confirmed that Thomas Markle had collaborated with Rayner.[389] The Palace was embarrassed, while Meghan and Harry were furious about Thomas's 'betrayal'.[390] Meghan's repeated calls to her father were unanswered. Mortified by her inability to tell the Palace officials what was happening, she blamed the media as irresponsible, harmful, ruthless and malevolent. She asserted that the *Mail on Sunday* had known about the collaboration for some time and had maliciously waited until the last moment to expose her father. That was untrue.

On Monday 14th May, Thomas woke late as usual at around 11am, which was 7pm in London. Thomas texted his daughter that he was sorry 'about all this', he loved her and he offered to make a public apology to both her and Prince Harry. To spare her and the Royal Family from any further embarrassment, he offered not to go to the wedding.[391]

After enduring months of silence from London and Harry's failure to meet his future father-in-law, the photo crisis sparked an outburst of calls. The first was from Harry to Thomas. Harry advised Thomas not to make an apology. That would only make everything worse. Thomas accepted the order. In turn, Thomas confirmed that after all he would come to the wedding. Harry replied that a British official would call at his home to drive him to the airport. Soon after that conversation, Jason Knauf called Thomas. An apology, said the official, would be after all advisable. No one in London could imagine Thomas Markle's confusion. Trapped in his isolated home, he festered without a sensible advisor.

Contrary to Meghan's account, Thomas insisted that Knauf's second call about the apology was his last. Knauf did not, as Meghan later claimed, speak to Thomas Markle 'on many occasions'.[392] Meghan would also claim that Knauf 'made significant efforts over many months to protect Mr Markle and to object to intrusions into his privacy'.[393] Thomas Markle denied that assertion. Not only was he abandoned but now he was utterly humiliated. That lunchtime he drove to a local McDonald's in Rosarito. After that meal he headed to a KFC.

Later that day, 14th May, Thomas felt chest pains again. Dizzy with palpitations he had the same symptoms as a previous heart attack. He asked a friend to drive him across the border to the Chula Vista hospital in California. While waiting for the friend, his phone rang. A man calling himself 'Sarge' announced that he would arrive soon to drive Thomas to Los Angeles airport. He was to fly two days later.

'Sorry,' replied Thomas. 'I've got to cancel. I have to go to hospital.'

'I'll pass that on,' said 'Sarge'. 'Thank you very much.'

Before going to the hospital Thomas spoke to TMZ, an American showbiz website. He confirmed that he had co-operated with Rayner to 'rehabilitate' his image but had been left looking 'stupid and hammy', and so he wouldn't be flying to London. Contrary to Meghan's later claim, he did not personally refuse to get into a waiting car to drive to the airport, nor had he 'turned away' a security guard sent by the British embassy.[394] Both arrived after Thomas had crossed the border.[395] Before entering the hospital, he texted Meghan to apologise and say that he could not travel to London.

Harry and Meghan were frantic. In a series of texts to Thomas Markle the prince was on the edge: 'Tom, it's Harry and I'm going to call you right now. Please pick up, thank you.' 'Tom, Harry again! Really need to speak to u. U do not need to apologise, we understand the circumstances but "going public" will only make the situation worse. If u love Meg and want to make it right please call me as there are two other options which don't involve u having to speak to the media, who incidentally created this whole situation. So please call me so I can explain. Meg and I are not angry, we just need to speak to u. Thanks.' 'Oh any speaking to the press WILL backfire, trust me Tom. Only we can help U, as we have been trying from day 1.'

With the eight-hour time difference between London and California, messages and more confusion dominated 16th May. Meghan awoke to read TMZ's report of her father's heart attack and hospitalisation. She would later claim that this was when she 'time learned' of Thomas Markle's condition.[396] That scenario is hard to believe. Both 'Sarge' and the British embassy security guard who had been sent to Thomas Markle's house were told he was going to hospital; and Meghan had received Thomas's text with the same news. In reality, Meghan doubted that his hospitalisation was genuine.

Meghan texted her father: 'I've been reaching out to you all weekend but you're not taking any of our calls or replying to any texts. Very concerned about your health and safety and have taken every measure to protect you but not sure what more we can do if you don't respond. Do you need help? Can we send the security team down again? I'm very sorry to hear you're in the hospital but need you to please get in touch with us. What hospital are you at?'

Ten minutes later, Meghan fired off another message about security. 'Harry and I made a decision earlier today and are dispatching the same security guys you turned away this weekend to be a presence on the ground to make sure you're safe. All of this is incredibly concerning but your health is most important.'[397] She added, 'Please, please call as soon as you can.' Sending a security guard to Thomas Markle in Rosarito while he was being prepared for surgery in California was odd. For 18 months, Thomas had been forlornly asking for help. He replied he would be in hospital a few days and refused the offer of security.

In an emergency procedure to prevent a heart attack on 16th May, two of Markle's arteries were unblocked by angioplasty. Emerging from the anaesthetic later that day Thomas Markle texted Meghan, 'Surgery went ok. Heart attack did some damage.' The doctors, he continued, forbade him to fly that day to London. He wished her the best. 'Love you and wish you the best of everything.'

Harry texted back: 'If you had listened to me this would never have happened.'

Stung by Harry's reprimand and silence about his health, Thomas reconsidered his position. In a text he asked Meghan who would give her away? If really required, he texted, 'I will come if you really need me. I'm sorry about this.' TMZ reported that, after all, Thomas had decided to fly to Britain.[398]

From London, Harry sent texts saying they were not angry; Meghan's final text ended 'Love M and H'.[399] Then Meghan telephoned Thomas. She pleaded that he come to London. Hearing her cry, Thomas became convinced that his daughter did not believe that he was in hospital.[400] The call ended acrimoniously. 'Maybe it would be better for you guys if I was dead,' snapped Thomas and hung up.

Harry fired off what Thomas regarded as three telling-off texts. First, Harry 'admonished' Thomas for talking to the press and accused him of hurting Meghan. To Thomas's distress, Harry did not ask about his health or the operation or send him good wishes. Deeply wounded, Thomas sent a curt reply: 'I've done nothing to hurt you, Meghan or anyone else…I'm sorry my heart attack is any inconvenience for you.' Harry would deny that the exchange occurred.[401]

Meghan, however, acknowledged she had received an 'unpleasant message' from her father. Within five minutes, she called him four times. He did not answer. Using Meghan's phone, Harry texted: 'Tom, it's Harry, please answer your phone, I need to know this is actually you because it doesn't sound like you at all.' Thomas later explained, 'There is a time and place to say what he said but not when I was lying in a hospital after a heart attack.'[402] Thereafter, Meghan never sent another text to Thomas, never telephoned him and ignored his calls forever. At 4:57 a.m. on her wedding day, Thomas called but unsurprisingly got no reply.[403]

On 16th May, three days before the wedding, Kensington Palace's official spokesman briefed that Thomas would not be coming to Britain because of ill-health. By then, several members of the Markle family had arrived in London to appear live on TV shows. Characterised as alcoholics, cannabis growers and jailbirds lured by money, they were angry not to be invited to a 'family reunion'. The visitors included Roslyn, Thomas Markle's first wife, and Tom Junior's ex-wife and her two sons. None had ever met Meghan.

Meghan's nephew Tyler used his visit to promote his latest cannabis product, Markle's Sparkle. Tyler was estranged from his father, Tom Junior: 'My dad, he's just a vile human being.'[404] By contrast his brother Dooley praised Meghan and denounced the media's reporting: 'I've always admired her.'[405]

At the last moment all the Markles were dropped by the broadcasters, but Samantha Markle would not be silenced. She wanted to promote her forthcoming book *The Diary of Princess Pushy's Sister* and denounce the descriptions of Meghan as a 'compassionate humanitarian'. Meghan, she said, had nothing in common with Diana. 'Early in the year,' she told US TV, 'we were asked not to speak to the public, but I'm pretty adamant about it. There's something in this country called freedom of speech. She doesn't have a copyright on that.'

Amid that background noise, Meghan's dilemma was who would walk her down the chapel's aisle? Harry agreed to ask Charles. 'He's our father,' Harry later said, 'so of course he's going to be there for us.' Charles replied, 'I'll do whatever Meghan needs and I'm here to support you.'[406] Harry later said about Charles: 'He was there for us. He was the one out of the two left to deal; he tried to do his best and to make sure we were protected and looked after.'[407]

Thomas Markle could not be airbrushed from the ceremony. His name was printed on the order of service. To square the circle, the Palace needed to secure his approval of the arrangement. To conceal the Markle family crisis, James Beal of the *Sun* was falsely told by Palace sources that Meghan had spoken to her father: 'Meghan said she loved him. He said he was recovering well and not to worry.' Thomas had 'told' Meghan that he was 'honoured' that Charles would give Meghan away.[408]

Unseen during the furore, Doria Ragland quietly arrived in London on 17th May. Escorted from the plane as a VIP, she was driven directly to the Cliveden House hotel outside London to prepare to meet Charles and the Queen at Clarence House and Windsor. Meghan had successfully suppressed the truth about her mother. In turn, Doria was ordered not to say a word. That appeared to include not making the slightest facial expression.

Doria was about to participate in one of Windsor's greatest theatrical performances, some would say a hapless Royal Family hijacked by Hollywood.

CHAPTER 23

Wedding

The fairytale – a rich prince weds a beautiful damsel in an imposing castle surrounded by 600 excited guests, and then departs in a horse-drawn coach to the ecstatic cheers of thousands of adoring citizens – was perfectly choreographed by the Windsors. Hollywood could not have rivalled its authenticity.

Few Kensington Palace staff approached that day without bruises and a tinge of disbelief about Meghan and Harry. The family was divided. William and Kate were sceptical, while Charles and the Queen were relieved that Harry had chosen a woman with sense and intelligence who was apparently prepared to undertake a public role. But like most families on the eve of a wedding, the inevitable tensions were expected to be put aside on the day.

Weddings symbolise the union of two families and their friends. The couple's guest-list defied that convention. It reflected Harry's deliberate detachment from his past. Several members of the Royal Family – cousins, uncles and aunts – were surprised not to be invited. Politicians were excluded, among them the prime minister and Donald Trump. Although scorned, he refused to criticise Meghan in a TV interview by Piers Morgan about Meghan's criticism of his misogyny. 'Well, I still hope they're happy,' Trump said with unusual tact.

Across the shires, many who had helped Harry through his early years, taught him to play polo, provided hospitality, taken him on safaris in Africa and cared for him in the years after Diana's death could not understand why they had been excluded. 'NFI', Not Fucking Invited, they cursed. Individually, none could understand the snub until they came to a common conclusion. All were deemed to be of no use to Harry in the future. The guest-list, strongly influenced by Meghan, ignored nostalgia and gratitude. The focus was on their reinvention. 'Mice shouldn't marry rats,' declared one disgruntled English landowner.

The most notable exclusion was Meghan's own family. Voicing the Queen's surprise, Charles was perplexed that besides Doria not a single relative had been invited. 'Meghan has climbed socially and left us behind,' said Mike Markle, her 80-year-old uncle. 'I think that's what happens when you're the underclass and trying to rise above the reality of your situation. She's a prima donna because he [Thomas] treated her really well.'[409] Samantha Markle believed that her half-sister had excluded all her relatives to protect the lies she had told Harry and others about her life.[410]

In their place, Meghan invited her girlfriends and admirers, including hotelier John Fitzpatrick, her close friend from New York. Less noticeable but more important were those engaged to maintain her Hollywood profile: her Los Angeles agents, lawyers and publicity advisors – Keleigh Thomas Morgan had a prime seat in the chapel. Behind them sat her fellow actors from *Suits*. Many had not been expecting the invitation. All stayed together in an Ascot hotel and noted they were not invited to the evening dinner. From their regular conversations with Meghan they assumed she would enhance her celebrity life with the Royal Family's approval.

Embracing celebrities was not unusual for the Windsors. Charles often invited actors and writers for weekend parties at Sandringham. Similarly, inviting an exceptionally helpful businessman to their wedding was acceptable. Kate and William included the head of Audi UK at their wedding, in thanks for supplying his cars on generous terms.

Wedding

Among the stardust to seal the glamour of Harry's and Meghan's wedding were David and Victoria Beckham, James Corden, Elton John, Serena Williams, and George and Amal Clooney. No one believed that Meghan knew the Clooneys but the Palace insisted that Harry had once met the actor. Priyanka Chopra, the Indian actress, was an acquaintance.

The biggest surprise was the inclusion of Oprah Winfrey, America's famous 64-year-old chat-show host, renowned for turning wounds into wisdom as the television Queen of Victimhood. Oprah was certainly not Meghan's friend. They had met for the first and only time two months earlier. Like so many other guests, Oprah knew that the relationship would be useful. So did Meghan. To be surrounded by Hollywood royalty would firmly establish her roots in America.

Unusually, the Palace did not publish a wedding guest-list. Identifying the guests depended on journalists spotting celebrities or following social media. Many guests could not resist posting messages and photos on Instagram about their clothes, hotels and journey to St George's Chapel.

The glittering ceremony had attracted tens of thousands to stand in bright sunlight along the streets outside the castle. For them the Royal Family epitomised Britain's identity – human and flawed, but also decent and considerate. Over ten million Britons watched on television as the guests arrived and took their seats. Meghan would not be pleased that 17.6 million had watched Kate's wedding and 28 million had watched Diana's. She could, however, be sure that many uncounted millions were watching in America and elsewhere.

Among them, lying on a hotel bed to avoid prying journalists, Thomas Markle grumbled that he knew more of the Hollywood guests in the first two rows than his daughter did. He had filmed with them all, including George Clooney in the sitcom *Friends for Life*. That was one of several reasons, he came to believe, why Meghan had abandoned him in the months before the wedding. 'She never really wanted me there,' he concluded. Doria, he became convinced, was also relieved about his absence.

Wearing the clothes and demeanour suggested by Meghan, Doria sat composed and alone. Few could understand why she had not arrived accompanied by a friend. Everyone assumed it was her own choice rather than Meghan's. Below Doria sat Kate and Camilla. Kate was inscrutable. Choosing to wear a traditional Alexandra McQueen tailored coat she had worn on a previous engagement, she signalled that Meghan should grasp that they were not rivals. Unlike Meghan, Kate would eventually become the Queen. Waiting by the altar, William and Harry, dressed in Blues and Royals uniforms, gave the firm impression of deep friendship and mutual support.

Exactly five minutes before the ceremony began, the Queen arrived. Beside her, Philip walked unaided. The proud 96 year old manfully disguised his recent recovery from hip surgery and the pain from a cracked rib. He refused to use a walking stick. The Royal Family sat facing Hollywood celebrity across the aisle.

Hailing Meghan as a boost to the monarchy had provoked a sombre discussion about how the monarchy would survive the Queen's death. The answer was in the service. Charles and the Archbishop of Canterbury had fashioned a celebration of multi-culturalism. For Charles, who had a strong relationship with Britain's Afro-Caribbean community, the invitation to the Afro-American Episcopalian Bishop Michael Curry of Chicago to read a sermon, and the inclusion of a performance by the 19-year-old cellist Sheku Kanneh-Mason, sent a message across the world that the British Royal Family sincerely embraced multi-culturalism.

At the precise moment set out in the timetable, Meghan arrived at the chapel in a Rolls-Royce, the same vehicle that had carried Wallis Simpson, the American divorcee and the Duke of Windsor's wife, to her husband's funeral in 1972. The official's choice was deliberate.

As she stepped out of the limousine, Meghan's bridal train was caught. The escorting officer who opened the door offered no help. The explanation foreshadowed what was to come. After her rudeness during the rehearsal the previous day, explained an officer, no one had any feelings of goodwill towards the bride.

The sight of the bride in her white Givenchy dress by the English designer Clare Waight Keller was pure Hollywood. Under the spotless blue sky and without her father at her side, Meghan stood at the entrance to the chapel as a proud performer. Unaccompanied, she walked into the chapel. That feminist gesture, reported CNN, proved Meghan to be 'a strong, independent woman who is prepared to challenge royal norms'. After she had walked alone halfway down the aisle, Charles joined the bride to complete the walk to the altar. 'Thanks, Pa,' said Harry. 'You look amazing,' he told his bride. She smiled. As she said, 'I will', broadcast across Windsor town, the loud cheers from the packed streets echoed back into the chapel and beyond.

The customary precision of royal events was lost after Bishop Curry ignored his instruction to speak for six minutes. In a barnstorming, unscripted 14-minute sermon, his exuberant appeals for the 'power in love' followed by a gospel choir singing 'Stand By Me' aroused smiles among some and exasperation among others. The doubts disappeared at the end of the service as Charles thoughtfully took the arm of the uncertain Doria and escorted her out of the chapel. As Harry and Meghan emerged into the sunlight, the wedding was hailed as a triumph.

'A magically modern royal wedding' was the *Daily Mail*'s front-page headline, echoing the resounding public acclaim. Universally, the ceremony was hailed as a perfect example of the monarchy's deft modernisation. No one doubted that the couple would be a benefit to the country and enhance the Royal Family. The monarchy's hope in William and Kate – a solid, loving, modern family – and now Harry and Meghan, symbolised Britain's confident entry into the twenty-first century.

Journalist and author Tony Parsons witnessed for the *Sun* the optimism among the crowds in Windsor. Standing on a packed pavement to watch Harry and Meghan pass by in an open Ascot Landau carriage, he recorded that the deep, bitter divisions inflicted on Britain by the EU referendum of 2016 seemed to have melted away: 'Here was a wedding to give us all reasons to be cheerful and the joy was everywhere. Here was a royal wedding for the multi-racial, multi-cultural country the UK has become.'[411]

The joy continued for the 200 guests greeted by Charles at the evening dinner in a glass marquee in the grounds of Frogmore House. Uninvited were Camilla's two children, Tom and Laura Parker Bowles, and several of Harry's oldest friends, including Tom Inskip. 'Meghan has changed Harry too much,' Inskip later said, shocked that he had been dumped. 'We've lost him.'[412]

Harry had switched his allegiances to the Hollywood set. Included at the dinner were Oprah Winfrey, Idris Elba, James Corden and notably George Clooney. The actor brazenly seized the moment for self-promotion. Princess Eugenie's future husband, Jack Brooksbank, a bar manager promoted to brand ambassador for George Clooney's Tequila Casamigos, was assigned to pour Clooney's brand for guests throughout the evening.

'My darling old Harry, I'm so happy for you,' said Charles during his post-dinner speech. Harry, he said, a 'big man with a big heart', had found his perfect wife.[413]

Meghan's speech was sentimental, but also a little threatening. Meeting Harry, she said, was 'love at first sight'. She had 'at last found my prince'. After thanking the Royal Family for their welcome she pledged to launch campaigns. 'That's why I am here,' she said to applause. 'Bring it on,' shouted the American guests.

By then – just two hours after the wedding – the Royal Family's official site had added the Duchess of Sussex's new web page. Meghan's pride, the page proclaimed, was being 'a woman and a feminist' and an activist on behalf of women, girls and the poor since the age of 11. Alongside her photo on a 'learning mission' to India, the website mentioned her interest in 'the stigmatisation of menstrual health management'.[414]

Some of the older British guests were wondering whether Meghan imagined herself to be the British equivalent of Michelle Obama. Gazing at the Californians who cheered Meghan's pledge to campaign, they were irked that their full white-teeth smiles revealed 'an awfully self-adoring crowd'.

Naturally, William tactfully praised Meghan as the sister he had never had and as the best thing that had happened to 'Haz', who he teased about his bald patch. Then the party began.

As Brooksbank handed out Clooney's tequila brand, James Corden hosted a dancing competition. Charles danced with his sons and waited for the fireworks. Impressed by the display, Charles asked Harry who had paid. 'You, Pa,' replied his son. Charles left the party early, uncertain how much of the £32 million bill was down to him. Regardless of this latest burden, he had hosted a memorable celebration on a special day.

Three days later, Meghan's wedding pledge to 'campaign' was highlighted by *The Times*.[415] 'Her legions of admirers,' commented the newspaper, 'see in her a princess, not a preacher.' Even the cheerleaders for her feminism, suggested the newspaper, hoped she understood the 'fine line to tread in public'. The newspaper continued, 'Clearly, she has no intention of giving up her activism and yet it carries clear risks. Activism strays easily into politics, and it is an iron law of the constitutional monarchy of which she is now a part that its members stay out of politics if they want it to survive.' The warning was explicit: 'In her new role she is a princess, not a politician. She will have to find a way to be content with that. Duchesses don't campaign and don't fight back.'

The measured caution did not appeal to everyone. Tom Bradby, a TV journalist known for his friendship with William and Harry, foresaw problems if Palace officials did not endorse Meghan's demands.

Writing in the *Sunday Times*, apparently on the Sussexes' behalf and aware of the tensions between Meghan and her staff, Bradby applauded Meghan who 'has yet to put a foot wrong in public'. He hailed her 'mixed-race background' as 'a PR department's dream…to refresh the royal brand.' Harry's friend put the burden on the Royal Family. The Sussexes, he warned, could be the family's 'natural rock stars [but] it's going to be a complicated balancing act'.[416]

Other writers were divided about the marriage. Margo Jefferson, the author of *Negroland*, elevated Meghan to the 'achievement conscious' Black bourgeoisie. Harry, she believed, was fortunate to be 'marrying up' to a woman with money and opinions. June Sarpong, the broadcaster, welcomed that 'the royals are beginning to resemble the rest of us'.

But Kehinde Andrews, a strident professor of Black studies at Birmingham City university, was scathing: 'The Royal Family is perhaps the most identifiable symbol of whiteness in the world. It is absurd to think that one Black woman could transform an institution so rooted in colonialism and whiteness.' For Professor Andrews, Meghan was not Black enough. Her skin, he said on CNN, was too fair, her hair was not Afro and her nose was not flat. 'She represents,' he wrote, 'the image of Blackness we have been sold as acceptable and marketable.'[417]

During those first days of the afterglow, Meghan maintained her control of events. Just as the wedding guest-list remained undisclosed, the couple's honeymoon destination was a guarded secret. 'If Meghan can't handle life in the royal goldfish bowl,' suggested one observer unaware of the growing tension in the palaces, 'no one can.'[418]

Unseen, Oprah Winfrey was texting Meghan. Thrilled to be acknowledged by Californian royalty, Meghan was delighted that Oprah had visited Doria. Her only misgivings were directed at those within Kensington Palace: her staff and the Cambridges. None realised that she remained in constant contact with all her advisors in California – the entertainment lawyer, her business manager and her publicists.

CHAPTER 24

Tremors

Over four days in June 2018, Meghan enjoyed the spotlight as a principal member of the Royal Family. The cameras lingered during her first appearance on Buckingham Palace's balcony after watching the Trooping the Colour. Her smiles, her close friends thought, looked forced. Still aggrieved by the royals' commitment to hierarchy during the conversations before stepping on to the balcony, she disliked the automatic assumption that she was junior to Kate. She believed she should be treated as an equal. Harry sympathised.

Three days later, her dissatisfaction became apparent again. After travelling with the Queen overnight on the royal train to Chester, Meghan emerged from the train the following morning at Runcorn looking reassured. The Queen had given her a pair of earrings during the journey. Meghan's demure smile on the platform gave the impression she had forged a bond of loyalty towards the monarch.

Throughout that day, opinions changed. While Meghan did perform, the Queen's aides noticed that she remained detached. Her refusal to wear a hat reflected, they believed, her disapproval of royal life as staid and stuffy. A few suspected from their conversations that while she enjoyed the privileges, Meghan appeared reluctant to become steeped in British traditions. She had already decided to resist the obligations of total commitment to public duty.[419]

Her return to London was ominous. At a leaving party in the private garden at Kensington Palace for Miguel Head, Prince William's former private secretary, Harry and Meghan were the last to arrive. They appeared reluctant to engage with others and left soon after William's speech, despite his frequent mentions of Harry. Head had reason to be surprised. He had worked with Harry during his deployment in Afghanistan.[420] Re-employed as a publicist for a corporation in San Francisco, Head asserted that his task in the Palace was to 'retain a sense of magic and mystery' for the Royal Family.[421] The importance of that mantra – to avoid public confrontation – had eluded Meghan.

Meghan's father remained a problem. Ever since their previous conversation three days before the wedding, Thomas Markle's attempts to re-establish contact with his daughter had failed. There was no reply to his text messages, his telephone calls were not answered and then her phone went dead. She had, he assumed, changed her number. For the first time, she had not sent a Father's Day card. Although Meghan would later insist that 'she did not ignore him', Thomas felt abandoned.[422] Even Jason Knauf did not reply to his text messages. Gradually Thomas Markle believed he was the victim of Meghan's blame-shifting and scapegoating. Psychologists identify a familiar cycle: 'idealise, devalue, discard'.

Amid much agonizing, he blamed Doria for poisoning their relationship. After all the support he had given her over the past 40 years, he believed that Doria had betrayed him. As for Meghan, he remembered her small hand clasping his as they walked to the ice-cream shop, and her excitement as he praised her school acting. He could not understand how that love had turned to hatred. Gazing at the sea, he wondered if she had any fears that her own children would treat her with such hostility? Perhaps as revenge for how she treated her father?[423] Isolated and mocked, his bitterness grew towards those who had ridiculed a hard-working, acclaimed lighting director. 'I wasn't going to be put away,' he recalled.[424]

Unexpectedly, on 18th June, Thomas Markle appeared on ITV's *Good Morning Britain*. Furious about his portrayal as a drunk living in squalor, he had agreed after lengthy negotiations to give his first live TV interview. He would be paid about £15,000. Since the wedding, he explained to the host Piers Morgan, despite being 'very forgiving' about the photographs, Meghan had ignored him.

In a mournful tone Thomas recounted his approval of Harry's request to marry Meghan so long as he 'promised me you'll never raise your hand against my daughter'; and about his sorrow at missing the wedding: 'I was jealous. I wish I'd been there…She was beautiful. It was incredible watching her. I cried a little bit about it. The whole world was watching my daughter. I was very happy about that. The unfortunate thing for me is that I'm a footnote in one of the great moments of history, rather than Dad walking her down the aisle.'

His reason for giving the interview was pride: 'I just want people to know I'm a normal guy. I'm a retired man and I was living a quiet little life and this happened. And lots of things happened around it but, more than anything, I don't want my daughter or new son-in-law hurt by any of this. I want to have a nice, normal relationship with my Royal Family as well now.' He added: 'I hope I haven't offended them, I don't think I have. They know I love them and I hope the Royal Family will understand my feelings as well.'[425] He hoped the interview would be seen as a peace offering.

'Friends' of Meghan told the media that Thomas Markle's surprise appearance was 'beyond disgraceful'.[426] In their version Meghan and the members of the Royal Family could give interviews, but not Thomas.

The following day, Meghan rode in the third carriage at Ascot after the Queen. Later she was seen laughing with Charles and Camilla. Her fury with Thomas was concealed. She had assumed that by refusing to take his telephone calls he would silently disappear. Meghan did not grasp the consequence of cutting herself off from her father and of spurning any notion of inviting him to London, or even meeting him in Los Angeles. In Mexico, her stubbornness provoked another outburst.

The interview, Thomas admitted on TV, 'put me in the penalty box', but he would not be silenced. 'If the Queen,' he said, 'is willing to meet our arrogant and insensitive president she has no excuse not to meet me, I'm nowhere near as bad.'[427] Trump was scheduled to meet the Queen on 13th July during a visit to Britain. One week later, after his calls continued to be blocked, Thomas admitted, 'I think that relationship is lost now.'[428]

Speaking to the media was becoming important to him. He decided to give interviews until Meghan talked to him. He also retained a lawyer to extract his share of the royalties – about $50,000 – from Jeff Rayner. 'I got screwed by Rayner,' said Markle, 'and I'm going to find a way to screw him over before I die. I want to tear him down. If they tell me I've got terminal cancer, then I'll kill him because I have nothing to lose.'[429]

'I could actually die soon,' he told the *Sun* the following week. 'Does she want this to be the last thing we've said to each other?' He went on: 'It is probably the longest time I have gone without speaking to her ever. I just want to clear the air and tell her how proud I am of her. If I had one message for her it would be: "I love you. I miss you. I'm sorry for anything that went wrong. I'd like to put our differences behind us and get together."'[430]

Rather than resting his case, the spurned father lashed out at the Royal Family for their 'asinine' anger about the paltry payment for Rayner's photos. 'Half of Great Britain,' he said, 'seems to make a fortune selling pictures of my daughter and her husband.' He could have earned $100,000 and more if he wanted. He extended his anger to the 'ridiculous' royal dress code. 'Meghan seems like something out of an old movie. Why in 2018 are we dressing like the 1930s? Why do they have to cover their knees?'

Stony silence from Meghan sparked another outburst to the British media: 'My daughter is very controlling. She likes to be in charge.' His conclusion was credible: 'I think she is terrified. I see it in her eyes. I see it in her face and I see it in her smile. I know her smile. I've seen her smile for years. I don't like the one I'm seeing now. This isn't even a stage smile – this is a pained smile. It really worries me. I think she's under too much pressure. There's a high price to pay to be married to that family.'

Meghan fumed about her impotence. Each rant from Thomas and Samantha dented her popularity. The previous day, photographers had noted the accuracy of Thomas's observation. In a staged photo opportunity to rebut the truth, Meghan and Kate had appeared for the first time together at Wimbledon for the Ladies' Final. Meghan's smile looked more forced than usual.[431] The physical comparison was unflattering to Meghan. On her own, Meghan's radiance won universal applause but beside the taller, authoritative future queen the duchess appeared diminished. Neither could conceal their mutual discomfort. Insiders drew a parallel with the relations between Harry and William. Days earlier, at a celebration of the RAF's 100th anniversary, the brothers had looked uncomfortable together.

Relations between the four had broken down. William and Kate refused to stay with Charles and Camilla at the Castle of Mey in Scotland at the same time as the Sussexes, and the Sussexes turned down the Queen's traditional invitation to stay at Balmoral in the summer with William and Kate. At the heart of their divergence was Meghan's unwillingness to be part of a team. There was no intimacy. She could not identify with the family's power – social, financial or political. She was also irritated by Kate's and William's refusal to be well-meaning partners.

Meghan's one-week visit to the Castle of Mey beginning on 28th July was used to brief the media that Charles had become attached to Meghan and admired her interest in history and furniture. Unspoken was Charles's bewilderment about the American. He had never really understood her or what she wanted. That week, his irritation about Thomas Markle's TV appearances, especially his criticism of the Royal Family, came to a head. 'Can't she just go and see him and make this stop?' Charles 'berated' Harry. His son, according to Meghan, was 'endlessly explaining the situation' about Thomas Markle's behaviour to Charles and Camilla, but the 'family seem to forget the context… they fundamentally don't understand.'[432]

Charles could not understand Harry's 'explanations' because his son withheld critical details. Harry did not tell his father about Thomas's fury at being ignored by his daughter and about Harry's insults while he was in hospital. Instead, Harry explained that Meghan refused to telephone Thomas Markle because she suspected that 'his phone was [not] in his possession' and 'his email account was compromised'. Charles could not have known that both reasons were untrue, but it was also possible that the Sussexes mistakenly believed their own version.[433]

The inconsistencies of Meghan's excuses not only irritated Charles but also the Queen. The monarch did not believe that Meghan could not resolve her differences with Thomas Markle. To persuade her to make an effort, she joined Charles in a conference call with Meghan and Harry.[434] At the outset, Charles and his mother urged Meghan to fly to America for a reconciliation.

Meghan rejected the Queen's suggestion. 'It was completely unrealistic to think I could fly discreetly to Mexico, arrive unannounced at his doorstep (as I had no means of secure communication with my father), to a location and residence I had never visited or known, in a small border town…and somehow hope to speak privately to my father without causing a frenzy of media attention and intrusion that could bring more embarrassment to the Royal Family.'[435]

Her argument avoided the truth. Although her father's telephone number was unchanged and the mobile was always in his pocket, she claimed, 'I had no secure means of communication with my father', and added, 'we could not trust that my father's phone was in his possession.'[436]

That did not prevent her from contacting him. Her father's telephone number was unchanged. They could meet discreetly in Los Angeles. The Queen was unaware that Meghan had never visited Rosarito.

Both Charles and the Queen realised that Meghan's excuse was far-fetched. Puzzled by her attitude, neither Charles nor the Queen had heard Thomas Markle's explanation for Meghan's stubborn refusal to meet him. Namely, that Doria had persuaded her daughter not to make that journey.[437] The conference call ended with both the senior royals perplexed by Meghan's conduct. 'I was especially sensitive,' Meghan later admitted, 'to this as I had very recently married into the family and was eager to please them.'[438] In turn, Harry fretted that Meghan needed protection. He sympathised with her resentment about the Palace's keen sense of deference and hierarchy. While he could not understand her intolerance of English reserve, he did fear he might still lose her.

'They fundamentally don't understand,' Meghan complained during her visit to Castle Mey. 'They' included Camilla. With nothing in common, Camilla was apprehensive about Harry's future.

Camilla epitomised the best – and probably some of the worst – characteristics of a practical, solid English upper-middle-class woman. Under-educated, expert as a horsewoman, a poor cook, keen to do good, with lots of old friends, she was grounded and not grand. As a no-nonsense, self-deprecating, plain speaker with a good sense of humour who, when necessary, displayed a stiff upper-lip, Camilla was most comfortable sloshing through the mud in a Barbour and gumboots.

For the hard-working American graduate and feminist, brought up enjoying the sunshine by the Pacific, the class-ridden hunting world galloping across the English shires, invariably under leaden skies, was unattractive. The stark differences between the Cotswolds and California aroused Camilla's sense that Meghan was an adventuress from Los Angeles. Unlike Charles, Camilla could see through the American actress's coquettish smiles and tactile performance. During her life-long experience among England's county set, Camilla had occasionally spotted self-important adventuresses. They were the sort she might call 'a minx'. In those circumstances, she found it hard to believe that Meghan would sacrifice her independence to serve silently as a team-player. But Camilla remained tight-lipped. As did Meghan in Castle Mey. Harry had his own reasons to distrust Camilla. He still blamed her for wrecking his parents' marriage.

Frustrated that she could not communicate with her admirers on the internet, Meghan was angry that Palace officials refused to protect her image. She refused to accept that Jason Knauf and the staff were not employed to promote her as an individual, but instead placed her within the grid of the entire Royal Family. In particular, Meghan fumed about Knauf's refusal officially to criticise Thomas Markle. Knauf, she complained, rejected her orders to 'set the record straight' by directly 'engaging' with the media to ask newspaper editors not to interview Thomas on the grounds that he was being 'groomed and exploited'.[439]

From her perspective, Meghan was isolated, vulnerable and stifled by conventions. Unwilling to accept that unlike Hollywood no one was counting the box-office receipts of the crowds she attracted, she was waging a struggle for which she was not suited, nor properly understood. Scornful of the Palace's explanation that attacking the media would rebound on her, she adopted Hollywood's rule-book and secretly took the initiative.

Gina Nelthorpe-Cowne, she heard from Knauf, had given an unfavourable interview to the *Mail on Sunday*. In the proposed article, Nelthorpe-Cowne described Meghan as 'picky, not only when it comes to her clothes but also her colleagues, instantly dismissing those who didn't share her "vision".' Describing how the duchess had 'given me a bit of a difficult time' in Edinburgh, she observed, 'Meghan likes to move on.'

Meghan was invited by the newspaper to give a comment. Instead, she asked Jessica Mulroney, her close friend and stylist, to intervene personally. To please her friend, Mulroney obliged. She called Adrian Sington, the literary agent. For more than two hours, she harangued him in what he politely described as 'a very unpleasant way'. Subsequently, Gina Nelthorpe-Cowne accused Mulroney of 'putting pressure on me to withdraw or change statements'.[440] After a complaint by the newspaper to the Palace about Meghan's conduct, Knauf said he would ensure 'this does not happen again'.

In reality, Knauf was powerless. The Royal Family had embraced a media junkie determined to exploit her new status to create a global image. Astutely, she found allies. Among those willing to help her was Bryony Gordon of the *Daily Telegraph*. 'She does not want to make the mistake of rushing in and giving critics an opportunity to trip her up,' wrote Gordon. 'Like Kate, Meghan will not shy away from duty…She has the opportunity to change the world.'[441]

In securing Bryony Gordon's support, Meghan had misunderstood the media. Her persuasive influence on one journalist's favourable portrayal of herself was an incentive for others to highlight the negative stories. Their search for harmful snippets started after an official visit by Meghan and Harry to Dublin. In a private conversation, Meghan told an Irish politician that she supported abortion. The politician posted the conversation on social media. Meghan was instantly criticised for expressing a political opinion. During the 24-hour trip the media delighted in reporting that she wore four outfits worth £28,000, mostly from Givenchy. A quick survey of her last 15 outings showed that she had worn clothes by Dior, Givenchy, Prada and Chanel, and never the same one twice. She was unfavourably compared to Kate, whose annual expenditure on clothes was about £100,000.[442]

Guilt by association extended to Buckingham Palace's announcement that Princess Eugenie's marriage to Jack Brooksbank would mirror Meghan's ceremony. It would include a carriage ride around Windsor. Meghan was indirectly blamed for feeding Eugenie's hunger for publicity.[443] And then came another blast from Mexico.

'I tell you. I've just about reached my limit on Meghan and the Royal Family,' Thomas said in yet another interview at the end of July 2018. 'I'm about to unload on them.' Angered by Meghan's latest denial that her father had paid her college fees, he was also infuriated by her assertion to have financed him out of her earnings from *Suits*. Thomas produced the bank statements to show that he was still repaying the loans for her college fees after she joined *Suits*.[444] In reply, Meghan would later reproach him. 'You've said I never helped you financially and you've never asked me for help which is also untrue; you sent me an email last October that said: "If I've depended too much on you for financial help then I'm sorry, but please could you help me more, not as a bargaining chip for my loyalty."'[445]

'What riles me,' Thomas told a newspaper during a long conversation on the eve of Meghan's thirty-seventh birthday, 'is Meghan's sense of superiority. She'd be nothing without me. I made her the duchess she is today.' Once again, his anger turned against the Royal Family. 'They have Meghan treating her father in a way that Harry's mother, Princess Diana, would have loathed. That's not what Diana stood for.' He added, 'I don't care if Harry never speaks to me again. I'll survive… Who cares these days about a dusty old crown? OK, maybe it's been polished but it's an ancient institution stuck in its ways.'[446]

Samantha endorsed Thomas: 'If our father dies, I'm holding you responsible,' she ranted at Meghan. 'The royals are an embarrassment for being so cold. You should be ashamed of yourselves. Act like a humanitarian. Act like a woman.' To her critics on social media, Samantha retorted, 'Meghan does not walk on water and she owes our father love and respect…It is morally unconscionable to ignore him, as he has made her everything that she is.'[447]

The battle about Thomas Markle spread across the airwaves. Sharon Osbourne, a TV chat-show host famous for confessions about her own life of violence, drugs, alcohol and adultery, expressed her sorrow to millions of viewers for 'dignified' Meghan's discomfort because she must 'feel so humiliated, so embarrassed by her father'. Accusing Thomas Markle of being disreputable – not least after being photographed carrying four beer-cans – she sniped, 'It is so obvious that you have a bad drinking problem. Get yourself clean and sober and then come back.'[448] Thomas Markle was photographed taking the beer to the guards of his compound.

'I'm worried he'll die of sadness,' said Samantha. 'I just want Meghan to get in touch before it's too late. You don't just throw a family away like a pair of shoes.'[449] For good measure, Thomas Markle damned the Palace in the *Sun* as 'secretive Scientologists and cult-like'.[450] He ridiculed the family 'like a Monty Python sketch' and mocked the idea of apologising to them: 'Perhaps you do it with gravy and flowers on the side?' To increase the pressure, Samantha headed for London. With cameras summoned she would arrive in her wheelchair at the gates of Kensington Palace to see Meghan. Denied entry, she left a letter addressed to 'Duchess Meghan' urging her sister not to leave their father 'hung out to dry'.[451]

No other member of the Royal Family had suffered as much embarrassment from their own family as Meghan. There was some equivalence in Meghan's contempt for Samantha and Thomas and now Harry's for Kate and William in particular. The Cambridges, she believed, were failing to offer the recognition and generosity she deserved. She hated the comparisons with uncomplaining Kate. Effortlessly, the Cambridges appeared to be perfect. She appeared to be influenced by envy of Kate. In turn, the future queen regarded her neighbour as dismissive of other people. Meghan's manner towards her staff, Kate observed, had become self-centred, manipulative and demanding.

The staff's complaints inflamed Meghan's growing sense of victimhood. Kate, she complained, did not have to live with the latest irritating revelation, such as the Urban Dictionary's newly published definition of 'Being Meghan Markled': a 'verb for ghosting or disposing of people once you have no use or benefit from them anymore, without regard to genuine human relationship.'

Stung by the criticism, Meghan forgot an actress's cardinal rule: pose with humility, even if it is false. Despite being raised in Hollywood's studios to work with others, Meghan became increasingly fragile, demanding that the Palace staff view the world from her perspective. Strangely, she appeared not to care whether she was liked. Empowered by her achievements, her standing was paramount. In self-defence she demanded retaliation against her critics. She urged Harry to become more combative.[452] In turn, he urged Knauf to protect his wife.

Eager to oblige the Sussexes, Knauf accepted Meghan's version that in the months before her marriage her difficult father had rejected a loving daughter's offers of help. He also assumed that her father's heart illness was suspicious and the hiatus which occurred in the days before the wedding was entirely Thomas's fault.

Knauf did not notice that whatever Meghan believed became a fact. In her mind she decided what she believed was true, and there was no possibility of contradiction.[453] Contradiction of her truth was persecution. As she would say, 'When you really know who you are and you know what your belief system is and you live by the truth, I think you can start to peel away the layers of where the fear comes in.'[454] Meghan's attitude towards 'truth' was common among Hollywood celebrities. In their new religion, the concept of a 'universal truth' was false. As she told an audience, 'Life is about storytelling, about the stories we tell ourselves, the stories we're told, what we buy into.' She sincerely believed that everyone had the right to 'create our own truth about the world'.

Seeking reassurance from fellow Californians, she flew in August with Harry in her host's private jet to stay with George and Amal Clooney on Lake Como. Amid extraordinary luxury she discussed coping with a medieval monarchy.

Before leaving for Italy she had considered how to appeal to her father to stop criticising her in the media. Instead of engaging in a conversation to rebuild their relationship, she would later say that two 'senior members of the Royal Family' advised her to write rather than telephone.[455] The two 'senior members' were the Queen and Charles. At Castle Mey, both had urged her to meet her father in America.

In drafting her letter on her iPhone to Thomas, Meghan blamed his co-operation with the media for destroying their relationship. Summarising the contents, her letter accused her father of 'breaking her heart, manufacturing pain, being paranoid, being ridiculed, fabricating stories, of attacking Prince Harry, and constantly lying.' She did not suggest reconciliation. On the contrary she later revealed, it was to 'make him stop his actions'.[456] So she ended her letter, 'I ask for nothing other than peace, and I wish the same for you.'[457]

Initially, she would publicly insist that 'she alone drafted' her letter.[458] Later she admitted that her signed declaration was incomplete. She had asked Jason Knauf to comment on her drafts. Her initial explanation for asking Knauf was to 'follow protocol'. Then she changed her reason. She had relied on Knauf, she admitted, to provide 'feedback' and 'general ideas'.[459] Some would later argue that by relying on Knauf, she anticipated or intended that the letter would be made public. She would deny that interpretation.

Knauf was in Tonga preparing for the Sussexes' official trip to Australia. Despite suffering from 'profound' jet-lag he replied encouragingly: 'The draft letter is very strong – enough emotion to be authentic, but all in resigned sadness rather than anger. Also, it is factually focused in a way that does not read like a legal filing – that is not easy to do.' He added: 'Also, there are a few tweaks to the order of events as you've set them out that could be a bit stronger – I think it's slightly even worse than you remember.' Before telephoning her he wanted to discuss the letter with Samantha Cohen, Knauf's superior. In a telling directive, Meghan replied that she would 'prefer' it if Cohen were not involved. Their detailed conversation about the letter adopted Meghan's version of events.

Knauf suggested that her letter reflected her justified suspicion about Thomas Markle's excuses for failing to fly to London for the wedding. 'The only thing I think it is essential to address in some way is the "heart attack",' he wrote. 'That is his best opening for criticism and sympathy. The truth is, you tried desperately to find out about the medical treatment he said he was receiving and he stopped communicating with you. You begged him to accept help to drive him to hospital etc, and instead of speaking to you to arrange this, he stopped answering his phone and spoke only to TMZ.'

Grateful for Knauf's help, Meghan sent back her redrafted letter for his approval on 22nd August, 2018, with a pertinent comment: her letter was carefully written so that 'it does not open the door for a conversation' with her father.[460] Her letter, she admitted, had been deliberately written 'not to put him in a good light.'[461]

The 'catalyst for doing this,' she texted Knauf, 'is seeing how much pain this is causing H.' She added that by writing, 'I protect my husband from this constant berating and, while unlikely, perhaps will give my father a moment to pause.' She added, 'Obviously everything I have drafted is with the understanding that it could be leaked so I have been meticulous in my word choice, but please let me know if anything stands out for you as a liability.'

With genuine sympathy, Knauf replied, 'It's such a strong and clear letter – with just the right amount of emotion. Hope you're ok after writing it.'

Bonded by the joint enterprise, Meghan replied, 'Honestly, Jason, I feel fantastic. Cathartic and real and honest and factual. And if he leaks it then that's on his conscious [sic] but at least the world will know the truth. Words I could never voice publicly.' She added, 'Trust me, toiled over every detail of the letter which could be manipulated.'

Even her opening words were manipulation, she admitted. She had started with 'Daddy', she had told Knauf, to 'pull at the heartstrings' of the public if her father leaked it. 'At least the world will know the truth.'

'Daddy, it is with a heavy heart that I write this,' she started her five-page handwritten letter, 'not understanding why you have chosen to take this path, turning a blind eye to the pain you are causing…Your actions have broken my heart into a million pieces, not simply because you have manufactured such unnecessary and unwarranted pain, but by making the choice to not tell the truth as you are puppeteered into this. Something I will never understand.'[462] She continued, 'If you love me, as you tell the press you do, please stop. Please allow us to live our lives in peace. Please stop lying, please stop creating so much pain, please stop exploiting my relationship with my husband.'[463]

In other paragraphs, she condemned him for giving interviews, for fabricating stories and criticising Harry: 'To hear about the attacks you've made at Harry in the press, who was nothing but patient, kind and understanding with you, is perhaps the most painful of all.' Her comment about the Rayner photographs was heartfelt: 'I believed you, trusted you and told you I loved you. The next morning the CCTV footage came out.'[464]

She told of her hurt from Samantha's attacks: 'You fixated and clicked on the lies they were writing about me, especially those manufactured by your other daughter, who I barely know. You watched me silently suffer at the hand of her vicious lies. I crumbled inside.'[465]

Her concluding pages appeared destined for an audience beyond her father: 'I have only ever loved, protected and defended you, offering whatever financial support I could, worrying about your health…and always asking how I could help…So the week of the wedding to hear about you having a heart attack through a tabloid was horrifying. I called and texted…I begged you to accept help – we sent someone to your home…and instead of speaking to me to accept this or any help, you stopped answering your phone and chose to only speak to tabloids.'[466]

Her next paragraph was calculated to rile Thomas Markle: 'You haven't reached out to me since the week of our wedding, and while you claim you have no way of contacting me, my phone number has remained the same. This you know. No texts, no missed calls, no outreach from you, just more global interviews you're being paid to do and say harmful and hurtful things that are untrue.'[467]

Her conclusion was damning: 'For some reason you choose to continue fabricating these stories, manufacturing this fictitious narrative, and entrenching yourself deeper into this web you've spun. The only thing that helps me sleep at night is the faith and knowing that a lie can't live forever.'[468]

To ensure the letter arrived, she forwarded it to her Los Angeles business manager Andrew Meyer, for delivery in Rosarito by FedEx.

Thomas Markle had never received a similarly long handwritten letter from his daughter. As he settled down to read it, he hoped it was an 'olive branch. Something that would be a pathway to reconciliation.' By the end, he was hurt by the absence of any love or inquiry about his health: 'I was so devastated I could not show it to anyone.' Meghan was right in her summary to Knauf. Her letter did not open the door for a conversation. Her lawyers would call the letter a 'heartfelt plea' to stop speaking to the press.[469] Thomas put the letter in a drawer and told no one except Doria about its existence.

'I don't know why,' he wrote to Doria, 'Meghan is being so hateful and sending me such hateful letters…Yes I have made a couple of stupid mistakes…I have apologised for those mistakes 100 times or more! I gave Meghan a good life and the best education I could. I love her very much and always will.' He received no sympathy from his ex-wife.

During Doria's visit to London in September she was taken by Meghan and Harry to the Grenfell mosque to launch *Together: Our Community Cookbook*, a volume of the women's recipes. To promote Meghan's philanthropy, Kensington Palace released a promotional film in which Meghan praised London as a city 'that can have so much diversity'. Invited journalists witnessed Doria introduce herself: 'Hi, I'm Meghan's mom.' The sincere event nevertheless attracted negativity in the media as 'a tiny bit self-serving' because Meghan had used the women 'to burnish her own caring credentials'.[470]

Her good work was overshadowed by the family row. Thomas Markle's appearances made Meghan an easy target for media lampoons. After breaking protocol by closing her own car door, one critic wrote: 'It is truly an inspiration. She humbles me, she makes me want to be a better person when it comes to exiting vehicles.'[471] Another hailed Meghan for having 'struck a greater blow for womankind'. Meghan, it seemed, could do little right. Later that week she was ridiculed for playing netball with children wearing a £1,636 Oscar de la Renta top and six-inch stilettos; for helping her friend Misha Nonoo advertise a 'Saturday Skirt' as 'Recently Worn by Meghan Markle, Duchess of Sussex'; and her flight on a private jet with Harry to Amsterdam to publicise the opening of a new Soho House. She was even criticised for not appearing at the wedding of a friend of Harry's.[472] The media constantly pricked Meghan's self-esteem. Matters came to a head during an argument between Harry and William.

At the end of September, while the Sussexes' office was finalising preparations for their first official visit – a 16-day tour of Australia and New Zealand – Harry suggested to William that Kate should be friendlier to his wife. Members of their family, said Harry, were not showing her sufficient support, respect and friendship. Meghan, Harry believed, should be just as appreciated as their mother.[473] William's reply was not sympathetic. Beyond the palaces, few were aware of the split between the brothers.[474]

The solution, Harry and Meghan decided, was to establish a separate office from the Cambridges. In an acrimonious meeting in Kensington Palace's garden between the brothers, William could no longer hold back. Meghan's behaviour, he told Harry, was unacceptable.[475] She had never intended to give up her career and become a loyal member of the family. Her workload was light. In the five months since the wedding, she had undertaken 26 engagements: at Ascot, a polo match, weddings, Wimbledon, and visits to the theatre including the musical *Hamilton*. Her proper royal duties were a day's visit to Sussex, a service in Westminster Abbey, a charity board meeting and a trip to Ireland. Meghan showed no interest in participating in the semi-anonymous, low-key visits to charities like those undertaken by Princess Anne, Philip and other members of the Royal Family. The Grenfell cookbook was a gesture but not a landmark.

That record, combined with her wish to be outspoken, William told Harry, had aroused suspicions among their staff. Did Meghan want to return to America, he wondered? If that happened, he believed, the monarchy could be embarrassed. As their conversation became heated, William mentioned staff complaints about being bullied by Meghan. Harry was outraged – but the accusations, whether justified or not, were firmly in the public domain.

Katrina McKeever, a member of Kate's communications team, had recently resigned. Kate believed that her departure had been provoked by Meghan's criticism of her performance in the run-up to the wedding. Meghan denied she had been critical. 'It's not my job to coddle people,' Meghan allegedly said.[476] In Meghan's defence Omid Scobie insisted that McKeever left 'on good terms' and was sent a huge bunch of flowers. That was disputed by insiders.

McKeever's grievances had been echoed by others to Jason Knauf.[477] Melissa Touabti, another personal assistant, had also resigned. Touabti was allegedly 'traumatised' by Meghan's unreasonable behaviour when she could not meet her 'unattainably precise demands'. Her departure was blamed on an outburst from Meghan, angry that embroidered blankets for guests at a shooting weekend were not the right shade of red. The Sussexes were said not to be disappointed by Touabti's departure but disagreed about the reasons.[478] A third member of staff had complained to Knauf of feeling undermined. Even Samantha Cohen, Knauf knew, 'felt stress'.

As the complaints accumulated, Knauf compiled a file. One

departing staffer, Knauf noted, said that her encounters with Meghan made her 'feel sick'. Others complained, 'I can't stop shaking', 'I feel terrified', and 'There were a lot of broken people. Young women were broken by [Harry's and Meghan's] behaviour.'

Knauf spoke to Harry. One member of staff, Knauf reported, was said to be 'completely destroyed'. Meghan, he explained, appeared to assume that her title automatically allowed her to forget her manners. Those who refused to be sycophantic were deemed to be unacceptable. To keep the peace, Harry apologised and, according to Knauf, 'pleaded' that the complaints should not be officially processed. In return, Harry said he would urge Meghan to show greater understanding. Knauf agreed, but the damage was done.

Meghan had convinced Harry that William's staff were smearing her. Whispers about the tiara, that Kate had cried, her own demand for an aerosol in St George's Chapel and now the staff's outrageous complaints about her behaviour were, she said, invented to undermine her. No one wanted to give her credit for the benefits she had brought to the monarchy, not least that the wedding generated an estimated \$1 billion for tourism.[479] The moment had arrived, the couple agreed, to break from the Cambridges. They needed their own court, their own staff and their own agenda.

Harry's support of Meghan persuaded Knauf, on the eve of Harry's and Meghan's departure for Australia, to compose a memorandum.[480] Addressed to Simon Case, William's private secretary, Knauf wrote, 'I am very concerned that the duchess was able to bully two PAs out of the household in the past year.' According to her staff, he continued, Meghan was vindictive: 'The duchess seems intent on always having someone in her sights.' The treatment of one person, he wrote, 'was totally unacceptable' and her 'bullying' of another seemed to be an attempt 'to undermine her confidence'. Meghan, it was said, played mind games with her staff. On one occasion, she had encouraged a staff member in a meeting to undertake a task, but at the next meeting she ignored that person and asked another to do the same work. 'We have had report after report from people who have witnessed unacceptable behaviour,' wrote Knauf about what was now called the 'Sussex Survivors Club'.[481]

Bullying was subsequently defined by Jenny Afia, Meghan's solicitor, as 'improperly using power repeatedly and deliberately to hurt someone, physically or emotionally'. Unsurprisingly, Afia said, 'It doesn't match my experience of her at all.' The lawyer added a contradiction: 'That story is absolutely untrue that she is a bully. That said, she wouldn't want to negate anyone's personal experiences.'[482]

Once again, Harry asked Knauf not to pursue the complaints. Since Harry and Meghan were about to leave for Australia, Knauf did not send his memorandum to Case. The alleged victims would be annoyed that their superiors had protected Meghan. Harry's lawyers would later deny that Harry had discussed the issue with Knauf or had interfered.[483]

On Friday 12th October, at Eugenie's wedding reception, Meghan told everyone she was pregnant. Many wondered why Meghan chose to reveal her news on the bride's big day. Two days later, the Sussexes flew to Sydney. Over 16 days, they would fly 14 times to 76 engagements. The full itinerary was normal for royal tours.

From the outset, the reception for the Sussexes in Australia was ecstatic. Large crowds cheered the couple, delighted by Meghan's special news. The Commonwealth, everyone agreed, would be enhanced by the birth of the Royal Family's first mixed-race child in the contemporary era. Harry and Meghan would be at the forefront of modernising the monarchy. In her accomplished manner, Meghan posed; her smiles exuded a special glamour.

Throughout those first days, the tour was perfect. Their visit on the second day to a family 500 miles east of Sydney, bringing a banana cake baked by Meghan the previous night, aroused euphoria. In parallel, Harry scored another triumph. He opened the Invictus Games and scaled up Sydney's Harbour bridge to replace an Australian flag with the flag of the Invictus. The couple were loudly praised for arranging free flights from Britain for participants of the games and members of charities, and warmly welcoming them at receptions. Their daily success, recorded by glowing photos, sent Australia's republicans into retreat.

The mood in the Sussexes' Sydney headquarters was by contrast miserable. Although the couple had arrived with four staff – Samantha Cohen, Amy Pickerill, Heather Wong and Marnie Gaffney – Meghan had decided that she needed to be surrounded by people she trusted. At her request, Jessica and Ben Mulroney had flown in from Canada to provide round-the-clock support. Mulroney doubled as Meghan's stylist, as she worked through her 'show-stopping' wardrobe.[484]

Boosted by the Mulroneys, Meghan was allegedly abrasive towards her four female staff and even towards the local British diplomats. According to one report, Meghan allegedly threw a cup of tea into the air. Her anger was partly fuelled by Harry. Every night, he trawled social media, searching for snide comments on the internet. Every morning he and Meghan turned on their phones to surf the internet. Thin-skinned, they were inflamed by the slightest criticism. Then, both bombarded their staff with demands for retribution and removal of the criticism.

Amid that turmoil, Harry read that once again the Markle family battle had resurfaced. The American media revealed that Thomas Markle had first heard about the prospective birth of a grandchild on the internet. Other scurrilous stories were dredged up. Radar Online quoted Tom Junior alleging that his father was absent during his first marriage because of alcohol and drug binges; while the *National Inquirer* accused Thomas Markle of snorting cocaine during a visit to the Playboy club in Manila. Markle denied all the accusations.[485]

Harry blamed British newspapers for those reports from America. But the only jibe he could attach to the accompanying British journalists was a report that one of Meghan's outfits cost £19,960. As a sign of

Meghan's intentions, she also wore a Serena Williams brand jacket. Soon afterwards, it was promoted on Instagram: '@Duchess Meghan in Our Boss Blazer. A collection fit for Royalty.'[486] Once again, Meghan was irate. Knauf and his staff were blamed for not suppressing, Hollywood-style, all those embarrassing media reports. Her mistake, she would lament, was 'believing them when they said I would be protected.'[487]

Unsurprisingly, Meghan's fury influenced Harry's attitude towards the small British media contingent accompanying the couple. 'Thank you for coming, although you weren't actually invited,' he sniped. He also brusquely snapped unprovoked abuse at a TV reporter.[488] The altercation bewildered the media. Beyond the Sussexes' entourage, no one was aware of the turbulent background in Kensington Palace and at the Sussexes' headquarters in Sydney.

In that maelstrom Harry inflamed the emotions by repeatedly telling his wife how closely she resembled Diana. Australia's huge welcome to them was comparable to Diana's tour of Australia with Charles and baby William in 1983. Tens of thousands had flocked every day to glimpse the princess. Australian republicans, and even the prime minister, credited Diana for sabotaging their campaign to remove the Queen as head of state. In hindsight, the tour became particularly important because the media concealed the evidence that the short marriage was already troubled. Their relationship irrevocably broke down after Harry's birth the following year. The more Harry drew parallels with his mother, the more Meghan became convinced of her importance to the monarchy.

The only clue to their preoccupation was Meghan's comment about a pair of jewel-encrusted earrings she was wearing from Diana's collection: 'It's so important to me to know that she's a part of this with us.'[489]

Harry, who was merely 12 years old at the time of Diana's death, could not fully understand his mother – her work, abilities, priorities and historic significance. She was both a traditionalist and an iconoclast, a mischievous revolutionary and a selfless loyalist to the monarchy. He did not appreciate that his mother did not collect a court of followers. She compartmentalised her friends from the courtiers. Sycophants and celebrities were summoned only if they served her purpose. Among those chosen were journalists Andrew Morton and BBC *Panorama*'s Martin Bashir. Her interviews with both, she knew, were dynamite but directed against Charles and Camilla, never against the Queen. Individual royals, Diana knew, must conform or the institution would lose its legitimacy. Diana's strength was the public's recognition of her vulnerability. As eyewitnesses to tragedy, both in her life and death, the public equated their own weaknesses to her experiences of betrayal, fear and grief, and even to their personal suffering after the death.[490]

The Sussexes had convinced themselves that their Australian success blessed them with Diana's magic. Never having studied British history, politics or shown interest in biographies, Meghan could not understand that Diana had won the public's affection after years of work. Neither she nor Harry could grasp that emulating Diana required time, to weave a narrative and create a brand from which influence would flow. Unlike Meghan, Diana had never needed to seek money or fame. Both had come naturally.

In her misunderstanding, and encouraged by Harry, Meghan conjured a fantasy that she could provide the leadership the monarchy required. Her activism would enhance the brand. To her staff, she gave the impression that she believed she personified the monarchy's importance.

Meghan's activism could partly be justified by Charles's example. Over the previous 40 years, the prince had controversially sought to influence key decisions in Britain: in architecture, medicine, the environment, GM crops, the army, foxhunting, and much more. British culture and history had been altered by his intervention. He had also created a series of charities, notably the Prince's Trust, benefiting thousands of young people's lives. Charles's impact was visible. Meghan wanted to do the same: just by addressing audiences – in front of cameras – about her causes.

Naturally, her American agents and lawyers were encouraging. For years they had struggled to land parts for her. Now they believed she could earn millions from her activism. Of course, she would need an American base and a Foundation to deposit the proceeds. There was even, she was told, an American billionairess who might provide the start-up sponsorship. Her advisors neither understood that their strategy was incompatible with the monarchy, nor did they care. In their uncluttered scenario, Meghan would earn millions and they would reap commission.

On 23rd October, one week into the tour, the die was cast. Harry and Meghan had convinced themselves that William was jealous of their success in Australia. The time was right for 'change'.[491] They needed to break out of Kensington Palace's claustrophobic fishbowl. Harry proposed that the Palace should rewrite the rule-book. Rather than Meghan being a dutiful member of the supporting cast she should star as a campaigner, independent of the Cambridges and even of the Queen.

Meghan watched Harry seek to finalise their agreement with London to create a separate court and administration. In that fundamental change, Harry and Meghan would no longer work with the Royal Foundation but operate a separate charity, Sussex Royal. Both were pledging to promote social well-being, to make the world a better place.[492] They also agreed that, before the birth of their child, Jason Knauf should be replaced.[493]

Jessica Mulroney was an eyewitness as Meghan balanced the stress of the tour, the news from London about the staff's complaints, and the discussions with her business advisor Andrew Meyer about re-establishing her presence in Los Angeles. That day, Meyer registered two foundations – the archefoundation.com and archefoundation .org. Five days later he registered @archefoundation on Instagram.

Arche is an ancient Greek term meaning 'beginning' or 'origin'. *Archon* is the Greek for leader. Her Los Angeles advisors, misunderstanding that as Harry's wife Meghan was not seeking approval on a stage but seeking respect, encouraged her to behave like a celebrity actress rather than as a royal.

Meghan's talent was to conceal the dramas. At the end of the Invictus Games she made a compassionate speech praising the competitors for stealing the show and her heart. Using her theatrical skill, her references to humanity and motherhood touched even the veteran royal photographer Arthur Edwards. 'I have been smitten with Meghan,' he wrote. 'She was absolutely brilliant.'[494]

The mood slightly changed after the couple arrived in Fiji. By any reckoning the brief stop on their way to New Zealand should have been uneventful. Just as in Australia, Meghan had requested to speak to groups of women and students. Unlike previous meetings, her address at the University of the South Pacific was reported. To her audience, her personally written speech was unexceptional: 'I am also fully aware of the challenges of being able to afford this level of schooling for many people around the world, myself included. It was with scholarships, financial aid programmes, and work study from my earnings from a job on campus that went directly towards my tuition that I was able to attend university, and without question it was worth every effort.'

In Rosarito, Thomas Markle exploded. 'I'm sorry but that is completely untrue,' he told the media. 'I paid every penny of her tuition and I have the bank statements to prove it. I told Meg I would pay for her education and I did. It's what any father would do. I paid for her trips to Spain and England. I paid for her internship in Argentina.' He had continued, he said, to pay off the loans, even after Meghan was earning a good income from *Suits*. He was furious that she claimed to have sent him money. 'I've never taken a penny from Meghan,' he mistakenly retorted.[495] In fact Meghan had given him at least $20,000.

Unaware of her father's latest outburst Meghan, wearing a £1,494 Figue printed silk dress, headed to a bustling Fijian street market for a 15-minute stop. About one thousand people, mostly women traders organised in 'Markets for Change', were waiting. Within minutes Meghan was unhappy. Many of the locals were wearing T-shirts emblazoned with the slogan 'UN Women'. She had been brought to a project sponsored by her old organisation. Unforgiving that Elizabeth Nyamayaro had refused to promote her to be an ambassador, Meghan berated Amy Pickerill for arranging the visit. Pickerill retreated to the official car where she was later seen, according to the *Daily Mail*'s Rebecca English, 'with tears running down her face. Our eyes met and she lowered hers, humiliation etched on her features.'[496]

Eight minutes after arriving, Meghan declared she was leaving. Meghan's spokesman explained that in the humidity, the unexpectedly large crowd was oppressive and threatened Meghan's 'security'. Hundreds of women expressed their disappointment. By the time the entourage returned to their hotel, the female Metropolitan police protection officer had decided to resign on her return to Britain.

The staff's unhappiness was transmitted to Jason Knauf in London. Amid talk of humiliated officials weeping in a febrile atmosphere, Knauf finally sent the complaint to Simon Case, William's private secretary. In summary, Case read that Meghan had bullied two assistants and shattered the confidence of a third, prompting all three to leave Kensington Palace.

The private secretary forwarded the memo to Samantha Carruthers, the head of human resources at Clarence House. After reading it, Carruthers appears to have done nothing formal. (Carruthers later worked for Elizabeth Murdoch.) Two years later, the Sussexes' lawyers denied all the allegations and claimed that the staff resigned amid allegations of their own misconduct.[497] Harry's relations with Knauf were fractured.

Showing no hint of the furore, Meghan smiled broadly during

her entrance to her first state dinner at Fiji's Grand Pacific hotel. Shimmering in a light-blue gingko cape dress, everyone was struck by her glittering Chopard diamond pendant earrings. Asked about the provenance of the amazing jewels, her spokesman said they had been 'borrowed', without stating from whom. The spokesman avoided giving the full explanation. They were a wedding present from Crown Prince Mohammed bin Salman of Saudi Arabia. Meghan had ignored her staff's warnings that wearing the jewels would be controversial. Three weeks earlier, the prince had approved the murder in Istanbul of the Saudi journalist Jamal Khashoggi.[498]

Meghan should have been shocked by the murder. Ever since meeting Loujain al-Hathloul, a Saudi activist, at the One Young World humanitarian summit in Ottawa in October 2016, she'd known about the regime's cruelty. In her speech at the conference, Meghan acknowledged Loujain's protests against 'human rights violations' and 'gender equality issues, discrimination and injustice' in Saudi Arabia. Since that conference, Loujain had been jailed, tortured and threatened with rape and death. Despite that link, Meghan would wear the earrings again on 14th November, 2018, for Charles's 70th birthday party at Buckingham Palace. Meghan later claimed to have been 'unaware' at the time of the global outrage about the prominent media reports the prince had ordered the murder.[499] Her lawyers denied to *The Times* that she had misled anyone about the provenance of the earrings.[500]

On 1st November, Harry and Meghan returned to London convinced they were 'royal rock stars' empowered to change the Royal Family. 'It was the first time,' said Harry excitedly, 'that the family got to see how incredible she is at the job. And that brought back memories.'[501] Not only his brother but all the courtiers, Harry believed, were dismissing Meghan just as they had shunned Diana. 'I just wish that we would all learn from the past,' he said.

Harry and Meghan were convinced, Omid Scobie reported,

that they had 'propelled the monarchy to new heights around the world'. Indeed, many women hailed Meghan as a symbol of modern womanhood, or as some said, the poster girl of aspiration. Utterly self-assured, she presented herself as a model for the new era. The problem was that Brand Markle was unacceptable to the Palace. As Scobie reported, the courtiers would 'rein them in' because they feared that Meghan 'might be bigger than Diana'.[502]

Soon after their return, Harry asked the Queen's permission to leave Nottingham Cottage and establish their lives beyond Buckingham Palace's control. To accommodate her grandson, the Queen agreed that the couple should be allocated the Frogmore cottages on the Windsor estate. Although it was hard to believe that Meghan wanted to live 25 miles from London and under the Heathrow flight-path, builders were contracted to rapidly convert the five dilapidated units into a luxury five-bedroom house.

But the line was drawn. Harry's request for his own office or court to build the Sussex brand of philanthropy and humanitarianism, separate from Buckingham Palace but financed by the Queen and the taxpayer, was rejected. On the Queen's orders, he was told that he would be allocated a small office inside Buckingham Palace – and under the Queen's supervision. While William had his own organisation, Harry was sidelined. The decision was supported by Charles.

Helping the second born, as previous 'spares' including Princess Margaret and Prince Andrew had discovered, was beyond the Palace's skills. Harry interpreted the Palace's decision to deny Meghan her independence as a blow to his own demand for freedom. Always on the edge, Harry's simmering anger was reignited.

Human nature dictated that the cracks in Kensington Palace could not be concealed. The brothers' arguments, the memorandum about Meghan's alleged bullying, Kate and Meghan's mutual dislike, and the niggling suspicion that Meghan was planning to return to Los Angeles prompted committed royalists to whisper secrets to their friends. The iron curtain imposed by uncompromising non-disclosure contracts on courtiers was breached on 10th November.

The first media report revealed the 'sudden' departure of 'Melissa' from the Sussexes' staff. Her surname, Touabti, was still unknown. It was, reported the *Daily Mail*'s Richard Eden, a 'real shock' for someone involved in the wedding preparations.[503] One week later, the *Mirror* added that Meghan had reduced Melissa to tears. Meghan asked the Palace spokesman to deny the allegation.[504]

On the same day, the *Sun*'s Dan Wootton reported 'Tiaragate'. Describing the 'temper tantrums', Palace 'insiders' mentioned that 'there was a very heated exchange that had prompted the Queen to speak to Harry. She said, "Meghan cannot have whatever she wants. She gets what tiara she's given by me."' The Queen also questioned why Meghan needed a veil for the wedding, given it was to be her second marriage.

More importantly, the *Sun* reported that Kate 'clashed' with Meghan over her 'rude' treatment of staff. 'That's unacceptable,' Kate had told Meghan.[505] An 'insider' said: 'Meghan is used to working in a Hollywood environment…However, there's a different level of respect in the royal household and Kate has always been very careful about how she has acted around staff.' Kensington Palace refused to comment to the *Sun*.[506]

The third revelation was reported by royal correspondent Robert Jobson. At the height of 'Tiaragate', he wrote, Harry was petulant and ill-tempered with Palace staff and even 'downright rude' and had shouted, 'What Meghan wants, Meghan gets.' The Queen, Jobson wrote, 'asked to see [Harry] privately and put him firmly in his place.'[507] Jobson blamed Meghan's original choice of the Vladimir tiara – set with emeralds or pearls and pendant emeralds and smuggled out of Russia after the revolution and sold to Queen Mary – for the dispute. The tiara's provenance, he suggested, made its public display sensitive. (However, that detail was undermined by photographs of the Queen wearing the same tiara at a Windsor Castle banquet in 2014.) Clearly, there had been an argument, but the reason remained ambiguous.

Harry and Meghan were incensed by the wave of media allegations.[508] Reports of their high staff turnover, they complained, were unfair – although Samantha Cohen had just disclosed that she too was planning to leave. Leaks about Meghan's 5am emails convinced them that her staff were disloyal. Everything she requested was referred to Buckingham Palace, filtered and invariably altered. She was, she complained, denied control over her own life. Harry was sympathetic. The media vultures, he believed, were to blame for everything. He and Meghan were innocent and the media were lying. Worse, Knauf was failing to turn negative headlines into positive ones. The newspaper headline 'Duchess Difficult' opened the floodgates.

In the *Daily Telegraph*, Camilla Tominey reported that Kate had burst into tears during the pre-wedding argument with Meghan about the bridesmaids' clothes – about wearing tights and the length of Charlotte's hem.[509] In the *Sun*, Dan Wootton described Kate's anger about Meghan's treatment of her staff and the breakdown of Harry and William's relationship.[510] William, the newspaper accurately reported, had – in the months before the wedding – advised Harry to consider his relationship with Meghan carefully. In addition, he was unhappy about the Sussexes' refusal to go to Balmoral with the Cambridges.[511]

To balance the anti-Sussexes reports, the *Sun*'s columnist Lorraine Kelly hit back, praising Meghan: 'Cut her some slack…Meghan has done incredibly well to tiptoe through the minefield of royal protocol… She's a fantastic addition to the Royal Family – approachable, sweet and with a genuine desire to make a real difference.'

Meghan would call the critical media reports the 'beginning of real character assassination'. She was particularly upset that Knauf 'refused to set the record straight' by promoting her point of view to disparage Kate. 'I think that's where everything changed,' Meghan later said.[512] She would give Omid Scobie an email that recorded she 'urgently requested' an official denial of an 'offensive' report in *The Times* that she had had made Kate cry. Meghan's request, Scobie wrote, was 'ignored'.[513]

Contrary to Meghan's orders, the Palace insisted that Harry and William were 'close'. As evidence that the Sussexes and Cambridges had not 'fallen out', an official briefed that the two families would spend Christmas together at Sandringham.[514]

Meghan hit back. In November 2018, she told Knauf and the Palace's communications staff that her friends were co-operating with Omid Scobie to write a book setting out Harry's and her lives and problems.[515] The background to that decision would challenge Harry's and Meghan's veracity.

During the summer of 2018, Kensington Palace had been approached to help Scobie and Carolyn Durand write a book called *Finding Freedom*. Their book, the authors promised, would be wholly favourable to the Sussexes. Knauf knew that Meghan would be interested. 'My view is that this is a very good idea,' Knauf texted Meghan. Knauf's opinion suited Meghan's agenda. She wanted the book to focus on the sacrifices she had made when she became a duchess. While supportive, Knauf advised against asking or authorising Meghan's friends to co-operate with the authors. There was a risk, warned Knauf, that the authors' opinion about the Sussexes might 'change'. Meghan disagreed. Scobie, she sensed, could be turned into a loyalist. 'I feel he needs to be back-briefed ASAP,' she replied about Scobie.'[516]

On 12th November, Meghan discussed the book again with Knauf.[517] She wanted to read 'Omid's outline'.[518] She was also worried by Doria's concern about what Meghan called 'these egregious paps'. Her mother felt unsafe.

Unaware of the book project, Prince Charles remained troubled by the upsurge of media reports about the strife within the Palace. To ensure his smooth succession to the throne, he wanted nothing to undermine the image of the House of Windsor as peaceful and unified. He understood the repeated criticism that Diana had suffered by being ignored. Now he was anxious that Meghan's unhappiness risked similar accusations. Just as he was seeking to boost the monarchy's prestige, he feared a monumental argument involving the Sussexes.

However, Prince Charles's own past behaviour undermined his plans. His admission of adultery to Jonathan Dimbleby during a TV interview in 1994 had damaged Charles. Rehabilitation had taken years and was still not complete. In recent media interviews he had enthused about Harry's energy, mentioned his pride escorting Meghan down the aisle, and vowed to stop campaigning about his passionate causes. 'I wasn't meddling. I always thought I was motivating,' he said. 'I won't meddle when I'm king.'[519] To help her son, the Queen's toast to 300 guests at his seventieth birthday dinner included praise for his wife. 'Most of all,' said his mother, 'sustained by his wife Camilla, he is his own man, passionate and creative.'

The Queen had moved a long distance since her son's wedding reception in 2005. After Charles's unglamorous ceremony at the Windsor register office, which she did not attend, the Queen had been reluctant to join the party in the castle. She was glued to the television in a side-room watching the Grand National horse-race. Eventually she emerged to make a short speech referring to Charles in the 'winner's enclosure'. After pausing briefly for photographs, she had left the party quickly.[520]

Over the following decade, opinion polls were harsh about Camilla's status. On Diana's anniversaries, Camilla's approval ratings sank and Charles's followed. Now, in the inevitably brief time available, Charles was determined not only to bury the past but build bridges with his eldest son. William's support was necessary, he believed, for Camilla to be crowned queen. Securing his sympathy went in parallel with the effort to craft William and Kate's image as a hard-working family embracing Britain's best values.

With some persuasion, William and Kate agreed to move back to London from Norfolk to undertake more royal duties. Yet Harry was going in the opposite direction. Getting the two brothers to smile together for Charles's seventieth birthday family photograph had not been easy for Kate. Thankfully, William agreed that Camilla could be included in the photograph alongside his children.[521]

The happy portrait could not deceive the public. The dam had broken. Publicity about the rift between the Sussexes and Cambridges combined with Thomas Markle's denunciation of his daughter had destroyed the blissful images recorded on Meghan's wedding day only six months earlier.

CHAPTER 25

Suicide

Meghan spotted an opportunity after Michelle Obama arrived in London to promote her bestselling autobiography. Having secured tickets to hear the former First Lady make her inspirational speech in the Royal Festival Hall on 3rd December, 2018, she went backstage afterwards to meet her hero.

Determined to fashion a special relationship, Meghan had also arranged that they would meet again for dinner at George Clooney's house near Windsor.[522] As an idol to be emulated, Michelle Obama was also a good source of advice and consolation for Meghan. However, the Duchess appears not to have appreciated how much the Obamas admired the Queen. Meghan's attitude alarmed Michelle. Her advice to Meghan was delivered in public.

'Take some time,' Obama said in an interview, 'and don't be in a hurry to do anything.' In a warning note, she added: 'Like me, Meghan probably never dreamt she'd have a life like this; no-deal, the pressure you feel can sometimes feel like a lot.' Meghan, Obama suggested, should be reasonable: 'What I'd say is that there's so much opportunity to do good with a platform like that and I think Meghan can maximise her impact for others, as well her own happiness, if she's doing something that resonates with her personally.'[523]

Within Kensington Palace, Meghan was still struggling to settle in. Purposefully, she had isolated herself from many former friends, including Gina Torres and other *Suits* actors.[524] One exception was John Fitzpatrick. 'I was amazed to see the difference in Meghan,' he recalled after a visit to the Palace. White-gloved footmen stood with the hotelier while he waited for her arrival. 'Meghan came in and her greeting was very formal.' Once the staff left, Fitzpatrick asked, 'How long have we got?' Looking at her watch, Meghan replied, 'We've got exactly twenty-nine minutes.' According to Fitzpatrick, 'she relaxed and the gossip began. At the end of the allotted time, the staff returned and Meghan's formal look came on again.'[525]

American girlfriends visiting Meghan in Kensington Palace found a troubled woman. Cooped up in Nottingham Cottage she complained that there were no staff to prepare meals – no one treated her as royal. Looking miserable, she mentioned being the 'most trolled person in the world'. People in the media were telling lies about her. 'It was so damaging to her mental and emotional health,' one friend concluded.[526] One cause of the difficulties was her reluctance to take on traditional royal duties.

By early December 2018, Meghan had completed only eight royal engagements since the summer. That included Trooping the Colour and the Remembrance Day service. Damaging stories appeared in the newspapers. The *Sun* offered the revelation that Meghan had been 'very excited' at her Jamaican wedding that each guest had received a gift-bag with five spliffs of cannabis.

That evening she made a surprise appearance at the British Fashion Awards at the Royal Albert Hall.[527] Wearing an off-the-shoulder black Givenchy gown with matching black-painted fingernails, Meghan told her audience, 'It is such an honour to be here celebrating British fashion and British fashion designers in my new home of the UK.' Some wondered why Meghan could not, for once, have compromised and worn a British-designed dress. Soon after the event, Meghan's photo on the British Fashion Council's Instagram site was deleted. On the same evening, Princess Anne visited the International Maritime Organisation's safety committee and the Queen celebrated the 600th anniversary of the Bar Association.

The revelations sparked Meghan's customary outrage about the media and Knauf's failure to suppress the embarrassment. In the midst of that argument Thomas Markle gave another interview. 'The treatment of me is harsh, hurtful and unforgiving,' he said. 'I'm being punished for things I didn't say.'[528]

Meghan's letter had failed to stop him speaking. Fuelling the flames, he also published a letter he had sent to Doria five days after the Duchess's speech in Fiji. 'Meghan,' he wrote, 'is saying she wants nothing to do with me and she worked her way through college all by herself. She cannot change history. I'm sick of the lies. I'm sick of being vilified and shut out of their lives. I always upheld my responsibilities as a father. Meghan's comments about paying her way through college are offensive to me.' Upset that his provocation had not encouraged his daughter to call him, Thomas Markle appealed days later on TV for Meghan to put aside their 'differences' in time for Christmas. 'I love my daughter very much…and I would really appreciate it if she would call me.'[529]

Thomas's outburst tipped the balance for the Sussexes. Meghan and Harry were exasperated. They agreed to co-operate with Omid Scobie.[530] As Knauf would later state, 'The book was discussed with the Duchess multiple times in person and over email.'[531] Her only irritation was Scobie's Tweet describing Jessica Mulroney as Meghan's stylist. 'You know,' Meghan told Knauf, 'how personally frustrating I find the "stylist" narrative (as it's the only thing I seem to still have any control over – my personal styling) but given we are being asked to co-operate with this evidently authoritative biography…I will not be comfortable doing so if this person is considered to be an authority.' Meghan was reassured that Scobie would be told the 'truth'. In an email to Meghan and Harry, Knauf opened himself up to subterfuge: 'Being able to say hand on heart that we did not facilitate access will be important.'[532]

Knauf's decision to trust Scobie was against his instincts and antagonism towards the tabloids. Inconsistently, with one breath he criticised *Vanity Fair* as 'tabloid-y', and on the other he trusted Scobie who recycled tabloid stories, even those which were patently inaccurate.[533] While planning a two-hour briefing for Scobie and Durand, Knauf was encouraged by Harry to be especially helpful. After two years of 'media onslaught, cyber bullying, puppeteering Thomas Markle, etc etc..,' Harry asked Knauf to cast Meghan in a positive light.

Early on 10th December, Knauf sent Meghan a list of questions that Scobie had submitted for their meeting two days later. Once again, Knauf reiterated the need for deniability. 'I think it is important,' he wrote to Harry, 'that we can say hand on heart they [Scobie and Durand] had no access' to Meghan's friends and the Palace.

Although Knauf advised against helping Scobie to meet Meghan's friends, he added: 'I am happy to facilitate either way.' Despite this, Harry agreed with Knauf: 'I totally agree that we have to be able to say we didn't have anything to do with it [the book].'[534] For Harry to encourage Knauf was noteworthy. So was Harry encouraging Knauf's co-operation: 'Equally, you giving the right context and background to them would help get some truths out there. The truth is very much needed and would be appreciated, especially around Markle/wedding stuff.' While he and Meghan criticised Thomas Markle for speaking to the media, they were doing precisely the same.

Determined to manage the narrative of the meeting to her advantage, that evening Meghan sent Knauf a 31-point briefing for his conversation with the authors. Amongst her priorities, listed over two pages, was a revised biography of her childhood.

Three years earlier, she had written in *Elle* magazine that her parents 'crafted the world around me to make me feel like I wasn't different, but special'.[535] She repeated the same version to *Vanity Fair* in 2017: 'What's so incredible, you know, is that my parents split up when I was two but I never saw them fight. We would still take vacations together. My dad would come on Sundays to drop me off, and we'd watch *Jeopardy!* eating dinner on TV trays, the three of us…We were still so close-knit.'536 But for Knauf she ignored the close relationship with her father and emphasised that she was 'very estranged' from her father's two other children: 'She [Meghan] was always referred to as an only child by both of her parents, and all of her friends through her entire upbringing, because the half-siblings were not in the picture (by their own choice).'537

Without explaining that Samantha was crippled in a wheelchair, Meghan wrote, 'She had lost custody of all three of her children from different fathers.' Meghan also asked Knauf to say about Thomas Markle, 'Meghan supported her father in spite of his reclusiveness. Despite countless efforts to support him through the last two years, they now no longer have a relationship.'

Meghan's version of 'Tiaragate' was that the Queen was present with Harry as she tried on five different tiaras. 'The Queen said they all suited her.' After choosing the 'diamond one', the Queen said it was 'perfect'. She also re-emphasised that Jessica Mulroney was not her stylist.538

'Are u planning on giving them a rough idea of what she's been through over the last 2 yrs?' Harry texted Knauf. 'If you aren't planning on telling them, can I?!'

'Of course – I've never stopped,' Knauf replied that night.

After sending Meghan further reassurances, Knauf met the authors on 12th December, 2018. 'I took them through everything,' he reported the next day. They had been briefed just as Meghan and Harry required. The book, said Knauf, would be targeted at an American audience. The authors, he assured Meghan, intended to 'position it as a celebration of you that corrects the record on a number of fronts. I will stay in close contact with them.' Later he added, 'It's going to be very positive.' Meghan was satisfied. Knauf had bent over backwards to help her. The Palace was in overdrive to protect her.

Two years later, Meghan would exhaustively claim that neither she nor Harry had 'co-operated with the authors to put out their "version of events" by means of the book.'[539] In a signed legal statement, Meghan added that neither she nor Harry had 'wished to be involved in any way with the book'.[540] Prior to his meeting with Scobie, she added, Knauf 'did not contact' Meghan about 'any matters relating to the book.'[541]

Knowing that the media would be watching her performance at Buckingham Palace's Christmas lunch and the Royal Family's celebrations, Meghan was persuaded to be on show with the Sandringham royal party on Christmas Day. Smiling and apparently chatting, the Fab Four walked together the half mile to St Mary Magdalene Church. To neutralise the damaging stories about bridesmaids and the move to Frogmore, Meghan agreed to join Harry for the Boxing Day shoot lunch.

Over 5,000 miles away in Mexico, Thomas Markle was spending Christmas alone. Grateful for the call from a British journalist, he poured out his anger that his beloved daughter had been dubbed 'Duchess Difficult'. She was, he said, just a pretty girl married to a former army officer who would never be king. 'It's ridiculous, cruel and heartless, and unless she proves me wrong by going around at night urinating on homeless people it needs to stop.'

Now aged 74, Thomas had convinced himself that within five years he would be dead. Markle men, he asserted, never made it to 80. 'To this day,' he concluded, 'I cannot think of anything I've done to deserve how I'm being treated now. I've been a good father, I've done nothing wrong. Axe murderers kill 19 people, and their daughters still come and visit them in prison. Now it's like a dream that has turned into a nightmare. The royals and Meghan can help end it by simply giving me a call.'[542]

Once again, Meghan was embarrassed by her failure to prevent Thomas broadcasting his wrath across the globe. She was also distressed by Frogmore's reconstruction. Despite spending £2.65 million to rebuild a five-bedroom house, she was dissatisfied. Dealing with the architects, designers, builders, and even the curator from Buckingham Palace responsible for the Queen's paintings had not produced the results she expected.

Friends and other clients heard from the contractors about Meghan's manner. Her constantly changing demands, said one contractor, seemed to be born from her assumption that a duchess was expected to behave like Marie Antoinette. Inevitably, their stories reached the media. Some were exaggerated, others were untrue, but the mention that the nursery would be painted with the Auro range from the Organic and Natural Paint Company exposed Meghan to ridicule in the tabloids.[543]

As the house neared completion, the contractors gained the impression that Meghan was unhappy. The new building, she appeared to suggest, was good enough for the staff but where was the Duchess's palace? Frogmore's kitchen was small, the living-room was cramped and there was no view of the ocean. On top of that, life under the flight-path to Heathrow was horrendous. Her dissatisfaction came to a head when she unfavourably compared Frogmore not only to the £4.5 million William and Kate had spent renovating their Kensington Palace apartment, but to the Californian mansions inhabited by Hollywood's celebrities.

The combination of the 'horrors' of Frogmore and the Queen's refusal to allow Meghan and Harry an independent court confirmed to Meghan that no one appreciated her. She also began to understand that the British monarchy, costing the public just £85 million a year, was neither flush with money nor an invincible luxury Rolls-Royce machine. The power and influence which she assumed to have acquired from her marriage to Harry was an illusion.

Harry's paranoia added to her sense of vulnerability. Gripped by fear of a random attack, they were both appalled by the prospect that members of the public could walk through Windsor Great Park, a short distance from their house. Media photographers, they realised, could breach their privacy because of the absence of 'a much-needed ring of steel'.[544] To satisfy Harry's demand for protection, the public were ordered not to approach Meghan or her dogs in Windsor Park.[545] The announcement did not win the Sussexes popular approval.

Once more, Meghan and Harry blamed Knauf and his deputy, Christian Jones. They had failed to halt the stream of negative media reports. Knauf replied that his staff were constantly working. Daily, they deleted abusive messages on social media websites posted by frenzied online trolls. Some supported Kate against Meghan. The worst messages, they suspected, were generated by an orchestrated campaign in Russia.[546]

Harry and Meghan were not convinced. Seizing on the criminal conviction of one student for calling Harry a 'race traitor' on social media, both accused tabloid newspapers of arousing racism. 'From the beginning of our relationship,' Meghan later complained, 'they were so attacking and inciting so much racism really.'[547] Hyper-sensitive to even reasoned criticism, both believed that Knauf was ordered by Buckingham Palace not to respond to 'a monster machine around us in terms of clickbait and tabloid fodder' because officials feared annoying the media. Buckingham Palace, said Harry, was 'scared of the tabloids turning on them'.

Yet again, Meghan pleaded that she was 'undefended by the institution' and 'prohibited from defending herself' against false stories.[548] Neither recalled Meghan's answer during her BBC engagement interview that she ignored the media. 'I made the choice not to read anything negative or positive,' she had told the world. Both knew that was not true. She couldn't resist reading the media. For over 30 years she had longed for fame, but now she was experiencing the consequences of what she called 'death by a thousand cuts'.[549]

Patrick Jephson, Diana's private secretary, partly endorsed the couple's grievance. He blamed the Palace's 'deep-rooted complacency, conceit and confusion' for not responding to Meghan's complaints. 'It has a fatal capacity for moral inertia when one of the big names is in trouble,' he would write. Just as Diana was 'cast adrift', continued Jephson, and Prince Andrew was not saved by the 'Palace elite', Meghan was let down by Knauf and the Palace's media staff. Jephson described the Palace's old-fashioned attitude towards relations with the media and its belief that the monarchy would survive regardless. Knauf and his superiors were unwilling to shape a strong narrative to suit Meghan. Jephson's opinion was partly contradicted by Knauf's efforts to help Omid Scobie, and by Knauf's willingness to deny it.

Often awake during the night, Meghan and Harry classed themselves as persecuted outsiders. 'I just didn't see a solution,' said Meghan.[550] Eventually, she decided, 'I just didn't want to be alive anymore.'[551] Harry would later say that Meghan had told him about her 'suicidal thoughts and the practicalities of how she was going to end her life.' [552] Suicidal feelings are usually the product of a profound psychological disorder, but Harry insisted that his wife, while she recited her thoughts, was 'completely sane' and 'absolutely sober'.

Meghan's reason for contemplating suicide was the critical media. 'I'm somewhat ashamed,' admitted Harry, 'of the way that I dealt with it.' He had good reason to feel remorse. Despite his expertise on mental health he did little to summon specialist help for his wife. He would accuse his family of 'neglect' but he also offered contradictory versions. In one, he did not tell them about Meghan's crisis. But in another version, Harry said that ever since Meghan had begun suffering suicidal thoughts he had discussed with his family the idea of leaving Britain. The conversations about the possibility of living in another country, revealed Harry, continued for over a year.[553]

The seriousness of Meghan's plight was dramatically revealed on 16th January, 2019. That evening, the Sussexes were the star guests at the Royal Albert Hall to see Cirque du Soleil. Although both smiled broadly as they arrived – and she looked as glamorous as ever – Meghan would later claim that she could only overcome the previous night's suicidal thoughts by holding Harry's hand particularly tight. Once the lights went down, she said, 'I was just weeping, and he was gripping my hand.'[554] She begged Harry not to leave her alone.

Although six months pregnant, said Meghan, she had not wanted to live. She said she had sought medical help from 'one of the most senior people' in the Palace. But, said Meghan, that help was denied by a woman employed in human resources with the explanation, 'It would not be good for the institution.'[555] 'My heart goes out to you,' the woman allegedly said, 'because I see how bad it is, but there is nothing we can do to protect you, because you're not a paid employee of the institution.'

After that snub, Meghan explained, 'I just didn't want to be alive anymore…and that was a very clear and real and frightening constant thought. And I remember how he [Harry] just cradled me.' She could not go to a doctor or a hospital, she explained later, because 'they' had taken 'my passport, my driver's licence, my keys.' She was 'trapped'.[556]

'The thing that stopped her from seeing it through,' added Harry, 'was how unfair it would be on me after everything that happened to my mum and to now be put in a position of losing another woman in my life, with a baby inside of her, our baby.'[557]

Verifying those events is difficult. Pertinently, Harry and Meghan gave conflicting accounts of the saga. In public they disagreed whether Meghan felt suicidal at night, in the morning or both. And they did not agree on the number of days. Neither explained why Meghan sought help from an unqualified Palace official rather than an experienced medical specialist. Harry never identified which member of his family had 'neglected' his wife.

Meghan's instability traumatised Harry. After sacrificing so much to marry into the Royal Family, she told him, she had become an unprotected target. Harry felt guilty for failing to shield her from the conspirators. He struggled to find a solution.

CHAPTER 26

Exposure

Meghan confided her misery to girlfriends in America. During their conversations, Meghan disclosed that her father had ignored her plea to cease his attacks. Her letter, she said, had reminded him of the extraordinary kindness she had shown towards him before and after the wedding. She mentioned her 'care for her father, her long history of looking after her father's welfare and trying to find solutions to his health problems'.[558] She also lambasted her father's refusal to come to the wedding. Above all, she felt 'abandoned' by the very Palace officials assigned to protect her.

At the same time, she consulted two publicists – Isabel May, a personal friend in London who she had met through Markus Anderson, and Keleigh Thomas Morgan, her Los Angeles publicity advisor. May denies giving Meghan any professional advice, but Thomas Morgan was sympathetic to Meghan's complaint. Persuaded that Meghan was regarded as an important part of the monarchy's future, Thomas Morgan was concerned that Meghan was not accorded the proper support. Thomas Morgan gave the impression that a high-powered publicist could close down the negative stories and simultaneously drive a totally positive story enhancing Meghan. She encouraged Meghan to fight back.

Over the Christmas holidays, Meghan's friends were dismayed to hear that the publication of Omid Scobie's book was delayed. They had agreed to be interviewed by Scobie to help broadcast Meghan's problems across the world. Now they believed it was urgent to find another platform to describe Meghan's plight.

One of the women was a personal friend of Dan Wakeford, the editor of *People* magazine, one of America's biggest circulation publications. After setting out her proposition to Wakeford he agreed to publish a profile of Meghan on the basis of interviews with five of her close friends. Lindsay Roth, Meghan's friend from Northwestern, was one of the magazine's principal sources.

Meghan would later insist that the article was initiated and researched without her knowledge. Meghan, her lawyers would plead, 'did not know that her friends were giving an interview to *People* magazine.'[559] Others believed that nothing would have been done by her five friends without at least one of them telling Meghan of their plan. After all, one of the key ingredients of the magazine's feature was Meghan's letter to her father. She would later deny using the letter as part of a calculated media strategy, or that her friends had even quoted her letter.[560] Others suspected that, without telling anyone at the Palace, she knew that her friends would outline its contents, which she had described in telephone conversations, to *People* magazine.

On the eve of publication, Meghan appeared to be emboldened. Visiting the One25 charity for marginalised women in Bristol, she wrote with a felt-tip pen on bananas 'You are strong', 'You are loved' and 'You are special'. Some were surprised by her sentiments. The media ridiculed her. She was infuriated. The criticism, she asserted, was clearly racist.[561]

She was similarly provocative during a visit to Manchester University. Many of the staff, she was told by the activist Rachel Cowan, were white and male. 'This is quite a shock to see and clearly we have some way to go,' Meghan replied.[562] Once again, observers were puzzled. After nearly three years as part of the Royal Family,

Meghan was breaching the golden rule of impartiality. Moreover, those two visits, meeting six groups for two hours, plus seeing two theatre shows in London and seven other outings was the total of her official duties in the first seven weeks of the year. In those weeks, critical officials compared to Meghan's 11 appearances to Princess Anne's 25 full days.

The question was: Did Meghan intend to play her part as a young royal, fulfilling her duties? Or was public recognition and celebrity more important? The question was answered on 6th February, 2019, by the publication of *People* magazine. Under the cover's headline 'Her best friends break their silence', the sub-heading was 'The truth about Meghan'. More telling was the headline 'Meghan's Media Fightback'. Meghan, the magazine implied, had authorised her friends to brief the magazine.

The article's substance was a flattering profile of a loving daughter living a frugal life in Kensington Palace who, despite being publicly maligned by a dreadful father, had sought heartfelt reconciliation. The breakdown in their relationship, Meghan's friends claimed, was entirely Thomas Markle's fault. The published article gave the impression that Meghan had informed at least one friend about the contents of her letter to Thomas Markle, and his reply to her. Summarising excerpts of Meghan's letter to Thomas, *People* magazine described the letter as a loving offer of reconciliation written days after the wedding. In fact, Meghan wrote it three months later. Contrary to what she would later claim, the magazine had put 'the contents of the letter into the public domain'.[563]

Meghan would emphatically deny being aware that the five had given interviews to the magazine or that the letters would be quoted.[564] She would also claim to have become aware of the magazine's publication only after Harry told her; and that Harry only heard on the day of publication from Kensington Palace's media team.[565]

Written by Michelle Tauber, the article described how Meghan had authorised five friends 'who know Meghan best [to] set the record straight'. The five women – described as 'a long-time friend, a former co-star, a friend from Los Angeles, a one-time colleague and a close confidante' – painted an image of Meghan's 'elegance, grace, philanthropy'. Rejecting the portrayal of Meghan as a 'demanding bride, an exhausting boss and an uncaring daughter', the magazine quoted one friend's eulogy: 'She is a diamond doing her duty'. The evidence was Meghan's purchase of 'an incredible ice-cream and sorbet stand' for her Kensington Palace staff. That, testified the friend, evoked 'heartfelt cheers for the best day of work ever'.

Portraying Meghan as an unselfish woman, living modestly, another friend described Meghan as lonely, frustrated and denied any staff in Nottingham Cottage. Nevertheless, she provided hand-warmers for the police guarding the palace gates, painted her nails while sitting next to a heater and was happy to rustle up a 'five-star meal out of the garbage in your refrigerator'.

'She's very self-service,' said a friend, describing an undemanding duchess with a 'close relationship with God' and 'a deep sense of gratitude and humility'. Sensationalising her 5am emails, the friend said, was a 'misreading' of her 'organised, diligent, focused and hard-working' nature.

Similarly, the staff turnover was 'all natural courses of employment'. Insensitive to the implication of Harry's incompetence, the friends said that Meghan helped him write his speeches. Finally, the friends dismissed the stories about the tiara and fragrance in the chapel as '100 per cent untrue'; and said there was 'nothing behind the feud with Kate'.

The five friends' significant contribution was their description of Meghan's relationship with her father. They claimed that it was 'false' to suggest that Meghan had 'shut' Thomas out. On the contrary, her letter had sought to 'repair our relationship'. The blame for not speaking or texting since the wedding fell entirely on Thomas Markle.

The magazine reported that Meghan had written, 'Dad I'm so heartbroken. I love you. I have one father. Please stop victimising me through the media so we can repair our relationship.' Their purpose, the friends told the magazine, was to 'tackle the lies', the 'emotional trauma' and expose the 'global bullying' inflicted upon a 'pregnant' person who 'loves her animals [and] loves her friends'.

Focusing on Thomas Markle, one friend said he had ignored over 20 telephone calls and texts before the wedding from Meghan: 'He knows how to get in touch with her. Her telephone number hasn't changed. He's never called; he's never texted. I think she will always feel genuinely devastated by what he's done.' Meghan, the magazine claimed, was hurt that Thomas refused to get into the car she provided to take him to the airport and had not even told her he was not coming to the wedding.[566] Clearly, the friend, relying on Meghan, did not believe that Thomas Markle had undergone heart surgery or even been ill in hospital.

'It's super-painful,' the friend continued, 'because Meg was always so dutiful. At the same time, because she's a daughter she has a lot of sympathy for him. She took care of her father with such incredible generosity. The fact that this could be flipped around, that she was acting out or not caring for him, is preposterous.' Meghan, that friend continued, had looked after her father financially and had 'been a rock for everyone in her family'. She could no longer tolerate the pain: 'Meg has silently sat back and endured the lies and untruths. We worry about what this is doing to her and the baby.' Thomas Markle was accused by *People* magazine of being an outright liar.

The source of all that information could only have been Meghan. Not least because she repeated the same version of the loving-caring-daughter-cruelly-spurned-by-her-wicked-father to Jason Knauf. The magazine's publication sparked a frenzied farce.

Buckingham Palace was profoundly shocked. The magazine's contents were dynamite. No one could understand Meghan's plan.

Since she was abrasive towards her father, Palace officials asked, how did she intend to treat the Royal Family? The blowback in the palaces surprised Meghan.

Knauf refused Meghan's demand for a fierce denial that she had any involvement. Meghan's claim to be 'upset and surprised' by the article was treated with scepticism.[567] The quotations from her private letter to Thomas Markle could only have come from her. Insisting that he only knew about the article after reading the British newspapers, Knauf's office replied 'no comment' to hundreds of media inquiries. Meghan would later protest about 'shared frustration' regarding Knauf's refusal to comment. That 'left everyone feeling silenced,' she complained.[568] Since neither Kensington Palace nor Buckingham Palace denied that the article was sanctioned by Meghan herself, most people assumed that the five had quoted her actual letter and spoken with her approval. *People* magazine never received a complaint about the breach of Meghan's copyright of her letter.[569]

In Mexico, Thomas Markle was once again fuming. 'The article is a total lie,' he cursed. 'It misrepresented the tone and content of the letter Meg had written.' Her letter had accused him of manufacturing pain, being paranoid, being ridiculed, fabricating stories, of attacking Harry and continually lying.[570]

'I quickly decided I wanted to correct that misrepresentation,' he said.[571] Meghan's letter, he claimed, was 'not an attempt at reconciliation. The letter didn't say she loved me. It showed no concern that I had suffered a heart attack...It actually signalled the end of our relationship. I just wanted to defend myself.'[572] He added, 'Meghan's a liar and very controlling.'[573]

To fight his corner, Thomas Markle showed parts of the two letters to the *Mail on Sunday*. In publishing the extracts, the newspaper justified their breach of Meghan's copyright and privacy by claiming that Thomas Markle was entitled to contradict the magazine's distortions. There was, the newspaper believed, a 'huge and legitimate' public interest in the

Royal Family and Meghan. She enjoyed 'immense privilege and wealth funded in part from public money' and she expected her 'elaborate' handwritten letter to be leaked and published.[574]

In reply, Meghan would claim that publication of her letter was part of the *Mail*'s campaign 'to publish false and derogatory stories' about her. In Los Angeles, Meghan's advisors were convinced that the British media's criticism of Meghan was racist, sexist and snobbish. They encouraged their client to launch a legal action against the newspaper.

Sunshine Sachs and her other publicists began searching for celebrities prepared to defend their client. Meghan suggested George Clooney. The actor was persuaded to enter the fray against the newspaper. Just as Meghan and Harry headed for an official visit to the Natural History Museum, Clooney's fusillade started. In a statement issued by his publicist, he attacked the media for reproducing *People* magazine's article: 'You're taking a letter from a daughter to a father and broadcasting it everywhere. She's getting a raw deal there. It's irresponsible.' Next, he compared Meghan's fate with Diana's. 'Pursued, vilified and chased' like the princess, thundered Clooney, 'it's history repeating itself. We've seen how that ends.'[575]

The American movie star roused the British tabloids' anger. No paparazzi were chasing Meghan and there had been no intrusion into her private life. Not even an unapproved snap of her while pregnant had been published. Clooney, they asserted, had invented his version of events. The *Sun* rolled out their veteran royal photographer, Arthur Edwards, a Diana expert. 'The biggest invasion of Meghan's privacy,' he wrote, 'was triggered by herself and her own family.' Clooney's 'hysterical mischaracterisation,' argued Edwards, missed the point. While Meghan had declared war on the media, she went simultaneously to *People* magazine arguing that she had the right to speak. Her father did not. Moreover, no one had forced Diana to sit without a seatbelt in a car recklessly driven by a drunk.[576]

Clooney was not thanked by many Britons for his intervention.

Yet even the *Sun* was unsure about the public's mood. Many readers still adored Meghan. To please them, the newspaper published Karren Brady's description of Meghan as 'gorgeous…and a positive person doing positive things' who had been appallingly treated by her fame-seeking father.

With Clooney on her side, Meghan persuaded Harry that her methods were right. They should abandon the royal press officers and rely on her Los Angeles publicists. In future, Harry and Meghan would distribute their own unfiltered message through social media.

CHAPTER 27

Baby Shower

Seven and a half months pregnant, Meghan wanted a traditional baby shower. With few friends in London, she would celebrate in America. In the thirty-second week of her pregnancy, she could safely fly to New York for a party. There she could plot her destiny. Her suicidal depression seemed to have disappeared.

Meghan would claim the party was organised and hosted by a university friend for 15 'close friends'.[577] The version in New York was different. After conversations with Oprah Winfrey and others, it was said, Meghan asked Serena Williams's publicists – Jill Smoller, Kelly Bush Novak and Celine Khavarani – to arrange the party. The result bore no resemblance to a traditional shower party to anticipate a child's birth. Rather, it was a launch-pad for a group of friends set on financially exploiting Meghan's status.

The Toronto friends invited were Jess Mulroney, two actresses (Abigail Spencer and Janina Gavankar), plus Meghan's hair-stylists Daniel Martin and Serge Normant and fitness trainer Taryn Toomey. The more important guests were the NBC executive Bonnie Hammer and Oprah Winfrey's close friend Gayle King, an ambitious CBS TV journalist, plus Amal Clooney. Naturally, Meghan's confidante Misha Nonoo was invited. Nonoo had already exploited their friendship by advertising another of her products, the 'Saturday Skirt', with the tag 'Recently Worn By Meghan Markle, Duchess of Sussex'.[578] With Meghan's blessing, other invitees intended to do the same. Celine Khavarani, a publicist, would use the event to promote her clients' fashions; Jess Mulroney hoped to capitalise on her friendship to get an enhanced TV contract; and Serena Williams, who funded the party, would re-advertise her brand citing Meghan's name. The guest-list was Meghan's latest shot at launching her own celebrity in America.

On 15th February, Meghan arrived in New York for five days. She headed for The Mark, promoted as 'NYC's most boldly lavish hotel'. Her suite's daily rate was £15,312. The Mark was one of the city's few luxury hotels that could guarantee full-frontal publicity for every arrival. A side door was practically unusable.

Meghan's dinner on the first night was with Markus Anderson, Jess Mulroney, Serena Williams and Gayle King. Meghan found it therapeutic to be among friends sharing her values in her own country. King was naturally fascinated to hear Meghan's complaints about life in Kensington Palace. Her misery, she described, was akin to survival behind a prison wall. While listing her grievances – just as she had to her five friends quoted by *People* magazine – Meghan's sincere loyalty towards the Royal Family appeared to be slender.

Meghan did not pretend to be modest. Having experienced the tough times she loved extravagance. She had no intention of following the Queen's notable frugality. Nor could she. Like those who financed the baby shower, she was determined to get her money's worth.

Journalists and photographers, briefed by the organisers, were crammed behind specially erected crash-barriers outside the hotel. Wearing an unmissable red jumpsuit and big sunglasses, Amal Clooney clearly wanted to be photographed walking towards the hotel door, possibly to show solidarity with Meghan. Some guests carried large gift-bags. A harp was slowly wheeled in. A trolley of 'Away' suitcases followed.

Everyone headed towards the £57,000-a-night penthouse suite of five bedrooms and two bars. Meghan's guests knew from photos already posted on Instagram that Darcy Miller, the party planner, had prepared a vast excess of food, including four macaroon towers from Ladurée, a Parisian bakery offering the 'elegance that Marie Antoinette would approve of', designer biscuits, cakes, mini-meringue pies on gold-rimmed plates, and an enormous display of flowers.

Less than two hours later, the guests departed. Each guest had been promised the home delivery of an 'Away' suitcase. Certain she would be photographed again, Amal Clooney stepped into her car in front of the hotel. Meghan left the hotel wearing a baseball hat and clothes promoted by Celine Khavarani.

The following day, Misha Nonoo appeared on NBC's *Today* programme to discuss her friend Meghan's passion for her fashion designs. With lightning speed, Meghan's make-up artist Daniel Martin posted pictures of the food, rattles and bibs – and his salon's address. Abigail Spencer promoted her new show called *Rectify*. Janina Gavankar blessed the publicity generated by the baby shower to be cast in a new acting role.

Gayle King, after appearing on CBS to plug her intimacy with Meghan during the shower party, successfully lobbied for a new lucrative contract. King's promotion owed much to Oprah Winfrey. 'Both of us,' said Oprah about King, 'grew up as Black girls striving to do better in our lives...She [King] is the mother I never had, the sister everybody would want, she is the friend everybody deserves. I don't know a better person.'

The following day, Meghan flew back to London on Amal Clooney's private jet. Soon after landing in Britain, her critics launched a ferocious onslaught. How could a self-professed philanthropist, they demanded, indulge in a junket estimated to have cost £325,000?[579] Her defenders retorted that the critics were racist. A more convincing reply might have been that Prince Charles sought out hospitality from shady donors on private yachts, jets and holiday islands.

Two days after returning to London, Meghan and Harry flew on a standard BA flight for an official two-day visit to Morocco. Meghan performed perfectly in public but in private continued to rage about the media's criticism of her trip to New York. In her state, she needed extra protection provided by private jets. Later she would claim that the media criticism had been dishonest. During the eight months of pregnancy in 2019, she said, 'I wasn't even visible. I was on maternity leave or with a baby.'[580] She would forget about her trips to New York and Morocco.

The New York trip appears to have settled Meghan's fate. Contemptuous of the Palace and the staff, she decisively set out to fashion her own career regardless of the monarchy. Once again she took the initiative and worked in secret.

Inspired by her Los Angeles publicists she had emailed British *Vogue* magazine's new editor, Edward Enninful. The 41 year old had worked in magazines since he was 17. His dramatic appointment as editor confirmed his skills. Without introduction, Meghan asked Enninful whether *Vogue* could promote Smart Works, a British charity she had joined in January.[581] The charity trained disadvantaged women for job interviews and provided suitable clothes. Intrigued by the approach, Enninful headed to Kensington Palace to meet a woman equally ambitious and hungry for publicity. Smart Works was not the only reason for approaching Enninful.

Enninful had developed a narrative about his ambition to be a positive force for change. As the son of immigrant Ghanaians, his passion was to promote Black women to embrace similar ambitions to white women. What followed during their conversation is inevitably disputed.

Meghan claimed that after consulting her 'two dogs nestled across me', she suggested to Enninful that she guest-edit *Vogue*'s next issue. The editor's staff ridiculed the notion. Enninful, rather than Meghan they insist, decided that the duchess would be a perfect money-making vehicle for the magazine. In his version, Enninful suggested that

Revenge

Meghan guest-edit the critically important September issue. She would be the first guest-editor at British *Vogue*, a magazine renowned as the fashion elite's bible. The woman who rarely stepped out of Kensington Palace in clothes costing less than £5,000 and high-heeled Manolo Blahniks to elevate her 5ft 5in to 5ft 10in saw no reason to inform Palace officials about her decision.

Enninful classed the project top-secret. With unprecedented disguise, Enninful assigned one team to produce the normal September issue unaware that it would never be published. In parallel, Enninful and a team of 13 produced the special issue. The focus would be on 15 women nominated by Meghan as her heroes, or 'Forces for Change'.

CHAPTER 28

Wellness

In March 2019, Harry crossed a boundary. 'Wellness' became his new religion. In the reinvention of himself he adopted Meghan's passion for organic products and treatments based on holistic meditation, numbers, gongs, crystal bowls, inner calm, chakra balancing, and special massages of the body and the inner mouth. The man who once reeked of tobacco, not least after smoking marijuana, also stopped drinking alcohol.

During a short stay at Heckfield Place hotel in Hampshire he used the spa's specialities, including a 'breathing workshop', a yoga studio and various natural treatments.[582] Prince Charles would have approved. As an advocate for alternative medicine, Charles had urged the NHS to offer coffee enemas as a cure for cancer. Harry's conversion to 'Full Blast Markle' had taken him further. He had become, wrote Jan Moir, 'an empty royal cipher into which Meghan has poured all her fresh-pressed dreamweaver jabber and he has swallowed it hook, line and sinker'. Accordingly, he spoke 'the kind of pseudo-profundo new-age blather that goes down a storm in Malibu juice bars.'[583]

The new Harry presented himself to 12,000 schoolchildren and students at Wembley Arena on 6th March for WE Day, a celebration of young volunteers seeking to influence their communities and the world. The prince urged the 'most engaged generation in history' who 'care about values and doing the right thing to shine the light'. They should not despair, he said, about 'the older generation when it seems they don't care'. Especially about climate change. 'Every blade of grass, every ray of sun and every raindrop is crucial to our survival,' he told them. Two days earlier, Harry had flown in a helicopter to Birmingham.

In his speech Harry damned social media for 'distorting the truth and trying to manipulate the power of positive thinking'. Harry forgot that Meghan's fame depended on her skill to orchestrate favourable social media. Those contradictions were buried by the audience's loud cheers as Harry 'dragged' Meghan on to the stage. The two were preaching to 'progressive, open-minded change-makers'. Their banner was, 'Be braver, be stronger, be kind to each other…change your thoughts and change the world.'[584] Their performance hid the contradictions about themselves.

Off-stage, the prince felt more than ever unfulfilled. Living in Frogmore, he was struggling through another bout of darkness. Still angry with his brother for refusing to support wholeheartedly his campaign against the media, or voice sympathy with his New Age politics, Harry felt sidelined. Palace officials were investing new energy to prepare William to be the future king. No longer in Kensington Palace, and feeling physically distanced from Buckingham Palace's officials, Harry became an agent for unrest.

In order to reassure Harry, a Buckingham Palace spokesman briefed the media that Charles had forged a new relationship with his two sons. Using the excuse of a party to celebrate Charles's 50th anniversary as the Prince of Wales, the Palace described Charles as always 'close' to Harry and now, thanks to Charles's excellent relationship with Meghan, they were bound even 'closer'.[585]

In reality, Harry had become an unpredictable contrarian. As a patron of expeditions for the Walking With The Wounded charity for former members of the military, Harry was eagerly welcomed at their annual meeting. On arrival, he was asked to show particular attention to Hans K. Rausing, a Swedish billionaire philanthropist who was expected to donate a six-figure cheque to the charity. Instead, Harry launched into a tirade about businesses' failure to limit climate change. Rausing nevertheless gave his donation. Insiders marked Harry down as disruptive.

In Kensington Palace, Amy Pickerill, Meghan's new assistant private secretary, followed Samantha Cohen and resigned after just one year. Like many junior staff, after her experience in Australia and Fiji, she found working for Meghan stressful.[586]

In an effort to negotiate an amicable solution, the Queen recruited Lord Geidt to help embed Meghan into the Royal Family. Acknowledging Meghan's description of herself as a leader to 'drive positive social change', Geidt organised her appointment as the first vice-president of the Queen's Commonwealth Trust responsible for education.[587] While doubting whether that position alone could resolve the antagonism between the Sussexes and the palaces, Geidt loyally discussed the option of settling the family in southern Africa, frequently described by Harry as his second home. That option had become highly problematic. Few could believe that Meghan would want to live in Africa. More insiders were speculating that she intended to return to California. Their suspicions were sparked by her plan to resume her role as an Influencer.

Meghan's ambition was to re-engage with her former followers and connect with millions of activists on Instagram. The @sussexroyal site would be her platform to respond to critics faster and independently of the Palace. 'She could call her "own shots",' explained her spokesman.[588] The Sussexes' celebrity guaranteed attention. Choosing Instagram as the social media platform for 'The Official Website of the Duke and Duchess of Sussex' was contentious. Instagram in particular was criticised for fuelling anxiety, depression and addiction, especially among young girls.

The new website was designed by Ryan Sax and David Watkins, alias 'Digital Dave', the head of Article, the creative agency based in Toronto that had established The Tig. Sussexroyal.com and sussexofficial.uk were registered using servers in Arizona.[589] Simultaneously, Meghan's long-term Los Angeles business advisor Andrew Meyer registered two websites, americanfriendsofsussexroyal .com and theamericanfriendsofsussexroyal.com. Later in the year, he also re-registered The Tig.[590]

To recruit new followers to her platform Meghan featured in London as a 'Thought Leader' on a panel to celebrate International Women's Day in early March 2019. Asked in public about social media descriptions of herself as 'woke', she replied, 'I don't read anything. It's much safer that way.' She also denied reading Twitter: 'I'm not part of any of that. I don't look at it.' Two fellow panellists, singer Annie Lennox and Julia Gillard, Australia's former prime minister, nodded in approval.

The two panellists also believed Meghan's declaration that her unborn child, even if it were a boy, was already a feminist. The baby's movements, she was certain, were 'the embryonic kicking of feminism'. Harry, she added, was a self-proclaimed feminist. He had benefited from what she called 'gender stereotype shifting'. Feminism, she explained, meant that a man should not feel threatened to have a 'woman by your side, not behind you'. By then, many believed that Meghan was leading Harry.

The speech coincided with a shift in the Sussexes' plans. Unknown to Geidt, in anticipation of the Sussexes' permanent move to America, Meghan's Los Angeles agents were negotiating with Oprah Winfrey. The broadcaster had pitched to land the first interview if Meghan returned to California. To sweeten the offer, she agreed to produce with Harry a TV documentary series about mental health.

Guided by Meghan, Harry had adopted the ideas of Brené Brown, an American psychological researcher. Her book *Dare To Lead* encouraged the famous to abandon their stiff upper-lip and display their frailty. 'If you develop skin so thick that you start to lose the ability to be hurt,' Brown wrote, 'you're at risk of feeling nothing at all.' Talking about his mental health, she advocated, would help other men to throw off the stigma. 'The only foolproof strategy I've come up with so far,' Brown wrote, 'is owning our story.' Focused on 'being real', said Brown, Harry would 'do the world a favour by speaking your truth.' Using their royal platform, agreed Meghan, would 'enable grass-roots change to create a better society.' Only prejudiced critics would object to their 'truth'.[591]

Contracted by Apple TV, Harry was paid to tell his personal story under the title *Mental Wellness*. Stepping into that area, Harry knew, would irritate his brother. Mental health, a cornerstone of William's work with Kate through the Royal Foundation, was the theme of his imminent BBC TV documentary *A Royal Team Talk: Tackling Mental Health*. Even more inflammatory was Harry's agreement with Apple to describe intimately his relationship with his family.

Harry was beyond caring about William's and Kate's sensitivity. The details of the two families' 'divorce' were nearly finalised. The Royal Foundation would be continued by the Cambridges. The Sussexes would create their own charity. Dissatisfied with Jason Knauf and his assistant Christian Jones, the Sussexes appointed a new press officer, Sara Latham. Recruited from Freuds PR, the American-born Latham had previously worked for Tony Blair, the Clintons and the Obamas.[592] Few watching Kate and Meghan warmly kiss at Westminster Abbey for the Commonwealth Day service would have realised that a major drama was about to be played out.[593]

On 14th March, Buckingham Palace announced that the Fab Four era was over – the Sussexes' and Cambridges' households were to split. The Palace's official spokesman denied that the divorce was evidence of a rift. Three weeks later @sussexroyal was launched on Instagram. 'Brand Sussex' promised to publish 'important announcements' and 'shine a light on key issues' direct to their followers. Within six hours the site had attracted one million people. That would rise within one year to nearly five million worldwide. The Cambridges had 7.4 million followers, David Beckham had 55 million and Kim Kardashian attracted 156 million admirers.

The Sussexes' Instagram account announced Harry's 'dynamic multi-part documentary series with Oprah Winfrey on mental health'.[594] The truth was now out. Meghan had committed herself and Harry to Oprah Winfrey. The Californian TV star had good reason to believe she was finally in control.

CHAPTER 29

Pitching

The exclusivity demanded by Oprah Winfrey matched Meghan's and Harry's mood for retaliation against the Royal Family, the media and the British public.

To build up Meghan's profile in America, Oprah Winfrey and Gayle King had an exclusive agreement with Meghan to produce a glowing CBS TV documentary about her first year of marriage. It would be transmitted at peak time, soon after the birth of her baby. In exchange, Meghan guaranteed that no other TV network would get access to her or the child. The strategy, kept tightly secret, was fully supported by Sunshine Sachs. The tripartite American agreement came under the headline label 'privacy'. Harry agreed that Buckingham Palace be given no choice. CBS would be given the exclusive rights to film the Queen being introduced to baby Archie. The birth and the aftermath would signal the Sussexes' break from the Palace.

In mid-April, Sara Latham, their new spokeswoman, announced that the Sussexes would 'keep the plans around the arrival of their baby private'. Not only would the hospital be kept secret, but even the identity of the godparents would remain undisclosed. On cue, Oprah Winfrey supported the Sussexes' unprecedented decisions. Meghan, she pronounced, would start her family 'in a different way than it's been done for more than a thousand years'. That was true. By tradition, royal births were always a cause for national celebration. And also, the publicity accompanying royal births had always been essential to establish the newborn's legitimacy.

Inevitably, the Sussexes' decision reignited controversy. Some were sympathetic to the Sussexes' self-protection from 'the hazards of fame'.[595] Others were perplexed how 'privacy' matched the Sussexes' agenda of 'modernising' and serving the people?[596]

Few understood the Sussexes' definition of 'privacy'. For the couple, privacy did not mean remaining 'secret and unseen'. Rather, it meant enforcing total control over their images and the accompanying narrative. If that strategy upset the Palace and tore up the royal rule-book, that was a bonus.

Meghan's original plan was to have a home birth, helped by her mother. For a 37 year old, there was an element of risk in that. Once her baby was overdue, the plan was ditched. On 5th May, Meghan was driven at speed from Frogmore to the Portland Hospital, a private clinic in central London. At 5.26am on 6th May, Archie Harrison Mountbatten-Windsor was born.

The deception started immediately.

At 2pm, just over eight hours after Archie was born, Buckingham Palace announced that Meghan had gone into labour. Twenty minutes later, at 2:20pm, his birth was announced on the Sussex Instagram site. Realising they had been fooled, Buckingham Palace officials caught up a few minutes later with a formal announcement: 'Her Royal Highness, the Duchess of Sussex, was safely delivered of a son at 0526hrs. The baby weighs 7lb 3oz. The Duke of Sussex was present for the birth.' By then, the Sussexes and baby were back in Frogmore. Meghan was in total control.

Torn between Meghan's strategy and sharing his own happiness, Harry could not resist appearing for the media in the early afternoon. Standing in the Queen's stables at Windsor Castle, the casually dressed prince trilled, 'I'm very excited to announce that Meghan and myself had a baby boy earlier this morning, a very healthy boy. Mother and baby are doing incredibly well. It's been the most amazing experience I could ever have possibly imagined. How any woman does what they do is beyond comprehension. I haven't been at many births, this is definitely my first. It was amazing, absolutely incredible, so we just wanted to share this with everybody.'

The Sussexes then made, through their spokeswoman, an important announcement. With Harry's agreement, the Palace also disclosed that the Sussexes had decided that Archie should not be a prince. The couple, said Sara Latham, did not want to be bound by convention or history. Meghan wanted her son to be plain 'Mister Archie' and not bear the title of a royal. They wanted to protect Archie's privacy.[597] The Sussexes knew that, under British law, Archie would automatically become a prince after the Queen died unless Charles changed the rules.[598] Regardless of the title, Meghan had been told, her family would continue to be fully protected by the Metropolitan Police. On Archie's birth certificate his mother named herself as 'Rachel Meghan, the Duchess of Sussex'. Three weeks later, the Palace lawyers ordered that certificate be altered to 'Her Royal Highness, the Duchess of Sussex'.[599]

Just after the birth, Thomas Woodcock, the Garter at Arms, called to discuss Archie's title. Her son, explained Woodcock, would automatically inherit the title Lord Dumbarton, since Harry, on marrying Meghan, was made Earl of Dumbarton. Meghan had also automatically become the Countess of Dumbarton. 'Hell no,' exclaimed Meghan. 'No son of mine is going to be called Dumb.'

Two days after Archie's birth, CBS's Gayle King was in Windsor for his first public appearance. BBC and ITV cameras were specifically excluded. At King's request, Meghan timed the photocall in St George's Hall in Windsor Castle with the start of CBS's morning show in New York. The photograph released by the Palace showed the Queen, Prince Philip, Doria and the Sussexes staring at a shawl.[600]

Neither CBS nor the single photographer present were allowed to record Archie's face.

King was nevertheless delighted. Her reward for securing exclusive access to Meghan in Windsor, and for the TV documentary to be shown ten days later, was an enhanced annual contract fee, estimated to have doubled to $11 million.[601] With every precedent broken, the critics of Meghan were forceful. Once again George Clooney was Meghan's defender. 'People should be a little kinder,' he said. 'She's a young woman who's just had a baby.'[602]

Meghan's own explanation of those arrangements to Oprah Winfrey nearly two years later was contradictory. First she said, 'We weren't asked to take a picture. That was part of the spin, that was really damaging.'[603] Then she admitted to Oprah that she had banned photos. That was, she said, her protest about the Palace denying Archie a prince's title and denying him police protection: 'I was very scared of having to offer up our baby, knowing that they weren't going to be kept safe.' Both those explanations she ought to have known were untrue. Forgetting her own announcement that Archie would be a 'private citizen' without a title, she would tell Oprah, 'A child who is not going to be protected and doesn't have a title. How does that make sense?'[604]

The turmoil continued at Archie's christening in Windsor. Meghan banned the Palace's accredited photographer and confirmed that his godparents' names would remain secret. In explanation, she would tell Oprah, 'The same people who have been abusing me want me to serve my child on a silver platter.' Among those nevertheless identified as godparents were Mark Dyer, a former equerry, Tiggy Legge-Bourke, Harry's trusted nanny, and Charles van Straubenzee, an old schoolfriend of Harry's.[605]

The media characterised Meghan's demands as a poseur's petulance. The tabloids she had hungrily sought until 2017 were now the enemy.

'She doesn't deserve all this negative press,' said Daniel Martin,

Meghan's make-up artist. The outrageous transformation of 'Meghan Markle, the Perfect Royal' into 'Duchess Difficult' was malicious, he pleaded. 'In the years I've worked with her, she's never had a diva fit. Never. Harry and Meghan are very philanthropic.'

Daniel Martin had good reason to be grateful to Meghan. 'That wedding,' he recalled, 'put me in a whole other stratosphere on social media that I can't understand.' Among many new lucrative appointments, Martin had become a brand consultant for Dior.

Capitalising on the wedding and baby shower had transformed other unknowns into celebrities. By associating her designs with Meghan, Misha Nonoo had opened a pop-up fashion boutique in central London and an 'intimate workshop' for 'group sound healing using crystal bowls'. Jess Mulroney, newly dubbed by *Harper's Bazaar* as 'the fairy godmother of Canadian fashion', had finally secured a contract on ABC's *Good Morning America*. Flaunting her relationship with Meghan, Mulroney modelled new clothes on Instagram alongside her three children. Abigail Spencer, an actor from *Suits*, was also delighted that her friendship with Meghan had increased her Instagram following from 100,000 in 2016 to half a million. Contrary to some expectations, her NBC TV show *Timeless* was not axed. Another beneficiary was Taryn Toomey, the fitness trainer. Meghan and Harry had urged their followers to 'explore' Toomey's retreats in Mexico and Mustique at £3,600 for four nights and buy a peach moonshine necklace for £1,200.[606]

The commercialisation plans, especially the transactional relationships orchestrated by the Sussexes, unnerved the Palace. Meghan's collaboration with her Los Angeles advisors and Gayle King convinced officials that the couple were heading beyond their control.

The struggle to find a replacement for Samantha Cohen concluded with the selection of Fiona Mcilwham, a Foreign Office diplomat. The high point of Mcilwham's 21-year service was as the UK's ambassador in Albania. Married to Daniel Korski, an aide to David Cameron,

Mcilwham had little in common with a Hollywood actress. From the outset, Mcilwham discovered that Meghan had no intention of sharing her intentions.[607] Even Sara Latham had failed, along with Heather Wong and Cara Madden, the duchess's projects manager, to win Meghan's complete trust.[608]

Meghan believed she had good reason to be suspicious. All her requests were now referred to Buckingham Palace, and regularly the Queen's officials directed her staff to prioritise the Palace's interests over Meghan's. More important, without consultation a legal constraint had been imposed on Sussex Royal, their foundation.

A solicitor regularly employed by Buckingham Palace had been asked to create 'The Foundation of the Duke and Duchess of Sussex'. The couple believed that the lawyer had been tasked to reproduce the Royal Foundation.

Under the law, a Foundation is private, the patrons have no legal obligations and there is no requirement to publish detailed accounts. However, a Foundation is complicated to establish and is usually financed before its creation. The couple's Foundation was registered as a charity, leaving the Sussexes future wide open to the financial scrutiny that goes with charity regulation. The difference was considerable. Easy to establish and without the need for original money, a charity is obliged to publish detailed accounts and is subject to scrutiny by independent officials employed by the Charity Commission. All the donations the Sussexes expected to receive, especially from America, would be itemised and published, as would the salaries of their staff. As an officer of the charity, Meghan would be subject to fiduciary laws. The charity was incorporated on 1st July, 2019.

At their first meeting in Kensington Palace, the Sussexes welcomed the Foundation's four trustees. All were personally unknown to them. Steven Martin Cooper was the chief executive of Hoare's Bank; Kirsty Jackson Jones and Karen Blackett, a British business-woman, had significant commercial and legal experience; and the chairman, Stefan Allesch-Taylor, was a well-known businessman and philanthropist. In a solemn atmosphere they discussed their objectives for the Foundation's success.

By the end of the meeting the Sussexes were shocked. The trustees, they discovered, were 'neither mates nor servants'. They were independents who would have complete control of the charity's money. Under the law, the Sussexes would be denied any privacy over the Foundation's management. For Meghan, a master of control, the legal requirement of transparency was unexpected. The Foundation's legal structure, she believed, was a deliberate bid to undermine her.

Once Meghan discovered that the Sussex Foundation could not operate in secrecy, another reason to stay in Britain had disappeared. Money was critical to her. As Gina Nelthorpe-Cowne had realised, Meghan was 'a businesswoman first and foremost'. Everything was calculated on commercial terms.[609] Financing her charities and her personal lifestyle were destined to be intertwined.

Harry was similarly incensed. Charles had assured him of a major role in the slimmed-down monarchy for at least ten years. Now, the discrepancy of treatment between William and himself confirmed the worst. He also wanted out. Meghan was not disappointed by his decision. 'I thought she'd stick with it for a few more years before she cracked,' Gina Nelthorpe-Cowne later reflected.

Meghan would later admit that she and Harry began the conversation about leaving Britain with the Queen even before their marriage. 'For two years,' she would say.[610] In Harry's recollection, he first mentioned to his grandmother in about January 2018 that the lack of support and understanding from both the media and his family were encouraging his thoughts about leaving Britain.[611] Even before he married he was looking to escape. 'I never blind-sided my grandmother,' he insisted. Harry would confirm that they had also discussed leaving Britain in January 2019, around the time that Meghan was suicidal, but his 'family tried to prevent him.'[612] In Harry's version, the conversations about departure continued throughout that year, spurred by Meghan's suicidal feelings. 'How bad does it have to get,' Harry rhetorically asked, 'until I am allowed to do this?'

The anger fuelling their urgency to leave Britain was transmitted to Los Angeles. Nick Collins was told to start looking for acting roles for Meghan.[613] Her business agent, Andrew Meyer, was also asked to look into the possibility of negotiating a mammoth deal, similar to the Obamas, with Netflix. In parallel, she was encouraged by David Furnish, Elton John's partner, to co-operate on an animation series.[614]

Meghan's veil fell on 14th July at the London premiere of Disney's *The Lion King*, Harry's favourite film. In the line-up that evening she did not hide her desperation. Pharrell Williams, the rapper, told her that he was 'so happy' about their marriage and added, 'We cheer you guys on.' Touching his arm, Meghan smiled: 'Thank you. They don't make it easy.'

Minutes later, Harry was speaking to Jon Favreau, the film's director. 'If anyone needs any extra voiceover work,' he began, only to be interrupted by Meghan. 'That's really why we're here,' she said. 'It's the pitch!' Harry praised Meghan's acting abilities.[615]

Next, Harry approached Robert Iger, Disney's chief executive famous for the quip, 'They only root for you in Hollywood when your cancer is terminal.'

'You do know she does voiceovers?' the prince asked Iger.

'I did not know that,' replied the executive.

'You seem surprised,' said Harry. 'She's really interested.'

'Sure, we'd love to try,' said Iger, grasping that the prince was touting for work. 'That's a great idea.'[616]

The Sussexes' successful pitch was only marred by their later realisation that all their exchanges had been recorded. Meghan did narrate Disney's documentary *Elephants Without Borders*, the story of a group of elephants at risk from poachers. The reviewers would not be enthusiastic: 'A spectacular of schmaltz, a sugary taste' and 'the right side of annoying' were among the more favourable comments in the reviews.[617]

Shortly after *The Lion King* premiere Meghan went to watch Serena Williams playing at Wimbledon. Dozens of professional photographers and TV cameras recorded and broadcast her presence in the royal box. Then an altercation occurred. Meghan ordered her bodyguard to tell a female spectator not to photograph her. She was at Wimbledon, she declared, 'in her private capacity'. The next day, Lorraine Kelly wrote in the *Sun*, 'Either they are private citizens and pay for their own loft extension, or they are royals and have to share the big events in their lives with the rest of the world. They really can't have it both ways.'[618]

Few in London, except possibly the Queen and Charles, realised during the summer that Meghan was already detaching herself from the Royal Family.

She was counting the weeks until her return to California. Her spokeswoman said that Meghan would not be taking maternity leave because she wanted to prove herself through work. Yet other than one engagement to promote Smart Works, she undertook no public work during the summer. She watched polo and tennis matches, and repeatedly flew in private jets for holiday trips with Harry and Archie. They stayed with Elton John in St Tropez, the Clooneys in Como, and in a friend's seven-bedroomed villa advertised at £100,000 per week in Ibiza's Vista Alegre estate. For Meghan, it seemed taking private jets was like ordering an Uber.

Inevitably, her critics, especially the *Sun* newspaper, objected: 'The couple want all the pluses and none of the minuses of royal life. They have imploded into an unhappy mess of self-pity and perceived victimhood, utterly disconnected from the much greater stresses ordinary people often endure.'[619]

To silence the calls of 'hypocrisy', Meghan's publicists once again contacted her friends. The result was a synchronised chorus of support. 'I am calling on the press,' said Elton John, 'to cease these relentless and untrue assassinations on their character that are spuriously crafted on an almost daily basis.'[620] Jessica Mulroney posted on Instagram, 'Shame on you, you racist bullies. Three years of undeserved hate and abuse. It's enough.'[621] Actress Jameela Jamil justified the private jets as protection for the public: 'It's not safe for us to be on the same planes…They are prime targets for kidnap and sometimes assassination.'[622]

Harry defied their critics. In early August he travelled by private jet and helicopter to the Google camp in Sicily to speak about the climate-change crisis. His plane was just one of the 114 private jets, as well as a fleet of super yachts, that had ferried billionaires and celebrities to the festival. Free from the constraints of palace etiquette, Harry tasted a movie star's freedom alongside Leonardo DiCaprio, Tom Cruise, Orlando Bloom and singer-songwriter Harry Styles.

As royals, both he and Meghan felt entitled to use their status to lecture others. 'Every choice,' Harry wrote at the same time on the Sussexes' Instagram page, 'every footprint, every action makes a difference.' Like his hosts, Harry justified his use of private jets 'to protect my family from these people'. The identity of 'these people' and the 'never-ending' threat Harry perceived remained unclear.[623]

There was a new arrogance to Harry's preaching. He resented scrutiny of his behaviour. Soon after his visit to Sicily, he staged a press conference in Amsterdam to promote his new online eco-travel campaign, Travalyst. He was outraged that his audience asked him to justify his use of private jets. In reply, Harry claimed that 99 per cent of his flights were commercial. Annoyed that his answers were scrutinised, Harry was encouraged by a hovering Sunshine Sachs executive to give evasive replies. He only flew private, he protested, to 'ensure my family is safe'.

In reality, at least 60 per cent of his flights were private.[624] 'No one is perfect,' he then declared. 'I plant trees to offset the carbon print.'

He was pressed to give answers. 'Where and how many trees?' he was asked. Questions sparked Harry's sense of persecution. Whatever he said, Harry believed, was 'the truth'. They were special people requiring protection. Just over one year later, Heather Wong, Travalyst executive director, resigned and was replaced by Sally Davey.[625]

The Cambridges retaliated. The media was summoned to film them flying on a low-budget airline from Norwich to Aberdeen for their summer holidays at Balmoral. In revenge, Meghan promptly announced that her family would not, after all, follow the Cambridges to Balmoral. Archie, she explained, was too young at three months to travel by plane to Scotland.[626] Instead, she flew with Archie to Ibiza. Later that same week, Meghan flew on a commercial flight to New York to watch Serena Williams play in the final of the US Open. Williams was defeated.

Days later, Meghan and Harry flew by private jet to Misha Nonoo's wedding in Rome. Nonoo's second husband, Mike Hess, was the son of an oil billionaire. Just the type Meghan enjoyed meeting – and Nonoo admired.[627]

CHAPTER 30

Vogue

Throughout August as Meghan jetted around Europe she anticipated the publication of the September issue of British *Vogue*. Edward Enninful's intense involvement and the secrecy surrounding the special issue convinced Meghan that the magazine would turbo-charge her launch in America. Her excitement was shared by the editor. 'I simply never imagined,' he wrote to the readers, 'that in my lifetime, someone of my colour would – or could – enter the higher echelons of our Royal Family.'

In tandem she was planning to launch *The Bench*, a children's book she had written. Hoping that both would be publishing sensations, she had asked Keleigh Thomas Morgan to oversee the publicity. In anticipation of her move to Hollywood, Andrew Meyer, her business manager and the director of Frim Fram Inc, once again renewed The Tig trademark. In August, on Harry's behalf, lawyers registered MWX Trading Ltd at Companies House to apply for trademarks, including Travalyst, Harry's sustainable travel company.[628] As an indication of Meghan's plan to end her role as a funded public servant in Britain, Latham and the Palace were initially excluded from giving advice.

Over the previous seven months as the magazine took shape, Meghan persuaded herself that she was editing the issue. Regularly, during telephone conferences, she made comments and demanded changes.

'I want to break the internet,' she exclaimed to the editorial staff, meaning that she would control her own image. Listening to the Duchess, the editorial team's expressions showed silent exasperation. Most of her contributions were superficial, lacking rhyme or reason. To avoid confrontation she was never asked to explain. The team wrongly assumed that her comments were inspired by Sunshine Sachs. They were her own ideas. Meghan's description of those conversations was 'philosophising with Ed over a steaming cup of mint tea'.

During the last weeks before publication, Meghan offered advice on publicity. She spoke about 'lighting up the internet' inspired by leaks. Enninful was unimpressed. Secrecy, Enninful repeated, was essential for a blockbuster launch. Nevertheless, the *Sun* regularly published snippets of information about the issue. The editorial team suspected the source was a friend of Meghan's, a female publicist in London.

Those irritations came with the turf for Enninful. Shaping a whole issue around the Duchess was a journalistic and commercial coup. Promoting Meghan as 'the country's most influential beacon of change,' he gushed in his editorial about this 'brilliant, bi-racial American powerhouse' who is a 'positive influence everywhere'.

None of *Vogue*'s staff witnessed Meghan ever pause to consider whether she had crossed the line in her relationship with Enninful. She never appeared to consider the conflict of using her marriage to promote herself. Meghan was uninterested in the boundary which Prince William had identified in a 2017 TV documentary. In a measured way, William had grasped the nettle regarding a royal's public openness with the media: 'One lesson I've learnt is you never let them in too far, because it's very difficult to get them back out again. You've got to maintain a barrier and a boundary, because if you cross it, a lot of pain and problems can come from it.' Meghan was dismissive of that caution. Thrilled by the opportunity, she would never have thrown it away.

Enninful and Meghan had selected 15 women identified as Game

Changers who 'reshape society in radical and positive ways'. Among them were the primatologist Dian Fossey, whose life was devoted to saving the Rwandan gorillas until her murder in 1985; 82-year-old Jane Fonda; Bonnie Hammer of NBC, who cast Meghan in *Suits*; Joni Mitchell, the singer-songwriter; and Toni Morrison, the winner of the Nobel Prize for Literature. There was also the transgender actor Laverne Cox; Adwoa Aboah, a model; Gemma Chan, an actress; Ramla Ali, a boxer; Adut Akech, a model; and the 16-year-old climate-change campaigner Greta Thunberg. The Swede must have wondered about her nomination among the gas-guzzling supermodels who criss-crossed the globe to pose in exotic locations. In reciprocity for their nomination, the women hailed Meghan as 'an ultimate force for change'. And in return, Meghan praised them for representing the unrepresented. The Queen was omitted.

That left the important decision of the cover. Meghan wanted to feature on the cover, just as Kate had done in 2016 to mark *Vogue*'s centenary. But during many discussions the editorial team persuaded her that it would be 'boastful'. In public, Enninful would say that it was Meghan's decision not to appear on the cover because she wished to remain 'humble'. The staff recall the decision being forced on her. The cover was given to Salma Hayek, a Hollywood star married to François-Henri Pinault – a French billionaire who happened to be one of *Vogue*'s leading advertisers.

'Forces for Change' was a thought-provoking headline. In the magazine's introduction, Meghan wrote about her intention to highlight 'the power of the collective' and focus on 'positivity, kindness, humour and inclusivity…to shine light in a world filled with seemingly daily darkness'. She added, 'Through this lens, I hope you will feel the strength of the collective in the diverse selection of women chosen for the cover.' Her language offered no philosophy. Nor did she identify her destination. 'Lens' was a recurring metaphor in Meghan's lexicon.

Within hours of announcing the magazine's scoop, the phones at *Vogue*'s office did not stop ringing. The whole world wanted to read

Meghan's special issue. The magazine's young female readers related to Meghan, a woman with a successful independent career using her platform in the Royal Family to campaign for change. To stay in the spotlight, the editor blitzed a news story every day. In regular calls Meghan urged Enninful to offer more stories to the hungry media. Finally, she had hit the ground running.

Buckingham Palace was blindsided. Sara Latham was told by Meghan to mastermind her latest publicity launch. Her first task, said Meghan, was to demand that the official publication date in Britain be delayed by one day to let publication in the US take the lead. America's reaction, she was certain, would be more positive than Britain's. Meghan's order revealed that she was relying on her American advisors and hoped that a Palace request to Enninful would be obeyed. Once Latham's demand was rejected, the relationship between Meghan and *Vogue*'s staff deteriorated. Their conflict was about control.

Keleigh Thomas Morgan called to tell *Vogue* that she, rather than Latham, would be representing Meghan's interests, and therefore also *Vogue*'s. Enninful rejected that demand. In the battle between Latham's aggressive demands on behalf of the Palace and the Los Angeles publicist, Enninful sided with the local power, namely the Palace. Facing the kick-back, his decision was questioned by Meghan. Within hours, their dispute was drowned out by a wave of antagonistic comment published in the British media.

Damned by the *Sun* as 'a Trump-hating Corbynista left-winger', Meghan's 'virtue-signalling *Vogue*' was called 'an epic misjudgement'. In *The Times* Melanie Phillips described the 15 women as 'aspirations of social justice warriors'. Most of the glossy acolytes associated with the magazine's world, she wrote, were 'non-white and have in common an attitude which is divisive and offends the royal code of neutrality to unite.' Phillips concluded about Meghan, 'When in a hole, she doesn't just keep digging. She keeps going until the earth caves in on top of her, and she doesn't stop even then.'[629]

Diktats poured down on Latham from Buckingham Palace to 'end it' as fast as possible. Aggressive and shirty, she called *Vogue*'s staff with demands to terminate the magazine's promotion. As each demand was refused, she abruptly ended the call. The blowback in Kensington Palace was instantaneous. Latham was seen weeping, 'broken by the system'.

Similarly emotional, Meghan called Enninful seeking reassurance. The *Daily Mail*'s headline, 'Memo to Meghan: We Brits prefer true royalty to fashion royalty,' Meghan said, was clearly racist. To be British meant to be born and bred in the UK – and therefore white.[630] Sounding terrified, she could not understand the reasons for the furore. 'I'm simply promoting a happier world,' she pleaded.

Giving up on Latham, she called Keleigh Thomas Morgan and James Holt, another new spokesman, to summon celebrity supporters. Holt telephoned personalities to urge that they publicly endorse Meghan. Among those who refused to be involved on screen was Enninful himself. Others booked themselves on to TV programmes, offered interviews and posted statements.

The Los Angeles actress Jameela Jamil wrote, 'Dear England and English Press, just say you hate her because she's Black and him for marrying a Black woman and be done with it. God dammit. Your bullying is so embarrassing and obvious.'[631] She continued, 'If Meghan was a white woman, all the bold things she's doing would be celebrated.' Meghan, she said, was 'the ultimate change-maker and rule-breaker and I am in awe of her.'

'Stop pushing this,' Sara Latham repeatedly urged *Vogue*'s editors. 'This should be quickly ended.' Under pressure from Buckingham Palace, Latham was fighting a thankless battle. Having published *Vogue*'s bestselling edition for 105 years, Enninful saw no reason to end the controversy. Nor did Meghan or her Los Angeles publicists and managers. The publicity was the prelude to the next stage of Meghan's strategy.

CHAPTER 31

Attack

Three weeks after Meghan declared that Archie was too young to fly to Aberdeen, the four-month-old baby and his parents boarded a BA flight to South Africa.[632]

Planning for the ten-day trip had started months earlier. At the outset the Palace considered that the Sussexes might live in South Africa to develop Harry's humanitarian programme. Towards the end of the planning, that option had disappeared. However, during their discussions the couple asked to meet the victims of South Africa's poverty, disease and violence. Ahead of their trip, Meghan's spokesman announced that she would be wearing cheap, sustainable clothes and would leave her unique engagement ring at home.[633] The tour would be billed by the Palace and Sunshine Sachs as an opportunity to rebuild the couple's image. Even Archie's face, the Sussexes agreed, would be exposed to the cameras.

Those same Palace officials who organised the tour were unaware that in the weeks before their departure, the Sussexes had jettisoned their future in Britain. Focusing on themselves, they decided to move to North America. They intended to use the South African tour as a branding operation, an opportunity to clarify their objectives.

Harry could not conceal his emotional turbulence as he travelled across South Africa. Speaking to an 18-year-old Christian student,

Peter Oki, he described how often he woke up and felt overwhelmed by the world's many problems. 'Sometimes,' he told Oki, 'it's hard to get out of bed in the mornings.'[634] During a speech to parents of seriously ill children in a township, beneficiaries of the Well Child Awards charity, Harry choked back tears describing his emotion about fatherhood and how it 'pulls at my heart-strings in a way I could have never understood until I had a child of my own.' The crying prince, the father of a healthy child, was comforted on the stage by impoverished parents struggling daily with overwhelming difficulties.[635] Unlike them, Harry could not manage the normal stress of life. Despite his unique privilege, he was a casualty without a purpose.

While Harry spilled out his suffering, Meghan threw herself into a personal campaign. With perfect poise she played the part of the campaigning Hollywood celebrity. Standing on a tree stump, she told a group of women in Nyanga – South Africa's 'murder capital' near Cape Town – 'May I say that while I am here with my husband as a member of the Royal Family, I want you to know that for me I am here with you as a mother, as a wife, as a woman and as a woman of colour and as your sister.' At private meetings across the country with businesswomen, politicians and academics, she advocated women's rights. At Johannesburg University, introducing herself as 'your sister', she told the audience, 'When we empower girls hungry for education, we cultivate women who are emboldened to effect change within their communities and globally.'

The missing link was explaining what women should be empowered to do. She offered no purpose for the power. She was also contradictory. After describing herself as a 'woman of colour', she said in the same breath how she hoped that her marriage would not be seen through the prism of race. Left dangling in the air were fundamental problems. Unlike South Africa's radicals, she could not explain the particular challenges of a mixed-race woman in a Western society. Nor did she question the values of Western society – because those were her values.[636]

No one told Meghan her messages were confused. Instead, she was praised for the fluency of her speeches and the sincere excitement of her audiences. Her popularity grew, but her disgruntlement increased and was aimed at her staff. The officials, Harry felt, 'simply didn't like Meghan and would stop at nothing to make her life difficult'.[637] In turn, her staff believed that Meghan assumed that her success justified her entitlement. Always present amid the tension was the Sussexes' relationship with the media.

The few British journalists officially allowed to accompany the Sussexes during the tour felt ostracised. Acting on the Sussexes' orders, Sara Latham denied the media normal, if limited, access to the couple. Nevertheless, anxious to placate the couple, even their sternest British critics suggested that their smiles for the cameras 'feels like the beginning of a rapprochement with the British public'.[638] The tour, the media proclaimed, was a resounding success. Meghan, Harry and Archie were hailed as heroes. The first photos of Archie were headlined as 'sensational'. Yet every olive branch incensed Harry. The 'positive' coverage of the tour, he believed, exposed 'the double standards of this specific press pack' that had 'vilified [Meghan] almost daily for the past nine months'.[639] Deliberately, he ignored even their benign questions.[640]

Harry and Meghan were shackled. Every night they scoured the internet to read the newspaper reports and the trolls' postings on social media. Irrationally, they grouped the two together and fed each other's frenzy about the media. Convinced that as champions of goodness they were being persecuted by mendacity and racism, they felt victimised by the mildest criticism. The British press, Harry later said, 'was destroying my mental health. I thought, "This is toxic".'[641]

Harry's instability fed Meghan's fears that friends were leaking stories to the media. In particular, she suspected Victoria Beckham of indiscretion. Harry called David Beckham to repeat the accusation. Outraged, Beckham's truthful denials damaged their relationship.[642]

The result, their staff saw, further aggravated their relations with the Royal Family. Just as in Australia, the Sussexes convinced themselves that their stardom in South Africa was unappreciated by Buckingham Palace. Their loyalty was being exploited. Having broken with her family, Meghan persuaded Harry to consider doing the same. At the same time, she poured out her anger to her Los Angeles advisors about the dark forces at work. Palace officials were briefing against them. They were being held back by Charles and William. They deserved better. Back came the reassurance that global recognition and her fame and fortune were guaranteed once she returned to America. But first, she needed to set the scene for her return. The gentle illusion of the benign Sussexes did not match their hunger for revenge against newspapers.

Harry was in the final stages of settling his claim against the *Daily Mirror* and *Sun* newspapers for hacking his telephone. That success, he believed, would be followed by another victory against the *Mail on Sunday*. He had complained to IPSO, the press standards watchdog, about an exposé of alleged dishonesty in a series of wild-life photographs. The images posted on Instagram showed Harry standing bravely close to untethered elephants. As the newspaper revealed, the photos were untruthful. They had been cropped to conceal restraining ropes around the elephant's legs.[643] Harry's hopeless complaint reflected his lack of judgement in pursuit of the media and any other enemy.

During August, the Sussexes crossed a Rubicon. Until then, Gerrard Tyrrell, the Royal Family's usual legal advisor, had led their threat of legal action against the *Mail on Sunday* for publishing Meghan's letter to her father. Tyrrell had sent the newspaper a draft claim for breach of copyright and Meghan's privacy. Her relationship with her father, claimed Meghan, was private. No public interest could justify her letter's publication.

As an experienced litigator, Tyrrell knew the risk of going to the next step and actually launching a legal action. Meghan would not only be exposed to cross-examination in the witness box, but she would be compelled before the trial to disclose embarrassing information, including every text and email to the five friends who spoke to *People* magazine, to Harry and to her Kensington Palace staff. Her denial that she did not know that her friends were giving an interview to the magazine or would refer to her letter would be rigorously tested under cross-examination.

There would also be the distasteful spectacle of a courtroom battle with her father. Her claim that she had repeatedly tried to contact him after the wedding 'which sadly went unanswered' was dangerous territory. She would need to provide proof of her 'care' for him.[644] Similarly, her claim that 'she did protect him from the media intrusion' before the wedding would be refuted.[645] And while she fumed that the *Mail on Sunday* had published stories showing her in 'a false and damaging light', she did not intend to sue the newspaper for defamation.[646]

Discounting the dangers, Meghan wanted action. Clearly dissatisfied with Gerrard Tyrrell's advice, her Los Angeles lawyers suggested that Keith Schilling, an aggressive London solicitor not previously employed by the Royal Family, was an ideal warrior for the case. Shabbily dressed and speaking sotto voce with traces of an East End lilt, Schilling was the antithesis of the pukka St James's lawyer. Loving a fight and charging high fees, Schilling and his staff boasted to potential clients about their successes. They rarely volunteered information about their failures.

Encouraged by Schillings to expect victory against the *Mail on Sunday*, the Sussexes had decided before they left London to attack the newspaper. The timetable was set by Schillings. Unexpectedly, the solicitors emailed that the claim would be filed while they were in

South Africa. Anxious Palace officials asked the Sussexes not to ruin the tour. To their horror, the Sussexes ignored their pleas. Their legal battle was launched in South Africa rather than in London.

Posted on the Sussexes' official website, Harry's aggressive script denounced their enemies. Partly drafted by David Sherborne, a media-hating barrister regularly parading in the spotlight, Harry's headline damned the 'press pack' for 'relentless propaganda' against Meghan by pursuing 'a game, and one that we have been unwilling to play from the start'.

Harry continued, 'Unfortunately, my wife has become one of the latest victims of a British tabloid press that wages campaigns against individuals with no thought to the consequences, a ruthless campaign that has escalated over the past year, throughout her pregnancy and while raising our new-born son. There is a human cost to this relentless propaganda, specifically when it is knowingly false and malicious, and though we have continued to put on a brave face, as so many of you can relate to, I cannot begin to describe how painful it has been. Because in today's digital age, press fabrications are repurposed as truth across the globe. One day's coverage is no longer tomorrow's chip paper.'

Clearly forgetting her trips during her pregnancy to New York and Morocco, Harry claimed that the media had created 'lie after lie at her expense simply because she has not been visible while on maternity leave.' While failing to identify the 'lies', he revealed their anguish: 'I have been a silent witness to her private suffering for too long… To stand back and do nothing would be contrary to everything we believe in. There comes a point when the only thing to do is to stand up to this behaviour, because it destroys people and destroys lives. Put simply, it is bullying, which scares and silences people. We all know this isn't acceptable.'

Finally, he played the Diana card. Meghan, he said, was 'falling victim to the same powerful forces' and his 'deepest fear is history repeating itself. I've seen what happens when someone I love is commoditised to the point that they are no longer treated or seen as a real person. I lost my mother and now I watch my wife falling victim to the same powerful forces.' Harry claimed that in publishing excerpts from Meghan's letter to her father the *Mail on Sunday* had misled readers by 'strategically omitting select paragraphs, specific sentences, and even singular words to mask the lies they had perpetuated for over a year'.

He would later assert about Diana: 'My mother was chased to her death when she was in a relationship with someone who wasn't white, and now look what happened.' Referring to Meghan, he said: 'They're not going to stop until she dies.'[647] He forgot that Diana had actually fired her bodyguards and that the only criticism of her relationship with Dodi Fayed was that the unemployed playboy fond of drugs had ordered a drunken driver to race through Paris.

Shortly afterwards, in the midst of the tour, Schillings issued a High Court claim on Meghan's behalf against the *Mail on Sunday* for publishing parts of her letter. Her resort to law was not unprecedented. Charles had sued the same newspaper in 2006 for publishing his revelatory 1997 journal about a trip to Hong Kong. Despite the weakness of his case, the judge sided with Charles. British judges could be trusted to protect the Royal Family from embarrassment.

In the claim, David Sherborne accused the *Mail on Sunday* of 'deliberately stirring up' a dispute between Meghan and Thomas Markle as part of an 'agenda'. Her father, described as a 'vulnerable and fragile individual,' had been 'exploited…harassed and manipulated' by the media. The claim also denied that *People* magazine had published 'any false or damaging information' about Thomas Markle which demanded any response.[648] Sherborne claimed that the newspaper's selection of quotations from Meghan's letter was 'dishonest' and reeked of 'clear malicious intent' and 'deceived and misled its readers'.

'Hysterical', 'ill-advised', 'hot-headed', 'self-indulgent' and 'over-emotional' were a few of the newspapers' verdicts about Harry's statement and the High Court claim. Their South African state tour had ended in embarrassment. For the first time, some suggested, the Sussexes ought to consider giving up their royal titles and become private citizens.[649]

Few realised that the Sussexes' assault on the media was a foretaste of a full-frontal attack on the Royal Family. An ITV documentary, *Harry & Meghan: An African Journey*, was filmed by Tom Bradby during their tour. Transmission was scheduled for a date two weeks after their return on 18th October. The broadcast coincided with the Cambridges' official visit to Pakistan. Not only was that visit critically important for British diplomacy, it was also intended to showcase Kate's transformation during her maternity leave into a more glamorous, self-confident woman.

With a more youthful, lighter cut of hair and a new wardrobe, Kate had been helped by Virginia Chadwyck-Healey, a former *Vogue* editor and stylist, to match Meghan.[650] Simultaneously, under Kate's influence, William had emerged as a calm heir, the 'People's Prince'. To focus the media's attention on the couple, Harry was asked to delay the broadcast of the ITV documentary. He refused. That was judged to be wanton sabotage of the Cambridges and the government. An almost unnoticed casualty was another TV documentary, crafted to promote Camilla.[651]

In planning *An African Journey*, Tom Bradby, a journalist sympathetic to the brothers, had planned to portray the Sussexes' experience of the continent's horrendous problems. He had become friends with Harry while filming a documentary in Lesotho after Harry left Eton. Accompanied by Bradby's film crew, Harry had posed in Angola with children who had lost their limbs to landmine explosions. Bradby had also filmed Meghan meeting girls who had survived wartime abuse, including multiple rapes. Whether those events matched Diana's homily – 'Anywhere I see suffering, that is where I want to be, doing what I can' – was debatable. Neither Meghan nor Harry chose, as she had done, to confront misery and console the homeless, sick and dying in shelters, hospitals and hospices in Britain. More pertinently, in Bradby's film, the Sussexes chose not even to focus on South Africa's human tragedies.

The Sussexes decided to use the African backdrop to express pain about their own plight. Anxious to display his vulnerability, Harry retold to Bradby how Diana's death had brought him repeatedly close to a breakdown. The trauma of walking behind his mother's coffin in public reminded him of the 'bad stuff' and 'a wound that festers'. He continued, 'I think being part of this family, in this role, in this job, every single time I see a camera, every single time I hear a click, every single time I see a flash it takes me straight back, so in that respect it's the worst reminder of her life as opposed to the best.'

Then Harry made his bombshell revelation. His relationship with William was fractured: 'We're on different paths at the moment.' Just why Harry exposed the family's turmoil at that moment in South Africa was hard to explain, except that he had been persuaded by Meghan's example of ghosting her father, her family and her lifelong friends that all relationships were dispensable.

Convinced that the audience also wanted to hear about her suffering, Meghan provided the more explosive interview. Standing in falling light outside a township of untold deprivation, she dramatically bit her lip while whispering to Bradby about how 'vulnerable' she felt during her pregnancy, how the pressure was 'hard' and the experience of 'just trying to be a new mother or trying to be a newly-wed' was 'made really challenging'. As tears welled up, Meghan regretted that she had ignored the warning from American friends that the British tabloids would destroy her life: 'And I very naively – I'm American, we don't have that there – thought, what are you talking about? That doesn't make sense, I didn't get it. In all fairness, I had no idea.'

Bradby failed to ask the 38 year old whether she had ever heard of the *National Enquirer*'s devastating exposés of famous Americans. Nor did he ask her to name one untrue tabloid story to justify her lament.

Instead, Brady nodded as she murmured, 'I tried, I really tried to adopt this sensibility of the British stiff upper-lip, but I think what that does internally is probably really damaging. I never thought this would be easy, but I thought it would be fair.'

Would it be fair, asked Bradby, to say that she is 'not really OK'? Her life has 'really been a struggle?' Another tear fell as Meghan replied with a swipe at the Royal Family: 'Yes. And also thank you for asking, because not many people have asked if I'm OK. But it's a very real thing to be going through behind the scenes.' With a hint of more tears, she deftly added: 'It's not enough to just survive something, right? That is not the point of life. You've got to thrive.' The audience was left to judge whether that eloquence had been rehearsed.

Asked about her future, Meghan replied, 'I don't know. You do just take each day as it comes.' Close by, South Africans took each day as it came to survive hunger, disease and violence. Meghan chose to say nothing about their lives. Bradby concluded that the Sussexes hoped to turn the 'relentless media interest in them into a positive force for good' but, he added, 'it became increasingly apparent to me the depth of their unhappiness and that what I was recording was to be their exit from public life.'[652] After spending so much time with the Sussexes, the journalist would have been aware of Harry's sentiment: 'I did what any husband and father would do. I needed to get my family out of there.'[653]

Palace officials in London were now aware that Meghan's separation from the Royal Family was underway. Reports from their staff in South Africa confirmed the worst. Acknowledging the existence of a problem, a Kensington Palace spokesman merely said that the Sussexes were in a 'fragile place'.[654] To escape the pressure, the Sussexes would fly to California for several weeks, but would return for Christmas at Sandringham.

William's original fear was materialising. Meghan had become a divisive agent. To please her, Harry had split from his old friends. He had even changed his telephone number without telling his family. William authorised an aide to tell the media about his hope that Harry and Meghan were 'all right'.[655]

Among Meghan's cheerleaders was Jessica Morgan, a 26-year-old British writer. Meghan's interview, said Morgan, 'absolutely broke my heart'. As a Black woman, Morgan sympathised with the Duchess suffering from feelings of rejection. 'She is not just a woman in the Royal Family, but a Black woman,' she continued. 'That she has come and started to experience what I've been experiencing in Britain for the past 26 years is sad. But I'm glad they are speaking out about it. This idea that you're rich, you don't get to be sad, is quite disgraceful.' Morgan spoke for many young women, especially those from diverse backgrounds. They sympathised with Meghan, a role model and a martyr. The young mother, oppressed by racism, was hailed for saving herself and Harry.

On the other side, Trevor Phillips, an outspoken Black commentator, criticised the assumption that Meghan was too fragile to handle the pressure. Jessica Morgan, he wrote, did not speak for the whole Black community. To suggest that Meghan was suppressed because of her colour, argued Phillips, was an insult to her and to legions of women like her who had fought their way to the top.[656] But Phillips's denial of racism in Britain, echoed by Priti Patel, the Asian home secretary, was derided by some Black activists, who called them 'coconuts'.[657]

'Meghan has made innocence look dirty,' was the contrary opinion by a white commentator.[658] Her sense of victimhood annoyed those who recalled that in 2017 Meghan had agreed to accept the limitations and duties of royal life in exchange for privilege, financial security and global recognition.

Gina Nelthorpe-Cowne was among those furious about the ITV interview: 'She made me laugh out loud. I know when nonsense is nonsense and this was demonstrable rubbish. Meghan was a grown-up woman when she met Harry. She had gushed in my ear, "We're going to change the world." She meant that she wanted to rule the world.'[659]

The next shot was fired by someone 'close' to Meghan. Max Foster, CNN's royal correspondent in London, was told by 'a source' that the Palace had no idea how to make the most of the Sussexes' potential. 'The institution around the British Royal Family', Foster reported, 'is full of people afraid of and inexperienced at how best to help, harness and deploy the value of the royal couple who, they said, have single-handedly modernised the monarchy.'[660] The CNN report led British news broadcasts.

Meghan's voice was loud and clear. The monarchy's fate, she thought, depended on her. Her critics were again bewildered. In the three years since she first met Harry, Meghan had clearly not grasped that the Queen had been modernising the 1,000-year-old monarchy since 1952. Under her direction, the family worked in unison as a team. Had Meghan heard the Queen's last Christmas message: 'As we all look forward to the start of a new decade, it's worth remembering that it is often the small steps, not the giant leaps, that bring about the most lasting change.'

Meghan skilfully concealed the widening gulf between herself and the Palace two days after the ITV broadcast. In a professional performance, she walked across the stage at London's Royal Albert Hall as a vice-president of the Queen's Commonwealth Trust to celebrate the opening of the One Young World summit. Five years earlier, the co-founder Kate Robertson had slotted Meghan into the Dublin event to give the ambitious actress a break. Now, Robertson welcomed the Duchess as 'a global champion for the rights of women and girls, activist and philanthropist'.

The sympathy Robertson showed for Meghan was shared by 72 female MPs. Led by Labour MP Holly Lynch, the cross-party group expressed in an open letter their 'solidarity' with Meghan as fellow women in public life. They sympathised with her struggle to cope with the pressure of being in the royal spotlight – and criticised what they claimed were 'outdated, colonial undertones' of stories written about her in the national press.[661] The newspapers' descriptions of the Duchess's character, wrote the MPs, were 'distasteful and misleading', and failed to 'accept your right to privacy'. Accusing the media of seeking to 'tear a woman down for no apparent reason', the MPs claimed 'an understanding of the abuse and intimidation which is now so often used as a means of disparaging women in public office from getting on with our very important public work'. The same day, Meghan telephoned Lynch to thank her.

To some it appeared that Meghan was becoming a prosecutor of the Royal Family. The nation's divisions about Meghan and Harry hardened. Depending on age, gender, race and politics, they were either applauded or condemned. Meghan's supporters were sceptical about the monarchy's so-called tradition of service, duty and impartiality. Viewed through the prism of privilege and misconduct, not least by Princes Charles and Andrew, they preferred Meghan's brand of feminism, environmentalism and wellness. Her supporters identified with her 'hopes, fears and insecurities'. Any disparaging reports about her were dismissed as racist prejudice.

Convinced that she was still misunderstood, Meghan invited Bryony Gordon, the sympathetic *Daily Telegraph* journalist, to join her at Luminary Bakery in Camden Town in north London.[662] The bakery employed vulnerable women. To express her sympathy, Meghan put on an apron and, while decorating cakes, listened to the women's accounts of their difficult lives. In less than two hours, Gordon was convinced that Meghan was 'not that much different from the rest of us.' She was, Gordon believed, 'a doer not a wallower'. She didn't want people just to love her but also to hear her thoughts. Gordon swooned as Meghan described humanity being like a 'wounded creature that needs to be healed'.

But the journalist failed to identify the contradictions in Meghan's recent ITV interview. She had told Tom Bradby of her own desire for sympathy. Like Bradby, Gordon agreed to label Meghan as 'the solution and not the problem'. Like Bradby, Gordon never asked Meghan whether she had understood that royal service demanded personal sacrifice. Or wondered whether Meghan would have visited the bakery without any publicity? Gordon did not ask whether her visit to the bakery was to help the women or to help Meghan? Was she genuinely compassionate? With considerable experience, Meghan knew how to craft her image. She posted on @sussexroyal's Instagram account a quotation by the American author Leo Buscaglia: 'Too often we underestimate the power of a touch, a smile, a kind word, a listening ear, an honest compliment, or the smallest act of caring, all of which have the potential to turn a life around.' Meghan's detractors wondered what sympathy she had shown towards her own father? And what about her kindness towards the Queen and the Royal Family?

Infused with American identity, Meghan had abandoned any pretence of interest in British culture. Endorsed by the Obamas, the presidential Joe Biden and the Clintons, she had become in America a courageous radical hero of her era. Michelle Obama and Hillary Clinton were her icons.

In early November, Hillary Clinton visited Meghan at Frogmore. As Meghan unloaded her anxiety, not least about the tabloid press, Clinton offered unqualified understanding. Meghan's treatment, the politician believed, was 'heart-breaking and wrong'. In Clinton's opinion, Meghan's meteoric rise had been spectacular. Living in the spotlight, with every move either scrutinised or distorted by racists, was difficult. Comparing the similarity of a life as US president with that of a member of the Royal Family, Clinton believed that the Sussexes were 'struggling to have a life of meaning and integrity on their own terms.'[663]

Two weeks later, the next stage of the Sussexes' departure from Britain was announced. Officially, they would not spend Christmas after all at Sandringham. They would stay instead for six weeks in Mille Fleurs, a newly fortified five-bedroomed waterfront mansion on Vancouver Island, guarded by six protection officers. Their stay as guests of a then unnamed American-Russian billionaire (later revealed to be Yuri Milner) had been arranged by the 71-year-old Canadian music producer David Foster. Five times married, Foster was a friend and neighbour in Santa Barbara of Oprah Winfrey, and occasionally appeared on her programme. He was also a friend of the Mulroney family.

The Sussexes' spokesman briefed that the couple would establish a presence in a Commonwealth country. From Vancouver, said her spokesman, Meghan could 'resume her business activities'.[664] Most assumed that Canada would be the location to launch their new lives and careers. Few speculated that it was a convenient half-way stop while finalising their exit from Britain.

Located in the same time-zone as Los Angeles, Meghan was in constant communication with Andrew Meyer, her business manager, Rick Genow, her lawyer, and Keleigh Thomas Morgan and others at Sunshine Sachs. Top of the agenda were the continuing negotiations with Netflix and Spotify, and the re-registration in Delaware on 22nd October, 2019, of Frim Fram Inc, the company behind The Tig. Their new Archewell Foundation – meaning 'source of action' – had already been registered in Delaware. Simultaneously, Genow had registered in Delaware a corporation called Loving Kindness Senior Care Management Inc. The corporation was run entirely by Doria Ragland. Unlike California, Delaware guaranteed secrecy for corporations' financial activities and accounts.[665] In parallel, Sussex Royal applied for trademarks on a range of products including bandanas, newspapers, sportswear, pens and 'emotional support services'.

Meghan consulted her Los Angeles team about the best terms for their departure from Britain. Buckingham Palace, she and Harry intended, should bear the blame for the fall-out. In Britain, the Palace understood that having rejected the Queen's invitation to visit Balmoral in the summer, the Sandringham snub at Christmas was irrefutable evidence of Meghan's intention to relocate, officials still believed, to Canada.[666]

The Sussexes' willingness to conceal the rift while they secretly considered their ultimate move to California coincided with Prince Andrew's BBC TV *Newsnight* interview with Emily Maitlis about his relationship with Jeffrey Epstein and his denial of any relationship with Virginia Roberts.[667] Andrew's lack of sympathy for Epstein's victims, his unconvincing denial that an incriminating photograph of himself with Roberts was genuine, and his absurd explanations of why Roberts's version of their encounters in a nightclub was untrue – the prince said he suffered a medical condition that prevented him sweating and he did not drink alcohol – totally destroyed his credibility. Worse, his misjudgement and lies jeopardised affection for the monarchy.

The combination of Andrew's car-crash appearance alongside Harry's ill-tempered contribution to ITV provoked the *Sun* to urge the Queen to rescue her family before it was 'driving off a cliff with no one at the wheel.'[668] The curtain was rising on another royal crisis.

The Queen, after consulting Charles and William, took control. Convinced that Harry and Meghan would never resume normal life in Britain, the trio agreed that the monarchy's future should be focused on reinvigorating Brand Cambridge. That was made easier by Charles and William becoming reconciled over the previous months. Memories of their heated arguments, rivalry and the resentment about Diana's treatment were buried. To avoid future disputes, they agreed that all foreign travel and duties would be planned to take account of their family life and William would begin to manage the Duchy of Cornwall, the source of his future income. Most important, without any formal announcement, the monarchy would be 'slimmed down'. The irritants, especially Andrew and Harry, would be removed earlier than planned.

Attack

Their agreement was conveyed by the Queen during her 2019 Christmas Day television broadcast. As Harry watched his grandmother from Vancouver, he was staggered. Four silver-framed family photographs had been carefully placed behind her. They showed the Queen's father George VI, Prince Philip, Charles and Camilla, and finally William and his family. To Harry's fury, there was no photograph of himself, Meghan and Archie. The Windsors were airbrushing the Sussexes from history.

CHAPTER 32

Transit

Isolation on Vancouver Island increased the Sussexes' sense of outrage. Listening to Harry's discussions with his family and officials in Britain, Meghan was furious that they were not accepted on their own terms. Rather, they were being bullied, pilloried and abused. Although hounded by the media and exploited by the Palace, they were left unprotected. 'Abandoned' was the sentiment Meghan soon adopted. The negotiations for their departure, she decided, would not be discreet.

The encouragement from her Los Angeles advisors was intoxicating. The Sussex brand, Meghan was assured, offered the same global opportunities as those reaped by the Obamas. They could exploit their royal status in films, books, finance and the digital world. By endorsing a major consumer corporation, the Sussexes would earn tens of millions of dollars. Their first step should be a major interview. Oprah Winfrey was waiting.

Together with Harry, Meghan intended to broadcast her frustration about the royals' crusty conservatism. It offended her can-do culture and the American Dream. In the propaganda battle, Meghan expected Hollywood to defeat the Windsors. Her publicists had produced an artful video to be shown on the sussexroyal website after the divorce was announced. Highlighting their lives during 2019, the couple thanked their 10.8 million followers for their 'continuing support' and assured them that they would be 'collaborating with the Queen' by pursuing a 'progressive' agenda. At the same time, the Sussexes also composed their proposed public statement announcing their departure from Britain. Harry believed that his family would accept their demands.

After several telephone calls with Charles, Harry was told to send his proposals in writing. Harry's message with their proposed statement broadly described the Sussexes' expectation to retain their titles, privileges and income while living in Canada. They would keep Frogmore, enjoy round the clock protection costing the British taxpayer annually about £2.5 million and continue to receive £1.5 million annual income from the Duchy of Cornwall. In exchange, they would occasionally return to Britain but otherwise represent the monarchy from Canada. Some would later suggest that Harry's proposal had been approved by Christopher Geidt.[669]

Charles prevaricated. He needed, he replied, more information. Harry appealed to the Queen. The Queen told her grandson that he should negotiate an agreement with his father. Although the monarch was deeply attached to Harry, her grandson's telephone calls to her and Charles and William about his future plans had unintentionally bound the three closer together. They were forging a united front against the Sussexes.

Just after Christmas, Harry's frustration increased. He heard that Dan Wootton, the *Sun*'s royal expert, had been told about their secret plans to leave Britain. The leak to Wootton convinced Harry of a conspiracy to destroy himself and Meghan. Harry demanded that Buckingham Palace take draconian action against the *Sun*. He was spurned. The Palace limited itself to simply denying to the newspaper that the Sussexes intended to leave Britain.

Obsessed about malicious forces in London, Harry was convinced that those in the Palace leaking his secrets were intent on destroying his marriage and himself. He could not imagine that Wootton's source might be one of the Sussexes' many advisors in Los Angeles and

Canada. Harry's only relief was that the scoop remained unpublished. Wootton was on holiday in New Zealand and unable to persuade the *Sun*'s editor to ignore the Palace's denials.

Harry and Meghan landed at Heathrow on 6th January, 2020, a cloudy, cold day. Archie had been left in Vancouver. Harry planned to drive directly to Sandringham for dinner with the Queen. To his dismay he was told that the engagement was cancelled. He telephoned the Queen and asked for another date that week. She replied that her diary was full.

Transferred to Edward Young, the Queen's private secretary, Harry disclosed that the solution to his recurring mental problems was to announce immediately their departure from Britain. Young asked Harry not to annoy the Queen by issuing his public statement before they met. At the end of their conversation, Harry believed that the Queen was receiving 'really bad' advice.[670]

The following night, the *Sun* published Wootton's exclusive. The couple, Wootton wrote, planned to 'step back' and live trouble-free in Canada alongside Meghan's many friends. And, helped by Sunshine Sachs, they intended to launch the Sussex Royal Foundation. The revelation dramatised the Sussexes' visit that morning, 8th January, to Canada House to say 'thank you' to the High Commissioner, Janice Charette, for providing sanctuary and protection. Their appearance was an excuse to provide a photo opportunity as they emerged into Trafalgar Square for their electrifying announcement.

Convinced of the Palace's plans to sabotage them, the couple decided to jump the gun. Despite the imminent negotiations with the Queen, their office issued their statement on the sussexroyal Instagram website. They would be 'stepping back' as full-time senior royals. They planned 'to carve out a progressive new role within this institution' and to 'balance our time between the United Kingdom and North America, continuing to honour our duty to the Queen, the Commonwealth, and our patronages. This geographic balance will enable us to raise our son with an appreciation for the royal tradition into which he was born, while also providing our family with the space to focus on the next chapter, including the launch of our new charitable entity. We look forward to sharing the full details of this exciting next step in due course.'

Their statement was read by the world as intended: a deliberate challenge to the Royal Family. Their promise of 'collaboration' in a 'progressive' future was, many thought, an insult to the Queen. Mentioning 'North America' was intended to persuade the public that the family would live permanently in Canada. Not least because Meghan had earlier pledged that she would stay out of the USA 'till after [Trump's] gone.'

The saga, now dubbed 'Megxit', gripped the nation. Meghan, once again in control, booked her return to Vancouver the next day. The Royal Family, she assumed, was blind-sided. Critics blamed Meghan for 'taking Harry hostage' and rupturing his relationship with the Queen. Others suggested that the Windsors' soap opera had been reinvigorated. William was upset. Charles was exasperated. Buckingham Palace's terse acknowledgement of the Instagram post concluded with a request for time. Harry waited for the summons. 'Megxit', Harry later claimed, was a term of misogynistic abuse invented by 'pirates with press cards'.[671]

In anticipation of the showdown, the Queen, Charles and William and their senior advisors agreed that, while they wanted to avoid appearing vengeful, British taxpayers would resent subsidising the Sussexes if they avoided serious duties. They were also puzzled why a 'progressive royal' would want the title, Her Royal Highness. 'Progressives', after all, were committed to changing an unequal society. Frivolity aside, they agreed that the monarchy could not risk the Sussexes' uncontrolled exploitation of their privileges and titles.

Their concern lay in one particular phrase: the Sussexes' intention to 'work to become financially independent' in Canada. Money, they knew, was at the heart of Meghan's thoughts, and it seemed that she intended to monetise the monarchy. Looking through the Sussex Royal filings in Delaware, officials were aghast that the couple intended to peddle pens and clothing under the Sussex Royal logo.

Although Harry had inherited about £27 million from Diana and his grandmother and Meghan had probably saved over £1 million from her career, that would not be sufficient to sustain their lives once they lost the Palace's financial support. Few in the Palace had forgotten the scandals involving the Countess of Wessex, Prince Andrew and his wife Sarah Ferguson, the Duchess of York.

Successful negotiations with Harry depended on striking a balance between keeping the Sussexes loyal and preventing them from 'leeching' off the British taxpayer. The options were not attractive. Either Meghan could be allowed to keep the privileges without the responsibilities; or her title could outrightly be removed. The latter option risked exciting those who were convinced that Meghan was a victim of racism, misogyny and class prejudice. (Harry would always remain a prince.) A compromise had to be agreed.

On 13th January, Harry was finally driven to Norfolk. Just before he arrived, Prince Philip headed to Wood Farm, his home on the estate. Harry's request that Meghan take part in the discussions by Zoom was rejected. The Palace assumed Meghan would allow others to listen – and their discussions would be recorded.

Those waiting for Harry at Sandringham – Charles, William and their advisors Edward Young, Clive Alderton, Simon Case and Fiona Mcilwham – assumed that Harry and Meghan would be prepared to agree to concessions. They also believed that Meghan controlled Harry. In reality, he shared Meghan's uncompromising demands. Over lunch, Harry intended to persuade the Queen that they could serve the monarchy in a semi-detached manner from Canada.

For his part, Harry did not realise that he would be met by an ultimatum. Half in, half out, he was informed, was impossible. He worked for the monarchy, he was bluntly told; the monarchy didn't exist to work for him. Once he was out, financial support would be quickly reduced, honorary titles would be removed and the Sussexes' duties sharply reduced. Moreover, they would not be allowed to accept payments as brand ambassadors for corporations. Police protection would also be withdrawn. Harry would subsequently claim that he had offered personally to pay for police protection.[672] [673]

Surprised by his family's hard line, Harry concluded that their terms amounted to punishment. As he tried to negotiate a better deal he remained aware that the British public was divided. While many supported the Sussexes' decision to leave the country, the majority opposed giving them any financial support or to them keeping their titles.[674]

'What has the Queen done to deserve this shoddy treatment?' asked the *Sun*'s Tony Parsons, previously an author of euphoric comments about the Sussexes on their wedding day. 'Let history record that no royal couple was ever as adored as Harry and Meghan. It is astonishing – and unbelievably sad, perhaps even tragic – that millions of us will be happy to see the back of them.'[675] The newspaper condemned the Sussexes' 'obnoxious behaviour' and continued: 'It's not just the Family they have betrayed. They are grotesquely abusing the generosity and goodwill of taxpayers too…They have decided to have their cake and eat it. They wanted all the money and privileges, but without the solid devotion to duty and hard graft that the Queen and latterly William and Kate exemplify. That is not how this institution works.'

Meghan's supporters were equally angry. The damnation of the Royal Family was led by the Anglophobic *New York Times*. Harry, asserted the newspaper, had angered Britons when he 'decided to take an American actress, with a bi-racial background, as his wife'.[676] 'Black Britons know why Meghan wants out,' wrote Afua Hirsch in the same newspaper. 'It's the racism. Only Blacks know the truth. The racist treatment of Meghan proved what many of us have always known: no matter how beautiful you are, whom you marry, what palaces you occupy, charities you support, how faithful you are, how much money you accumulate or what good deeds you perform, in this society racism will still follow you.'[677]

'Every Black person knew this was coming,' agreed Gina Yashere, again in the *New York Times*. Meghan faced 'constant racist vitriolic abuse disguised as criticism'. Delighted by the Royal Family's struggle to prove their own relevance, *The Oprah Magazine* went even further. As a mixed-race divorcee who wore dark nail-polish, asserted the publication, 'Meghan has not been made to feel welcome in the United Kingdom.'[678] *People* magazine quoted a 'friend' of Meghan: 'There is so much bad blood in that family – it's toxic...Meghan and Harry's hand was forced.' Meghan, reported the magazine, complained about her 'outsider status as a bi-racial American'. Neither she nor Harry 'got enough comfort or solace from [the royals].'[679]

None of the American media acknowledged that racism was a bigger problem in their country than Britain; or named a person or incident to illustrate the racist abuse suffered by Meghan in Britain. They appeared to be thrilled by Meghan's defiance towards the Queen and identified with her reasons for leaving the country.

Meghan's secret weapon was leaked by her 'friends' in California. If the Royal Family rejected her demands, they would be denounced as racist on *The Oprah Winfrey Show*.[680] Her threat of a 'no-holds barred' interview with Winfrey was confirmed by Tom Bradby in the *Sunday Times*. 'I don't think it would be pretty,' he predicted.[681] Tom Bradby damned William for having 'bullied [Harry] out' of the Royal Family. He accused William and Kate of snubbing Meghan before the wedding. The Cambridges, Bradby wrote, were 'insufficiently welcoming...Quite early on they decided, "Right, we are going to tell these people their place and we are going to push them away".' The result, wrote Bradby, was 'Harry and Meghan's escape from the poisonous palace.' Buckingham Palace used just one word in reply to Bradby's accusations: 'False'.[682]

In Britain, Clive Lewis, a mixed-race Labour MP, blamed Megxit on 'structural racism and sexism'. The Duchess's lack of interest in her royal responsibilities was irrelevant. 'We can see it with Meghan Markle and the way that she's been treated in the media…After 400 years of racism, you can't just overturn it overnight.'[683] To like-minded Britons, including the writer Philip Pullman, Meghan was a brave Black woman hunted by racists. The Royal Family had betrayed Meghan, every woman and every Black person.[684] 'Of course Meghan Markle is attacked by the British press because she's Black,' said Pullman, 'and of course Prince Harry is right to defend her.' North America, advised Pullman, was a natural refuge from Britain's intolerance.

The threats and the abuse by commentators did not influence the Royal Family's negotiating position. The trio had seen enough. The notion of any shared interest with the Sussexes to protect the monarchy was abandoned. Even seeking a compromise was ruled out. Meghan, they believed, clearly felt no qualms about who was insulted. She would exercise no self-censorship. Nothing would be held back to defeat her enemies. As they had witnessed, dumping unneeded people and burning bridges was natural to her. For Meghan, disloyalty was evidence of conviction. Nevertheless, the Queen wanted to appear fair.

On the Queen's insistence, Harry and Meghan were persuaded to attempt a trial separation – a transition period to divide their time between Canada and Britain – rather than an instant divorce. Harry agreed, but insisted that he would not change his mind. In his mind, they were leaving forever.

Some speculated that Christopher Geidt might have fashioned an amicable compromise, but now that was an unreasonable expectation.[685] The Sandringham Agreement, as the separation document became known, was tough. The Sussexes would cease to be working members of the Royal Family and would no longer use their HRH titles. Harry would lose his military roles, including Captain

General of the Royal Marines, and Meghan would lose her role within the Commonwealth. They would repay the £2.4 million for rebuilding Frogmore and, after one year, lose all financial support.[686] Harry assured his family that he and Meghan would 'never' use their royal titles 'to make money'.[687] Finally, they agreed to express mutual platitudes. The Queen said, 'I recognise the challenges they have experienced as a result of intense scrutiny over the last two years and support their wish for a more independent life.' The Sussexes pledged to 'uphold the values of Her Majesty'.

Harry returned to Vancouver knowing that Meghan was 'raging' about their treatment. He and Meghan shared a sense of grievance: the loss of his security and financial support, and the hostility of Charles, William and Kate. In search of consolation, he regularly telephoned senior officials in London for support but they, furious about Meghan's rudeness and preparing for their own redundancy, were unsympathetic.[688]

In their eyes, Meghan's well-publicised dash by seaplane to Vancouver for a hastily arranged visit to a women's refuge was intended to embarrass the Palace.[689] With one hour's notice, the refuge's staff welcomed Meghan. But after a brief stay she disappeared on the same plane, never to be seen again. The media was then tipped off by her staff. No one could explain why she did not choose instead to visit a women's refuge near her home.[690] The cynicism in London about the escapade fed Harry's and Meghan's hunger for revenge. Buckingham Palace, Harry fumed, was staffed by 'vipers' who deserved to be punished.

In early February, Buckingham Palace officials heard from the Sussexes' protection officers that Meghan had been house-hunting in Malibu in California. She had often mentioned her wish to live near the beach.[691] Senior Buckingham Palace officials were only half-surprised. Living in Canada, they believed, was a smokescreen. On the other hand, they also heard from a senior Canadian official about his long telephone conversation with Harry about the advantages of staying in the country. At the end, the official was convinced that Harry intended to remain in Canada.

In the Sussexes' version, they would have remained permanently in Vancouver if Harry had not been told 'at short notice that security was going to be removed'.[692] Their remote home had been identified and, he concluded, 'It's not safe.' Buckingham Palace's 'lack of support and lack of understanding,' he said, left them no alternative but to leave the heavily-guarded remote house. Harry spoke about being 'able to protect my son' – but from what danger was unclear. His principal enemy seemed to be the tabloids. The newspapers, Harry believed, were 'incredibly angry' about their move to Vancouver. 'They've come out fighting, and they will try and destroy our reputation, and you know, sink us.'

Fortunately, said Harry, he and Meghan had been able to 'stand up for what we believe together'.[693] How a move from Vancouver to a home in Los Angeles would better protect the Sussexes from the tabloids or from an unknown assassin was unclear, but logic played no part in the Sussexes' conduct.

Their true intentions were highlighted by Harry's agreement to speak at a JP Morgan event in Miami. Hosted by Gayle King, he flew to Florida on a private jet from Vancouver to earn an estimated $1 million for exposing his wounds. In an emotional address, Harry described once again the childhood trauma of losing his mother. More controversially, he told the world that he had no regrets about giving up his royal duties. To protect his family, he said, Meghan and his children should not experience a similar childhood to his own.

Buckingham Palace officials were aghast. This was exactly the commercialisation of the monarchy which Harry had agreed at Sandringham to avoid. Worse, Harry was negotiating with the Harry Walker Agency a contract to receive $500,000 per speech. His spokesman's insistence that Harry did not intend to speak about the

Royal Family was doubted.[694] Fearing ridicule, Harry was told by Buckingham Palace officials that the SussexRoyal Instagram account and brand should immediately be closed down.[695] The Palace's deadline for them to cease being royals was set for 31st March. Just six weeks after saying they were 'stepping back' as senior royals, the Sussexes announced they were 'stepping down'. The Canadian government immediately withdrew funding for their protection.[696]

'We were excited,' said Harry wistfully. 'We were hopeful. We were here to serve…For those reasons it brings me great sadness that it has come to this.'[697] To maintain their lifestyle, some calculated they would need an annual income of $10 million. The Sussexes' spokesman denied they had any plans to be interviewed by Oprah Winfrey.[698] But in a long statement drafted by their lawyers and publicists about losing their 'Royal' HRH title, the couple took a swipe at the Queen.[699]

The Queen, the Sussexes declared, had no 'jurisdiction' overseas about the word 'Royal'. If they chose to use the word, the monarch – and the government – were powerless. After all, they emphasised, Harry was sixth in line to the throne and an HRH by birth. 'The preference of the Duke and Duchess of Sussex was to continue to represent and support Her Majesty the Queen, albeit in a more limited capacity, while not drawing on the Sovereign Grant.' Their simmering resentment against William, Kate and other royals was not concealed. The Cambridges, after all, were allowed to operate the Royal Foundation, while Andrew's two daughters Beatrice and Eugenie were also employed, in a fairly modest way, in the art world.

Meghan was not to be defeated. She told her advisors to find a director in Los Angeles for their new charity, Archewell. Her frantic pace could not be hidden from senior officials in Buckingham Palace. In their opinion, the Sussexes' new jigsaw was nearly complete. The public and the media were still uncertain of the Sussexes' plans as they arrived in London for a final farewell.

CHAPTER 33

Farewell

'Without question,' Harry would say about Meghan, 'she saved me.'[700] Unsure about her precise future in Los Angeles, Meghan hid her emotions from the public during the brief return to London on 5th March, 2020. Her script required a dramatic finale. The Sussexes needed to spin their narrative of leadership, modernity and victimhood. Boosting her commercial value entailed constant visibility. Emphatically, her advisors advised that the optics should remind Americans that she was a duchess married to a prince.

Their first photo-opportunity was styled as if for a Hollywood star. On a rainy night outside the Mansion House in the City, Meghan, wearing a startling electric-blue dress, stood close to Harry under an umbrella. Brilliantly choreographed, the image showed two celebrities enjoying their freedom. The composition and lighting enthralled even the veteran royal photographer Arthur Edwards: 'It was the best royal picture of the year,' he judged. *Vanity Fair* described the photo as 'cinematic and affectionate'. On that day, those who had dubbed Harry 'a hostage' were flummoxed. In the photograph, the prince appeared to have escaped to the Pacific Ocean, leaving William with the royal burden.

The Sussexes were undertaking their last royal task, awarding prizes for the Endeavour Fund. During a military ceremony, Harry solemnly reaffirmed to serve 'Queen and Country' and 'never leave' his band of brothers – the wounded military.

Two days later, his final engagement as Captain General of the Royal Marines at the Royal Albert Hall was more emotional. Wearing his red ceremonial uniform to anticipate the seventy-fifth anniversary of the end of the Second World War, he came close to tears as the audience cheered the loyal soldier. At that moment, many recalled his happiness in the army and wondered how he would cope with exile. Some speculated that he would despair about losing contact with his friends and family. 'It was so unnecessary,' Meghan said angrily to a friend about Harry losing his military appointments.[701]

Reality hit two days later, on 9th March. A monumental argument blew up after Harry was told that he and Meghan could not join the family's procession through Westminster Abbey for the annual Commonwealth Day Service. Although the order of service listed Harry and Meghan walking behind the Queen, Palace officials had revised their decision. Suspicious about the Sussexes they decided to publicly humiliate them. Harry was told that having stepped down from royal duties, he and Meghan would sit and wait with the congregation. The prospect of the televised image of their isolation in the Abbey appalled them.

By then they were keenly aware of Kate and William's antagonism. William had not offered a brotherly welcome and Kate was outright distant towards her sister-in-law. Eventually, to end the dispute, William and Kate agreed they too would wait with Harry and Meghan. As the members of the Royal Family filed into the Abbey, the frayed relationships could not be concealed. Kate had blanked the Sussexes and William's greeting was cold. Harry looked strained. Meghan's face showed bemusement.

During that same day, Meghan bid farewell to the last few members of her staff. In Omid Scobie's version, 'Staff who had been with the couple from day one were in mourning at the end of what was supposed to be a happy story.'[702] Especially invited by Meghan, Scobie also watched her last private engagement in Buckingham Palace. After meeting 22 students who had received Commonwealth scholarships, he wrote, 'Reality finally set in as I gave Meghan a goodbye hug… Tears that the Duchess had been bravely holding back are free to flow among familiar faces.' Meghan apparently said to Scobie: 'It didn't have to be this way.'[703]

Even on her last day, Meghan did not want to understand that the Royal Family could not compromise. To the end, she could not understand why her demands were not met. 'I gave up my entire life for this family,' she apparently told a friend in London. 'I was willing to do whatever it takes. But here we are. It's very sad.'[704]

Meghan's personal regret was not the lasting memory of her in-laws as she sped from Westminster Abbey to Heathrow for the flight to Vancouver. They recalled an angry adventuress denied the power to dictate her own fate. Despite all the efforts to welcome her – the wedding, the house, the staff, the foreign tours and limited duties – Meghan had refused to accept that a monarchy epitomised continuity. There was no place for someone to overturn one thousand years of evolution to spearhead a 'progressive new role'.

The nation was bewildered and divided. Tom Bradby's criticism of the Royal Family – 'few meaningful attempts were made by anyone to heal the wounds' – resonated with those who blamed the Windsors. In their opinion, the family had also abandoned Diana. They lamented a lost opportunity.[705] Others were outraged by Meghan: 'It's deeply unfair to the Queen, who doesn't deserve to be treated this way. It is a shoddy way to treat her,' wrote a *Mail* contributor.[706] The majority were perplexed by Meghan's lament: 'I gave up my entire life for this family.' She spent only three years in Britain. She left behind former staff and a world which was misled about her intentions. The following day, the *New York Times* reported that Meghan had departed to 'decamp for one of the frontier outposts, western Canada, and an uncertain life as semi-royals'. The Sussexes, declared the headline, would 'head to Canada to patch together a new life and build their brand.'[707]

There was good news from Los Angeles. Meghan's team had recruited Catherine St-Laurent, a Canadian-born philanthropic organiser and formerly a key aide to Melinda Gates, to be Archewell's director and the couple's chief of staff. St-Laurent would describe her new employers as global leaders who 'embark on this journey of learning, listening, and inspiring all of us to act'. She would add, 'I am thrilled to be able to play a supporting role in realising their vision and enabling them to achieve impact on the issues that matter most to them.'[708]

St-Laurent's task was to entrench the Sussexes as global Influencers. Her description of Meghan's mission was perfectly crafted jargon: 'At Archewell we unleash the power of compassion to drive systemic cultural change. We do this through our non-profit work within Archewell Foundation, in addition to creative activations through the business verticals of audio and production.'

Described as a non-profit charity, Archewell had no money in the bank. There was no explanation of how, in the future, they would divide their income to support their personal lifestyle, pay their employees – and fund Archewell. Nor would they list all Archewell's beneficiaries. Unlike the transparency laws in Britain, the Sussexes would be protected from scrutiny. Everything was ready for their new life. Or as Meghan called it, 'the next chapter'.

Secretly, in mid-March the Sussex family boarded a private jet and dashed from Vancouver Island to Los Angeles, shortly before entry into American airspace was restricted by the escalating Covid crisis.

The jet was owned by Tyler Perry, a film producer occasionally represented by Keleigh Thomas Morgan. Typically among the interlocking relationships, Tyler had sold his TV series *The Have and The Have Nots* to Oprah Winfrey's TV network. Perry also lent the Sussexes his eight-bedroom home in Beverly Ridge. Worth $18 million, the biggest house in the area was set in 22 acres. Although not inhabited by the same prestigious A-listers as in Beverly Hills or Malibu, the Sussexes could cast off their memory of those unpleasant months in Frogmore. There was no reason for any doubts when Meghan exclaimed, 'For so many reasons, I'm glad to be home.'[709]

One of the few not to welcome her return was Donald Trump. In the past, she had called the President 'divisive', 'misogynistic' and added, 'You don't want that kind of world he is painting for us.'[710] After their arrival, the President tweeted that America would not pay for their security. No one had asked America to pay, Meghan replied.[711] Unusually, Trump did not rise to the bait: 'She was nasty to me and that's OK for her to be nasty. It's not good for me to be nasty to her and I wasn't…She's doing a good job. I hope she enjoys her life. I think she's very nice.' The President's emollience was rewarded by Harry telling a hoax caller, 'The mere fact that Donald Trump is pushing the coal industry, is so big in America; he has blood on his hands.'

Meghan was returning to California after a nine-year absence. For the wealthy, Los Angeles is glorious – sunshine, sea, spectacular countryside, excellent restaurants, unlimited reservoirs of staff, and a perfect environment for children. Mothers like Meghan cared about organic philosophies and natural foods. Rich enough to enjoy the beaches and lifestyle, Meghan could easily convert Harry to the pleasure of wading in the Pacific and watching the surfers in Santa Monica. Better than shaking hands with the public in a rainy English town. Free and independent, she promised they would build exciting, rewarding lives.

Their prospects in the short and long term were different. The city's society hostesses were certain to seek to adorn their parties with a duke and duchess. California's great and good would undoubtedly flock to experience the novelty. Harry's celebrity guaranteed attention. But in the long term their lasting success depended on their message and manner. The challenge was to sustain their status. That required not only building a solid network of famous sympathisers but also retaining the loyalty of millions of people. The couple's hyper-sensitivity made the job harder for St-Laurent. Both expected obsequiousness and the exclusion of critics. Finding like-minded people for long-term relationships would be a challenge.

To their misfortune, their relaunch coincided with the world going into lockdown. Covid's imposition of solitary lifestyles was causing desperation among millions of people. At that dark moment the Queen offered sympathy to all. Her televised address to the nation ended emotionally by recalling the wartime song 'We'll Meet Again'.[712]

On Sunshine Sachs's recommendation, the Sussexes posted a rival message about the global crisis. 'We will be sharing information and resources to help all of us navigate the uncertainty,' their Instagram post declared. 'From posting accurate information to learning about the measures we can take to keep ourselves and our families healthy.' The presumption that the Sussexes should be trusted to distil the accuracy of the science was audacious.

In the countdown to bid farewell at the end of March to the followers of Sussex Royal and end their royal lives, they pledged not to embarrass the Queen or rely on financial support from Charles: 'We look forward to reconnecting with you soon. You've been great. Until then, please take good care of yourselves, and of one another. Harry and Meghan.'[713]

Tony Parsons articulated the voice of disillusioned Britons:

'As the UK struggles with the worst health crisis in living memory, the message from Harry and Meghan's borrowed Beverly Hills mansion to the country they abandoned is loud and clear — you think YOU'VE got it bad? It is all stunning – the arrogance, the hubris, the self-regard, the self-pity, the lack of self-awareness. You can see how we went right off them. The abiding memory of 2020 will NOT be Harry and Meghan phoning in their woke messages from Los Angeles. It will be the Queen's stirring, profoundly moving and genuinely inspirational 'We'll Meet Again' address to the nation at the height of the pandemic. If they were not quite so full of themselves, Harry and Meghan could have been national treasures during this crisis. Imagine Harry turning up to talk to frontline health workers! Imagine Meghan showing the nation how to look drop-dead gorgeous in a face mask! It was not to be. And as our nation struggled with the worst health crisis in a lifetime, these empty, self-obsessed, self-pitying celebrities left Granny to do the heavy lifting. And at 94, the Queen did it brilliantly. But how pathetically shallow the Queen makes Harry and Meghan look. And how empty, how trivial, how redundant they seem outside the context of the Royal Family.'[714]

At least, Meghan no longer had to remember to cross her legs when sitting.

CHAPTER 34

Paradise

In May 2020, Meghan could say she had achieved the American Dream. She and Harry bought a nine-bedroom, 14-bathroom, 18,000-square-feet hillside house in Montecito, Santa Barbara for $14.65 million (£11 million). With eight acres of lawns and views over the Pacific for what local agents called a bargain price, the property included a gym, a spa, cinema, tennis court, swimming pool, a children's cottage, a two-bedroom guest house and a five-car garage. Finally, Meghan's hard work had been rewarded with a palace in a part of California's paradise.

Her neighbours offered the key to her future. Among the celebrities were Ellen DeGeneres, the host of a popular daytime TV show. In 2016, Obama had awarded her America's highest civilian honour, the Presidential Medal of Freedom. Nearby, Oprah Winfrey owned a house with 40 acres. Next to Oprah was her associate and close friend, Gayle King. A few blocks away was Ted Sarandos, responsible for Netflix's $17 billion annual budget for content. Sarandos lived with Nicole Avant, America's first Black ambassador to the Bahamas, a friend of Oprah Winfrey and the daughter of Motown's former chairman, Clarence Avant, alias the 'Black Godfather'.

Dotted around were Hollywood celebrities including Gwyneth Paltrow and Katy Perry. The most important was David Foster, the Canadian music producer. Living in Montecito with his fifth wife

Katharine McPhee, Foster had become a guiding spirit. 'David has a really, really beautiful relationship with Harry,' said McPhee. 'They're so cute. They're like father and son.'[715]

Reports of their happiness in Montecito excited speculation in Britain about the future of their marriage. Many doubted it could last. Some predicted that Harry would regret abandoning his royal life and miss his family and friends. His ultimate humiliation would be overwhelming, once Meghan's true agenda was exposed. They misunderstood the prince. Harry blessed Meghan for rescuing him from the British press and Kensington Palace. Now he could walk freely across the sandy beach with Archie to paddle in the Pacific. Harry felt liberated. Those who predicted the same misery as Edward VIII, who was surprised after his abdication when Britons turned against him, made the wrong comparison. Harry was never heir to the throne. Although the Queen gave the couple a chance to reconsider their departure after a year's trial of independent life, Harry had no intention of returning.

Meghan had power and influence. All those directors, producers, agents and actors who had witnessed her earlier struggles feared speaking out about their experiences. One negative word from Meghan could terminate their careers. 'I'm not feeling comfortable speaking of Meghan at this time,' said David Bartis of *Suits*, a typical reply to journalists' inquiries. Terrified of being blackballed or cancelled, the only heroes in Los Angeles were invented by Hollywood for the screen. The Sussexes were protected as Hollywood stars. Embedded in Hollywood's culture, both transformed their image into warriors eager to brave the crossfire.

Harry had been persuaded by Meghan about the evils of white privilege and the justification of Black Lives Matter. 'My wife said recently,' Harry told the young people being honoured with Diana Awards in July 2020, 'that our generation hasn't done enough to right the wrongs of the past. I am sorry. Sorry, that we haven't got the world to the place you deserve it to be. Institutional racism has no place in our societies. Yes, it is still endemic. Unconscious bias must be acknowledged without blame to create a better world for all of you.'[716] Harry was echoing a speech Meghan had given two weeks earlier in a video about Black people killed by the police.[717] Her audience were graduates of her old school, the Immaculate Heart: 'The first thing I want to say to you is that I'm sorry. I'm so sorry that you have to grow up in a world where this is still present.'[718]

In Montecito, Harry separated himself from his family and roots. Transforming himself into a campaigner he attacked the Commonwealth as colonial and racist with an 'uncomfortable' history. Just four months earlier, as vice-president of the Commonwealth Trust, he had spoken with unquestioning praise about his grandmother's achievement.[719]

'When you look across the Commonwealth,' Harry told young Commonwealth leaders from his garden in Montecito, 'there is no way that we can move forward unless we acknowledge the past.' Meghan repeated his attack on the Commonwealth's 'unconscious racial bias'. Adopting BLM's argument, Meghan advocated equality. 'We're going to have to be a little uncomfortable right now, because equality does not put anyone on the back foot, it puts us all on the same footing – which is a fundamental human right.'[720]

Both possibly confused the Commonwealth, a voluntary organisation embracing one-third of the world's population to rectify inequalities of the past, with the British Empire. Some blamed Nicola Brentnall, the Commonwealth Trust's chief executive, for encouraging their criticism. She resigned soon after.[721] Their spokesman, Omid Scobie, shared their criticism. The Commonwealth, he wrote, existed to 'uphold white supremacy'.[722] One month later, both partially corrected themselves. In a video conference Meghan gushed about her 'incredible pride' to work with the Commonwealth but still urged Britain to 'right the wrongs'.[723] Even Meghan could not have anticipated how her sentiment would be echoed in the Commonwealth, especially in the Caribbean – a cauldron of growing resentment against Britain, the white colonialists who rejected their demands of reparations for the slave trade.

The couple's declarations coincided with a further draconian lockdown across the world to stem the spread of Covid. Britain was in crisis. Deaths were increasing, the economy was in freefall and suffering was widespread. From Montecito, Harry urged the British government to do more for seriously ill children.

Their tub-thumping damaged the couple's popularity. Harry's negative rating in Britain increased from 35 per cent to 47 per cent. Meghan's rose from 46 per cent to 59 per cent. Their positive ratings fell to the mid-30s per cent. The Queen scored 83 per cent positive and William 80 per cent positive.[724] In America Meghan and Harry remained popular.

CHAPTER 35

The Trial

'It was destroying my mental health,' Harry said about the British media. He blamed them for fleeing from London. 'I was like…this is toxic. So I did what any husband and father would do – I need to get my family out of here.'[725] Privacy and protection from Britain's tabloid newspapers was repeatedly cited by the Sussexes as their principal reason to escape from Britain. Safe in Los Angeles, the couple announced a campaign against the tabloids.

'She believes there was a pattern of intrusive and offensive articles,' David Sherborne, Meghan's barrister, wrote in his complaint against the *Mail on Sunday* in April for publishing her letter to Thomas Markle. Launching the claim for breach of privacy was the Sussexes' moment of truth, a calculated bid for revenge.

Posing as champions of a free press, Sherborne, on the Sussexes' behalf, sermonised: 'When power is enjoyed without responsibility, the trust we all place in this much-needed industry is degraded.' Citing nine articles to prove the newspaper's 'dishonesty and malicious intent', the barrister portrayed Meghan's 'distress' about the *Mail on Sunday*'s 'agenda'.[726] In her mind, Britain's unaccountable media had printed 'hundreds of thousands of inaccurate articles about her' knowing they were 'distorted, false, or invasive beyond reason'.[727] The Sussexes were honourable people 'completely pulled apart for no good reason' other than to earn profits. Refusing to 'offer themselves up as currency for an economy of click-bait and distortion', their staff were forbidden to speak to tabloid journalists.[728]

Reading Meghan's declamation online in Mexico, Thomas Markle was outraged. *People* magazine had not only distorted Meghan's letter but had defamed him. 'It was a total lie,' he would say. 'It misrepresented the tone and content of the letter Meghan had written. The letter was not an attempt at reconciliation.'[729] Even worse, the *People* article had 'vilified' him as 'dishonest, exploitative, publicity-seeking and cold-hearted.' Yet in suing the *Mail on Sunday*, Meghan was attacking him, the honest father. She also, Thomas believed, refused to accept responsibility for the media's negative portrayal of herself. Not only by her hypocritical preaching about the environment while using private jets, but her repeated advocacy of 'compassion' while treating her father harshly. Her self-delusion, he believed, sparked the courtroom battle. The juxtaposition of Meghan's 'core purpose' with Archewell's mission to 'uplift and unite communities – one act of compassion at a time' – fuelled her self-delusion and, he believed, had sparked the courtroom battle.

Thomas Markle was particularly annoyed by Meghan's claim, written by David Sherborne, that the *Mail on Sunday* caused the rift between the two by 'deliberately seeking to dig or stir up issues between her and her father'. She claimed that the *Mail* had 'harassed, humiliated, manipulated and exploited...this vulnerable man into giving interviews'. She went even further. Her signed statement alleged that she was 'concerned that her father's narrative that she had abandoned him and had not even tried to contact him (which was false) would be repeated, when in fact she had tried to call him, and text him, and had even written a letter to him to try and persuade him to stop dealing with the media'.

Thomas Markle was furious. Media harassment had definitely occurred – but that was before the wedding – and when she had ignored all his appeals for help. Convinced that he would die like all the Markles before he was 80, he wanted to give evidence – 'a High Noon showdown' – before it was too late.[730]

'It will be quite stunning for everybody,' he promised, and 'excruciatingly embarrassing' for the Royal Family. His particular target was Harry for his insults before the wedding. 'Meghan,' he said scathingly, 'has turned into Harry's mother. He's candy-ass. He's whipped.'[731] To his misfortune, his anger spilled into self-harm. 'It's time to look after Daddy,' he told British TV. 'Meghan owes me.' It was time she repaid 'Daddy' for all he had done.[732]

High Court trials for privacy in London follow a complicated route. Long before Meghan and other eyewitnesses would be asked to give their evidence – and be cross-examined – the judge would highlight during several hearings what issues were to be decided and how the relevant law should be applied. In the very nature of the process and the prejudices, the judge's decisions were unpredictable. With the addition to that potent mix of a member of the Royal Family as the claimant, neither side could be certain what facts would influence the judge and what bias would determine his interpretation of the law. Both sides could only agree that Meghan's claim was a landmark case that could determine England's privacy law for many years.

Conscious about their image before the trial started in London, Meghan's and Harry's publicists authorised the distribution of photographs of the two handing out meals to the homeless in Los Angeles. Organised by Project Angel Food founded by Marianne Williamson, the author of self-help books and a friend of Oprah Winfrey, the couple stood in safety by the open boots of their black Porsche SUV and a six-litre Cadillac Escapade to distribute the packages.[733] After a short spell of charity, they drove back to their Montecito haven.

The trial's first hearing started in London on 24th April, 2020. Although it was early morning in Los Angeles, Meghan was watching on TV with her lawyer.[734] The judge, Mark Warby, was rated by newspapers as fair minded. Experienced in media law, he had encountered as a barrister many capricious judges.

Representing the *News of the World*, he had acted against Max Mosley. The head of Formula One motor-racing had objected to the newspaper's exposé of his sado-masochistic orgy with four paid-for women dressed in German military uniforms. Mosley won his action for privacy because the judge declared that since there were no Nazi overtones in the orgy itself, the newspaper could not assert there was a public interest to expose Mosley's unusual behaviour. Many criticised the judge as biased.

The same criticism was levelled at another judge in Warby's case against Prince Charles. Representing the *Mail on Sunday*, Warby argued that the newspaper was justified in publishing Charles's widely distributed Hong Kong journal. The newspaper lost the case, and its executives were reassured that Warby was as surprised as themselves about the judge's bias in Charles's favour. Some believed that the judgements in both cases exposed the judiciary's prejudice against the media.

Based on his advice as a barrister, the *Mail on Sunday* might have trusted Judge Warby to consider carefully its robust defence against Meghan's claim. Namely, that she constantly sought publicity and could have 'no reasonable expectation of privacy'. First, because she had 'knowingly' allowed her five friends to leak details of the letter to *People* magazine; second, because Thomas Markle was entitled to expose the magazine's false claims that Meghan had been reaching out to repair the relationship; and third, because she wrote her letter in the expectation that it might be leaked to the media.[735]

Three weeks into pre-trial hearings the newspaper's hopes rose. Warby made a series of dramatic decisions. Meghan's claim that the *Mail on Sunday* had deliberately 'exploited' her father was struck out of the case. Similarly, Meghan's claim that the newspaper had 'harassed and humiliated' her father and 'deliberately manipulated and exploited a vulnerable and fragile individual' was ordered to be dropped. There was no 'credible' evidence, ruled the judge. The judge also rejected Meghan's claim that the *Mail on Sunday* had waged a 'dishonest' campaign against her. He called her case 'wholly inadequate', 'impermissibly vague' and 'irrelevant'. All of Sherborne's hyperbole was struck out.[736] Meghan was ordered to pay the *Mail*'s £67,888 costs. As a side swipe, the judge criticised Schillings, who instructed Sherborne to help Omid Scobie to post pro-Meghan messages on Twitter.[737]

'For Meghan,' commented the media lawyer Mark Stephens, 'this judgement is like a train ploughing into a petrol tanker at a level crossing...she's been humiliated.' Stephens advised Meghan to give up because she had no chance of winning a case wholly focused on whether the public interest and freedom of expression overrode her rights to privacy and copyright.[738]

The defeat galvanised Schillings and Meghan. David Sherborne was replaced by two expensive QCs, including Justin Rushbrooke, Boris Johnson's great friend.[739]

Meghan's strategy dramatically changed. Instead of exclusively attacking the newspaper she also criticised her Palace advisors. Not only had they left her 'unprotected' while pregnant, she now pleaded, but when faced by an onslaught of 'hundreds of thousands of inaccurate articles about her', Kensington Palace's spokesmen would only say 'No comment'. To her fury, 'without any discussion', she was 'prohibited from defending herself'. Compelled to suffer in silence, her closest friends – a 'special sisterhood' – became 'deeply worried for her mental health'. To save her, they had spoken 'anonymously' to *People* magazine.

For the first time, Meghan admitted that two of those friends had been told about the letter.[740] But she still denied authorising them to speak publicly and claimed she was unaware of the *People* article until its publication.[741] The *Mail on Sunday* expected to discover the truth once all Meghan's text and email messages to the five friends were disclosed. Meghan condemned the *Mail*'s attempt to discover the five friends' identity as 'playing a media game with real lives and vicious.'[742] She never complained to *People* magazine's editor about their inaccuracies.

Meghan also adopted a different attitude towards the media promotion of Scobie's and Durand's book, *Finding Freedom*. In the months before publication in August, Scobie attracted controversy about his age – he claimed to be 33 but was said to be about 39 – and about his appearance. As Meghan's acknowledged cheerleader everyone believed Scobie's assertion that the book was written 'with the participation of those closest to the couple'. Kensington Palace, Scobie wrote truthfully, had also introduced the authors to people 'close' to Meghan. Scobie left the reader in no doubt that he had also enjoyed close access to Meghan and Harry, claiming to have spoken 'when appropriate [to] the couple themselves.'[743]

The bestselling book cast Meghan as the victim of 'sexist and prejudiced' Palace courtiers who snidely referred to 'Harry's showgirl' who 'comes with a lot of baggage'. The book's narrative portrayed Meghan as a popular outsider distrusted as a 'successful woman of colour'.[744] Royal aides were described as 'vipers', William was criticised for provoking a rift with Harry; Thomas Markle was portrayed as a bankrupt, unloving and deceitful father who deliberately failed to arrive at the wedding; and Kate was blamed for snubbing Meghan. Strangely, Scobie dismissed the allegations about the pre-wedding argument between Kate and Meghan. 'No tears from anyone,' Scobie wrote.[745] According to the Sussexes' rules of privacy, media criticism of themselves was unacceptable. But they could assist Scobie in criticising the Royal Family. Then, unexpectedly, Meghan changed her 'truth'. The Sussexes somersaulted.

'They did not collaborate with the authors on the book,' said Meghan's spokesman. 'Nor were they interviewed for it.' In a signed statement, Jenny Afia, her Schillings solicitor, denied on Meghan's behalf that the Duchess had spoken to Scobie or gave authority to anyone to speak to the authors on her behalf. Meghan herself described the *Mail*'s allegations that she had helped Scobie as 'false', 'fantastical' and 'a conspiracy theory'.[746] She denied knowing how much help the authors got from her staff[747] and denied being given the opportunity to make changes or fact-check.[748] 'It was not me and had nothing to do with me,' she said. Meghan's 'truth' was supported by Omid Scobie.

On 16th September, Scobie signed a statement: 'Any suggestion that the Duke and Duchess collaborated on the book is false.'[749] At the end of his statement, Scobie acknowledged that signing a misleading statement was punishable as a contempt of court. Scobie knew that the two-hour briefing with Jason Knauf required the Sussexes' approval, as did the help provided by Keleigh Thomas Morgan and Sara Latham. The author had signed a misleading statement to support Meghan against the *Mail on Sunday*. The Sussexes were now indebted to Scobie to maintain the pretence. In future, he could leverage that to obtain exclusive information to sell to newspapers and TV. Among his early bonuses was his revelation about the Sussexes' private video-call with the Queen on her ninety-fourth birthday.

Armed with Scobie's cast-iron denial, Meghan's lawyers asked Judge Warby to dispense with a trial – so that she could avoid being subject to cross-examination – and just issue his summary judgement about privacy. Her letter, the lawyers claimed, was 'private, personal and sensitive' and was never intended to be made public. The *Mail* argued that during her consultation with Knauf, Meghan anticipated the letter being made public; and that she had breached her own privacy by allowing her friends to speak to *People* magazine on her behalf.[750]

Forty-nine examples of intimate details described by Scobie were listed as evidence of Meghan's co-operation with Scobie. They included their holiday plans, Meghan's hygiene and bathroom routines in Botswana, details of her first meeting with Harry in Soho House and who first said, 'I love you.' The details were so precise, claimed the newspaper, that they could only have come from the Sussexes. The Sussexes refuted the *Mail*'s assumption. Meghan listed many of the book's errors, inventions and 'creative licence' as proof that she had not co-operated with Scobie.[751]

Meghan's conviction that her misleading statement would not be exposed was not an aberration. For years she had made incorrect assertions about her childhood, parents and career. But this was different. Although she would later assert that she had forgotten her conversations, emails and her two-page memorandum to Jason Knauf, others would conclude that she had decided to take a gamble. If she admitted co-operating with Scobie her claim against the newspaper would go to trial. Subject to cross-examination, she would also have to reveal all her text messages.

By nature, Meghan viewed other people through self-interest, or as she called it, 'being kind to yourself'.[752] Her outspoken complaints in *Finding Freedom* and again in her court statement that she felt unprotected in Kensington Palace irritated her former staff. Although bound by stiff non-disclosure agreements, some staff revealed in whispered conversations that Meghan's statement to the court about not co-operating with Scobie was inaccurate. Four officials – Knauf, Cohen, Latham and Jones – intimated their readiness to testify in a trial without taking sides about the 'creation of the letter' to Thomas Markle.

In September 2020, the *Mail on Sunday* filed a statement challenging Meghan's original claims that she had not spoken to the authors of *Finding Freedom*. In November or December 2018, the newspaper declared, Meghan had told the Kensington Palace communications' team led by Jason Knauf that 'her friends were assisting the authors'.[753] The newspaper questioned why Meghan did not protest that excerpts of her letter to her father were quoted in the book? Why had she objected only to the newspaper's alleged offence?[754] If she co-operated with Scobie's flattering account, declared the newspaper, she had not been telling the truth. By implication she could not claim privacy.[755]

Seven weeks later Meghan changed her statement. She now admitted authorising a friend to explain to Scobie 'the true position' about the relationship with her father 'to prevent any further misrepresentation...that she had abandoned him.'[756] She also admitted that Sara Latham had helped 'fact-check' for the authors. She sought to minimise her latest admission by volunteering that she 'does not know if and to what extent the communications team were involved in providing information for the book.'[757] Her two page briefing note to Jason Knauf had apparently been forgotten.

As Meghan's version crumbled, Keleigh Thomas Morgan was also named as providing introductions for the authors.[758] Meghan admitted that Knauf did contribute to drafting the letter,[759] and that one of her friends spoke to Scobie about the letter.[760] She also admitted that her letter was not an attempt at reconciliation.[761] The *Mail on Sunday* was delighted. The newspaper believed that Meghan's admissions reinforced their defence that she could not have 'reasonable expectation of privacy'.

Their cause appeared to be aided by Scobie's contradictions. First, asserting in the book that he had spoken to the Sussexes, then denying in a signed statement their help. Francesca Kaye, a Master of the Chancery Division, decided that Scobie's honesty should be tested. 'It's not what he says but what he does not say which may be instructive at trial,' Kaye declared. Pertinently, she also noted Meghan's contradictions. 'It's a simple case,' Kaye anticipated. 'If it's a house of cards, then it will fall down quickly at trial. But I'm satisfied it is arguable.'[762] Meghan was again ordered to pay all the lawyers' fees, totalling £178,000 – so far.[763] Everything seemed set to test Meghan's veracity in the witness-box.

No one in Buckingham Palace had anticipated that Meghan would go through with the case. Accordingly, the four Palace staff instructed David Engel, a solicitor, to send a clear message to the newspaper's lawyers. While the four did have evidence as to whether Meghan anticipated that her letter would be leaked, wrote the lawyer, he refused to describe their evidence.[764] However, Engel added, 'They are willing to provide to the Court such assistance as they can. That would, if appropriate, include giving oral evidence at trial and/or providing to the parties any relevant documentary evidence.' Warby was left in no doubt that the Palace Four could provide critical eyewitness evidence in a trial.

In the sunshine 5,000 miles away, the soothing assurances of her lawyers minimised the glitches of the legal battle in London. Meghan was busy laying the groundwork for the starring role in the next greatest appearance of her career.

CHAPTER 36

The Jigsaw

The branding of Meghan as an Influencer benefited from her marriage to Prince Harry. Despite the undemocratic overtone, the social justice warrior was trading as a duchess with a mission. To forge a composite image of a unique woman, her communications staff were tasked with slotting together the jigsaw pieces: compassion, victimhood, fake news, racism, feminism and motherhood. Each piece of the jigsaw illustrated Meghan's suffering.

Based in Montecito, Christine Weil Schirmer, the communications chief, and Toya Holness, the 'global' press secretary, collaborated with London-based James Holt, previously a Downing Street aide of the former deputy prime minister Nick Clegg, to deliver the Sussexes' slogan, 'Build compassion around the world'. In true believer's jargon, Schirmer explained that her employers offered 'diverse and open access to their work by engaging with global, specialist and grass-roots outlets.' In the same vein, she spoke of Archewell's purpose to 'unleash the power of compassion to drive systemic cultural change'. The trio were on a mission to spread Meghan's gospel.

The curtain-raiser was the 'Most Powerful Women Summit', a *Fortune* magazine conference.[765] Although virtual because of Covid, tickets cost $2,426 each. Meghan featured in the 'Courageous Leadership' session. Describing herself as the 'most trolled person in the entire world in 2019' – an exaggeration, since Adele and Gemma Collins were among the many who were even more trolled – she recited how abuse had left her 'isolated' and 'othered'.[766] Being the victim of the racist antagonism that was 'manufactured and churned out' was, she said, 'almost unsurvivable'.

At the heart of Meghan's argument was the 'unfairness of her mistreatment'. Facebook and other social media platforms always carried hate-filled posts after she spoke about mental health, well-being and gender equality. While her statements were obviously true and 'not controversial', the reaction to her on social media was callous, poisonous even. 'I am cautious of putting my family at risk…What ended up inflammatory is people's interpretation. That's so big, you can't even think about what that feels like.'[767]

Using the phrases which viewers of the Netflix documentary *The Social Dilemma* would find familiar, she advocated to the conference, 'Stop Hate for Profit'. The world's biggest companies, she urged, should stop advertising on Facebook until founder Mark Zuckerberg tackled hate-speech.[768] Her criticisms were somewhat undermined by denying that she read any social media: 'For my own self-preservation, I have not been on social media for a very long time…I have made a personal choice to not have an account.'[769] Meghan claimed to have stopped using Facebook: 'I don't know what's out there, and in many ways that's helpful for me.'

That declaration sat oddly with Meghan having been once the dedicated producer of The Tig, followed by over three million on Twitter, Facebook and Instagram.[770] On sussexroyal.com, Harry had just posted on Mental Health Day: 'Showing vulnerability in today's world is a strength.'[771] On the same website, Meghan had posted a message from herself as 'the Duchess of Sussex' commiserating with the trials of their followers during the Covid lockdown: 'We recognise the unique perspectives through which different communities view the world. And though this is a time of unprecedented challenges and polarisation, our communities have the capability to deliver solutions that will build a better future for all'. She had added in a YouTube address from Montecito on International Day of the Girl that the Covid lockdown had allowed the Sussexes to enjoy 'really good family time'.[772]

Even that was not quite accurate. Six weeks later, she revealed in an article for the *New York Times* that she had suffered a miscarriage in July. Under the headline, 'The Losses We Share', Meghan described how she felt the first pain while changing Archie's nappy. 'I knew as I clutched my first-born child that I was losing my second.' Hours later, she was holding Harry's hand in hospital: 'I felt the clamminess of his palm and kissed his knuckles, wet from both our tears. I tried to imagine how we'd heal.'[773]

To some, her newspaper article was an outright invasion of her own privacy. To others, she blessedly breached a taboo. A quarter of all pregnancies in Britain ended in a miscarriage. 'Losing a child,' she wrote to her sympathisers, 'means carrying an unbearable grief, experienced by many but talked about by few.' To add a sting to her revelation, she blamed the miscarriage on the pressure of 'going through a lot'. Namely, her legal action against the *Mail on Sunday*. In reality, in July on the eve of the publication of *Finding Freedom*, she had anticipated an outright victory in her privacy litigation.

The revelation of her miscarriage was accompanied by a reference to her royalty, an essential element of the jigsaw. She disclosed that in the aftermath of her interview with Tom Bradby in South Africa – so memorable in her opinion because she posed as 'a mother, feminist and advocate' – the Queen and Charles had 'reached out' to her.[774] No evidence was provided for her assertion.

All those pieces supported the key ingredient to Brand Meghan: her political support for the Democrats. On the eve of the fractious presidential election in the midst of the Covid crisis, the Sussexes supported Joe Biden against Donald Trump. The president's low poll ratings suggested his defeat. Keen to play a part in Trump's humiliation, Meghan enjoyed a virtual meeting with Gavin Newsom, California's Democrat governor.[775] Thereafter, she and Harry broadcast a message to Americans from their Montecito garden. Celebrating their inclusion as one of *Time* magazine's 100 most influential people on the planet, Meghan urged Americans to 'build communities of compassion' and spoke about 'the most important election of our lifetime'. In a clear anti-Trump appeal, Harry asked Americans to register to vote: 'As we approach this November, it's vital we reject hate-speech, misinformation and online negativity.'

The Sandringham agreement for the couple to 'uphold the values of Her Majesty' was broken. Endorsement of a political party was not acceptable for the Royal Family. On reflection, Harry's snub of Ivanka Trump during her visit to Buckingham Palace with her father in December had been clearly inspired by Meghan. Meghan had not appeared at the state dinner in Buckingham Palace for Trump. Her partisanship did not surprise the President. 'I am not a fan of hers,' he said. 'I wish a lot of luck to Harry because he's going to need it.' The question was whether Harry would loyally abide by the other terms of the Sandringham agreement and to the Queen, or would he adopt Meghan's attitude? Money influenced the answer.

Cut off from London's purse, the financial jigsaw-piece became important. A podcast deal with Spotify was estimated to be worth between £18 million and £30 million. Rumour estimated that the long-negotiated contract with Netflix was worth $100 million. The Sussexes had agreed to produce documentaries and films to 'share impactful content that unlocks action'. Approved by Ted Sarandos, the Sussexes' neighbour who was head of Netflix's content, the Sussexes' statement said more about themselves than the programmes they would produce:

'Our lives, both independent of each other and as a couple, have allowed us to understand the power of the human spirit: of courage, resilience, and the need for connection. Through our work with diverse communities and their environments, our focus will be on creating content that informs but also gives hope. As new parents, making inspirational family programming is also important to us, as is powerful storytelling through a truthful and relatable lens.'[776]

The surprise was Harry's readiness to partner with the producer of *The Crown*, the sensational TV series that unashamedly distorted the truth about the Royal Family.[777] Some wondered whether Harry even recognised the conflict of interest after he proclaimed in a broadcast, 'Every single raindrop that falls from the sky relieves the parched ground. What if everyone of us was a raindrop, and if every single one of us cared?'[778] Harry was fond of mentioning raindrops in his speeches.

Buckingham Palace was faced by another unprecedented problem. Harry was approaching his thirty-sixth birthday. Normally, the Palace would celebrate the event by issuing photographs of the prince surrounded by his family. That was no longer an option. To make the point, officials released three-year-old photos of Harry. All excluded Meghan.[779] The process of excluding Harry was also underway. To highlight the Covid crisis, the Queen visited Porton Down, Britain's secret science park. Seen for the first time in seven months, she was accompanied by William.[780] The unmistakable message was confirmed soon after. Harry requested that a wreath be laid on his behalf at the Cenotaph during the Remembrance Day ceremony. His wish was rejected. He raged against Palace officials but he knew that the Queen had personally approved that decision.

Any suggestion from London that the Sussexes were excluded threatened their celebrity ranking in America. Their finances depended upon their status as royals. Recognising the danger, Meghan and her advisors produced a riposte. With a photographer in tow, Meghan took Harry on Remembrance Day to Los Angeles's National Cemetery, the home of 90,000 war graves. As an aide followed with flowers, they headed for the grave of two Commonwealth soldiers. Wearing his military medals attached to his suit, Harry's card read: 'To all of those who have served, and are serving. Thank you.' After the photographs were released for global distribution, Harry denied he had orchestrated a publicity stunt to reassert his abandoned royalty. On the contrary, he would not allow his family to deny him his birthright.

At the same time, Harry followed Meghan's lead into the most sensitive issues. Meghan had supported Joe Biden's government's removal of gender identity from official statements. Making the terms mother, father, daughter and brother unacceptable was part of the administration's policy to obliterate biological sex.

Meghan's support for cancel culture included the censorship of her opponents like Trump on Facebook and Twitter. But then she ran into a problem. Supporters of Black Lives Matter proposed the 'cancellation' of presidents George Washington, Thomas Jefferson and Abraham Lincoln because they owned slaves. Others wanted to ban classical literature books because they were allegedly racist. For the moment, remembering that Harry's misstep and hers about the Commonwealth had exposed them to criticism, she resisted joining the extreme end of the movement. But the race issue had become too important in their careers for her to ignore the reasonable debate.

Ever since writing the *Elle* article in 2015 about her experience of race, Meghan had spoken as the victim of racism. Although she provided no specific evidence of suffering any personal disadvantage, she explained that after returning from Britain she realised that America's racial tensions were 'devastating'. She added, 'It was so sad to see where our country was.'[781] After the murder of George Floyd in May 2020 she found a 'silver lining'. Across America, 'the peaceful protests…people were actually owning their own role. It shifted from sadness to a feeling of absolute inspiration because I can see the tide is turning.' In Meghan's opinion, the Black Lives Matter movement was 'a beautiful thing'.[782] She accepted BLM's arguments about white privilege and saddling whites with their guilt of oppression. Although critics labelled BLM as Marxists fomenting social discontent, Harry shared her opinion about white man's guilt.

Harry criticised a 'world created by white people for white people'. Britain, said Harry in an interview from Montecito, suffered from 'structural racism'. Institutional racism was 'endemic' across society.[783] White society, he believed, produced 'bias' with an 'effect on young people of colour'. White Britons, Harry said, needed to understand people 'of a different coloured skin'.[784] Influenced by Meghan's experience, he added, 'You know when you go into a shop with your children and you only see white dolls, do you even think: "That's weird, there's not a black doll there?"'[785] White Britons, he implied, benefit from racism.

Even London, he asserted, was not sufficiently diverse. Many white Britons were bewildered by this. Over 40 per cent of the city's population were non-white. The Mayor of London was the son of a Pakistani bus driver. His main rival in the last election was from a Jamaican family. The Home Secretary was the daughter of Ugandan Asian refugees. The Chancellor of the Exchequer was an Indian Hindu. The Foreign Secretary's Jewish father arrived in Britain from Czechoslovakia in 1938 to escape the Nazis. The government's business secretary and education secretary were children of immigrants from Africa.

Trevor Phillips, a Black commentator, criticised the Sussexes for styling themselves as the 'next generation of trailblazers' in their introduction of a new TV show, *Black History Month*. The Sussexes' TV programme, wrote Phillips, 'made me want to look away. Not only was their programme similar to Britain's Black History Month broadcast since 1987 but their video said less about Black Britain and more about a couple pleading "Let me entertain you".' Phillips's comments probably never reached the Sussexes. Negativity was banned in Montecito.

As the family approached Christmas, to be celebrated in Santa Barbara with David Foster and his wife Katharine McPhee, Meghan was drawing ever closer to Oprah Winfrey. Her show would be the perfect platform to lay out her experience of racism.

Reputedly America's most important TV star and worth $1 billion, Oprah Winfrey promoted herself as the nation's leading cultural personality. She had 19 million followers on social media. Those employed on her programme were tightly controlled by lifelong non-disclosure agreements to prevent the publication of any damaging insights. Not least, to provide information for her critics that Winfrey earned her fortune by exploiting 'victims'. Meghan's repeated homilies about suffering trolls, racism and prejudice made her a natural guest on Oprah's programme.

Oprah's seduction of Meghan was masterly, albeit of an eager supplicant. To include her in the Montecito family, Meghan had been persuaded to support Clevr Blends, a woman-led local company producing instant SuperLattes coffee – a premixture of dried oat milk, coconut cream, monk fruit, mushrooms and stress-reducing, focus-enhancing adaptogenic herbs. Like Oprah, Meghan claimed to 'personally love' the SuperLattes' 'holistic approach to wellness'.[786] She also endorsed Clevr Blends' $120 'Home Ritual Kit' containing two SuperLatte bags, an 'Everlasting Strawflower Garland' (a string of decorative dried flowers) and a 12-inch x 12-inch print of mushrooms with a message about 'gratitude'. Meghan invested a small amount in the fledgling company that employed six people.

This was the influence which Oprah Winfrey exerted as she prepared the biggest scoop of her career. She had pencilled-in the transmission date on the CBS network. All was set to launch Brand Meghan in America.

CHAPTER 37

Netflix

The scene was memorable. Seated in front of a giant screen at the sprawling Santa Barbara hacienda of Tom Barrack, a Trump-supporting billionaire, Meghan and Harry were watching the latest series of *The Crown*. Introduced to Barrack by Oprah Winfrey, the Sussexes had driven to the 1,200-acre mountain ranch near Santa Barbara to meet the controversial father of six, who controlled a multi-billion-dollar property empire linked to Arab investors.

On the eve of their host becoming embroiled in a criminal prosecution, Harry indiscriminately commented during the show on the fictionalised version of his grandparents' reign and his parents' hostile relationship. 'Oh, it's much worse than that,' he repeatedly pronounced.

Living among Hollywood celebrities had undermined Harry's understanding of discretion and loyalty to his family. His remarks reflected the Sussexes' mission. First, to extract revenge against the Royal Family, and second, to fashion their brand. To stay in the spotlight and earn millions of dollars, the Sussexes sought maximum publicity. The normal understanding of privacy was discarded.

Soon after their visit to the Barracks, Harry was driving around Los Angeles on an open-top bus with James Corden and a camera crew. The British star of the play *One Man, Two Guvnors* was filmed serving tea and biscuits to the prince, who in turn sucked up to the comedian's pranks and flattery.[787] The interview, Corden's producer would reveal, was the result of Harry pestering the star to appear on his show.[788]

Once again, this time for the camera, Harry repeated his praise for the Netflix series. Despite *The Crown* being branded 'a hatchet job' on his parents, Harry told Corden with self-pity, 'I am way more comfortable with *The Crown* than I am seeing the stories written about my family, or my wife or myself.'[789] He added, 'Of course, it's not strictly accurate, but loosely it gives you a rough idea about that lifestyle, the pressures of putting duty and service above family and everything else, and what can come from that.' Few forgot that Harry was contracted to Netflix.

Harry was untroubled that the Corden interview was broadcast in February, 2021, on the same night as Prince Philip spent his thirteenth day in hospital and the Queen urged Britons on television to be vaccinated against Covid. In his bid for publicity, Harry appeared to ignore his grandparents' grief. Breaking custom, he also disclosed that the Queen gave Archie a waffle-maker for Christmas. 'I am actually dying for a pee,' Harry was filmed telling the owners of a Bel Air house. They agreed he could use 'their bathroom'.

Self-humiliation had become an occasional essential ingredient in the Sussexes' search for publicity. Even Archewell's first podcast for Spotify relied on coaxing 19-month-old Archie to appear. 'You can speak into it,' Harry urged his son, pointing at the microphone. 'Archie, is it fun?' asked Meghan a mite desperately. 'Fun,' Archie replied. 'After me, ready?' Harry commanded his son. 'Say, "Happy New Year".' Prompting nervous laughter from the couple.[790]

The heart of their Spotify podcast featured 13 guests invited by 'Prince Harry, The Duke of Sussex, and Meghan, The Duchess of Sussex' to speak about the 'power of connection'. The radio station was billed for people to 'share their vulnerabilities within that safe space'.[791] Among the helpless was Elton John. He chose to confess that he was a 'recovering' alcoholic who had survived the Covid lockdown, thanks to Zoom. More confessions flowed. To capture public attention, the Sussexes relied on self-exposure, including themselves. Meghan's pregnancy featured as a celebration of her importance.

Misan Harriman, a Nigerian-born photographer educated at Bradfield, a minor English public school, and known for his support of the Black Lives Matter movement, was hired for the shoot. The result was spectacular. Harriman's black-and-white portrait showed Meghan lying on the ground under a willow tree with her head on Harry's lap. Her right arm was resting on the baby bump. Guaranteed to appear on front pages across the world, Harriman shot the photo of the 'free spirits' with an iPad from London.

'With the tree of life behind them,' he wrote, 'and the garden representing fertility, life and moving forward, they didn't need any direction, because they are, and always have been, waltzing through life together as absolute soulmates.' The willow tree, it later transpired, was superimposed on to the photograph by Harriman in London.[792] Soon after the shoot, Harriman was appointed the chairman of London's Southbank Centre, one of the city's largest arts and music complexes.[793]

'Publicity-shy woman tells 7.67 billion people I'm pregnant,' was the *Daily Star*'s headline over the photograph. The newspaper echoed Piers Morgan's quip: 'They quit the country for privacy and they have hardly shut up since…It's all complete hogwash.'[794] Meghan's supporters agreed with her own definition of privacy: 'I think everyone has a basic right to privacy. We're not talking about anything that anybody else wouldn't expect. It's about boundaries…respect.'[795] Meghan represented a powerful strand of opinion among Influencers.

The Sussexes' publicity offensive flummoxed the Queen's private secretary Edward Young and his staff. Young faced a popular couple promoting themselves at the Palace's expense. One year after Sandringham, the Sussexes had sealed their breakaway, including, officials suspected, an interview with Oprah Winfrey. Never before in the modern era had the monarchy been challenged in quite this way. Instead of summoning expert strategists to plan a counter-attack and undermine the Californians, Young panicked.

The conundrum Young faced was complicated. Meghan's case against the *Mail on Sunday* was progressing through the court; and the Palace staff who complained about Meghan's alleged bullying were dissatisfied that their grievances had been buried. For her part, during 2020 Meghan had good reason to believe that Jason Knauf's memorandum describing the allegations of her bullying had been forgotten. Similarly, she assumed Knauf would not expose the inaccuracy of her own High Court statement about the letter to her father and her denial of any assistance to the authors of *Finding Freedom*. Timid Palace officials would resist open warfare. Her gamble appeared to pay off.

David Engel, Jason Knauf's solicitor, had not been overly helpful to the *Mail on Sunday*. He explained that the Palace Four knew how the letter was created, but gave no hint about their evidence. The newspaper's editor was disappointed. Much more surprising was Judge Warby's conclusion. Sceptical that the newspaper could produce evidence contradicting Meghan, Warby decided that there was no need for a trial. Meghan would be handed victory without submitting to cross-examination.

The judge refused to hear the evidence of the four Palace employees.[796] He decided that most of the evidence submitted by the newspaper in its defence, including Meghan's text messages, was irrelevant.[797] The newspaper, he said, had refused to 'see the light'. Their defence, he declared, had been 'reduced to speculative hypotheses founded on hearsay from an unknown source, which lacks corroboration and is contradicted by both key individuals'. Dramatically, Warby gave a summary judgement in Meghan's favour. The newspaper, he ruled, had breached her copyright and privacy.

In his judgement, Warby damned the newspaper's publication

of the excerpts of the letter as 'manifestly excessive and therefore unlawful'. Being royal did not make 'one' public property. Her letter, ruled Warby, was from a distressed daughter – and private. There was no 'public interest' in Meghan's relationship with her father being exposed; nor did Thomas Markle have a right to challenge *People* magazine's defamation of himself. Her relationship with the authors of *Finding Freedom* was equally irrelevant. Meghan's credibility and reputation was protected from any challenge by the judge. Meghan and Schillings had won an outright victory.

The newspaper and the media industry were baffled by Warby's decision. To deny a trial offended the meaning of justice. No one could explain the judge's about-turn. Representing the shock across the media, Camilla Long described Warby's judgement as 'a dream decision for the powerful wishing to escape scrutiny. The public, who allowed Harry and Meghan to use a British brand to make money, were denied the truth by a judge.'[798] Unsurprisingly, Meghan disagreed.

'We have all won,' Meghan said in a statement. 'You cannot take somebody's privacy and exploit it,' she added. 'I share the victory with each of you – because we all deserve justice and the truth, and we all deserve better.' Her treatment by the media, she said, was 'illegal and dehumanising'. The public, she insisted, was entitled to 'reliable, fact-checked, high-quality news'.[799]

On 16th February, buoyed by that victory, Meghan sat in a Santa Barbara garden ready for an interview with Oprah Winfrey which had been planned prior to her wedding. Meghan was now ready to shame her in-laws and assert her narrative against the Cambridges. To some, this was a reject's revenge – against the Royal Family who plotted to deny her destiny. Those who smeared her reputation in London with lies about the pre-wedding arguments and her bullying were in her sights. 'Life is about telling stories, right?' said Meghan. 'Telling stories through a truthful lens.'[800]

Over the previous weeks Meghan's lines had been written, rewritten and rehearsed. She knew precisely the moments she would hesitate, draw in her breath, touch a carefully poised strand of hair, portray her reluctance to deliver a withering condemnation of the Royal Family and then, overcoming her hesitancy, bashfully recite her obligation to tell the truth.

The interview lasted three hours and twenty minutes. Harry would be included after about two hours. During the shoot, Meghan disclosed that she was expecting a girl. She made no reference to Prince Philip nearing the end of his life. Oprah Winfrey thanked her guests. Hours later, the star announced her scoop. 'The best interview I have ever done,' declared Oprah Winfrey to the world. The recording would be edited for worldwide broadcast on Sunday 7th March.

There was shock in Buckingham Palace. The Sussexes' failure to tell the Palace in advance was deemed to be an insult. Officials feared the worst. Edward Young could now understand Harry's recent haste to persuade the Queen that the couple could do commercial deals, yet remain working, impartial royals. Trust in Harry rapidly declined.

Young recommended retaliation. The Queen decided that the Sussexes should resign their remaining royal patronages. Harry's last military titles and his patronage of the Rugby Football Union and Commonwealth Trust were stripped. Since he was born a prince, he kept that title. Meghan lost her patronage of the National Theatre and the Association of Commonwealth Universities, yet she could also keep her royal title.[801]

All that remained was to negotiate an agreed statement. Fraught and unsuccessful, the Palace unilaterally announced: 'In stepping away from the work of the Royal Family, it is not possible to continue with the responsibilities and duties that come with a life of public service.' Instantly, the Sussexes snapped back, 'We can all live a life of service. Service is universal.' The Sussexes' riposte, drafted by Meghan's advisors, appeared just as 99-year-old Prince Philip re-entered hospital.

The Royal Family was fighting on uncertain terrain. Amid the turbulent emotions, not least Prince Philip's inevitably imminent death, there was anger about the Sussexes' behaviour. Someone decided to launch pre-emptive retaliation. The popular suspect, without any evidence, was Prince William. Some would say the information was delivered to the editor of *The Times*, while Valentine Low, the newspaper's royal expert, described his report as the product of several weeks of hard work.[802] Either way, the result was striking.

On 3rd March, *The Times* revealed that Jason Knauf had reported allegations of Meghan's bullying to a senior official at Kensington Palace. The newspaper's unnamed source also claimed that Meghan's behaviour had compelled two personal assistants to resign and a third, suffering a loss of self-confidence, to say 'I can't stop shaking.' None of the four involved were identified. All claimed they had been operating in a 'climate of fear' where employees were routinely 'humiliated' by both Meghan and Harry in front of their peers and repeatedly subjected to 'unreasonable demands'. One aide told *The Times*, it felt 'more like emotional cruelty and manipulation, which I guess could also be called bullying'.[803]

Valentine Low wrote that he had been approached by 'sources' who felt that 'only a partial version had emerged of Meghan's two years as a working member of the royal family and they wished to tell their side'. Traumatised and broken by the Sussexes' behaviour, the officials objected to the Palace's mismanagement of their complaints. To protect Meghan, the Palace had refused to investigate the allegations: 'All the men in grey *Suits* who she hates have a lot to answer for, because they did nothing to protect people.'[804]

'Those concerned,' reported Rebecca English later in the *Daily Mail*, 'are fed up with the sheer hypocrisy of it all. The suggestion that they, the Sussexes, were being bullied and forced out when others were experiencing that very treatment at their hands!'[805]

Meghan's lawyers had one week's advance notice of *The Times*' allegations. Buckingham Palace was asked for evidence – documents, texts and emails – of her bullying. In the end, the Sussexes' representatives could produce no legal grounds to prevent publication. Meghan's riposte had been prepared. 'Let's just call this what it is,' said Meghan. 'A calculated smear campaign based on misleading and harmful misinformation.'

Her lawyers lamented that the newspaper was 'used by Buckingham Palace to peddle a wholly false narrative…We are disappointed to see this defamatory portrayal of the Duchess of Sussex given credibility by a media outlet.' The Duchess, the lawyers added, was 'saddened by this latest attack on her character, particularly as someone who has been the target of bullying herself and is deeply committed to supporting those who have experienced pain and trauma'.[806]

The Sussexes interpreted the newspaper report as yet another malicious attack by the Palace on themselves, the innocent victims. Harry and Meghan had no doubt that the leak was instigated by William to sabotage their big moment – a pre-emptive strike before their big interview. Since Jason Knauf had written the memorandum, either he or his superiors had leaked it to *The Times*. The Sussexes knew that the Palace would not be given the right of reply or even invited to comment about their harmful allegations against the Royal Family to Oprah Winfrey.[807] But that, in their opinion, was different. They were speaking the truth and Knauf's memo was utterly false.

Whatever the motive, the character assassination of the Sussexes misfired. Delivered without sufficient evidence, many readers sensed the newspaper's source lacked conviction. The Palace's caution suggested that Edward Young was fretting about whether the Palace could accuse Meghan of bullying, yet protect Prince Andrew. Belatedly, the Palace hired a new firm of solicitors to investigate the bullying allegations, but hinted that only after an exhaustive process might the lawyers ask the Sussexes to answer the allegations. Sensing that weakness, Meghan's communication staff orchestrated a wave of sympathetic statements by her friends against the Palace.

'The Duchess of Sussex,' said Jon Cowan, a *Suits* scriptwriter, 'is a good person thrust into an unimaginable world. Having spent three years working with her...I saw a warm, kind, caring person.' 'No one,' agreed Kristen Meinzer, a friend and writer, 'could have been prepared for the level of racism and misogyny and vitriol she's faced.' She, as Meinzer described herself, blamed the 'inbred, messed-up, dysfunctional family' who were up against a 'highly educated self-made millionaire who knew how to do the PR game...A lot of people think you were so lucky to get her, and you blew it.'[808] US television producer and author Lindsay Roth, a close friend of Meghan's for more than two decades, said that 'kindness, goodwill runs in her bones'.

Patrick J. Adams, her *Suits* co-star, described the Royal Family as 'at worst, seemingly archaic and toxic. It's obscene that the Royal Family is promoting and amplifying accusations of "bullying" against a woman who herself was basically forced to flee the UK in order to protect her family and her own mental health.' Referring to the accusations of her bullying, Adams continued, 'This newest chapter and its timing is just another stunning example of the shamelessness of an institution that has outlived its relevance, is way overdrawn on credibility and apparently bankrupt of decency. Find someone else to admonish, berate and torment. My friend Meghan is way out of your league.'[809]

Jessica Mulroney, famous for calling Meghan's critics racist bullies but now herself 'cancelled' after being accused of racism by a Black blogger, said that Meghan treated her staff with 'kindness, empathy and love'. Meghan was also supported by Serena Williams, Katy Perry and Orlando Bloom, friends and neighbours in Montecito who, as friends of Oprah Winfrey, had all holidayed together on business magnate David Geffen's yacht.[810] In that circle Meghan was in safe hands. Yet none of her defenders had directly accused the Palace Four of lying about the alleged bullying. And Meghan's lawyers did not issue a claim for defamation against *The Times*. In Canada, the Reitmans crew recognised the truth.

To promote Sunday's programme, CBS broadcast a clip of Meghan on Friday 5th March. Perfectly poised, Meghan sat in a Montecito garden, a wisp of hair hanging down on to her cheek – an excellent prop for her to touch while confessing her anguish and anger. For the trailer she disclosed that she had been banned by the Palace from giving Oprah an interview in 2018. Now liberated, she was 'able to just make a choice of your own. And to be able to speak for yourself.' But even speaking with honesty, the victim volunteered, 'comes with the risk of losing things. I mean, there is a lot that has been lost already.' Some viewers did not spot genuine sadness in her eyes.

At CBS's headquarters in Los Angeles, there was excitement. Reduced to 85 minutes, CBS had pre-sold the interview around the world. Oprah Winfrey had hit a goldmine. ITV in London had paid about £1 million for the broadcast rights. Like CBS, ITV was demanding premium rates for advertisements. In the USA, CBS had sold prime spots to manufacturers of lavatory paper, wrinkle-remover and almond milk.

On the eve of the broadcast, the Sussexes' spokesman announced that their interview would be the 'last word' about their rift with the Royal Family. Having 'needed to have their say', they now considered the matter closed and wanted to 'move on'.[811]

That sentiment was grasped by Buckingham Palace's spokesman. On Saturday night, he predicted that the interview would be a quickly forgotten sideshow – 'lost in the mists of time'. People, he believed, were more worried about Covid. The Queen was reportedly 'calm' and believed in the long game. She was said to have considered it 'best not to react' to what would be 'their final word'. Doing her duty, she along with the Royal Family would spend Monday celebrating virtually the annual Commonwealth Day service. Aptly, she had chosen to speak about 'friendship and unity'.[812]

Edward Young failed to anticipate the sensational radio and TV headlines that would dominate the waking hours on Monday 8th March. With his passive approach Young also did not foresee the onslaught from America. Naively, Young believed that the interview would be the Sussexes' 'last word'.

On Saturday night in Montecito, Meghan was in bed crying. Not because she felt any remorse for her shattering allegations against the Royal Family, but because The Firm had orchestrated a 'smear' about her alleged bullying. 'I held her,' said Harry. 'We talked, she cried and cried and cried.'[813] Certain they had spoken the 'truth in the most compassionate way possible' to Oprah, Harry believed they had left 'an opening for reconciliation and healing'.

As she cried, Meghan might have recalled telling the *Fortune* magazine audience five months earlier, 'If you live knowing the truth, regardless of what anyone says, you'll be able to go to sleep with a clear conscience.'[814] At the same time she had probably also forgotten informing the same audience, 'If you listen to what I actually say, it's not controversial.'

That night, Harry and Meghan apparently believed that their interview with Oprah Winfrey was true and not controversial. 'What ended up inflammatory,' Meghan had said, 'is people's interpretation [of what I say].'[815] In their opinion both were victims of the racist tabloids, and now Buckingham Palace was stoking hatred about fictitious bullying.

CHAPTER 38

The Interview

Oprah Winfrey's introduction to the interview was unforgiving. In the peaceful setting of an enormous, sun-drenched garden Meghan sat on wooden furniture, seemingly relaxed. Perfectly made-up, she adopted the pose of a harmless, defenceless soul. Oprah's opening comments set the tone of victimhood.

Meghan, said Oprah, had been the target of 'constant criticism [and] blatant sexist and racist remarks by British tabloids'. As she spoke, the screen was covered by a spread of apparently racist headlines in the *Daily Mail* and other British newspapers. The word 'niggling' was highlighted as causing offence, although critics noted the sixteenth-century Scandinavian origin of the word has no connection to race. Even before the broadcast had ended, British newspapers had denounced CBS for doctoring the headlines – and concealing the truth that the overwhelming majority of the headlines were taken from American and Australian publications. Despite Associated Newspapers proving the distortion, Oprah Winfrey refused to take down the fake headlines from her package. All the British media, she claimed, was racist. The show's principles were fixed: This was Meghan's 'truth'.

Meghan's sad story was of a naïve American who, without 'a plan', fell in love with a prince about whom she knew nothing – before the blind date, 'I hadn't googled Harry online'. Written into her script, she likened herself to Disney's Little Mermaid who lost her voice after falling in love with an unknown prince. 'I didn't have a plan,' she said.

Meghan's innocence was compounded by her ignorance about the consequence of marrying Harry: 'I didn't do any research about what that would mean.' Once smitten, she 'honestly' thought The Firm would look after her interests. 'Genuinely' she had never thought of profiting from her royal connections. To her horror, heartless flunkies refused to 'reach out'. Her admission to Gina Nelthorpe-Cowne over lunch that she had researched the royals was forgotten, as was Nelthorpe-Cowne's warning about the inevitable consequences. Even her own admission in South Africa to Bradby that she had naively ignored her friends' warnings about the tabloids was forgotten. 'Thank God, I hadn't researched,' Meghan told Oprah.

Speaking with dramatic pauses, her kohl-lined, long-lashed, dancing eyes emphasised the sheer emotional toll she was reliving. Her first culprit was the media for creating a 'false narrative'. She denied reading newspapers but was still horrified. She had never, she said, ever raised the issue of privacy. 'I mean, I've never talked about privacy. That's just a basic understanding.' Her privacy suit against the *Mail on Sunday* in London was forgotten. The 'bigoted' media, as Harry said, had created a 'toxic environment of control and fear'. That partly fuelled her collapse into suicidal thoughts, which climaxed on the day they were due to star at the Royal Albert Hall. Thinking about that night reminded her of the 'dark place' she had inhabited. She had sat up all night considering suicide.

Verifying the events leading towards Meghan's thoughts of 'suicide' is difficult. Pertinently, Harry and Meghan gave conflicting accounts of the saga. In the interview they disagreed whether Meghan felt suicidal at night, in the morning or both. And they did not agree on the number of days she felt suicidal. Neither could explain why Meghan sought help from an unqualified Palace official rather than an experienced medical specialist. Moreover, Harry never identified which member of his family had 'neglected' his wife. Since Oprah failed to ask any follow-up questions, her producers chose to broadcast the Sussexes' inconsistent answers.

The same suicidal threat apparently happened again after Archie's birth. Harry would later in the show confirm returning from work in London to find Meghan crying while breastfeeding Archie. He did not tell his family. 'I was ashamed of admitting it to them. I didn't know what to do. I wasn't prepared for that. I went to a very dark place as well, but I wanted to be there for her. And I was terrified.'

Winfrey did not ask Harry, the patron of a mental health charity with seven years' experience of receiving medical help for his own problems, living in a city with thousands of medical specialists, why, after witnessing his wife unsuccessfully seek help from a heartless human resources specialist in the Palace, he did little to seek specialist help. The same question was also not asked of Meghan. Instead, Winfrey watched her guest shed a tear, but not enough to smudge her immaculate make-up. Oprah did not ask for any evidence or the name of the Palace official. Meghan's truth was not questioned.

Seventeen million American viewers, far below the 96 million viewers for the Super Bowl, were undoubtedly gripped – but the next revelation would resonate among the British even more.

Oprah Winfrey had scripted an attack on Kate. Whereas Meghan, she stated, was popularly portrayed in Britain as the 'villain', Kate was hailed 'a hero'. The reason, Oprah suggested, was because Meghan was 'the first mixed-race person to marry into the family'. With race established as the dominant theme, Oprah moved on to the newspaper revelation that Meghan had reduced Kate to tears about a bridesmaid's dress before the wedding. That story had turned many Britons against the Duchess. The interview was Meghan's opportunity to tell her truth.

At the appropriate moment Oprah asked if Meghan had made Kate cry. Perfectly rehearsed, she replied: 'The reverse happened...It had made me cry and it really hurt my feelings…And I don't say that to be disparaging to anyone, because it was a really hard week of the wedding. And she was upset about something, but she owned it, and she apologised. And she brought me flowers and a note, apologising.'

Having turned the narrative against Kate – or in Meghan's terms not wanting 'in any way to be disparaging about her' – Meghan continued: 'And she did what I would do if I knew that I hurt someone, right, to just take accountability for it.'

Not only was Kate guilty but she had admitted her bad behaviour. And then Meghan added another twist. While she had politely remained silent to 'protect' Kate, she blamed her sister-in-law's friends for leaking a false story, turned against her. 'What was hard to get over was being blamed for something that not only I didn't do but that happened to me…The narrative about, you know, making Kate cry I think was the beginning of a real character assassination. And they knew it wasn't true.' Gracefully, she added, 'But I have forgiven her.' The result, Meghan believed, was irreversible. 'I think that's when everything changed, really.'

'I don't know how they would expect that after all this time we would still just be silent if there is an active role that The Firm is playing in perpetuating falsehoods about us.' Her staff and she herself were stopped by Palace officials from denying Kate's lies and telling Meghan's truth.

Silenced and unprotected, Meghan concluded, 'I thought, well, if they're not going to kill things like that, then what are we going to do?' The Firm's 'lies', said Meghan, were not just confined to 'Kate's tears' but other issues: 'I came to understand that not only was I not being protected but that they were willing to lie to protect other members of the family – but they weren't willing to tell the truth to protect me and my husband.'

No other examples were offered about the false accusations she had suffered or the 'real character assassination', but her supporters were roused by her lament. She had been thrown into the deep end where 'nobody tells you anything'.[816]

Amid her wave of assertions Meghan's credibility was reinforced for most Americans. In particular they were impressed by her claim that during her marriage, especially while pregnant, she had effectively been held under house arrest. Her passport, driving licence and keys had been confiscated. Officials had prevented her from independent travel in the last four months of her pregnancy: 'I left the house twice in four months.' British viewers were puzzled how that accorded with her two private trips to New York for the baby shower and the tennis match, and four holidays in Europe.

'I couldn't even meet my friends for lunch,' complained Meghan, who had enjoyed many social visits around London and to her country-house in Oxfordshire. 'It's like you were trapped?' the interviewer confirmed. 'That's the truth,' replied Meghan.

'Trapped' was the same word later used by Harry to describe his life as a royal. 'Like the rest of my family I was trapped but I didn't know I was trapped. Trapped within the system, like the rest of my family are. My father and my brother, they are trapped. They don't get to leave. And I have huge compassion for that.' Their smiles in photographs, he revealed, were all 'a part of the job'.

Next came an unprecedented disclosure by Meghan: 'You know, three days before our wedding, we got married. No one knows that.' In Meghan's version they were privately married in Kensington Palace before the big day at Windsor. 'So, like, the vows that we have framed in our room are just the two of us in our backyard with the Archbishop of Canterbury.' The globally televised Windsor ceremony was, implied Meghan, a sham.

Just what Meghan imagined she achieved by that crude invention has not been explained. Under British law a marriage must be in a public place with two witnesses; and Meghan's marriage certificate stated the wedding was on 19th May in Windsor. Possibly she believed that, like in California, marriage certificates can remain secret and can only become available to the public on the explicit order of a judge. Again, Oprah Winfrey gave Meghan a free run. On reflection, it appeared that Meghan was manipulating her interviewer – and the Archbishop of Canterbury. The prelate refused to comment about the marriage date. Instead the Archbishop lamented for Harry's and Meghan's fate: 'It's life without parole.'[817]

Other injustices which Meghan had suffered tumbled out. She was given 'no class on how to speak, on how to behave, how to properly cross your legs, how to be royal…There was none of that training that might exist for other members of the family. That was not something that was offered to me.' She even had to google the national anthem and had to take a rushed lesson in curtsying in Windsor Park.

During the interview she could not quite decide whether she had been shocked when the security guards were withdrawn (and they were not withdrawn), or had she happily confided after all to the Queen that she did not want protection? Oprah did not query Meghan's contradiction. Instead she seized on Meghan's criticism of the Queen: 'Believing them when they said I would be protected.' That unimaginable conversation was not challenged by Oprah after Harry endorsed his wife. 'A lack of support and lack of understanding,' he agreed.

American viewers, Meghan knew, had no reason to doubt any of her truth. Especially not after Oprah Winfrey raised the bombshell – racism. Nothing, Meghan knew, was more sensitive in America. On cue the woman glorified in America as a popular icon and even as the 'Black Princess' delivered the payback to the family who denied her stardom.

With theatrical hesitation, her sweet tone described 'several conversations with Harry' involving his 'family' about her unborn child. During her pregnancy she revealed 'there were concerns and conversations about how dark his skin might be when he's born'.

With gasped surprise Oprah asked whether 'they were concerned that if he were too brown, that would be a problem?'

Meghan confirmed the horror: 'If you're making an assumption that someone thought Archie would be too brown, it feels like a pretty safe one.' She described her predicament: 'The idea of our son not being safe, and also the idea of the first member of colour in this family not being titled in the same way that other grandchildren would be.'

Oprah Winfrey asked Harry later to explain the racist comment. Meghan had asserted there were 'several conversations' and they occurred while she was pregnant. Harry's version was starkly different from his wife's.

'Right at the beginning' of the relationship, Harry said, there had been a single, 'general remark' about the 'kids'. Harry's contradiction was critical. Meghan had described the conversations occurring during her pregnancy, but Harry insisted it happened once long before they were engaged. 'That conversation,' said Harry, 'I am never going to share. At the time it was awkward. I was shocked.'

The enormous discrepancy was ignored by Oprah Winfrey. She did not explore the 'conversation', an exchange in his father's house with Charles and Camilla. Five years later Harry reinterpreted what he knew was innocent speculation as a doom-laden finale to relations with Charles and Camilla: 'Like, there were some real obvious signs before we even got married that this was going to be really hard.'

Harry and Meghan held off naming and shaming those responsible. 'That would be very damaging,' she explained. Although Harry mentioned his 'deep respect' for the Queen because 'she's my colonel-in-chief and she always will be', some viewers were left wondering whether the 94-year-old monarch and her 99-year-old husband, now spending his third week in hospital, might be guilty of racism.

During that exchange Meghan smiled. She appeared unfazed that Harry had undermined her script. Effortlessly, she moved on to her terrible discovery while pregnant. The unborn Archie, she was told, would not only be denied a title as prince but would also remain unprotected. Delivered in a disarmingly calm tone, Meghan's accusation was again explosive.

Asked by Oprah why Archie wasn't a prince, Meghan replied: 'I can give you an honest answer.' The same reason, said Meghan, as why her son would be denied security: because with brown skin he would not be treated 'in the same way that other grandchildren would be'. The Palace, according to Meghan, was infected by racism from top to bottom. 'It was a decision that they felt was appropriate. There's no explanation.'

Damning the Queen and the Royal Family as racist for not making Archie a prince was breathtaking. Meghan knew her argument was inaccurate. Under a protocol signed by George V on 30th November, 1917, Archie could become prince only after his grandfather, Charles, was crowned king. Moreover, on Archie's birth, Meghan's spokesman announced that his parents did not want their son to have a title. But in the interview Meghan went further. She asserted that because her son would be brown, 'They said they wanted to change the convention for Archie.' She did not identify 'they' or explain how the convention would be abandoned.

Facts could never undermine Meghan's truth. She knew that Archie's security was never withdrawn. So long as his parents lived at Frogmore or anywhere in Britain and continued their royal duties, he would be protected by the state. Once again, Oprah Winfrey visibly registered her disdain for the royals and failed to probe Meghan's version.

Wearing an unusually ill-fitting blue suit, Harry was introduced into the interview after two-thirds of the programme had been broadcast. Racism generated by the 'bigoted' tabloids, he had previously said, had 'played a large part' in persuading the couple to leave Britain. Plus, taking away 'at short notice' their security, a norm since his childhood. Although he had been warned that the British taxpayer would not pay for protection if he moved to America, he had refused to accept reality. 'I inherited the risk,' he told Oprah Winfrey, 'so that was a shock to me.' And now he told millions, he feared 'history repeating itself'. Meghan, he implied, would be 'murdered' just like Diana.

'My family literally cut me off financially,' he told Oprah Winfrey. 'I got what my mum left me. I had to afford security for us.' Charles's unexpected refusal to help financially, he implied, had left them penniless and without a 'plan'. His shock disclosure was that Charles had stopped taking his calls. Negotiating the contracts with Netflix, Spotify, Disney and others, Harry claimed, all started out of financial necessity only after they arrived in California. In fact, Prince Charles's audited accounts showed that Harry had received over £1 million after leaving Britain.[818]

'It's really sad that it's gotten to this point,' said Harry as the programme drew towards the end. 'But I've got to do something for my own mental health, my wife's and for Archie's as well. Because I could see where this was headed.'

'It's a happy ending,' said Meghan. Her closing thoughts, drafted by a scriptwriter. 'Greater than every fairytale you've ever read.'

For three days the Sussexes' accusations ranked among the world's most discussed topic. A majority of Americans and most non-white Britons believed Meghan: the Royal Family was racist. The majority of Britons were also left with the impression that the interview was a preliminary. The Sussexes threatened more if necessary.

The immediate reaction was predictable. Buckingham Palace was momentarily paralysed; the British media was hostile; and the American media voiced euphoric support. Across the Commonwealth many were persuaded by Meghan and Harry that the whole Royal Family was racist. The irretrievable consequences were truly bad.

In the opinion polls Britain was divided by age: 83 per cent of the over-65s were negative about the couple, while 95 per cent of the 18 to 24 category were positive about them. The young and ethnic minorities were gleeful that Meghan had represented their thoughts.[819] Overall, both drew negative ratings: 48 per cent negative for Harry, 56 per cent negative for Meghan.[820]

Support for Meghan and Harry was eloquently argued by a mixed-race American history professor, Christy Pichichero.[821] Meghan's prejudiced abusers in the Palace, she wrote, were questioning the truth of her recollections by 'discriminatory gaslighting' to psychologically manipulate and undermine her self-confidence. In brief, because the Palace failed to apologise for its list of sins, Pichichero judged the Palace to be guilty of 'racism and other forms of bigotry'.

Janina Gavankar, an actress and Meghan's friend for 17 years, revealed that post-interview Meghan feels 'free'. Despite her devotion to the Royal Family and sacrificing her identity, 'They just didn't want to listen.'[822]

Meghan's most important supporters were the Democrat party's aristocrats. President Joe Biden's press secretary praised Meghan's 'courage', portraying the Royal Family as backward racists. Michelle Obama sympathised with Meghan as a victim of racism: 'Race is not a new construct in this world for people of colour, so it wasn't a complete surprise to hear her feelings and to have them articulated.' Yet noticeably, after reflecting on Meghan's accusations, the Sussexes were not among the four hundred guests invited to Barack Obama's sixtieth birthday party at Martha's Vineyard.

Hillary Clinton, quite familiar with serious scandals in her own family, observed that 'It was heart-breaking to see the two of them sitting there having to describe how difficult it was to be accepted, to be integrated. Not just into the Royal Family as they described, but more painfully into the larger society whose narrative is driven by tabloids that are living in the past.' Certain that Meghan was treated with 'cruelty' by the tabloids and suppressed by the Palace, Clinton said, 'Well, this young woman was not going to keep her head down. You know, this is 2021 and she wanted to live her life. She wanted to be fully engaged and she had every right to hope for that.'[823]

No supporter was more eloquent than Amanda Gorman, the young Black American poet globally famous for reading 'The Hill We Climb' at Joe Biden's inauguration, a poem depicting a message of hope about America's racism. 'Meghan,' she tweeted on 8th March, 'was the Crown's greatest opportunity for change, regeneration and reconciliation in a new era. They didn't just maltreat her – they missed out on it.' Later in the day, Gorman told her followers, 'Meghan is living the life Diana should have had, if only those around her had been as brave as she was. Meghan isn't living a life without pain, but life without a prison.'

Meghan's supporters ignored the reports from London listing 17 inaccuracies and contradictions in Meghan's answers to Oprah Winfrey. None questioned Meghan's failure before the marriage to consider whether she could adapt to fit in with the Royal Family's culture. Among many Americans, Meghan's strength would define their struggle against the Royal Family. A victim was always beyond reproach.

There was just one loud dissenting voice in America. 'Her lies are almost psychotic,' said Thomas Markle, echoing the same anger in Britain about Meghan's blatant falsehoods. 'The delusional, one-sided ravings of a couple drunk on their own drama,' wrote Sarah Vine.[824] Many Britons wanted the Sussexes stripped of their titles for casting the Royal Family and the country as racist.

Britain's Black community was divided. Many outrightly sympathised with Meghan, identifying with her anger. Others, like Dr Rem Adekoya, an academic at York University, argued that many Black people regarded Meghan as white and would not rally around her.[825] Wendell Pierce, her 'father' in *Suits*, condemned the Oprah interview as 'quite insensitive and offensive' while 3,000 people were dying every day in America from Covid.[826]

Soon after the broadcast, Meghan's spokesman rushed out a

clarification. The person questioning the unconceived child's colour was neither the Queen nor Philip. That left Charles, William and Kate. Palace officials had resisted instant reaction. After careful thought their statement was measured: 'The whole family is saddened to learn the full extent of how challenging the last few years have been for Harry and Meghan. The issues raised, particularly race, are concerning. Whilst some recollections may vary, they are taken very seriously and will be addressed by the family privately. Harry, Meghan and Archie will always be much-loved family members.'

Most Britons hailed that statement as a work of genius. Omid Scobie would report that the Sussexes scoffed and 'were not surprised that full ownership was not taken' by the Royal Family. In their words, he outlined, the Sussexes apparently asked, 'How can you move forward with that?'[827]

On the Sussexes' behalf, Scobie also damned Kate Robertson, the founder of One Young World and an early supporter of Meghan. 'The Sussexes have grievances,' Robertson had tweeted, 'but should sort it out in person privately. Hurting the Queen in public is really low.' She praised the Queen for being 'the world's most stunning example of public service'. Omid Scobie's criticism sparked a 'Sussex Squad' onslaught on Robertson. She quickly surrendered to the trolls. 'Everyone has a right to tell their story,' Robertson retreated. 'Commenting on people's lives is wrong. I'm truly sorry.'[828]

Piers Morgan was not as restrained on ITV's *Good Morning Britain*. The journalist whose career was built on provoking outrage introduced the programme at 6:32am on 8th March. 'I'm angry to the point of boiling over today,' he told his record audience. 'I'm sickened by what I've had to watch...A two-hour Trashathon of our Royal Family.'

Instantly, he was challenged by co-presenter Susanna Reid. Following ITV's editorial guidelines, Reid defended Meghan. Looking at the camera she declared that Meghan's claim to have felt suicidal was serious. It could not be 'brushed over'. She should be believed.

Morgan interrupted. Meghan, he demanded, should give the details and names of those who shunned her. 'I don't believe a word she says,' he said. 'I wouldn't believe it if she read the weather report.' Once again, Reid dismissed Morgan's scepticism. The reaction in America to the race allegation, Morgan retorted, would be used against the monarchy.

At that watershed moment, GMB's audience was as divided as the programme's presenters. Some cast Meghan as the villain who lied about the Royal Family and race. Others believed her accusations. No fewer than 41,500 complaints about Morgan would be registered by the TV regulator, Ofcom. Added to the mix, Meghan's solicitor formally complained to ITV about Morgan's prejudice.

The temperature rose the following morning. Morgan's damnation of Meghan's 'diatribe of bilge' had infuriated the programme's weather presenter, Alex Beresford. Clearly siding with Meghan, he was invited to debate their differences. Participating for the first time in a TV debate, Beresford repeatedly hailed Meghan's courage to call out racism. He cited his own experience as a mixed-race person to support her.

Morgan's attack on Meghan, he complained, was 'incredibly hard to watch'. Her race, he said, was not just the colour of her skin but her identity and her ideas. Morgan, he believed, did not understand the racism experienced by non-whites. As a mixed-race woman, he continued, she automatically ranked among the oppressed and, as a white man, Piers Morgan was unquestionably an oppressor.

'If Meghan is telling you that she suffered racism in the Palace,' Beresford said, 'then she did. Anyone who suggests otherwise is not Black.' [829] Even to expect Meghan to prove her allegations was deemed to be racist. As a person of mixed race, he said, she was entitled to 'tell her own truth', even if any inaccuracy defamed members of the Royal Family. Beresford denied that actual 'facts' were different from Meghan's personal 'experience' or 'perception'.

Beresford's outburst was a complaint against Morgan's performance.

'Meghan Markle,' Beresford told Morgan, 'is entitled to cut you off if she wants to. Yet you continue to trash her.' Beresford expected Morgan to stay quiet if Markle decided to ghost him.

'I'm done with this,' said Morgan, and walked off the set. 'Sorry,' he snapped. Seconds after his dramatic exit, Beresford expressed his fury that Morgan had criticised Meghan's truth.

There was an irony in Morgan's exit. For months the acerbic journalist had been mercilessly haranguing government ministers about Covid. Repeatedly, he humiliated politicians about their supposed errors. But when confronted with the same tactics, he fled. In the furore which followed the comparison was not highlighted.

In normal times, fiery TV confrontations merit a passing mention or a frisson of excitement. But Morgan's clash with Beresford mirrored not only the sharp racial divisions in Britain and America, but also the irreversible damage the Sussexes had inflicted on the monarchy. The dispute raised a fundamental issue in debates across the world: Does a self-proclaimed 'victim' have the unquestioned right that her 'truth' be accepted without challenge? By then, Meghan's truths, or lies according to her critics, were established and explained in broadcasts.

Carolyn McCall, ITV's chief executive, disputed Morgan's right to disagree with Meghan. She was particularly critical of Morgan for doubting Meghan's claim to have been suicidal. Morgan, declared the *Guardian*'s former chief executive, was not allowed to question Markle's 'truth'. Having received a protest from Meghan as a woman and a mother, McCall demanded that Morgan apologise on air. Under her edict, Morgan was not allowed to doubt Meghan's suicidal thoughts. Morgan refused to 'do a grovelling apology'.

In Morgan's opinion, self-diagnosis of a mental health problem had become a celebrity's excuse after being caught out. Even Prince Andrew had mentioned his 'mental health issues' as a protective shield from recrimination for his wrongful conduct. McCall, however, was unwilling to enter that debate. Bowing to Meghan, she immediately terminated Morgan's appearances on GMB.

'I thus became the latest victim of the cancel culture,' boasted Morgan, enjoying the glory of front-page headlines about himself. 'If I have to fall on my sword for expressing an honestly held opinion about Meghan Markle and that diatribe of bilge that she came out with in that interview, so be it,' puffed the martyr outside his house. In between, he mentioned that he'd just enjoyed a £400 bottle of Krug and a cigar.

Some suspected that he had been looking for an excuse to leave ITV with a bang. Overnight, the programme's record 1.89 million audience crashed to under 500,000.

McCall decided to audition Alastair Campbell, formerly Tony Blair's Downing Street spokesman, as Morgan's replacement. Reported to be a liar and a bully, Campbell was not only accused in a BBC report of responsibility for 'sexing-up' the tendentious Iraq dossier but also, despite serious warnings, for outing David Kelly, a government scientist, as the confidential source for BBC News about the Iraq intelligence dossier. The publicity approved by Campbell provoked Kelly's suicide.[830] Despite those serious accusations, Campbell duly sat on Morgan's studio chair.

Six months later, Ofcom rejected the 58,000 complaints about Morgan's performance. Among those rejected complaints was Meghan's. 'Mr Morgan,' declared Ofcom, 'was entitled to say he disbelieved the Duke and Duchess of Sussexes' allegations.' To silence Morgan, Ofcom continued, would be 'an unwarranted and chilling restriction on freedom of expression'. Morgan was vindicated. 'A resounding victory for free speech,' he said, 'and a resounding defeat for Princess Pinocchio.' Carolyn McCall remained silent. Someone murmured it was all about the inconvenience of truth and the convenience of blame.

In Montecito, Meghan was more certain than ever that she was the victim, but with a purpose. Her triumph on Oprah Winfrey's show proved the Sussexes' power to manipulate the media to broadcast their message on their terms.

Meghan did not anticipate one consequence. Watching events unfold in London, Jason Knauf, Sara Latham, Samantha Cohen and other former staff were aghast. They had worked tirelessly to help the couple. In her own words Meghan had admitted the truth in her court statement: 'I had privately endured the media onslaught surrounding my father with the support of…Mr Knauf.'[831] However, she told the world on Oprah a different story: Knauf and his team had not only done nothing, but conspired against her and Harry. In California, she mistakenly sensed that she was secure from exposure.

CHAPTER 39

Backlash

'I've lost my father. I lost a baby. I nearly lost my name. I mean, there's the loss of identity,' said Meghan on the same day as she admitted that she had, after all, been married at Windsor.[832]

For Meghan, who had complained to both of her husbands of her childhood without a family, the Oprah Winfrey interview condemned her own children to a similar fate. Except for Doria, the Sussexes' children, at that moment, could expect to grow up without grandparents, uncles, aunts and cousins. The Windsors were a troubled family, but no one had expected Harry to sabotage all the relationships.

In London, the public repercussions continued for days. 'We're very much not a racist family,' declared William as he was door-stepped by journalists entering an east London school to promote a mental health project.[833]

Despite his anger about Meghan's denunciation of Kate, William telephoned Harry. Heal and mend, he agreed with Charles, was their only option before the estrangement became irreversible. Hours after the call, Gayle King appeared on CBS TV. After revealing the private conversation she ridiculed the peacemakers. The conversation, she disclosed, was 'not productive'.

Speaking, as briefed by the Sussexes, King criticised William's attitude: 'The family has to acknowledge there are issues, and right now no one is acknowledging that.' She went on to describe 'what is still upsetting' to Meghan. Namely, that the Palace wanted to settle their dispute privately, yet had not stopped false stories appearing in the media.[834] They had certainly failed to stop the stories broadcast in Oprah Winfrey's interview.

The Palace warned Harry there would be no more conversations, or even contact, if there were further leaks to the media. That, the royal advisors believed, would intimidate Harry. They were mistaken. Certain that the Oprah interview was a huge success in America, the Sussexes were set to establish themselves – not as beleaguered royals in exile but as A-list celebrities and social activists in California.

On the eve of her fortieth birthday, Meghan welcomed the watershed. Hailed by millions as an uncompromisingly authentic superstar, she had defied the odds. Standing in the global spotlight she had humbled the Royal Family.

Control of the media was critical. Nothing could be left to chance. Meghan's status and income depended entirely on media exposure. Denigrating the media, not least by legal threats, was part of her armoury. At her request CNN withdrew a report exposing her inaccuracies in the Oprah Winfrey interview.[835] The Sussexes' skill was to deny access to anyone unwilling to fawn on their terms. In turn, their authority bestowed considerable influence across Hollywood. In Los Angeles, the media acknowledged, Meghan had become a significant force. Fearful of Meghan's negative influence among her neighbours and other power-brokers, past associates greeted journalists inquiring about her career with aggressive silence. Their abrupt refusal to comment was a measure of Meghan's new authority.

Introduced on their insistence as the Duke and Duchess, the Montecito Windsors had created their own celebrity image crafted in skilfully orchestrated photo-opportunities as multi-racial, multi-cultural humanitarians. Rather than service and sacrifice, their brand of royalty was shaped for lucrative political careers. The only uncertainty was Meghan's destination. Her ultimate ambition was shrouded in mystery.

The Sussexes' routine had changed. They no longer troubled themselves to be filmed handing out food packages or visiting women's hostels. On Remembrance Sunday in November 2021, Harry did not visit a cemetery to salute the fallen. With their shrewd team of advisors, they also concluded that any appeal to Britons was wasted. In the aftermath of the Oprah Winfrey show they focused their energy entirely on America – not only to relate to their bedrock of support but also to maximise their income.

To benefit from Delaware's secrecy, Meghan's lawyers had registered 11 companies in the state.[836] The Archewell Foundation and the Sussexes' personal finances were hidden from view. Confusingly, besides the charity Archewell Foundation they had simultaneously created two commercial corporations, Archewell Audio and Archewell Productions. Outsiders would be unable to discover where the couple had deposited any of their income from Netflix and Spotify. Or whether their income had been used for charitable purposes.

There was also no evidence that Netflix and Spotify were earning any revenues from their relationship with the Sussexes. On the contrary, executives in both corporations were reportedly frustrated by the lack of products and profits.[837] The only new venture agreed by the Sussexes was a partnership with the Center for Humane Technology. Together with Archewell they would research the development of 'safer, more compassionate online communities'. That flagged the Sussexes' interests but was not the source of money to sustain their lifestyle.

In the dragnet cast by the Sussexes' team among Silicon Valley billionaires and headhunters to find suitable employment for Harry, their first catch was Better Up. 'Prince Harry, The Duke of Sussex', announced the corporation founded in 2013, had been employed as the Chief Impact Officer. Delivering 'hyper-personalised coaching' to improve motivation and productivity, Harry would oversee the corporation's counselling and mentoring services.

Despite his promise not to cash in on his royal connections, Harry offered to the Californian money-machine his expertise as a sufferer of mental health as a prince.[838] As a sufferer of 'burn-out' he would join a programme to urge sufferers to seek mental wellness by meditation with the help of a Better Up coach. 'I'm being schooled by the universe,' Harry would say about finding the cure to his own personal burn-out.[839] A sufferer's mental health, he advocated, would improve if they quit their job.[840] Their alternative source of income was left unexplained.

To promote Better Up, Harry arranged that the Californian corporation should be linked to the Queen's Commonwealth Trust (QCT), a royal charity. In return, the QCT promoted Better Up as an invaluable help to the Americans.[841] Harry was dipping into murky waters. Contrary to British charity practices, nearly the entirety of QCT's total annual £796,106 income was paid to its staff rather than to listed beneficiaries. Without any understanding of finance or law, Harry risked trouble.

Describing himself as a 'humanitarian, military veteran, mental wellness advocate and environmentalist', Harry's second position was as a member of the Aspen Institute's Commission on Information Disorder. The Commission was investigating how 'misinformation' was causing a 'modern-day crisis of faith in key institutions'. Among Harry's fellow members was Kathryn Murdoch, the wife of James Murdoch, whose London newspaper had illegally hacked Harry's telephone, although Murdoch claimed to be unaware of the crime.

As a victim of the 'digital dictatorship' Harry felt he could contribute to the investigation into 'a crisis of trust and truth…which is a global humanitarian issue.' The Commission's report would call for accountability from the 'superspreaders' of 'online lies' which were harming 'hundreds of millions of people every single day.'[842]

Harry went further. He described inaccurate journalists as 'the pirates with press cards who have hijacked the most powerful industry in the world'. He asked, 'If the news media is supposed to be holding us to account, who is holding them to account? I would love to see a movement to expose the unethical, the immoral and dishonest amongst them.'[843] The 17 inaccuracies in the Oprah Winfrey interview and Meghan's misleading statement to the High Court in the *Mail on Sunday* case passed unmentioned.

Ethics were so important to Harry that he and Meghan joined New York's Ethic Bank as 'impact partners'. The $1.3 billion asset management fund founded in 2015 focused on sustainable investments. Their purpose, said the Sussexes, was to 'rethink the nature of investing to help solve the global issues we all face'. The Sussexes had invested their own money in the fund, and were paid to become brand ambassadors, even though that was forbidden by the Sandringham agreement.

The bank was controversial.[844] Presenting themselves as environmentalists and hippies, the bank's founders were accused of 'greenwashing' investment for the super-rich by conjuring a 'do-good' smokescreen. Critics highlighted that Ethic Bank had invested in goldmines, social media, airlines, oil corporations, pharmaceuticals, Amazon, Raytheon, the precision-guided missile manufacturer, and even Rupert Murdoch's Fox Corp – all of whom were condemned as unethical by pressure-groups, and by Harry himself when appearing under a different guise. Above all, he hated those in the media who criticised him.

Harry's understanding of the media was revealed by his denunciation on American television of the First Amendment as 'bonkers'. America's cornerstone of freedom of speech and an uncensored media was described by Harry as 'vulgar'. In America, 'vulgar' meant 'crazy'. Subsequently, he admitted he did not understand the constitutional protection.[845]

There was a good reason for Harry to renew his criticism of the media. On 16th April, 2021, David Engel, the solicitor, told the *Mail on Sunday* that although his client Jason Knauf would not voluntarily help the newspaper he would provide a statement if Meghan's case came to a trial.[846] Knauf's latest approach was prompted by Judge Warby's refusal to allow a trial. Knauf was also taken aback by the Sussexes' inaccuracies in the Oprah Winfrey interview, as well as Meghan's story that Thomas Markle was a liar who she, as a loving daughter, had tried to help. Warby, the Palace Four complained, had protected Meghan's 'duplicitous' behaviour, allowing her to traduce the reputations of 'good people and brilliant professionals'. Namely, the Palace Four. If the four testified at Meghan's trial the consequences for the Sussexes would be serious. With that in mind, Harry set off for London.

One week earlier, on 9th April, Prince Philip had died. His funeral was set for 17th April. Neither the Palace nor the media understood the Sussexes' mindset when Harry arrived in London just before the service.

The mood in London was sombre. Daily, the media extolled Philip's remarkable life and devotion to the country. The Duke had planned a simple funeral at St George's Chapel, Windsor. The rehearsals displayed faultless military drill. Few would not be touched by the perfection of British ceremonial tradition. The weather was forecast to be perfect. The only uncertainty was the relationship between Harry and his family. How would he cope with his father and brother? Meghan had cited her seven months' pregnancy as the reason for not travelling.

In Windsor Castle the Queen was preparing to face the public on one of the saddest days of her life. Philip had been her rock for the previous 70 years. To comply with Covid restrictions she would grieve alone inside the chapel. 'Thank goodness Meghan is not coming,' the monarch said in a clear voice to her trusted aides. There was no mistaking the Queen's dislike for the disruptive actress.

Harry's presence remained a problem. As a private citizen stripped of his military titles he could not dress in uniform. To minimise the embarrassment for both Harry and Andrew, who was mired in allegations of sexual sleaze, all the male members of the Royal Family dressed in morning suits. To avoid any problems with William, the brothers were separated as they walked towards St George's Chapel by their cousin Peter Phillips.

During that short procession many watched whether Harry signalled any regret towards his family. Some interpreted his sideways glance towards William as the outsider's unease. No one grasped the truth about Harry's nervousness. None realised that in four weeks' time his Apple TV series about mental health would confirm not only his disloyalty but his disregard for his family's privacy. Transmission had been delayed until after the funeral. Once again, Harry had shafted the Windsors.

Looking at his family standing in St George's Chapel, Harry knew that his damnation of them in the Apple TV series would widen the rift. Sitting alone and isolated, the 94-year-old monarch's grief was concealed behind a black mask. Everyone was moved by her dignity. William looked tense, Kate serene, Charles visibly anguished. Only Harry's expression defied accurate reporting. Flapping his order of service against his thighs as he left the Chapel, he was clearly impatient. None knew that Harry, the once adored young prince, had betrayed his whole family.

After the service, eager for signs of reconciliation, the media seized on Kate's manoeuvre to engineer a conversation between the brothers. Cameras followed them as they walked up the hill towards the castle. Later reports of the aftermath veered between a two-hour conversation between Harry, William and Charles, and a perfunctory exchange before everyone departed. Few realised that Harry had no interest in reconciliation. He wanted to return to California as fast as possible. The three princes spoke briefly before Charles drove to his cottage in the Brecon Beacons in Wales. William was handed the burden of rescuing the monarchy from the damage caused by his brother and his uncle Andrew.

Buckingham Palace finally understood very precisely on 14th May that the Sussexes were beyond control. Apple TV released Harry's broadside. Called *The Me You Can't See*, Harry denounced William whom he had previously praised as the only person he 'could trust', and later in a podcast called *Armchair Expert* dishonoured Charles whom he had previously thanked for being so 'kind', for causing a cycle of 'genetic pain'. He had even criticised the Queen, despite saying she was 'hugely admired'.[847] All were cast as villains responsible for his 'cycles of suffering' and 'unresolved anger'. Comparing his life as 'a mixture between *The Truman Show* and being in a zoo', he said of his family: 'I've seen behind the curtain. I've seen the business model. I know how this operation runs…I don't want to be part of this.'

Instead of being reconciled with his family, he had monetised his anguish. The trigger for his anger was once again his family's 'total neglect' of Meghan while she was suicidal. 'She was going to end her life. It shouldn't have to get to that,' he said, adding, 'That was one of the biggest reasons to leave, feeling trapped and feeling controlled through fear, both by the media and by the system itself which never encouraged talking about this kind of trauma. I was ashamed to go to my family. Because I know that I'm not going to get from my family what I need.'

Ramping up his earlier accusations aired in the Oprah Winfrey interview, Harry described how he and Meghan felt 'bullied into silence…I thought my family would help, but every single ask, request, warning, whatever it is, just got met with total silence, total neglect. We spent four years trying to make it work. We did everything we possibly could to stay there and carry on doing the role and doing the job. Meghan was struggling.'[848] Even while they negotiated their departure – 'hunted and helpless' in London – there were 'forces working against us'. Who rebuffed Harry's pleas remained unidentified.

While the Palace struggled to understand why Harry should publicly criticise the Queen and his dead grandfather for their upbringing of Charles, Harry enjoyed the reports that he was trending at No.1 on social media. America's men were gripped by Harry's advocacy of therapy. He was credited for removing the stigma of admitting to anxiety and depression. By contrast, Palace officials decided there was no way for them to reason with a man who 'shared' his anger in order to help others have a 'positive impact'.

The gulf between the Windsors and Harry was widening. Five days earlier, Harry nailed his colours to political campaigning. At Vax Live, a Los Angeles charity concert, Harry told an audience that Pfizer and other pioneers of anti-Covid vaccines should abandon their intellectual property rights and let poorer countries have their patents free.[849]

President Biden supported that gesture, but it was opposed by Britain and the EU. Harry's participation would have been impossible as a member of the Royal Family. As would Meghan's two-minute video. She weighed in by asserting that women of colour had been disproportionately affected by Covid. Women's progress, said Meghan, had been 'wiped out' for a generation. She offered no evidence for that proposition.

Harry knew that the couple's political activism and the monetisation of their anger was causing Charles grief. Powerless over events in California, Charles knew he had good reason on his accession to strip the Sussexes and their children of their titles. The Sussexes' status depended entirely on their royal titles. Every appearance or statement was issued under the label 'The Duke and Duchess of Sussex'. Neither considered it odd to honour the Queen yet damn her as a bad parent to Charles, or label her whole family as racist and neglectful of Meghan. In America, the Sussexes assumed, no one would be aware of those contradictions. But Harry could not assume that Charles would tolerate the enmity without retribution. In the possibly brief time before the Queen died, Harry needed to cement his status.

To remain in the public eye, the Sussexes organised a Lilibet website before their daughter was born.[850] Lilibet was the name used by George V, the Queen's grandfather, as he imitated his young granddaughter's attempts to say her own name. After his death in 1936 the name stuck, but was only used by the closest members of the Queen's family.

Harry's daughter was born at Santa Barbara's Cottage Hospital on 4th June. On the same day, but two days before the birth was announced, Meghan's lawyers registered the lilibetdiana.com website. After the birth, but before the public announcement, Harry called the Queen. He told his grandmother about the birth and their decision to call their daughter Lilibet.

To stymie the Sussexes, the Palace told the BBC that the Queen was 'never asked' for permission for the use of her name. In his telephone call, Harry was 'telling' the Queen about the name. Once the BBC broadcast that report, the Sussexes' 'truth' machine was activated. Toya Holness, Meghan's spokeswoman, claimed that Harry would not have chosen the name if the Queen had not been 'supportive'. Fired up by the Sussexes' anger, Schillings announced that unless the BBC apologised and withdrew that report, the Sussexes would sue for defamation. Pitching Harry against the Queen was an extreme tactic to control the Sussexes' image. The Palace supported the BBC. Faced with the factual truth, the Sussexes retreated. Schillings' threat evaporated. The Sussexes were defeated.

Legal wrangles in London could be easily forgotten in California. Only when the whole Royal Family descended on the G7 summit hosted by the prime minister in Cornwall on 12th June, and Kate was filmed laughing with Jill Biden, did Meghan understand the unequal struggle for attention. For the British, the sight of William, Charles and the Queen walking through a garden, and alongside the world's leaders, represented the monarchy's enduring strength, and William and Kate represented its future. The Windsors felt reassured by the international accolades. The Sussexes plotted their counter-attack. All their future public appearances were carefully scheduled and inserted onto a grid, building up to a climax later that year in New York. Their own royal event was planned to consolidate their status in America.

In their timetable, the unveiling of a bronze memorial to Diana in Kensington Palace's Sunken Garden on her sixtieth birthday became a sideshow for Harry. In the bitterness sparked by the Sussexes, only the Spencer family were present alongside the brothers. Everyone else, including Diana's grandchildren, stayed away. Meghan's absence passed without comment, except in those parts of America where Diana was revered.

Standing in front of an uninspiring depiction of Diana, William and Harry defied speculation. The ceremony would not trigger a reconciliation. William's reluctance to attend the ceremony was well known. By then he knew it was pointless to appease the Sussexes. Harry's destiny was built on undermining the Windsors. Harry's reinvention required a clean break, retribution and possible reconciliation on the Sussexes' terms. The only blip was the risk of the truth emerging.

At the end of July 2021, the *Mail on Sunday*'s lawyer wrote to Jason Knauf. She asked the official whether he might after all give a statement for the forthcoming court hearing against Meghan. Knauf's reply arrived the next day. To avoid any challenge to his veracity, he subsequently sent a statement based entirely on his exchange of text messages and emails with Meghan and Harry. Knauf's statement and Meghan's later statement signalled a public somersault. Knauf revealed that he commented about Meghan's draft letter to her father and that, at Meghan's request, he had also briefed Omid Scobie.[851] In addition, Kensington Palace's communication team was believed to have given the journalist a copy of Meghan's letter to Thomas Markle. Scobie was alleged to have later discussed the letter with one of Meghan's American friends.[852] In the event, Scobie had been furious when *People* magazine had scooped him.[853]

Now, Knauf intimated, the Palace staff were prepared 'to tell the truth' in Meghan's trial.[854] The other three former members of Meghan's staff had also prepared witness statements. All four would challenge Meghan's truthfulness. Knauf's statement was delivered simultaneously to the *Mail*'s and the Sussexes' lawyers. The Sussexes had good reason to be fearful.

Tellingly, Knauf had switched lawyers. A new firm of solicitors was also employed by the Palace to investigate Meghan's alleged bullying. Not mentioned in Knauf's statement was his memorandum that recorded the staff's allegations of Meghan's bullying. For the Sussexes, preventing the media from publicising Knauf's 'truth' had become essential.

CHAPTER 40

Grandstanding

Ceaselessly, the social media trolls were spreading vicious gossip. Their posts were unrelenting: Meghan had insulted Tyler Perry's staff and the Sussexes had left his house after an argument; Meghan was cursing that Harry spent too much time with 'Brits' living in Los Angeles; George Lucas, the film director and a neighbour in Montecito, was irritated by the Sussexes; Meghan wrote on stationery embossed with a gold 'M' under a golden crown; Netflix and Spotify were dissatisfied by the Sussexes' lack of product; Archie was never seen playing with local children; and Harry was seen every morning smoking weed in his garden. Richard Mineards, a former journalist living near Montecito, gave the *London Evening Standard* the opposite report. The Sussexes, he said, were happily integrated into the neighbourhood.[855]

The Sussexes had good reason to ignore the trolls. Their astute team were completing the jigsaw to establish them as major players in America. Their deadline was three months away.

Negotiations were nearly completed to sign a four-book deal. The first title, to be published in late 2022, was to be Harry's 'intimate and heartfelt' memoir.[856] Ghost-written by the American journalist J. R. Moehringer, Harry's book promised to deliver an 'accurate and wholly truthful definitive account' about the 'losses and life lessons that have helped to shape him'. To earn the estimated advance of about £20 million, Harry would be expected to give Moehringer emotional confessions and secret details. These would settle his scores with his family and friends. Meghan was expected to help the ghost-writer understand the pain inflicted by the Royal Family on herself and Harry.

Among the targets besides William, Kate and Charles would be Camilla. Meghan had identified her as racist. Publication was sensitively timed for after the end of the celebrations of the Queen's Platinum Jubilee in June. By definition Harry excluded describing the advantages bestowed on himself. By any count, Harry was one of the world's most privileged men. The further threat was the announcement that his second book would be published after the Queen's death.

The announcement of Harry's deal coincided with the publication of Meghan's illustrated children's book *The Bench*. She anticipated a sensational bestseller for the 34 pages inspired by a poem she wrote for Harry on Father's Day after Archie was born. Dedicated 'For the man and boy who make my heart go pump-pump', she wrote about the inspiration 'to depict the special bond through an inclusive lens'. In particular, she wanted to highlight the 'softness of masculinity and fatherhood' through 'the warmth, joy and comfort of the relationship between fathers and sons'. Meghan failed to spot the irony that she and Harry were estranged from their own fathers.

The critics were harsh. Meghan was too controversial to attract generosity. The *Daily Telegraph* commented that her 'semi-literate' book 'leaves Harry holding the baby'. Another complained that the 'semi-literate vanity project...limps along'. Others questioned the book's remarkable similarity to *The Boy and the Bench* published in 2018. Ranked 4,934 on Britain's Amazon after two weeks, *The Bench* reached the Top 2000 in America. Within days the bad reviews were unimportant. Meghan had successfully executed two other appearances.

On her fortieth birthday, she issued a video launching her 40x40 initiative. Filmed in her house behind a large table piled with her book, she explained how a clutch of famous women had been recruited to devote 40 minutes to each help one woman return to work after the pandemic. Although she did not explain what could be achieved in 40 minutes, and the humour in the brief video of comic actress Melissa McCarthy fell flat, the snapshot raised her profile and reaffirmed her commitment to women's empowerment. The results were never revealed. The next jigsaw piece was more profound.

Two Republican senators, Susan Collins from Maine and Shelley Moore Capito of West Virginia, received cold-calls.[857] Introducing herself as 'Meghan, the Duchess of Sussex', she asked the surprised politicians to vote in favour of paid parental leave. She wanted more mothers to get paid-time off work to spend with their babies. Both senators appeared underwhelmed by the calls. Not least, both found it 'ironic' that Meghan should use her royal title. After all, she had told *Vanity Fair* that she 'never defined myself by my relationship'. Nevertheless, the Sussex publicity machine successfully spread the news of Meghan's surprise coup.

The two telephone calls were preceded by letters from Meghan to House Speaker Nancy Pelosi and Senate Majority Leader Chuck Schumer.[858] To support her cause, the Duchess of Sussex described her childhood to the politicians as poor: 'I grew up on the $4.99 salad bar at Sizzler.' She also repeated once more that she had worked at the age of 13 in the local yoghurt shop.

Harry and Meghan were on a roll. They voiced concern that 'the world is exceptionally fragile'; felt 'speechless' with 'many layers of pain' after the Taliban began its victorious advance towards Kabul; and were 'left scared' by the new variants and constant misinformation about Covid.[859] They were less concerned that after a polo match Harry flew on a private jet from Aspen to Santa Barbara, despite telling Oprah Winfrey that climate change was 'one of the most pressing issues' facing the world.[860]

That was the same Oprah Winfrey whose clip of the Sussexes' interview was booed at the National TV Awards ceremony in London in September. There was a dispute whether the boos were for the Sussexes or for Oprah for seeking accolades for the interview. Either way, the Sussexes relied on Toya Holness to suffocate any negative voices directed against them.

Holness recruited in New York Genevieve Roth, the founder of Invisible Hand, to promote the couple. Roth was paid to oversee the Sussexes' 'strategy on storytelling'. In 2020, Roth told *Good Housekeeping* magazine, 'I am rife with internalised racism and unconscious bias.' Married to an African-American man, she confessed that 'race is an issue in our marriage because as a white woman of privilege I have racist tendencies written in at a cellular level'.[861] In New York's prevailing atmosphere, Roth was helped by *Time* magazine's editors.

Every year, *Time*, historically among America's most prestigious publications, named the nation's 100 most influential people. The Sussexes' staff had worked hard to persuade *Time*'s editors that Harry and Meghan ranked as America's Number One 'icon'.[862] They succeeded. In the distant past, the nomination would be written by a famous political or cultural personality. The best *Time* could produce to nominate the Sussexes was José Andrés, a chef who pioneered the charity World Central Kitchen (WCK), part financed with $25,000 from Archewell. Andrés' operation belied the title. Beyond America, WCK had only opened small kitchens in Haiti, Puerto Rico and Tonga.

Andrés' praise for the Sussexes was effusive. The couple, he wrote, were 'blessed through birth and talent, and burned by fame. The Duke and Duchess have compassion for people they don't know. They don't just opine. They run toward the struggle. They give voice to the voiceless through media production.' Critics might question associating the Sussexes' with 'struggle', but Clare and Nina Hallworth, famous for creating the image of Jennifer Aniston in 2019, were hired to produce a perfect image for the Sussexes' cover photo.

The stylists positioned Harry, all in black, standing behind Meghan dressed in white. Meghan had clearly had a change of heart about stylists. Three years earlier, she had told Knauf that she didn't use stylists: 'You know how personally frustrating I find the "stylist" narrative (as it's the only thing I seem to still have any control over – my personal styling).'

Time magazine was the prelude for the Sussexes' next big event: a mini-royal three-day tour of New York starting on 22nd September. They arrived on a private jet with Mandana Dayani, newly appointed as Archewell's chief operating officer, who had formerly worked for Hillary Clinton. The media would be restricted to just photographs. No interviews.

Based at The Carlyle, Princess Diana's favourite hotel, the Sussexes were assured by the city's power-brokers of maximum security. Their SUV convoy would be surrounded by police motorcyclists – sealing off roads – as they drove across Manhattan. On their first visit early on Thursday morning to the Twin Towers Observatory, they were welcomed by Bill de Blasio, New York's mayor, and the state governor, Kathy Hochul. Treated as members of the British Royal Family, they were escorted to the 9/11 Memorial and the 102nd floor of the Freedom Tower of the World Trade Center. After paying their respects, they walked from the building to their police-guarded convoy.

Onlookers were surprised that Meghan was wearing a turtleneck and thick overcoat despite the 80-degree humid weather. Over the three days, she would wear heavy winter clothes, pieces by Armani, Loro Piana and Max Mara, over Valentino dresses. Accessories were Valentino, Cartier and Manolo Blahnik. As Meghan walked with Harry they were overheard on a microphone Harry was wearing for a Netflix documentary. Speaking in strained voices they discussed a plan to take Lilibet to Britain for her baptism. That did not happen.[863]

Next stop was the UN building to meet America's ambassador to the UN, Linda Thomas-Greenfield. Then to a discussion about Covid vaccine equity with Chelsea Clinton at the offices of the World Health Organisation, which included the virtual appearance of WHO's director general, Dr Tedros Adhanom Ghebreyesus.

The following day, the couple visited the Mahalia Jackson elementary school in Harlem. Meghan was filmed reading *The Bench* to a class of children. Reporters were told that the Sussexes had donated a washing and drying machine, two garden boxes filled with vegetables and herbs, and copies of her book. Critics questioned whether the schoolchildren from broken homes would welcome a narrative of a happy family, and whether Meghan's $15,000 outfit was appropriate. From there, they went for a lunch of Southern fried chicken and waffles at Melba, a Harlem comfort-food restaurant. They pledged $25,000 for the restaurant's Covid relief fund.

The highlight of the tour was on Saturday afternoon. In front of a 60,000 crowd in Central Park, a Global Citizen Live concert promoted vaccine equity. The Sussexes were cheered for urging manufacturers to donate free vaccines to poor countries. 'The ultra-wealthy pharmaceutical companies are not sharing the recipes to make them,' Harry told the crowd. 'Recipes' is the word he used. Adopting Meghan's language, he continued, 'When we start making decisions through that lens, every single person deserves equal access to the vaccine.' None of the audience appeared to question how Harry, trading on his inherited title and inherited wealth, was qualified to launch a socialistic campaign.

Before the concert ended, the couple were driven to Teterboro airport. As they flew on their private jet back to Santa Barbara, the Cop-26 climate summit was meeting in Glasgow. 'The Duke and Duchess of Sussex have a long-standing commitment to the planet,' Archewell announced. The Sussexes, the charity added, would be net-zero by 2030, and be offsetting their carbon footprint.

One month later, the Sussexes returned to New York by private jet to star in a gala for veterans.[864] Walking into the hall dressed in a stunning red designer dress, Meghan was hailed by the *New York Times* as an A-list celebrity and social activist.

The same newspaper invited the Duchess of Sussex to appear on a platform with Mellody Hobson, the chairwoman of Starbucks, co-chief executive of an investment fund and the wife of *Star Wars* director George Lucas. Together, they urged the Biden administration to pay for family leave as a 'humanitarian issue'.[865] On the same day, at a Re-Wired conference, Harry attacked the British media for 'creating news with a vested interest' to provoke Meghan's untimely death. 'The incentives of publishing,' Harry read from his script, 'are not necessarily aligned with the incentives of truth. Misinformation is a global humanitarian crisis.'

Their two speeches in New York coincided with the opening of the appeal court hearing of Meghan's case against the *Mail on Sunday*.

CHAPTER 41

Victory

From the outset on 9th November, 2021, the three appeal judges in London showed little interest in the arguments offered on the newspaper's behalf by Andrew Caldecott to allow a trial. Leading the three judges, Geoffrey Vos, the Master of the Rolls, had never shown in his career particular concern for the freedom of the press.

Alongside him, Victoria Sharp was a renowned trenchant critic of the media. Early in her career she had eagerly represented the press tycoon Robert Maxwell to crush journalists' criticism. More telling, in a previous judgement Sharp had undermined a critical statutory protection of the media in defamation cases. She was overruled by the Supreme Court.

As a class, Britain's judges were unsympathetic to the *Mail* news-paper group whose 2016 headline 'Enemies of the People' had damned the judiciary for alleged prejudice against Brexit. (Two judges had declared that the referendum in favour of Brexit could only be implemented with parliament's approval. In a hung parliament, getting that vote was unrealistic.) In Meghan's trial case, the three judges' lack of sympathy for the *Mail* was apparent from their impatient expressions as Caldecott outlined his case. 'You're wasting court time,' was the impression the judges gave.

Just as Meghan was visiting a US military base in New Jersey as part of her 'royal' duties, Caldecott spelled out the importance of Jason Knauf's statement. He argued that Judge Warby had been misled by Meghan's misleading statement to the court. He also showed how Warby had ignored some of Thomas Markle's text messages. The judge was wrong, Caldecott said, to deny the *Mail* the right to cross-examine Meghan and produce the testimony of the Palace Four in a trial.

The judges openly dismissed Caldecott's argument about the importance of Jason Knauf's description of his 'multiple' discussions with Meghan.[866] The judges preferred to latch on to Meghan's excuses for her misleading the court in her signed statement.

'I had forgotten about the email exchanges I had with Mr Knauf,' wrote Meghan in a new contrite statement, 'and his meeting with the authors.'[867] She continued, 'When I approved the passage...I did not have the benefit of seeing these emails and I apologise to the court for the fact that I had not remembered these exchanges at the time. I had absolutely no wish or intention to mislead the defendant or the court.'

The judges accepted Meghan's explanation. Her misleading statement, said Vos, was 'at best an unfortunate lapse of memory'. The newspaper lost its appeal. According to the judges, Meghan was empowered to determine the narrative and the media were not allowed to challenge her truth in a trial. Meghan's right of privacy was more important than press freedom and the public interest. The newspaper would not be given the chance to defend itself.

Inevitably, the media's reaction to the judgement was critical. How could she have forgotten her exchanges with Knauf? many asked. She was guilty of a 'falsehood' and 'lies'.[868] No other claimant in an English court had ever escaped a trial and justice because of 'an unfortunate lapse of memory'. Many were outraged that once again the rich and powerful had won. Insiders said the outstanding victor was Judge Warby, protected by his fellow judges. The victim was Thomas Markle. He had no redress for the defamation published by *People* magazine.

'Markles die at 80,' he said. 'I've got just three years to live. I'll never see my daughter again, or my grandchildren.'

Meghan Markle was euphoric: 'This is a victory not just for me but for anyone who has ever felt scared to stand up for what's right.' She accused the *Mail on Sunday* of dragging the case out and twisting the facts to generate more headlines – 'a model that rewards chaos above truth.' She added, 'In the nearly three years since this began, I have been patient in the face of deception, intimidation and calculated attacks…These harmful practices don't happen once in a blue moon – they are a daily fact that divides us and we all deserve better.' She urged a change of law: 'While this win is precedent-setting, what matters most is that we are now collectively brave enough to reshape a tabloid industry that conditions people to be cruel and profits from the lies and pain that they create.'

The Times in London criticised the Duchess for attacking the media: 'It is improper to exploit the platform granted by hereditary privilege, in her case through marriage, to press a political case.'[869]

A substantial argument against the British media and in Meghan's defence was written for *New York* magazine by Safiya Umoja Noble, an associate professor of Gender Studies and African Studies at UCLA, the director of the Center for Critical Internet Inquiry, and the author of *Algorithms of Oppression: How Search Engines Reinforce Racism*. Noble asserted that Meghan had been targeted by an unprecedented sexist and racist Twitter campaign fuelled by 'harassment and hate'. Black women, she wrote, were 'relentlessly targeted online' by 'misogynoir'. The attack on a 'Black woman suing for her privacy and winning is too much for the tabloids to bear,' wrote Noble. She did not mention in her article that her studies were part-financed by the Archewell Foundation to 'illuminate the problems of inequality and structural racism'.[870]

Meghan's triumph was sealed by her appearance on the Ellen DeGeneres TV chat show.[871] Both women, neighbours in Montecito, were united by accusations of bullying.[872] Both were also desperate to stay relevant for the American public. In the celebrity economy, remarkable additional effort was required by middle-aged women to secure the publicity which kept their status at the top of the index. Many, Meghan knew, disdained the fickle superficiality of maintaining one's celebrity, but since her childhood in ABC's studio she had embraced that world. The trick was to avoid obsolescence by constantly refreshing her appeal.

Fearing that her New York success two months earlier had been forgotten, Meghan agreed to an extraordinary subversion of her royal image. First, she appeared in the studio for an interview with DeGeneres covering all the very familiar milestones in her life.

Next, dressed in an Oscar de la Renta top, Meghan left the studio and went into the street. Instructed via an earpiece connected to DeGeneres, she was ordered to interact with market traders selling quartz crystals and hot sauces. 'Let's get the spiciest, let's get the hottest,' screeched Meghan with eye-opening foolery. Ordered by DeGeneres to 'eat like a chipmunk', she chanted at the bemused traders, 'Oh lordy, lordy, lordy.' The studio audience cheered. Viewers were baffled. 'I'm feeling hot, hot, hot,' shouted Meghan as she danced alone. Obeying DeGeneres' orders to squat and touch her nose while swigging from a baby's bottle, she intoned, 'Mommy wants some milk.' The studio audience was encouraged to cheer more. Viewers were even more perplexed. Her finale was to act like a cat. For one minute, she recited, 'I'm a kitten, meow, meow, meow.'

CHAPTER 42

Revenge

The scene was now set for the final divorce between the Sussexes and the Royal Family.

Harry fired the opening shots. His refusal to seek any reconciliation at Diana's memorial or fly over to London for Prince Philip's memorial service on 29th March, 2022, confirmed that the Windsors of Montecito had no intention of rebuilding their relationship with the Royal Family, except on their own terms. Similarly, he appeared to be looking for an excuse not to fly to London for the Queen's Platinum Jubilee celebrations in June.

Although the Queen had invited Harry and Meghan to join the nation's extravaganza, the couple appeared to seek reasons to avoid humiliation. As private citizens they could not expect to be invited on to the Buckingham Palace balcony or ride in the carriages.[873] Isolated on the periphery, the image would undermine their royal status in America.

To forge a valid excuse, Harry applied to the High Court in London for an order to compel the Metropolitan police to provide protection for himself during his visit, or allow him to pay for police protection.[874] Predictably, his £400,000 case failed. As a private citizen Harry was told he could not force the government to provide police protection.[875] He showed no disappointment, nor embarrassment that he would be visiting Holland for the Invictus Games in April.

Any doubts about Harry's antagonism towards his country and family were dispelled by his stony silence after the Queen announced on Accession Day that Camilla would be Britain's next queen.[876] Seventeen years after their controversial marriage, Charles had persuaded his mother and a majority of Britons that Camilla should be crowned during his own coronation. Harry's refusal to acknowledge the Queen's decision foreshadowed the problems to come. Charles had good reason to fear that Harry's dislike of Camilla had been re-energised by Meghan. The Sussexes' suspicion that the Duchess of Cornwall had made racist comments about the unborn Archie had fuelled their fearsome denunciation of the entire Royal Family.

Most Britons could not understand Harry's hostility towards his country and family. His disloyalty to his grandmother was particularly mystifying. Occasionally, he seemed willing to betray every value he formerly held dear. No one realised how his hostility had grown during his conversations with John Moehringer, the ghost-writer of his memoirs. To secure vast sales and recoup the huge advance, the publishers had encouraged Harry to criticise his family in the most extreme terms possible. Easily persuaded, Harry edged towards betraying his father, Camilla, the Cambridges and even the Queen. And then, the deed was done. To earn out the publisher's advance, nothing and no one had been sacrosanct.

Charles got an inkling of the horrors to come in early 2022. Two Sunday newspapers alleged that Charles had accepted £1.5 million from a Saudi billionaire businessman, Mahfouz Marei Mubarak bin Mahfouz, in questionable circumstances. Mahfouz had given the money to help maintain Charles's Scottish project, Dumfries House. In return, Charles had met Mahfouz in Scotland and Saudi Arabia; and then in 2016, in a private ceremony in Buckingham Palace, Charles had awarded the Saudi a CBE for charity. Those transactions were not unusual in Charles's life. During over 30 years of fundraising for his charities, Charles had encouraged the rich to pay for access to himself. The unusual exception in the Mahfouz case is what followed in 2017.

During that year, Charles had not prevented his close aide Michael Fawcett from writing to the Saudi a compromising letter. After acknowledging the Saudi's financial gifts, Fawcett offered to support Mahfouz's application for British citizenship and he pledged that Charles's office would attempt to augment the CBE awarded to Mahfouz into a knighthood or KBE. Once Fawcett's letter was exposed by newspapers, Scotland Yard was compelled to open an investigation of cash-for-honours, a criminal offence since 1925. Charles's fate depended on Fawcett denying that the prince was aware of his written offer.

In the midst of Charles's crisis, Harry aimed a blow at his father. He released emails showing that unlike Charles he had broken his own relationship with the Saudi businessman. In 2014, Mahfouz had promised £1 million to Harry's charity, Sentebale. After Harry had offered his thanks, Mahfouz's representative stipulated that as a pre-condition of the gift, Harry should visit the businessman and his family in Saudi Arabia. On Harry's behalf, the invitation to visit Saudi Arabia was rejected as a questionable offer of cash-for-access. There was no further communication. Charles had done the opposite. Adding to Charles's predicament, Harry highlighted his 'concern' about his father's conduct.[877]

That discomforting news broke in the same week as Prince Andrew agreed to pay off Virginia Giuffre, the American woman who had accused him of sexual abuse when she was an underaged girl of 17. The multi-million-pound settlement avoided a devastating trial in a New York court. The curse of Jeffrey Epstein was very damaging. Andrew was instantly stripped of his honours and public positions, banned from public life and permanently relegated to the shadows.

In combination, all those embarrassments destabilised the

monarchy's reputation as the Queen's health noticeably deteriorated. Just as Charles feared, Harry might not support his own and Camilla's accession to the throne. Camilla, he suspected, would be cited in Harry's memoir as a reason for the couple to turn away from Britain. Under Meghan's influence, Harry had embraced America's toxic political battle about race as a platform for his wife's and his own advancement.

Through assiduous networking, Meghan had forged relationships with Black America's leaders. Few were more controversial than the lawyer and Brandeis professor, Anita Hill. She had unsuccessfully sought in 1991 to prevent the Black conservative Clarence Thomas from being appointed as a Supreme Court judge. Thirty-one years later, Meghan featured in Hill's welcome for Ketanji Brown Jackson's nomination as the first Black woman to the Supreme Court.

In her article, Hill referred to another 'Black woman of stature and credential – Meghan, the Duchess of Sussex'.[878] Citing Meghan at length, Hill described the Duchess as a historic figure in Black women's empowerment. 'The civil rights history of tomorrow is being written today,' Hill declared. In the context of Black women's achievements, attested Hill, Meghan was written into the history books. Meghan represented 'a fabric woven into the entire chronicle of the American story'.

It was no coincidence that Hill's elevation of Meghan as a political champion of Black Americans was published simultaneously with the Sussexes making a star appearance at the 53rd NAACP Image Awards in Beverly Hills. The National Association for the Advancement of Colored People, established in 1909, is America's largest civil rights organisation. In the theatrical relaunch of Meghan, the couple were noticeably accompanied to the ceremony by Doria, Meghan's mother. Just before walking on to the stage in a shimmering blue outfit, British newspapers revealed that Meghan's approval ratings had fallen to 8 per cent. Harry's rating was merely 13 per cent.[879]

Their appearance at the awards was part of a deal negotiated by

Meghan's staff. The NAACP's President's Award was given to the Sussexes in 'recognition for their distinguished public service and philanthropic contributions'.[880] Previous recipients of the award included Muhammad Ali, Jesse Jackson, Colin Powell and Rihanna. Meghan's achievement looked impressive until the organisation announced at the same ceremony a new NAACP-Archewell Digital Civil Rights Award. Worth $100,000, the recipients would be recognised for inspiring the next generation of activists.

The first person to be acknowledged was Safiya Noble, the UCLA professor already financed by Archewell to study how digital technologies intersect with culture, race and gender. The publicity for the event was organised by Sunshine Sachs. Just as José Andrés, the chef who nominated the Sussexes to be *Time* magazine's icon, had himself received $25,000 from Archewell for his kitchen charity, the Sussexes' charity had promoted the couple and their causes with the NAACP.

Transactional arrangements to promote the Sussexes were questionable and possibly contrary to the Internal Revenue Code. There were legal limits of giving financial help to an individual associated with a charity, and the source of the $100,000 was inexplicable.[881] In its first year's accounts, Archewell had raised less than $50,000.[882] The charity's finances remained shrouded in mystery. But its prime purpose was clear: publicising the Sussexes.

CHAPTER 43

Fall-Out

At the end of March 2022, Kate and William became victims of Meghan's and Harry's fevered self-promotion. Within hours of arriving in Jamaica – the second stop during an eight-day visit to the Caribbean – anti-British sentiment wrecked their goodwill tour. Neither had been adequately warned that Meghan Markle's message about the Royal Family's racism was ingrained across the region.

Planned for months as a celebration of the Queen's Platinum Jubilee, the Duke and Duchess of Cambridge's tour was focused on three Commonwealth countries – Belize, Jamaica and the Bahamas – where the monarch remained head of state. To the Cambridges' misfortune, their senior advisors in Kensington Palace, the British Foreign Office and the British High Commission in Jamaica had failed to grasp some feelings of hostility towards the British. None of those panjandrums had reported to the Palace the consequence of Meghan's sermons. Namely, that the Commonwealth was a relic of white colonialism; and that the Royal Family lacked sympathy for the descendants of slaves.

Meghan's denunciation of the Royal Family fuelled existing demands for reparations from Britain for slavery and the anti-monarchists' protests that their countries should become republics. British officials had dropped the unwary Cambridges, the future hope of the monarchy, into the crossfire.

Revenge

Insensitive photo opportunities in Kingston followed the Cambridges' humiliating appearance in front of Jamaica's prime minister, Andrew Holness. Marooned like schoolchildren in a contrived televised show-trial, the Cambridges were compelled to listen to Holness berate the British monarchy to promote his republican agenda and political ambitions.

The Cambridges' discomfort became worse after William, wearing a white dress uniform adorned with military medals, took the salute in an open-topped Land Rover. Criticised as caricatures of arrogant colonialists, the Cambridges were doomed once anti-British critics highlighted Kate's expensive clothes and glittering jewellery, and photographs appeared of her speaking to local children through a mesh-wire fence. The crisis climaxed after William made an abject apology for slavery. His words irritated most Britons and failed to satisfy those Jamaicans who disapproved of the visit. Foolishly, on his return to London, William failed to follow the Queen's example and remain silent. Instead, he issued an embarrassed statement acknowledging that the Commonwealth's fate should be reconsidered.

William's performance highlighted another of Meghan's complaints: the Royal Family was surrounded by incompetent advisors. The anti-monarchy protests had been predicted by the media in Jamaica and New York. *Newsweek*'s royal correspondent, Jack Royston, foresaw problems in the Caribbean for the Cambridges after Meghan's allegation that Archie's brown skin had denied him a title. *The Gleaner*, Jamaica's leading newspaper, had asked, 'Why should Jamaica persist in loitering on colonial premises' since the Queen was 'the matriarch of a dysfunctional British family'? The opprobrium heaped on the Cambridges was inflamed by the memories of Harry's acclaimed visit to Jamaica in 2012, and by the Sussexes' successful and informal tour of South Africa in September 2019.

In the aftermath, many speculated that royal visits and even the monarchy itself were relics. Wounded by the criticism, William appeared like a lost soul. By contrast the savvy Sussexes were trampling on what remained of the Cambridges' pristine reputation.

Over the previous months Harry had been preparing for the Invictus Games being held in The Hague in April 2022. His involvement would be featured in a Netflix series. In successive Netflix episodes, the Sussexes would feature as members of the Royal Family. Visibly retaining their relationship with the Queen was critically important for the Sussexes' status and income.

By March 2022 the ailing 95-year-old monarch had repeatedly cancelled public engagements. The exception was her appearance at Prince Philip's memorial service. To the Royal Family's misfortune, the event was overshadowed by Andrew's bold appearance centre-stage, escorting his mother to her seat in Westminster Abbey. Defiantly ignoring his banishment from public duties, Andrew also indicated that he expected to appear in the spotlight during the Queen's Jubilee celebrations in June.

Keeping Andrew out of sight was one problem. Another was Harry's and Meghan's demand also to appear with the Queen on Buckingham Palace's balcony. If the three outcasts did successfully appear in the spotlight, the media's focus would no longer be the Queen's achievements over 70 years, but on her dysfunctional son and grandson. Inevitably, the public reaction would be unenthusiastic.

The obstacles for Meghan and Harry to appear centre-stage were considerable – not least because their presence was opposed by Charles. Charles preferred that the Sussexes, as private citizens, were not invited on to the balcony or to ride in a royal carriage. Instead, they would be confined to the VIP enclosures. In Meghan's view those optics were unsatisfactory, partly because her value to Netflix was to stand near the Queen.

To achieve this goal Harry badgered the Queen's resistant advisors. When this failed he asked the Queen if he could visit her in Windsor on his way to the Netherlands. To secure her agreement, Harry appeared to give the impression that the meeting would offer an 'olive branch' to 'clear the air'. At the last moment, keen to see her grandson and instinctively forgiving of Meghan, the Queen agreed to meet the couple on 14th April. Charles was suspicious, while William avoided the problem with a previous arrangement to ski with his family in France.

After spending the night with his cousin Eugenie, Harry and Meghan were driven to Windsor Castle. Some would say that on the way they were seen walking through the sunlit park to allow Netflix to record their 'journey'. On the Queen's insistence they met Charles and Camilla before her. The Sussexes arrived late. Their first encounter was civilised but failed to resolve the fraught relations created by their Oprah Winfrey interview. By contrast, there was no tension drinking tea with the Queen. Yet the issue of their appearance on the balcony remained unresolved. Their visit was leaked to the *Sun* after they arrived in the Netherlands on the same day. The danger of allowing the meeting surfaced six days later.

Followed by Netflix cameras, the Sussexes proved themselves modern and compassionate as they faultlessly mixed in The Hague with the athletes. Always smiling and dressed in an unending change of expensive clothes while watching the events, Meghan played the stunning hostess pledged to offer 'service' to the world. But festering was their fury that the Palace had refused all of their demands for a prominent role at the Jubilee in return for returning to Britain with their children. Harry could not resist venting his anger to an American NBC TV reporter.

His 'special' relationship with the Queen, he told the world, meant that the Queen confided in him secrets unknown to others of her family. Her four children and seven other grandchildren, he implied, were excluded from her confidence. More inflammatory, he declared his duty was to make sure his grandmother was 'protected and got the right people around her'. Charles, Anne, William and all the Queen's staff, suggested Harry, were inadequate for the task. He appeared to speak from the heart, not as a thoughtless man totally manipulated by his wife. Harry, like Meghan, had resumed the war against his family. The 'olive branch' media headline about his visit to Windsor splintered.

Predictably, Harry's assertion of his special status aroused accusations about his 'breathtaking arrogance' with 'no bounds to his self-delusion'. Responding to the public fury, Downing Street even issued a statement that the Queen was well-protected.

Clearly unwilling to limit the damage, the most wounding moment of his TV appearance was his refusal to answer whether he missed his 'brother and dad'. Ignoring his family, he knew, would be offset among most American viewers by warmly responding to any mention of his mother. Asked about Diana's 'presence' in his life, he replied: 'It's constant. It has been over the past two years, more so than ever before.' In a bid to own Diana he added, 'It's almost as though she's done her bit with my brother and now she's very much helping me. She got him set up, and now she's helping me set up.'

Unconvincingly, the multi-millionaire implicitly linked his mother to a plea for 'a more equal world'. Finally, he volunteered that America was his 'home'. That was a direct contradiction of his recent submission to the High Court while appealing for special protection. Britain, his lawyer told the judges, 'is and always will be his home'.

Within those few minutes on television Harry had indicated the danger of his appearance at the Jubilee celebrations. Everything was about himself and Meghan. Disloyal to the Royal Family, the Sussexes cast doubt on whether they could be trusted.

Merely four years since their wedding the Sussexes had transformed the Royal Family from a relatively harmonious group, embracing multi-culturalism as part of their service to Britain and the Commonwealth, into a beleaguered institution uncertain of its future. Single-handedly, and for considerable financial gain, the Sussexes had tarnished the Queen's global reputation for unblemished decency. To their harshest critics, they had become agents of destruction.

Revenge

Meghan never appeared to understand that the Queen was much more than a celebrity. She represented Britain's national identity and charitable values. The constitutional monarchy was the reason for Britain's historic liberties and stability while many neighbouring European states had succumbed to dictatorships. Through every crisis the Queen symbolised continuity to Britons.

Unwilling to grasp that she could not share the spotlight with the Queen, Meghan had accelerated her return to California. Disloyal to the Windsors, she and Harry showed no concern that their Oprah Winfrey interview had compromised the eventual transition from the Queen to Charles. They appeared delighted that their outspoken revenge had complicated the management of an inevitably difficult time.

Charles's challenge would be to disarm the Sussexes, who would not remain silent and compliant. The Sussexes' credibility and coffers required them to grandstand from California as members of the very family they unceasingly damned. The doubt remained whether Charles possessed either the skill or ruthlessness to expel the Sussexes from the Royal Family – and strip them of their titles. Yet anything less jeopardised his reign and William's inheritance. Charles's problem was the Queen's determination to unite her family on possibly her last state occasion.

On 6th May, the Royal Family and their officials finally agreed to act. At 3pm, the Palace announced that Meghan, Harry and Andrew were banned from the balcony for the Trooping the Colour. Only working royals would stand with the Queen for the start of the celebrations on 2nd June in front of loyal Britons. The Queen and Charles had ended the damaging farce created by the Sussexes.

The news media had been forewarned about the announcement one hour earlier. Among those notified was Omid Scobie. Alerted by their unofficial spokesman, the Sussexes became desperate. They had lost the battle. Their status and Netflix demanded their presence in London. With little hesitation, Harry abandoned his demands for special protection and Meghan agreed to the downgraded role. Eighteen minutes after Buckingham Palace's announcement, Scobie revealed that the Sussexes would after all be coming to London with their children. 'Excited and honoured,' was their face-saving phrase. The next problem for Palace officials was to limit any damage the Sussexes might cause over the weekend amid their angry family. Any attempt to milk the Jubilee for Netflix would cause a scandal.

Unexpectedly, financed by a TV company, Thomas Markle decided to visit London during the Jubilee. 'I'm coming to see the Queen,' he said from Mexico, aware that he risked disrupting the celebrations. His principal objective, he knew, would be to embarrass his daughter, herself anxious to be filmed with her children meeting the Queen. The sudden resignation of Toya Hollness just before the Sussexes' arrival in London reflected the couple's problems to keep their show on the road. Netflix's interests, the Sussexes knew, ran counter to the Palace's. If the Queen's officials failed to suppress the Markles' family feud, the weekend threatened to become a media-inspired bloodbath.

Then suddenly the threat was averted. On 23 May, Thomas Markle suffered a stroke. Driven across the border to a Californian hospital, he had lost his ability to speak. His trip to London, financed by a British TV station, was abandoned. The danger of the Markle family feud dominating the Jubilee disappeared. Instead of driving south for three hours to see her ailing father, Meghan flew in a private jet to Uvalde in Texas, to lay flowers at a shrine for 19 schoolchildren and two of their teachers, slaughtered by a teenage gunman. In her absence, the Palace and Harry agreed that the Sussexes would meet the Queen on Lilibet's first birthday but not seek the limelight. While invited to the service of Thanksgiving on St Paul's Cathedral, they would not seek any further attention.

During the Jubilee celebrations few believed that Britain would abandon the monarchy. But equally, few did not recognise that the public's enthusiasm for the Royal Family had, within just four years, been diminished. This was caused by Andrew's behaviour, and partly by Megxit.

In her own terms Meghan's career had been an astounding success. Thanks to her father she had prospered despite her parents' divorce and, during her school years, her mother's frequent absence. Thereafter her acting career and personal relationships had been a mixed success. At 34 she had faced an uncertain future. Meeting Harry had delivered the fame and fortune she had sought since childhood. Engineering that encounter and overcoming the justified doubters among Harry's family exposed the determination of a Hollywood survivor. Toughness came with a price.

Concealing humiliation to achieve success had transformed a compassionate young woman into a merciless opportunist. To advance herself she not only abandoned her father and close friends, but first misled Harry's relations and then been accused of lying to Oprah Winfrey. The consequences for the Windsors were irrelevant to Meghan. She only considered the advantages for herself. Her television appearance with Winfrey had reinforced her global celebrity. The question was whether her damage to others, in revenge for their refusal to meet her demands, would eventually result in self-destruction.

Even Meghan's fiercest critics could not convincingly predict the outcome after the Oprah Winfrey interview. In the short term she and Harry would remain a contented family enjoying extraordinary wealth in the sun.

In the medium term her fate is uncertain. Until now the Sussexes' only guaranteed income is trading off the family they have betrayed. But at 40, Meghan remains ambitious – if only to finance her lifestyle. Money remains a permanent incentive. Earning millions of dollars every year depends on the Sussexes' originality and celebrity. Both are limited by reality and time. Her singular bold move would be a political career.

California's Democrats might well be prepared to select the Duchess of Sussex as a candidate for Congress. Even if her royal title was temporarily dropped, she possesses celebrity appeal. Her appearance and speech at the Invictus Games confirmed her fluency and charm. Whether her self-interest is sufficiently robust to ignore the inevitable conflicts and criticism that politics throws up is uncertain, but it would not deter her at the outset.

Meghan's good fortune is that she does not appear to suffer a bad conscience for the hurt she caused the Queen and her family, nor for the disappointment to millions of Britons. She retains the power to damage the institution to which they have been compelled by birth to dedicate their lives.

With her fixed Hollywood smile, Meghan was too savvy to reveal her feelings as she walked into St Paul's Cathedral. Harry looked tense. Meghan barely stopped rubbing his back. They were seated in the second row on the other side of the aisle from the senior members of the Royal Family. Charles, William and Kate studiously avoided looking in their direction. The Cambridges had ensured that they would not meet the Sussexes over the weekend. Netflix were also denied the panning shot associating the couple with the Queen. Unable to walk any distance, the monarch watched the service from Windsor Castle. However, to the delight of thousands packed from Admiralty Arch down the Mall and in front of the Palace, the Queen had appeared the day before with the working royals on Buckingham Palace's balcony for an extended Trooping the Colour. Banned from that appearance, the Sussexes were restricted to a snap photograph looking down at the parade from a small office window. That was the totality of their exposure.

With unusual skill, Palace officials had excluded the Sussexes from any other public appearance. Labelled as second division royals, Meghan concealed any sign of regret. By contrast, Harry's grim expression signalled disappointment about his exclusion from the front line. Over the weekend, the message he witnessed was the succession – The Queen to Charles to William to George. He was eliminated from the scenario. He and Meghan were spectators as the Cambridges basked in universal applause during the sunlit coach ride with their children to the Trooping the Colour and for their star billing during the spectacular Saturday night concert outside the Palace. Before the Sunday pageant began, the Sussexes left Britain's grey skies and were on their private jet returning to sunny Santa Barbara. Meghan was undoubtedly relieved to be home. Harry had faced the reality of exclusion and exile. Their 10,000-mile round trip did not end with heartfelt smiles.

The appearance of Meghan exacting revenge will harm the Queen. Shrewd, modest and frugal, the mother, grandmother and great-grandmother would want to end her days amid a happy family. Meghan and Harry appear determined to deny Britain's much-loved and longest serving monarch that final happiness.

Acknowledgements

Several people urged me to write this book but no one was more persistent than Tom Mangold. Over the past 50 years, Tom has given me pertinent advice – both as we travelled together across the world for *Panorama* and more recently as friends. He was right about Meghan Markle. I am grateful to him for that and much more.

Discovering the real story whilst being denied access to the subject of the book depends on the trust of reliable witnesses and the determination to dig deep. Fortunately, many agreed to help. No one was more important in writing this book than Claudia Wordsworth, an outstanding, determined researcher and an invaluable guide to previously untold aspects of this extra-ordinary story.

For further vital research I relied on Mary Jo Jacobi in Washington and Barbara McMahon in Los Angeles. Both were staunch allies. In Toronto, I was helped by Shinan Govani, the city's society columnist. At the outset, I consulted a remarkable group of journalists. They include Patrick Jephson, Matthew Drake, Andrew Morton, Ingrid Seward, Camilla Tominey, Katie Hind, David Jones, Hugo Daniel, Caroline Graham, Alison Boshoff, Charlotte Griffiths, Richard Kay, Hugo Vickers and Dan Wootton. I am also grateful to David Ambrose, Clive Sydall and Anne Marie Thompson for their assistance.

Many gave me information but asked not to be named. Indeed, this book was noteworthy for the number of people who asked this. Many spoke on the basis that their identities would never be revealed. I am indebted to all of them.

As always, I am especially grateful to my loyal agent Jonathan Lloyd of Curtis Brown, friend and ally. My publishers, Blink Publishing, have been hugely supportive.

The most important thanks are due to Veronica, my wife, best friend, wise consigliere, and irreplaceable supporter. Without her, this book would not have been written.

London, June 2022

Endnotes

I interviewed over 80 people in the United States, Canada, Britain and Ireland. All the revelations are from eyewitnesses. Those who are on the record are listed in the endnotes. For understandable reasons, the majority insisted on anonymity. With a few exceptions, I have included the information from unnamed sources in the text and avoided the irritating footnote 'Private source'. The exceptions are where I felt it was important. Meghan Markle's life is a media story – fought over in newspapers, magazines, books, TV interviews and court proceedings. So I make no apology for citing the many different public sources and naming the journalists who have observed this saga since 2016.

A great many citations and references in this book come from a select core of sources, predominantly from printed news media and books. For this reason the below abbreviations are used throughout the Endnotes for those sources employed most regularly.

Tel – *Daily Telegraph*
ST – *Sunday Times*
T – *The Times*
MoS – *Mail on Sunday*
DM – *Daily Mail*

Endnotes

AM – Andrew Morton, *A Hollywood Princess*, Michael O'Mara (London, 2018)

SM – Samantha Markle, *The Diary of Princess Pushy's Sister*, Central Park South Publishing (New York, 2021)

RL – Robert Lacey, *Battle of Brothers*, William Collins (London, 2020)

[1] DM15.8.17; MoS21.10.18
[2] AM p.30
[3] Author interview with Thomas Markle
[4] DM31.10.16
[5] DM15.4.19
[6] SM p.52 & p.64
[7] SM p.72/3
[8] Author interview with SM; author interview with Thomas Markle; SM p.73
[9] SM p.9
[10] SM p.31
[11] *Elle*, July 2015; DM31.10.16
[12] Omid Scobie, *Finding Freedom,* HarperCollins Publishers (USA, 2020) p.176
[13] Author interview with Thomas Markle
[14] *Elle* magazine, 2015
[15] DM2.4.18
[16] DM2.12.17; *Sun* 15.7.18
[17] *Finding Freedom* p.13
[18] DM5.11.16, Alison Boshoff
[19] https://afrotech.com/meghan-markle-businesses-duchess-of-success?item=2
[20] DM2.12.17
[21] Author interview with Thomas Markle; SM p.151
[22] DM5.6.20
[23] https://www.youtube.com/watch?v=FWstrgBr6Xg
[24] *Vanity Fair*, October 2017
[25] MoS3.12.17
[26] Author interview with Thomas Markle
[27] AM p.56
[28] *Sharp* magazine, 2016; AM p.56
[29] DM31.10.16; DM15.8.17, David Jones
[30] Author interview with SK; Larry King 8.8.13; DM2.4.18
[31] DM25.10.18; author interview with Thomas Markle
[32] *Sun* 15.7.18
[33] MoS12.8.18
[34] https://www.*dailymail*.co.uk/video/*dailymail*tv/video-1766720/Video-EXCLUSIVE-14-year-old-Meghan-Markle-gives-graduation-speech.html
[35] *LA Times*, 18.5.18
[36] *Finding Freedom* p.16
[37] DM15.8.17, David Jones

Endnotes

38   DM31.10.16
39   https://web.archive.org/web/20160324100245/http://thetig.com/birthday-suit/ [accessed Winter 2020]
40   Samantha Brett & Steph Adams, *The Game Changers,* Penguin Books Australia (Aus, 2017)
41   Meghan Markle, letter to Congress; DM21.10.21
42   https://www.youtube.com/watch?v-Mp91w4qQ32k; https://youtu.be/dLp1eFoiC5Q
43   Author interview with Lisa 25.3.21
44   DM30.3.18
45   DM12.8.17, David Jones
46   DM2.12.17
47   DM2.4.18
48   *Vancouver Sun* 1.11.2016
49   SM p.172
50   T16.5.18, Valentine Low
51   AM p.64
52   Ancestry, US school yearbooks, 1900–1999
53   DM16.8.17
54   MoS9.12.18, Caroline Graham
55   DM2.12.17, David Jones; *Sun* 2.9.19
56   *Sun* 10.5.18
57   Author interview with Linda Gater
58   DM7.5.2019
59   AM p.72
60   MoS22.4.18, citing *Marie Claire*
61   DM2.12.17
62   The Tig, June 2014
63   DM2.12.17
64   DM11.5.18
65   *Sun* 10.5.18; M11.5.18
66   https://www.scriptsandscribes.com/2016/04/podcast-trevor-engelson/
67   AM p.89
68   DM21.4.18, David Jones
69   DM21.4.18, David Jones
70   The Tig, 4.8.14, https://web.archive.org/web/20160324100245/http://thetig.com/birthday-suit/ [accessed winter 2020]
71   SM p.189
72   *Finding Freedom* p.20
73   *Finding Freedom* p.32
74   https://www.youtube.com/watch?v=pFKleWOhehs
75   AM p.101, quoting 'Working Actress'
76   AM p.100
77   T19.5.18
78   DM31.10.16
79   *Allure,* April 2020
80   Author interview with Thomas Markle
81   Unattributable Source
82   Unattributable Source
83   Unattributable Source

84 DM21.4.18

85 AM p.110

86 Author interview with Thomas Markle

87 *Air Mail*, March 2021, Shinan Govani

88 Author interview with Phaedro Harris

89 *Air Mail*, March 2021, Shinan Govani

90 AM p.112

91 AM p.111, quoting Lesley Goldberg

92 MoS9.12.18

93 AM p.114

94 DM14.4.18, David Jones

95 Larry King, 22.7.2013

96 AM p.117

97 *Air Mail*, March 2021, Shinan Govani

98 AM p.117

99 DM2.12.17

100 https://thetig.meghanpedia.com/for-the-love-of-dogs/

101 ST3.12.17

102 ST3.12.17, Bedell Smith

103 *Air Mail*, 20.3.21, Shinan Govani

104 AM p.124

105 Abby Wathen, ITV doc, *Prince Harry and Meghan: Truly, Madly Deeply*, 21.4.18

106 Abby Wathen, ITV doc, *Prince Harry and Meghan: Truly, Madly Deeply*, 21.4.18

107 DM2.12.17; DM21.4.18, David Jones

108 DM2.12.17

109 Author interview with Thomas Markle; *Sun* 15.7.18

110 MoS1.9.19

111 *Finding Freedom*, p.31

112 Legal documents: Case Number BD586850, Stanley Mosk Courthouse

113 *Elle*, 2015

114 DM15.8.17, David Jones

115 https://www.marieclaire.com/celebrity/news/a7733/meghan-markle-interview/

116 https://www.youtube.com/watch?v=b6LOQnO6lyo

117 DM21.4.18

118 https://www.elle.com/culture/celebrities/news/a16293/women-in-television-2013
-celebration/Inside ELLE's Second Women in Television Celebration ELLE hosted the
second annual Women in Television Dinner.

119 https://extra.ie/2018/07/11/entertainment/celebrity/meghan-markle-dicyes-tweet-2015

120 DM3.12.17; MoS27.10.19

121 DM31.10.16

122 MoS27.10.19

123 DM25.5.19, Alison Boshoff; *Finding Freedom* p.82

124 https://youtu.be/sVLzHkBXyxl [accessed 2020]

125 https://www.canadianliving.com/style/fashion/article/fashion-advice-from-meghan-markle

126 DM5.11.16, Alison Boshoff

127 Larry King, 2016

128 https://variety.com/2014/tv/news/usa-network-renews-suits-season-5-1201279977/

129 DM14.8.17

Endnotes

130 DM14.4.18, David Jones
131 https://www.irishcentral.com/culture/entertainment/rory-mcilroy-returns-to-new-york-as-conquering-hero [accessed 2020]
132 https://www.golfpunkhq.com/news/article/when-meghan-markle-and-rory-mcilroy-took-the-ice-bucket-challenge
133 https://soundcloud.com/user-682413562-561358898/charlie-bird-meets-john-fitzpatrick
134 https://www.her.ie/celeb/rory-mcilroy-steps-out-with-actress-for-cosy-dinner-in-new-york-173288
135 *Finding Freedom* p.66
136 Instagram: 4.10.14, message from Meghan Markle to Ashley Doyle
137 Author interview with Gina Nelthorpe-Cowne
138 https://strategyonline.ca/2015/08/07/un-women/turn-on-the-light/
139 https://www.her.ie/celeb/rory-mcilroy-steps-out-with-actress-for-cosy-dinner-in-new-york-173288
140 https://soundcloud.com/user-682413562-561358898/charlie-bird-meets-john-fitzpatrick
141 https://goss.ie/showbiz/rory-mcilroy-isnt-dating-suits-star-meghan-markle-as-she-has-a-secret-boyfriend-16610
142 Author interview with Gina Nelthorpe-Cowne; MoS20.1.20
143 DM16.9.17, Alison Boshoff
144 https://ew.com/article/2013/07/17/suits-costume-designer-on-the-shows-tailor-made-wardrobe/
145 https://v5.femalefirst.co.uk/celebrity_interviews/jolie-andreatta-interview-292307.html
146 Vanessa Pascale, *Miami Living*, 2016.
147 *Vanity Fair*, October 2017
148 DM14.4.18
149 http://www.prweb.com/releases/2014/12/prweb12370444.htm
150 https://www.youtube.com/watch?v=8XfvJeiUed8
151 DM29.11.17
152 https://www.cosmopolitan.com/entertainment/a20145547/meghan-markle-lifestyle-blog-tig-facts-photos
153 https://www.irishcentral.com/culture/entertainment/meghan-markle-friend-of-liam-neeson-and-hillary-supporter
https://www.independent.ie/style/celebrity/celebrity-news/theyre-on-the-list-the-irish-guests-attending-the-british-royal-wedding-36923472.html
154 Tom Bower, *Broken Vows*, Faber & Faber (London, 2016) p.xiii
155 https://rwanda-podium.org/book-i-am-a-girl-from-africa-a-powerful-memoir-by-elizabeth-nyamayaro/= [accessed 2020]
156 Larry King, Feb 2016
157 AM p.153
158 AM p.276
159 *Toronto Star* 1.11.16, Leanne Delap
160 AM p.157
161 https://lovinmalta.com/lifestyle/celebrities/future-british-princess-rocks-a-traditional-maltese-look/
162 https://bay.com.mt/why-meghan-really-loves-malta/
164 https://www.irishtimes.com/culture/heritage/meghan-markle-s-great-great-great-grandmother-was-a-belfast-catholic-1.3767214

Endnotes

https://www.walesonline.co.uk/news/uk-news/meghan-markles-great-great-great
-20695180

Forces War Records online archive, https://www.forces-war-records.co.ukrecords
/8529343/private-thomas-bird-british-army-1st-battalion-22nd-foot-cheshire/

164   Gracie Delicata

165   Author interview with Thomas Markle

166   https://www.elle.com/uk/life-and-culture/news/a26855/more-than-an-other/

167   Meghan Markle, The Tig, 27.3.15, https://web.archive.org/web/20160426114329/http:
/thetig.com/malta/

168   Meghan Markle, The Tig, 27.3.15, https://thetigarchives.tumblr.com/post
/175614202520/ the-tig-archivestravelmalta-pt-1-originally

169   https://soundcloud.com/search?q=Charlie per cent20Bird per cent20interviews

170   https://www.independent.ie/entertainment/radio/ryan-tubridy-recalls-meeting-old-friend
-meghan-markle-as-he-praises-actress-as-great-fun-36106748.html.

171   https://www.livingly.com/Fun+Facts+About+Meghan+Markle/articles/ghNy9n49Ojn
/met+President+Obama+2015

172   https://www.unwomen.org/en/news/stories/2015/3/press-release-galvanizing-global
-attention-world-leaders-celebrities-and-activists

173   https://www.unwomen.org/en/csw/previous-sessions/csw59-2015/official-meetings

174   DM16.8.17, quoting *US* magazine or *Glamour*

175   https://thetig.meghanpedia.com/international-womens-day-2015/

176   AM p.155

177   AM p.142

178   DM7.1.17

179   https://www.youtube.com/watch?v=NrrC3HkJMzM

180   The Tig: 29.8.14 & 8.9.14

181   https://screenrant.com/suits-usa-season-5-jessica-rachel/ JUNE 15 2015

182   DM5.11.16, Alison Boshoff

183   https://thetig.meghanpedia.com/international-womens-day-2015/ Tig Archives 8.6.15

184   *Finding Freedom* p.24

185   MM22.1.17

186   DM14.4.18, David Jones

187   DM14.4.18, David Jones

188   https://www.Youtube.com/watch?v-Mp91w4qQ32k

189   *Living Well with Meghan Markle of The* TIG (thechalkboardmag.com)

190   https://strategyonline.ca/2016/03/24/world-vision-plays-on-bold-promises/

191   https://static1.squarespace.com/static/5c807307d7819e55018dfc31/t/5fbca5e2b474932ca
25fa8a8/1606198754947/GABOR+JURINA.pdf

192   https://www.worldvision.ca/about-us/media-centre/meghan-markle-brings-clean-water-to
-children
http://meghanmarklereview.com/2017/05/tig-archives-meghans-world-water-day-article/
https://strategyonline.ca/2016/03/24/world-vision-plays-on-bold-promises/

193   https://www.worldvision.org.uk/about/blogs/meghan-markle-rwanda/

194   The Watercolour Project, https://youtu.be/kfpiezABvOU

195   https://www.youtube.com/watch?v=IepMamRWnJU&t=89s

196   http://meghanmarklereview.com/2017/05/tig-archives-meghans-world-water-day-article/

197   Larry King 5.2.16

198 https://uk.news.yahoo.com/liam-neeson-doesn-apos-t-160249215.html.
https://www.irishcentral.com/culture/entertainment/meghan-markle-friend-of-liam
-neeson-and-hillary-supporter
199 DM14.4.18, David Jones
200 *Mirror* 6.12.20
201 *Daily Mail* Australia, 19.7.19
202 https://www.youtube.com/watch?v=FWstrgBr6Xg
203 https://www.irishtimes.com/news/world/us/bill-clinton-advises-irish-politicians-to-work
-together-1.2615881
204 https://cassies.ca/reitmans-really/
205 *Toronto Star* 1.11.16, Leanne Delap
206 Author correspondence with Jeannie Vondjidis-Miller
207 https://www.youtube.com/watch?v=wi45nKVv3UQ
208 *Toronto Star* 1.11.16, Leanne Delap
209 https://www.youtube.com/watch?v=JeUJUCzEMzY
https://www.youtube.com/watch?v=Uj0YTm4FNJU
https://www.youtube.com/watch?v=wi45nKVv3UQ
210 https://www.youtube.com/watch?v=Lksnk6Wtzy8
211 https://strategyonline.ca/2017/02/22/cassies-silver-reitmans-pitches-a-younger-crowd/
212 *Fashion*, 20.4.16, Jeanne Beker
213 MoS14.3.21
214 *Finding Freedom* p.33
215 T31.10.16 iV
216 MoS9.12.18
217 MoS8.4.18 Gina Nelthorpe-Cowne; author interview with Gina Nelthorpe-Cowne
218 MoS15.4.18; author interview with Gina Nelthorpe-Cowne
219 RL p.147
220 RL p.136
221 RL p.97, citing Wendy Berry
222 RL p.98
223 RL p.240
224 MoS25.6.17
225 Dax Shepherd, Apple TV, 2021
226 MoS25.6.17
227 DM7.5.18
228 RL p.162
229 MoS25.6.17
230 MoS25.6.17
231 *Finding Freedom* p.65
232 www.independent-360.com/presenters/Cressida-bonas/#
233 RL p.244
234 HeadsTogether event, Kensington Palace, 25 July 2016
235 RL p.240
236 DM14.5.21; Dax Shepard, Apple TV, 2021
237 ITV, *Elizabeth: Queen, Wife, Mother*
238 *Finding Freedom* p.65
239 ST8.5.16
240 DM25.5.21

Endnotes

241 *Finding Freedom* p.36
242 Tel28.11.17
243 *Dave TV*, 12 July
244 Author interview with Gina Nelthorpe-Cowne; MoS12.1.20
245 *Finding Freedom* p.53
246 Tel28.11.17; MoS8.4.18; author interview with Gina Nelthorpe-Cowne
247 Tel1.4.17
248 https://www.judiciary.uk/wp-content/uploads/2021/02/Duchess-of-Sussex-v-Associated
     -2021-EWCH-273-Ch.pdfhttps://www.judiciary.uk/wp-content/uploads/2021/02
     /Duchess-of-Sussex-v-Associated-2021-EWCH-273-Ch.pdf
249 Tel29.7.20
250 Tel19.11.21; Ellen DeGeneres show
251 DM31.10.16
252 AM p.207; DM31.10.16
253 DM9.3.21
254 T30.10.16
255 DM2.11.16
256 DM9.11.16
257 DM2.11.16; DM3.11.16
258 Tel5.11.16
259 DM21.4.18, David Jones
260 *Sun* 6.11.16
261 DM3.11.16 DM4.11.16
262 *Finding Freedom* p.103
263 *Finding Freedom* p.104
264 *Finding Freedom* p.104
265 MoS6.11.16; *Finding Freedom* p.104
266 *Finding Freedom* p.89
267 *Elle*, 2016
268 T19.11.20
269 *Finding Freedom* p.106
270 DM26.11.16
271 Tel9.11.16
272 DM9.11.16
273 AM p.214
274 *Finding Freedom* p.186
275 *Newsweek* 21.6.20
276 CBS, *Oprah with Meghan and Harry*, 7.3.21
277 *Finding Freedom* p.124/5
278 CBS, *Oprah with Meghan and Harry*, 7.3.21
279 DM5.5.19, Alison Boshoff
280 DM1.12.16
281 ST12.1.20
282 Tel17.12.16
283 RL p.236
284 Tel17.12.16
285 https://www.youtube.com/watch?v=b6LOQnO6lyo 21.2.16
286 *Newsweek* 21.6.17

287 DM3.2.17
288 DM7.12.16; DM15.12.16; DM24.12.16
289 MoS18.12.16
290 DM10.12.16; *Finding Freedom* p.111
291 DM2.10.17
292 DM8.1.17; DM21.1.17
293 Tel8.3.17; DM22.4.17
294 Tel6.3.21, Camilla Tominey; *Finding Freedom* p.102 & p.106/7
295 *Finding Freedom* p.114
296 RL p.249
297 *Time* magazine, 8.3.17
298 Legal Documents: Re-Amended Particulars of Claim 1 p.1
299 DM7.5.17
300 DM12.6.17
301 DM8.4.17; AM p.219; *Finding Freedom* p.115 & p.128
302 Tel17.4.17
303 Tel23.9.17
304 Tom Bower, *Rebel Prince*, William Collins (London: 2018) p.331
305 *Newsweek* 21.6.17
306 *Newsweek* 21.6.17
307 MoS25.6.17; *Newsweek*; DM22.6.17; Tel23.6.17
308 DM22.6.17
309 DM24.7.17
310 RL p.271 & p.304
311 https://www.heart.co.uk/news/royals/meghan-markle/meghan-markle-engagement
-ring/#:~:text=Here's%20all%20the%20details.,gorgeous%20three%2Ddiamond%20
engagement%
312 *Vogue*, 24.6.19
313 https://youtu.be/Ape4M6jXw0s
314 *Finding Freedom* p.129
315 Author interview with Thomas Markle; *Vanity Fair*, October 2017
316 DM7.8.17
317 https://www.smh.com.au/lifestyle/life-and-relationships/the-girl-power-speech-that-put
-meghan-markle-on-the-map-20181009-p508lb.html
318 DM5.9.17
319 RL p.249
320 CBS, *Oprah with Meghan and Harry*, 7.3.21
321 CBS, *Oprah with Meghan and Harry*, 7.3.21
322 *Finding Freedom* p.147
323 DM23.9.17
324 T3.2.19
325 DM26.9.17
326 MoS1.10.17
327 Legal Documents: Re-Amended Reply 15.2D(xi) p.25
328 Tel29.10.19
329 DM19.10.17, Richard Kay
330 CBS, *Oprah with Meghan and Harry*, 7.3.21
331 BBC News, 27.11.17

Endnotes

332 BBC News, 27.11.17
333 Kelsey Castanon, 14.5.16
334 Tel28.11.17
335 DM26.11.17
336 Tel29.11.17, Matthew Bell
337 ST3.12.17
338 DM28.11.17, Jan Moir
339 DM29.11.17, Sarah Vine
340 AM p.6
341 DM9.12.17
342 DM29.11.17
343 DM30.11.17, Stephen Glover
344 *Finding Freedom* p.230 & p.229
345 *Finding Freedom* p.127 & p.159
346 SM p.233
347 Legal Documents: First Witness statement of Duchess of Sussex 13.10.21, para 7, p.3
348 Author interview with Thomas Markle; T4.2.21; SM p.233
349 Author interview with Thomas Markle; SM p.236
350 Tel28.11.17
351 DM14.5.21; Apple TV, *The Me You Can't See,* May 2021
352 AM p.245
353 Tel1.12.17; *Finding Freedom* p.160 & p.162
354 T3.3.21
355 ST7.3.21
356 T2.3.21; *Finding Freedom* p.250
357 CBS, *Oprah with Meghan and Harry,* 7.3.21
358 DM11.1.18
359 23.3.18; author interview with PD
360 DM16.2.18, Jan Moir
361 *Finding Freedom* p.181
362 Tel14.2.18 & Tel6.3.21CT; author interview with Gina Nelthorpe-Cowne
363 DM9.3.21
364 DM17.4.18; RL p.275
365 *Finding Freedom* p.180; Tel30.1.18
366 T19.1.18
367 DM8.3.18
368 *Finding Freedom* p.207
369 DM27.11.19, quote from *Woman* magazine
370 DM25.4.18
371 T3.8.20
372 *Finding Freedom* p.256
373 Tel6.3.21, Camilla Tominey
374 Tel4.12.21
375 *Sun* 1.12.18
376 *Finding Freedom* p.245
377 CBS, *Oprah with Meghan and Harry,* 7.3.21
378 Author interview with Thomas Markle; T13.8.18 re-MoS
379 Contra, *Finding Freedom* p.191

380 DM2.12.17, David Jones
381 Author interview with Thomas Markle; MoS12.8.18
382 Author interview with Samantha Markle; Tel15.5.18
383 DM18.4.18; ST22.4.18; DM8.3.21, Rebecca English; RL p.478
384 DM12.5.18, Patrick Jephson
385 https://twitter.com/scobie/status/1367236572928761860?lang=en 3.3.21
386 DM12.5.18, Patrick Jephson
387 Legal Documents: Re-Re-Amended Defence 15.6.4 p.27
388 Legal Documents: Statement, LH, para 641
389 MoS13.5.18
390 CBS, *Oprah with Meghan and Harry*, 7.3.21
391 Author interview with Thomas Markle; MoS 29.7.18, Thomas Markle
392 Legal Documents: First Witness statement of Duchess of Sussex 13.10.21, para 7 p.3; author interview with Thomas Markle
393 Legal Documents: Letter Addleshaw Goddard to court;' Mail 6 May 2021
394 Legal Documents: Re-Amended Reply 14.8(c) p.31
395 *Finding Freedom* p.197 & p.199
396 Legal Documents: Re-Amended Reply 14.2e(ii) p.28
397 T16.5.18
398 T16.5.18
399 Legal Documents: Re-Re-Amended Defence 17.8.2 p.41
400 Author interview with Thomas Markle; DM21.4.20
401 *Finding Freedom* p.198
402 T13.8.18
403 Author interview with Thomas Markle; *Sun* 21.4.20
404 Tel16.5.18; 17.5.18
405 T30.10.18
406 Tel8.11.18
407 Tel5.3.19
408 *Sun* 19.5.18
409 *Woman* magazine, *Sun* 27.11.19
410 Author interview with Samantha Markle
411 *Sun* 26.7.20
412 *Finding Freedom* p.220
413 *Finding Freedom* p.218
414 T22.5.18
415 T22.5.18
416 ST20.5.18, Tom Bradby
417 CNN Opinion, 21 May 2018, RL p.294
418 T21.5.20, Anne Murphy
419 MoS12.1.20
420 ST12.1.20; RL p.227/8; Tel6.3.21, Camilla Tominey
421 Christina Pazzanese, Harvard Staff, 26.4.2019
422 Legal Documents: Response 14 to Defendants CPR
423 Author interview with Thomas Markle
424 Author interview with Thomas Markle
425 DM18.6.18
426 *Finding Freedom* p.228

Endnotes

427 *Sun* 27.6.18
428 *Sun* 7.7.18; DM6.7.18, Jan Moir
429 Author interview with Thomas Markle
430 *Sun* 15.7.18
431 Tel16.7.18
432 Legal Documents: First Witness statement of Duchess of Sussex 13.10.21, para 12 p.5
433 Legal Documents: First Witness statement of Duchess of Sussex 13.10.21, para 12 p.5
434 Legal Documents: First Witness statement of Duchess of Sussex 13.10.21, para 11 p.4
435 Legal Documents: First Witness statement of Duchess of Sussex 13.10.21, para 12 p.5
436 Legal Documents: First Witness statement of Duchess of Sussex 13.10.21, para 12 p.5
437 Author interview with Thomas Markle
438 Legal Documents: Meghan statement November 2021
439 T19.8.18; T3.10.19, Valentine Low
440 Author interview with Gina Nelthorpe-Cowne.
441 Tel21.5.18
442 DM12.7.18; DM14.7.18
443 DM24.7.18
444 T18.7.20
445 *Sun* 13.2.19; Legal Documents: Re-Re-Amended Defence, para 15.9 p.29/30
446 MoS29.7.18
447 DM19.7.18
448 *Sun* 19.7.18
449 T30.7.18
450 *Sun*; T19.8.18
451 DM8.10.18
452 Tel23.4.19
453 Elliot D. Cohen, *Psychology Today*, 'The Epistemology of Narcissistic Personality Disorder', September 2017.
454 Fortune conference, 14 October 2020
455 Legal Documents: 7th witness statement of Jenny Afia, 10(a)
456 Legal Documents: Re-Re-Amended Defence para 40.6, ref. para 56, Third Response
457 Legal Documents: Re-Re-Amended Defence para 15.9
458 Legal Documents: 7th witness statement of Jenny Afia, 10(a)
459 DM19.11.20; T12.2.21; Legal Documents: Warby's judgment
460 Legal Documents: Witness statement of Jason Knauf Exhibits
461 Legal Documents: First Witness statement of Duchess of Sussex 13.10.21, para 6 p.2
462 https://www.judiciary.uk/wp-content/uploads/2021/12/Sussex-v-Associated-News-judgment-021221.pdf, para 18
463 *Finding Freedom* p.232
464 *Sun* 13.2.19
465 T19.11.20
466 *Sun* 13.2.19 Letter's text: Re-Re-Amended Defence 15.9 p.29/30; https://www.judiciary.uk/wp-content/uploads/2021/12/Sussex-v-Associated-News-judgment-021221.pdf, para 6
467 https://www.judiciary.uk/wp-content/uploads/2021/12/Sussex-v-Associated-News-judgment-021221.pdf para 14
468 https://www.judiciary.uk/wp-content/uploads/2021/12/Sussex-v-Associated-News-judgment-021221.pdf. Para 12

Endnotes

469 T20.1.21; MoS10.2.19, Caroline Graham
470 DM21.9.18, Jan Moir
471 DM28.9.18
472 DM29.9.18, Amanda Platell; MoS2.6.19; DM27.9.18
473 *Finding Freedom* p.262
474 *Sun* 1.12.18
475 RL, p.332/3
476 *Finding Freedom* p.248; DM4.3.20
477 T4.3.21
478 DM8.3.21; *Finding Freedom* p.244
479 https://meghanpedia.com/the-royal-family-the-media-and-sussexit-part-4/
480 T3.3.21
481 DM4.3.21
482 T7.1.22
483 T3.3.21
484 *Sun* 28.10.18, Tracey Sayer
485 DM25.10.18
486 MoS2.6.19
487 CBS, *Oprah with Meghan and Harry*, 7.3.21
488 DM27.10.18
489 Tel17.1018
490 MoS4.7.21, Patrick Jephson
491 CBS, *Oprah with Meghan and Harry*, 7.3.21
492 ST28.10.18
493 Royal Foundation report
494 *Sun* 28.10.18
495 MoS12.8.18
496 DM4.3.21, Rebecca English
497 DM4.3.20; DM4.3.21, Rebecca English
498 MoS7.3.21
499 DM4.3.21
500 *Sun* 5.2.19
501 CBS, *Oprah with Meghan and Harry*, 7.3.21
502 CBS, *Oprah with Meghan and Harry*, 7.3.21
503 DM10.11.18
504 DM4.7.20, Richard Kay
505 *Sun* 1.12.18
506 T10.11.18
507 DM28.10.18, Robert Jobson
508 Tel6.3.21Camilla Tominey
509 Tel26.11.18, Camilla Tominey
510 *Sun* 1.12.18, Dan Wootton
511 *Sun* 8.12.18
512 CBS, *Oprah with Meghan and Harry*, 7.3.21
513 DM12.3.21, citing Scobie's *Harpers Bazaar* website
514 DM13.12.18, Rebecca English
515 Legal Documents: Re-Re-Amended Defence p.11 13.8A.5
516 Knauf text message to Meghan Markle 30 August 2018

Endnotes

517 12 November 2018 Meghan Markle email to Knauf
518 Legal Documents: First Witness statement of Duchess of Sussex 13.10.21 Exhibit p.6, email 19 November
519 DM8.11.18
520 *Rebel Prince*
521 MoS31.1.21
522 MoS11.11.18
523 T3.12.18
524 https://www.glamour.com/story/gina-torres-interview
525 https://soundcloud.com/user-682413562-561358898/charlie-bird-meets-john-fitzpatrick
526 ST11.10.20
527 *Sun* 11.12.18
528 MoS9.12.18
529 Tel18.12.18; *Sun* 29.12.18, Thomas Markle
530 Legal Documents: First Witness statement of Duchess of Sussex 13.10.21, para 42 p.17
531 Legal Documents: Witness statement of Jason Knauf 16.9.2021 para 12
532 Legal Documents: Witness statement of Jason Knauf 16.9.2021 para 12
533 Legal Documents: First Witness statement of Duchess of Sussex 13.10.21, Exhibit p.13 & 15
534 Harry to Knauf 10 December 2018
535 *Elle*, 2015
536 *Vanity Fair*, October 2017
537 Legal Documents: First Witness statement of Duchess of Sussex 13.10.21, Exhibit, p.11
538 Legal Documents: First Witness statement of Duchess of Sussex 13.10.21, Exhibit p.11
539 Legal Documents: Re-Amended Reply para 5.1 signed by Jenny Afia
540 Legal Documents: Re-Amended Reply para 9B.1 & 14A.3 signed by Jenny Afia
541 Legal Documents: Re-Amended Reply para 9B.4 & 14A.3 signed by Jenny Afia
542 *Sun* 29.12.18
543 DM24.1.19
544 *Finding Freedom* p.273
545 DM29.7.19
546 Tel9.3.19; T10.1.20
547 CBS, *Oprah with Meghan and Harry*, 7.3.21
548 Tel3.7.20
549 *Finding Freedom* p.280
550 CBS, *Oprah with Meghan and Harry*, 7.3.21
551 CBS, *Oprah with Meghan and Harry*, 7.3.21
552 CBS, *Oprah with Meghan and Harry*, 7.3.21
553 *The Me You Can't See*, Apple TV, 2021
554 *The Me You Can't See*, Apple TV, 2021
555 CBS, *Oprah with Meghan and Harry*, 7.3.21
556 CBS, *Oprah with Meghan and Harry*, 7.3.21
557 *The Me You Can't See*, Apple TV, 20 May 2021
558 Legal Documents: Response 8 & 13 to Defendants CPR
559 Legal Documents: Re-Amended reply paras 3.5.5
560 Legal Documents: Re-Amended Reply 12.7A p.13
561 DM2.2.19; *Finding Freedom* p.251
562 *Finding Freedom* p.264
563 Legal Documents: First Witness statement of Duchess of Sussex 13.10.21, para 45 p.18

564 Legal Documents: Re-Amended Reply 3.5 p.2/4; 12.8e p.18
565 Legal Documents: Meghan statement, ct case; Tel2.7.20
566 Legal Documents: Re-Re-Amended Defence 17.8.2 p.41
567 Legal Documents: First Witness statement of Duchess of Sussex 13.10.21, para 47(a) p.19
568 Legal Documents: Meghan statement, ct case; Tel2.7.20
569 M8.2.19, Richard Kay
570 Legal Documents: Re-Re-Amended Defence 15.9 p.29
571 Author interview with Thomas Markle
572 DM, Thomas Markle; T20.1.21
573 Author interview with Thomas Markle
574 T15.1.20; Tel2.7.20
575 DM13.2.19
576 *Sun* 14.2.19
577 Legal Documents: Response 27 (5) to Defendants CPR p.12
578 MoS2.6.19
579 DM22.2.19, Jan Moir
580 T12.10.20
581 *Finding Freedom* p.262
582 DM6.4.19; DM31.7.19, *Vogue*
583 DM8.3.19
584 DM7/8.3.19
585 Tel5.3.19
586 DM9.3.19; DM4.3.21
587 RL p.278; DM8/9.3.19
588 *Finding Freedom* p.297 & p.300
589 RL p.299 & p.327
590 MoS26.1.20
591 *Sun* 25.9.19
592 DM15.3.19
593 DM12.3.19
594 DM11.4.19
595 DM7.5.19, Sarah Vine
596 DM12.4.19
597 *Finding Freedom* p.10
598 *Finding Freedom* p.285
599 DM9.2.21
600 DM19.5.19
601 MoS2.6.19
602 DM9.5.19
603 CBS, *Oprah with Meghan and Harry*, 7.3.21
604 *Finding Freedom* p.302
605 DM12.4.19
606 MoS2.6.19
607 *Sun* 12.5.19
608 DM19.8.19
609 MoS 12.1.20
610 CBS, *Oprah with Meghan and Harry*, 7.3.21
611 CBS, *Oprah with Meghan and Harry*, 7.3.21

612   *The Me You Can't See*, Apple TV, 2021

613   *Sun* 2.3.20

614   DM19.8.20; *Variety*

615   T20.1.20

616   Tel14.7.2019

617   *Sun* 1.4.20

618   *Sun* 6.7.19

619   *Sun* 12.1.20

620   DM20.8.19

621   T14.1.20

622   DM22.8.19

623   DM11.3.20, spoke to Harry on 31/12 and 22/1

624   DM4.9.19

625   https://www.dailymail.co.uk/femail/article-9368653/Prince-Harry-loses-key-member-staff-sustainable-tourism-venture-Travalyst.html

626   DM6.9.19

627   DM7.9.19

628   ST13.9.19

629   T30.7.19

630   *Finding Freedom* p.87

631   DM22.8.19; ST11.8.19

632   DM24.9.19

633   *Washington Post* 28.9.18

634   *Sun* 25.9.19

635   T16.10.19

636   DM24.9.19

637   DM26.7.20

638   DM26.9.19, Sarah Vine

639   Tel2.10.19

640   Tel2.10.19

641   *Sun* 27.2.21; James Corden interview

642   *Sun* 12.1.2020

643   IPSO, 30 January 2020

644   Legal Documents: Re-Amended Reply 13 p.21

645   Legal Documents: Re-Amended Reply 14.2(a) p.27

646   Legal Documents: Response 26/7 to Defendants CPR

647   CBS, *Oprah with Meghan and Harry*, 7.3.21

648   Legal Documents: Re-Amended Reply 12.10 p.20

649   *Sun* 3.10.19; *Sun* 5.10.19; *Lorraine Kelly*

650   DM30.3.19

651   *Sun* 19.10.19; DM19.10.19

652   T16.1.21

653   *Sun* 27.2.21; James Corden interview

654   T22.10.19

655   DM22.10.19, Richard Kay

656   T10.1.20, Trevor Phillips

657   T & DM14.1.20

658   *Sun* 21.10.19

659 Author interview with Gina Nelthorpe-Cowne, MoS12.1.20
660 T23.10.19
661 DM30.10.19
662 Tel1.11.19
663 BBC Radio 5, bbc.in/34OB0kY; https://people.com/royals/meghan-markle-meets-hillary-clinton-at-her-home-first-time/
664 Legal Documents: Re-Amended Reply 6. p.7
665 https://apps.irs.gov/app/eos/detailsPage?ein=852213963&name=Archewell per cent20Inc.&city=Beverly per cent20Hills&state=CA&countryAbbr=US&dba=&type=CHARITIES, per cent20DETERMINATIONLETTERS, per cent20EPOST CARD&orgTags=CHARITIES&orgTags=DETERMINATIONLETTERS&orgTags=EPOSTCARD
666 DM14.11.19
667 BBC TV 16.11.19
668 *Sun* 19.11.19
669 RL p.326
670 CBS, *Oprah with Meghan and Harry*, 7.3.21
671 Tel10.4.21
672 *Newsweek* 22.3.22
673 CBS, *Oprah with Meghan and Harry*, 7.3.21
674 DM11.1.20
675 *Sun* 12.1.20
676 *New York Times* 9.1.20
677 DM11.1.20
678 DM10.1.2020
679 DM15.1.20
680 DM14.1.20
681 ST12.1.20
682 DM14.1.20; ST12.1.20
683 Sky News, Clive Lewis
684 T10.1.20
685 MoS19.1.20
686 T25.9.20
687 *Mail*-online 11.3.20
688 DM14.2.20
689 DM26.1.20
690 https://www.cbc.ca/news/canada/british-columbia/meghan-markle-dtes-womens-shelter-1.5427270
691 DM23.9.20, lawyer's statement
692 CBS, *Oprah with Meghan and Harry*, 7.3.21
693 *Mail*-online 11.3.20
694 DM25.6.20
695 DM19.2.20
696 DM28.2.20
697 Tel21.1.20
698 DM20.1.20
699 DM24.2.20
700 CBS, *Oprah with Meghan and Harry*, 7.3.21

Endnotes

701 *Finding Freedom* p.236

702 *Finding Freedom* p.5

703 *Finding Freedom* p.9

704 DM26.7.20; *Finding Freedom* p.329

705 RL p.348

706 DM9.1.20

707 *New York Times* 9.3.20

708 https://www.marieclaire.com/career-advice/a37003705/catherine-st-laurent-meghan-markle-melinda-gates/

709 DM27.8.20

710 DM31.3.20

711 T2.4.20

712 DM20.3.20

713 DM31.3.20

714 *Sun* 26.7.20

715 DM21.5.20

716 DM2.7.20

717 https://www.youtube.com/watch?v=FWstrgBr6Xg 2.6.20

718 DM5.6.20; T2.7.20

719 Tel6.7.20

720 DM8.7.20; DM28.1.20; DM7.7.20

721 https://www.msn.com/en-gb/news/uknews/prince-harry-and-meghan-cheerleader-nicola-brentnall-quits-her-role/ar-BB1ffovr

722 DM12.3.21

723 20.8.20

724 T29.10.20

725 T8.2.21

726 Tel25.4.20

727 Tel3.7.20

728 T21.4.20

729 Legal Documents: First witness statement Thomas Markle, para 2 & 5

730 Author interview with Thomas Markle; T30.10.20

731 Author interview with Thomas Markle; *Sun* 27.1.20

732 Tel24.1.20; Channel 5, Thomas Markle Interview

733 MoS19.4.21

734 DM25.4.20

735 DM21.4.20

736 Legal Documents: Supplemental Response to the Defendant's Third CPR 19.4 p.10

737 T9.8.20; T13.6.20

738 DM2.5.20

739 T21.9.20; https://www.judiciary.uk/wp-content/uploads/2020/05/sussex-v-associated-judgment-010520-1.pdf

740 Legal Documents: Re-Amended Reply para 9B.5

741 DM2.7.02

742 Tel20.11.20

743 *Finding Freedom* p.349

744 DM24.7.20

745 *Finding Freedom* p.245

746 Tel19.11.20
747 Legal Documents: Re-Amended Reply 4 p.9
748 Legal Documents: Re-Amended Reply 5.4 p.4
749 Legal Documents: Scobie statement para 6
750 DM20.1.20
751 DM23.9.20; T23.9.20
752 https://youtu.be/dLp1eFoiC5Q
753 DM22.9.20
754 DM2.10.20
755 DM22.9.20
756 Legal Documents: Re-Amended Reply 5 p.9
757 18.11.20
758 Tel20.1.21
759 Legal Documents: Re-Amended Reply para 12.7A.5, Mathieson para 15(b)
760 Legal Documents: Re-Amended Reply para 9B.5, Mathieson para 15(a)
761 Legal Documents: Ted Verity statement, para 5
762 *Sun* 30.9.20
763 T30.9.20
764 Legal Documents: First Witness statement of Keith Mathieson paras 6 to 8. Sent 21 December 2020
765 T30.9.20
766 ST11.10.20; Tel13.10.20
767 Tel13.10.20
768 DM29.6.20; T30.9.20; *Fortune* 29.9.20
769 *Fortune* 13.10.20
770 T10.1.21
771 T12.10.20
772 Tel13.10.20
773 T26.11.20
774 Tel26.11.20
775 T8.2.21
776 DM3.9.20
777 DM5.9.20
778 T19.12.20
779 DM16.9.20
780 T16.10.20
781 DM16.8.20
782 DM2.10.20
783 DM2.10.20
784 DM2.10.20; T2.7.20
785 T2.10.20 interview for *Evening Standard* for Black History Month
786 T8.1.21; T15.12.20
787 T8.2.21
788 DM25.6.21, quoting *The Hollywood Reporter*
789 *Sun* 27.2.21
790 T30.12.20
791 T23.2.21
792 BBC Radio, Private Passions 20.3.22

793 Tel17.2.21
794 *Sun* 5.1.21
795 *Sun* 10.3.21
796 Legal Documents: Second Witness statement of Keith Mathieson para 5(c)
797 Legal Documents: Judgement, paras 111/2/3; 11 February 2021
798 ST14.2.21, Camilla Long
799 Tel16.2.21
800 CBS, *Oprah with Meghan and Harry*, 7.3.21
801 RL pp484
802 Private information.
803 T3.3.21
804 T4.3.21
805 DM4.3.21, Rebecca English
806 DM4.3.21
807 T15.3.21
808 T6.3.21
809 DM6.3.21
810 DM6.3.21, Alison Boshoff
811 DM8.3.21
812 MoS7.3.21
813 Apple TV, *The Me You Can't See*, May 2021
814 *Fortune* conference 14 October 2020
815 Tel13.10.20
816 CBS, *Oprah with Meghan and Harry*, 7.3.21
817 DM9.4.21
818 DM24.6.21
819 DM10.3.21
820 DM13.3.21
821 Christy Pichichero, *Think* newsletter, 28 March 2021
822 DM11.3.21; T11.3.21
823 https://www.vanityfair.com/style/2021/03/hillary-clinton-meghan-markle-prince-harry
     -oprah-interview-suits-writer-defends-royals. Washington Post event, 8.3.21
824 DM6.3.21
825 *Spectator TV*, issue b26, 11.3.21
826 LBC interview; DM9.3.21
827 *Finding Freedom*, epilogue
828 DM5.3.21
829 *Sun* 11.3.21, Nana Acheampong
830 *Broken Vows* p.382
831 Legal Documents: First Witness statement of Duchess of Sussex 13.10.21, para 10 p.4
832 DM24.3.21
833 DM12.3.21
834 T17.3.21
835 DM4.5.21
836 https://www.nytimespost.com/harry-and-meghan-are-setting-up-a-network-of-11
     -companies-in-delaware/
837 https://perezhilton.com/prince-harry-meghan-markle-spotify-podcast-deal-hiring
     -producers/

https://www.dailymail.co.uk/news/article-10438993/Are-Netflix-taking-matters-hands-too.html
https://www.dailymail.co.uk/news/article-10437119/Spotify-takes-Sussexes-podcasts-hands-Streaming-giant-hiring-producers-project.html
https://www.dailymail.co.uk/news/article-10380379/Harry-Meghans-Archewell-outshone-tiny-cat-sanctuary-boy-tent.html
https://www.dailymail.co.uk/femail/article-10068835/Meghan-Markle-amazing-leader-says-Pearl-director-David-Furnish.html

838 DM24.3.21; Tel28.3.21
839 T4.2.22
840 T2.12.21
841 DM21.2.22
842 T16.11.21
843 "The Internet Lie Machine," organised by *Wired* magazine.
844 https://www.dailymail.co.uk/news/article-10084113/Now-Harry-Meghan-banking.html
https://www.dailymail.co.uk/news/article-10086147/Inside-Harry-Meghans-hippy-investment-firm.html
https://www.dailymail.co.uk/news/article-10088227/British-hippie-banker-33-hung-Harrys-10million-Los Angeles-mansion.html
845 Dax Shepard, Apple TV, 2021
846 Legal documents: First Witness statement of Keith Mathieson para 12
847 DM14.5.21; Dax Shepard, Apple TV, 2021
848 *The Me You Can't See*, Apple TV, 2021
849 T9.5.21
850 DM22.6.21
851 Legal Documents: Re-Amended Reply para 9B.4 signed by Jenny Afia
852 Legal Documents: Re-Re-Amended Defence paras 13.8.13/4 & 40.6; Keith Matheson 6th statement para 15 (a)
853 Legal Documents: Keith Mathieson 6th statement, paras 8
854 Legal Documents: Ted Verity statement para 16;
855 https://www.standard.co.uk/insider/prince-harry-meghan-markle-montecito-mansion-california-life-b981179.html
856 M20.7.21
857 *People* 4.11.21
858 *People* 20.10.21
859 https://archewell.com/news/haiti-afghanistan-relief/
860 MoS22.8.21
861 *Tatler* newsletter
862 *Time*, 15.9.21
863 https://www.entertaintimes.com/articles/9457/20211007/prince-harry-meghan-markle-s-public-fight-lilibet-christening-allegedly.htm; https://www.entertaintimes.com/articles/9446/20211006/prince-harry-allegedly-fought-meghan-markle-new-york-refused-talk.htm; https://pagesix.com/2021/09/24/meghan-markle-does-the-talking-on-nyc-date-with-\prince-harry/
864 T13.11.21
865 *New York Post* 9.11.21, *New York Post* 10.11.21
866 https://www.judiciary.uk/wp-content/uploads/2021/12/Sussex-v-Associated-News-judgment-021221.pdf

Endnotes

867 Legal Documents: First Witness statement of Duchess of Sussex 13.10.21, paras 33 & 40 p.14 & p.16

868 DM3.12.21

869 T3.12.21

870 https://www.c2i2.ucla.edu/2020/12/31/ucla-center-for-critical-internet-inquiry-to -collaborate-with-the-duke-and-duchess-of-sussexs-archewell-foundation/ 12.12.21

871 https://www.youtube.com/watch?v=FOKEE67MexM

872 DM18.11.21

873 https://www.dailymail.co.uk/news/article-10433739/Prince-Charles-asks-son-Harry-stay -Queens-Platinum-Jubilee.html

874 T16.1.22

875 https://www.gbnews.uk/news/prince-harry-files-a-claim-for-judicial-review-against -home-office-decision-over-police-protection/206063 https://www.pedestrian.tv/news/prince-harry-prince-andrew-police-protection-uk/

876 DM6.2.22

877 DM6.12.20

878 https://url-media.com/anita-hill-ketanji-brown-jacksons-nomination-to-the-supreme- court-signals-historic-change/

879 DM12.2.22

880 https://www.harpersbazaar.com/celebrity/latest/a39244491/prince-harry-meghan-markle -naacp-image-awards/

881 Legal Documents: Internal Revenue Code, section 501 (c)(3)

882 https://www.dailymail.co.uk/news/article-10353787/Prince-Harry-Meghan-Markles -Archewell-charity-raised-50-000-2020.html

Index

Index

Index

Index

Index

Index

Index

Index

Index

Index

Index